STJEPAN RADIĆ, THE CROAT PEASANT PARTY, AND THE POLITICS OF MASS MOBILIZATION, 1904–1928

The Croatian nationalist leader Stjepan Radić is generally considered one of the most important politicians in Yugoslavian history. In 1904 Radić mobilized the peasantry to form a populist movement that resulted in the Croat Peasant Party. The CPP fought to reform Yugoslavia's centralist state system and to amend the structural flaws of the parliamentary system. His assassination in 1928 marked the end of the country's short democratic experience; a royalist dictatorship immediately followed. Croatia failed to achieve statehood or autonomy within Yugoslavia, but Radić's indisputably dominant role in the formation of Croatian national consciousness is widely celebrated among Croatians today.

The story of this charismatic, ideologically eclectic politician and his role in nation-building makes for fascinating reading. In North America, with our increasing involvement in the political conflicts of the former Yugoslavia, we cannot afford to remain ignorant of the major historical forces involved in the early Serb/Croat struggles for power and identity. This is an essential work for political scientists, historians, and other specialists in the area.

MARK BIONDICH was a post-doctoral research fellow at the Institute on East Central Europe, Columbia University, while working on this book. He is currently with the Centre for Advanced Holocaust Studies at the U.S. Holocaust Memorial Museum, Washington, DC. He also holds a position at the Centre for Russian and East European Studies, University of Toronto.

MARK BIONDICH

Stjepan Radić, the Croat Peasant Party, and the Politics of Mass Mobilization, 1904–1928

UNIVERSITY OF TORONTO PRESS
Toronto Buffalo London

© University of Toronto Press Incorporated 2000
Toronto Buffalo London
Printed in Canada

ISBN 0-8020-4727-0 (cloth)
ISBN 0-8020-8294-0 (paper)

Printed on acid-free paper

Canadian Cataloguing in Publication Data

Biondich, Mark
  Stjepan Radić, the Croat Peasant Party, and the politics of mass
  mobilization, 1904–1928

  Includes bibliographical references and index.
  ISBN 0-8020-4727-0 (bound)   ISBN 0-8020-8294-7 (pbk.)

  1. Radić, Stjepan, 1871–1928.   2. Hrvatska seljačka stranka – History.
  3. Croatia – Politics and government – 1800–1918.   4. Croatia –
  Politics and government – 1918–1945.   I. Title.

  DR1589.R33B56 1999   949.7201′092   C99-932733-X

University of Toronto Press acknowledges the support of the Canada Council and
the Ontario Arts Council for our publishing program.

This book has been published with the help of a grant from the Humanities and
Social Sciences Federation of Canada, using funds provided by the Social Sciences
and Humanities Research Council of Canada.

University of Toronto Press acknowledges the financial support for its publishing
activities of the Government of Canada through the Book Publishing Industry
Development Program (BPIDP).

Canadä

Contents

cally with the issues that separated Radić and the peasant party–movement and Croatia's (and subsequently Yugoslavia's) very diverse intellectual élite. By examining their relationship over a range of political, socioeconomic, and ideological issues I have tried to provide a nuanced discussion of Radić's peasantism while addressing the issues posed above. This study consists of eight chapters. Chapter 1, an introduction, offers historical background about nationalism, the Croat national movement, the character of the Croat–Serb antagonism, and the nature of Croatian society to the turn of the century. I have also tried to shed light on the character of the chasm between the city and the village and the consequences this had on the process of national integration. Chapter 2 examines Radić's early years and the formation of his *Weltanschauung*, and assesses the causes of the split between himself and both the older and younger generations of the intelligentsia. Chapter 3 deals with the Croat Peasant Party's agrarian–peasantist ideology and how it relates to the process of national integration and modernization. In the course of researching this topic, it became evident to me that particular emphasis had to be placed on Stjepan and Antun Radić's concepts of 'peasant right' and 'peasant state.' Chapter 4 examines Radić's national ideology and the party's national program as well as Radić's relationship with the Croato-Serb Coalition, the political group most representative of the majority of Croatia's intelligentsia, both Croat and Serb. A significant segment of the Croat intelligentsia adopted Yugoslavist ideology, and by 1918 most Croat intellectuals supported unification with Serbia. Radić long opposed this course of action, and it is therefore imperative to examine his national ideology, especially since he became the only Croat leader of significance after 1918. The issue of Yugoslavism, one of the main questions dividing Radić and the intelligentsia, is of great significance in relation to the process of national integration. In its evolution among the Croats, Yugoslav ideology had many variants, and few were unitarist. The purpose of this ideology in the vast majority of cases was to affirm Croat national individuality and statehood in cooperation with the other Southern Slavs. Radić falls into this tradition, which was increasingly challenged by unitarist Yugoslavism in the pre-1914 period. A much shorter version of this chapter has appeared as an article in volume 27 of *Austrian History Yearbook* (1996). In Chapter 5 I examine Radić's wartime policies. By 1918 the Croatian countryside was in revolt against the city and the urban élite. The Croat Peasant Party's agrarian and national ideologies, as well as its organization, placed it in an excellent position to tap into the peasantry's new radicalism.

In the aftermath of the Great War, the Croat Peasant Party became the only significant political force in Croatia. In Chapter 6 I examine Radić's policy *vis-à-vis* Belgrade and his attempt to create a neutral Croat peasant republic. It was during this struggle that the Croat Peasant Party became a national movement, encompassing Croatia's peasants and intellectuals. The first part of the chapter discusses the new Yugoslav state's major political parties and their national ideologies. The second part provides a more traditional narrative and attempts to assess the evolution of the Croat Peasant Party's policies and tactics to 1925. Chapter 7 analyses Radić's brief stint in government (1925–7) and his second bout of opposition, which ended with his death in August 1928. It also explores the important political role of King Aleksandar and the growing factionalism within the two major Serbian parties, the National Radical Party and the Democratic Party. Chapter 8 is a conclusion.

A brief clarification of the terms Croat/Croatian, Serb/Serbian, and Slovene/Slovenian is in order. Throughout the text, Croat, Serb, and Slovene refer to peoples, regardless of the territory which they inhabit, whereas Croatian, Serbian, and Slovenian refer to land, language, and literature: Serbs (not Serbians) of Croatia, Croat people, Slovenian language, Serbian state, Croatian history, and so on. In a few instances, however, Serbian refers to the Serbs of Serbia, as reflected in the Croatian and Serbian distinction between *Srbijanci* (Serbians; Serbs from Serbia) and the generic *Srbi* (Serbs, regardless of the territory they inhabit). Furthermore, the reader familiar with Croatian should note that the Radićes employed an orthography that does not in all cases correspond to modern literary Croatian.

This study was originally a doctoral dissertation. It would not have been possible without the generous financial support of a number of institutions and the advice of many individuals. I am grateful to the Social Sciences and Humanities Research Council of Canada for its financial support, in the form of a Doctoral Fellowship, between 1993 and 1995. I am equally indebted to the Andrew Mellon Foundation, the Centre for Russian and East European Studies at the University of Toronto, and to the Associates of the University of Toronto for their research and travel grants. The assistance of the staffs of the Archive of Croatia, the Institute of Contemporary History, and the Historical Archive of Zagreb is greatly appreciated.

I owe a great deal of thanks to Professor Andrew Rossos, my PhD adviser at the University of Toronto, for his guidance at the doctoral level. Professors Harvey L. Dyck and Paul R. Magocsi suggested a number of important revisions at both the doctoral and postdoctoral levels that have undoubtedly strengthened the final draft. I am grateful to my very good friend and colleague Robert C. Austin, who commented on parts of the dissertation, and offered many useful insights of a comparative nature about Radić and his equally ill-fated Albanian contemporary, Bishop Fan Noli. I would also like to thank Christian A. Nielsen of Columbia University for offering a number of suggestions that have improved the revised manuscript. In Croatia both Branka Boban of the Institute for Croatian History and Zvonimir Kulundžić provided a number of suggestions and comments. I would like to thank Professor Ivo Banac of Yale University for his many helpful suggestions. I have been interested in Radić for many years, but it was Professor Banac who first raised the issue of Radić and the intelligentsia, as well as a number of questions that this study attempts to resolve. His suggestions gave my general interest in Radić a much more focused edge and coherent form. I also owe a great debt of gratitude to Virgil Duff, executive editor of University of Toronto Press, for agreeing to take the manuscript under consideration in the first place, to my copy-editor, Harold Otto, and to the Aid to Scholarly Publications Programme in Ottawa for its financial assistance. I would also like to thank the two anonymous readers who provided numerous helpful suggestions that have helped to strengthen the final version.

I am indebted to my friends in Croatia, the Kasun and Sorko families, with whom I spent a lot of time during 1993 and 1994. They not only provided me with a home, but made my stay much more enjoyable than it otherwise would have been. I extend my thanks to Branko and Ana Kasun, Krunoslav and Jasna Sorko, and especially to my very good friend Vesna Kasun. Above all, I am indebted beyond words to my family: my parents Marko and Katarina (née Kovačić) Biondić, and my sister Branka. Their help and support proved to be most important, which is why I dedicate this work to them.

MARK BIONDICH
NEW YORK, JANUARY 1999

Abbreviations

ČSP	Pure Party of Right	JMO	Yugoslav Muslim Organization
HFSS	Croat Federalist Peasant Party	KPJ	Communist Party of Yugoslavia
HPSS	Croat People's Peasant Party	NRS	National Radical Party
HRSS	Croat Republican Peasant Party	SDS	Independent Democratic Party
HSK	Croat-Serb Coalition	SLS	Slovene People's Party
HSP	Croat Party of Right	SSS	Serb Independent Party
HSS	Croat Peasant Party	SZ	Alliance of Agrarian Workers
HZ	Croat Union		

STJEPAN RADIĆ, THE CROAT PEASANT PARTY, AND
THE POLITICS OF MASS MOBILIZATION, 1904–1928

1

Introduction and Historical Background

Two great forces have shaped the modern age. The first is nationalism, normally associated with the French Revolution of 1789, although its antecedents predate that event. The second is the Industrial Revolution. Combined, these two revolutions inaugurated a period of tremendous political, social, and economic upheaval in Europe, for they undermined the traditional loyalties and tenets of the *ancien régime*. Although their impact was not felt immediately and uniformly throughout Europe, in the course of the nineteenth century they left an indelible mark on the entire continent. Old loyalties associated with feudal society, whether dynastic, corporate, regional, or religious, gradually lost their legitimacy. The diversification of European society and the emergence of new social groups gave rise to new loyalties.

One source of legitimacy became the nation, which for the newly emerging social groups in the West became a means to gain access to political power. In this sense the concept of nation, including the lowest social orders, was democratic both in theory and in practice. But the nation was defined and perceived differently in the European West and East. The French revolutionaries espoused a political concept. The nation was a community of people residing within the borders of the French republic and possessing one government. The concept of nation that emerged in East Central Europe was different and requires a brief elaboration. Under the impact of German romanticism the nation came to be defined primarily by cultural criteria. Above all this meant a single language, but the romantics also posited a common historical consciousness, customs, and a historical mission. The nation was therefore seen as a community of people possessing a single language, culture, and historical tradition.[1] This point requires further clarification, however, because in the West the term 'nation' has been closely associated with the state, or loyalty to a state or country. Many scholars prefer the term 'nationality,' as opposed to nation, to refer to a com-

munity of people who have acquired a national consciousness, that is, an awareness of belonging to a national group distinct from all others.[2] Thus the reader
should keep in mind that nations, particularly in East Central Europe, are
defined by cultural criteria, but for the purposes of this study 'nationality' will
refer to people.

The formation of, and new emphasis on, nations and nationalities gave rise
to nationalism. To some, nationalism is a social and political movement
attempting to realize the national will; to others, it is a consciousness of
belonging to a particular nation (national consciousness); still others see it as
the process of forming and, once formed, of maintaining, a nation or nation-
state.[3] But nationalism should always be defined as an ideology resting on a
comprehensive world-view, which seeks to achieve and to assert the cultural
and political unity of a community which considers itself a nation. Thus
nationalism is distinct from national consciousness, although it obviously
relies on a broad dissemination of the latter among a particular social group or
community defined as the nation.

As an idea, nationalism can take form in a variety of nationalist ideologies
that are shaped by various political, social, cultural, and historical factors. One
key distinction was between romantic and integral nationalism. The former
predominated in the era before 1848. Romantic nationalists saw Europe and
the whole of humanity as a family of peacefully coexisting nations. Resting on
liberal precepts, romantic nationalism preached that each nation had a right to
its existence and full expression. This approach was delivered a crushing blow
in 1848, when many of the latent contradictions between liberalism and
nationalism were revealed. The liberal utopia of the romantic nationalists was
crushed and gradually replaced by the ideology of integral nationalism, which
was intolerant of other nations.

The varieties of nationalist ideology notwithstanding, the diffusion of
nationalism to all social groups of a nation is a process that often takes
much time. In other words, in order for a community of people to be transformed into a modern nationality, they must first acquire a national consciousness. This process, which may be referred to as 'national awakening'
or national integration, is in turn influenced by a number of criteria. Among
the most important of these is increased social mobility. Education is even
more critical, for it broadens the horizons of those not hitherto conscious of
nationality and facilitates their self-conscious inclusion in the national
group. In the case of East Central Europe, the relatively late arrival and uneven distribution of the Industrial Revolution and the resultant slow rate of
modernization meant that the process of social mobility and educational
advancement was rather slow. A further complication to national integration

was the domination of the region by the Prussian-German, Habsburg, Russian, and Ottoman empires.

In discussing the process of national integration among the smaller peoples of Europe, particularly those of East Central Europe, it is useful to make reference to the work of the Czech scholar Miroslav Hroch. According to Hroch, the process of national integration proceeds through three stages. In the first stage (phase A) a group of learned individuals, who may be referred to as the intelligentsia, initiates a study of the culture, history, and language of a people. This leads to the second stage (phase B), during which this work is transmitted to a broader section of society by patriots, who become politically active in the national cause. The third and final stage (phase C) is reached when the national idea or cause is embraced by the broadest sections of society, that is, the masses. At this point the process of national integration is completed and the people have been 'awakened.'[4] Although this analytical construct is useful in examining national integration in East Central Europe, Hroch does not explain how the transition from one stage to the next is achieved. This is, of course, a critical issue, and even Hroch has recently raised the question of why people successfully "awaken" to nationalism,[5] as an issue in need of further scholarly inquiry.

It is the broader objective of this study to determine how the basis of a national mass movement was formed among the Croats. After 1918 this occurred under the aegis of the Croat Peasant Party, but the underlying question of how this was achieved, of how the leaders of that party were able to mobilize peasants to the national cause, needs to be examined for a better understanding of the process of national integration.

Hroch's three-stage process is discernible in the Croat national movement, although a precise periodization of the three stages is problematic. According to Mirjana Gross, the first stage among the Croats occurred between the Renaissance and the eighteenth century.[6] Renaissance literature in the native language and different forms of identification with other Slavs contributed to the integration process, although it must be stressed that this process was limited to segments of the Croat élites in Croatia proper and Dalmatia. One of the most notable writers of this period was Pavao Ritter Vitezović (1652–1713), who claimed all of the South Slavs for the kingdom of Croatia. But it must be emphasized that Vitezović's writings, like those of his contemporaries, were protonationalist: they were based on historicist thinking and he paid virtually no attention to the cultural, linguistic, and religious attributes of modern nationhood.[7] Nevertheless, the writers of this era emphasized Slavic reciprocity, which was primarily a reflection of the fragmentation of Croat lands and the concomitant threat (or reality) of foreign domination. The separation of

Croat lands in the medieval and early modern periods gave rise to regional identities which could be overcome through reference to a wider Slavic framework. Thus, once posited, the notion of Slavic reciprocity would remain an important feature of many modern Croat national ideologists.

I would argue that Hroch's phase A conforms in most cases either to the late eighteenth or early nineteenth century. This would mean that in the Croat case this phase began with the Illyrianist movement (1836–49), which Gross identifies as phase B.[8] The Illyrianists initiated the process of national awakening among the Croats, which was particularly complex. If language is the defining characteristic of a nationality, then the Croats were in a difficult situation, because they spoke three dialects (Kajkavian, Čakavian, Štokavian). This impeded the creation of a Croat literary language. Moreover, although after 1878 all Croats lived within the Habsburg monarchy, they were divided into a number of separately administered provinces (Croatia–Slavonia, the Military Frontier, Dalmatia, Istria, Medjimurje, Bosnia–Herzegovina, and southern Hungary). This regional division, combined with the different levels of social and economic development in these areas, meant that the process of national integration differed, sometimes markedly, from one region to the next. Further complicating the process was the presence in the Croat lands of a considerable Serb minority that spoke virtually the same language as the Croats.

To overcome these difficulties, the leaders of the national movement in Croatia employed the label Illyrian. Confronted by the growing threat of Magyarization in the 1830s and 1840s and by the regional identities of the Croats, as well as the previously noted linguistic dilemma (on which dialect to base the national literary language), the Illyrianists, who were led by Ljudevit Gaj, turned to the neutral Illyrian name to mobilize the articulate segments of Croat society as well as the Serbs.[9] Rejecting the Kajkavian dialect of Zagreb and its environs for the Štokavian dialect, which was spoken by most Croats and virtually all Serbs, the Illyrianists hoped to construct a national culture for the South Slavs. At no time did they attempt to impose one South Slavic name (Croat, Slovene, Serb, Bulgar) on the others; the Illyrian name would serve as a neutral appellation leading to a single culture. Based on this common culture and identity, the Illyrianists hoped to unite the South Slavs of the Austrian Empire to defend their interests against the growing tide of Magyarization. They failed, however, for they were unable to recruit any substantial number of Slovenes or Serbs. The Illyrianists' success was limited largely to Croat intellectual circles, first in Croatia–Slavonia and later in Dalmatia, Istria, and Bosnia–Herzegovina.

The social origins of the Illyrianists varied. The most influential class in

Croatia at the time was the landed nobility, but generally speaking it did not support, or provide the leadership for, the national movement, although some nobles, such as Count Janko Drašković, did play an important role. Since there was little industry to speak of in this period, the members of the national movement came from the educated element of society, the intelligentsia, which played the central political and cultural role in Croatian society. The intelligentsia included civil servants (bureaucrats), the clergy, the poorer nobility, teachers, professors and members of the free professions, particularly lawyers.[10] The intelligentsia would continue to play the dominant role in the national movement and the struggle for Croat political autonomy throughout the nineteenth century and well into the twentieth. This was equally true for most other regions of East Central Europe; the intelligentsia retained its leading position in large part because of the region's relative socioeconomic backwardness.

Although originating as a cultural movement and the dominant intellectual current in the Croat lands from the 1830s, the Illyrianist movement soon acquired political overtones. In September 1841 Gaj and his associates established the Illyrian (later National) Party to safeguard Croat political individuality within the Habsburg monarchy. During the revolutions of 1848–9 it demanded the unification of all the empire's South Slavs into a united Triune Kingdom consisting of Croatia–Slavonia, Dalmatia, the Military Frontier, the port city of Rijeka (Fiume), and Medjimurje. Even though the Illyrianists wished to create a single culture for the South Slavs under the neutral Illyrian name, their political activities remained centred around the Croatian kingdom. Moreover, they expressed their approval of the 'Austro-Slav' federal program as articulated by the Czech historian–politician František Palacký. They also advocated an end to all feudal obligations, among other liberal reforms. But the revolutionary events of 1848–9 were to have disappointing consequences for the Illyrianists. Lajos Kossuth's Hungarian revolution, with its imperative call for the assimilation of all non-Magyars, was defeated, but the imposition of Alexander Bach's absolutist system dashed any hopes that the Triune Kingdom would be territorially integrated as an autonomous unit within the monarchy.

Although the Illyrianist movement corresponds to phase A (phase B according to Gross) among the Croats, it also represents a quick transition to phase B, that stage of the national movement when political agitation begins. In this case, the period between phases B and C, which represents that point at which the national movement acquires the attributes of a mass movement, was a protracted one. Indeed, the second half of the nineteenth century and the early twentieth represents a long transitional stage between phases B and C.[11] In this period the Illyrianist movement was succeeded by two competing Croat national ideologies. The first of these was shaped by Bishop Josip Juraj Strossmayer and Canon Franjo Rački during the 1860s and 1870s.[12] Both of these men, and the National Party (NS, *Narodna stranka*) that they founded, continued to operate within the Illyrianist tradition in that they attempted to create a single South Slavic culture, this time called Yugoslav. But their national ideology, predicated on cultural Yugoslavism, had a pronounced emphasis on political 'Croatism,' even more so than the Illyrianists. In other words, though prepared to work towards Yugoslav cultural unity and to recognize the 'genetic' distinctiveness of the Serbs and Slovenes, they nevertheless laid claim to Croatia's historic state right to virtually all of the South Slav territories of the Habsburg monarchy, which they wanted federalized.[13]

Such plans had little chance of success after 1848–9. Strossmayer and Rački were no more successful than Gaj and the Illyrianists in winning over the Serbs, largely because their Yugoslavism was coupled with a strong emphasis on Croat political rights. Moreover, the political circumstances after 1848–9 militated against Habsburg federalism and the creation of a united and autonomous Croat state. In the 1850s, under Bach's centralized system, Croatia–Slavonia was divided into six districts ruled by officials appointed by Vienna. The Croatian *Sabor* (Diet) did not sit at all in this decade. The Unionist (or Magyarone) Party of Croatia was committed to Croato–Hungarian cooperation and thus naturally opposed the Bach system and any cooperation with Vienna. The National Party eventually split over the issue of cooperation with Vienna. When the February Patent (1861) was issued, establishing a central Imperial assembly (*Reichsrat*), the Unionists and most of the National Party, headed by Strossmayer, refused to send delegates to the assembly.

A new element entered Croatian political life in 1861: the Party of (Croat State) Right (*Stranka prava*). Established by Ante Starčević and Eugen Kvaternik, this party stood for Croat state rights.[14] Starčević and Kvaternik shaped an exclusivist Croat national ideology. Since there could only be one political nation on the territory of the Croatian state, all of the Southern Slavs, with the exception of the Bulgars, were considered to be 'Croats.' Starčević argued that Croatia was an independent state and opposed any political linkages with either Vienna or Budapest, although he was prepared to accept a personal union with Austria; Croatia was to be joined to the rest of the Dual Monarchy only through the person of the monarch. Starčević and Kvaternik opposed any collaboration with Vienna in 1861 or thereafter, especially since they considered Habsburg despotism to be a greater threat to Croat interests than Budapest.

The events of the late 1860s delivered a decisive blow to Croat national aspirations, represented in both the Strossmayerist and Starčevićist variations. The *Ausgleich* (Compromise) of 1867 between Emperor Franz Joseph and the

Magyar ruling oligarchy, which created a dualist framework for the Habsburg monarchy, and the Croato-Hungarian *Nagodba* (Agreement) of the following year, resulted in outright disillusionment and consternation in Croatia.[15] The *Ausgleich* confirmed Croatia-Slavonia's historic, eight-centuries-old relationship with Hungary and perpetuated the division of the Croat lands, for both Dalmatia and Istria remained under Austrian administration. The *Nagodba* stipulated the precise provisions of the Croato–Hungarian relationship, and its terms were to regulate Croatia-Slavonia's status until the Habsburg dénouement in 1918. Although the *Nagodba* provided a measure of political autonomy to Croatia-Slavonia, it was subordinated politically and economically to Budapest.

Croatia-Slavonia was recognized as a separate political unit within the Kingdom of Hungary. In 1868 an autonomous Croatian government was established in Zagreb; thereafter, until 1914, it possessed three departments: internal affairs and finance, religion and education, and, justice. The first had the widest array of responsibilities, from administration and maintaining public security and order to agriculture, health, and public works, as well as social policy.[16] In 1914 a fourth department was added for national economy. Croatia-Slavonia thus gained autonomy in the areas of internal affairs, justice, religion, and education. Croatian became the official language of administration, and it could be used by the forty Croatian deputies assigned to the Hungarian parliament when Croatian matters were being discussed. The *Nagodba*'s terms provided the Hungarian government with considerable influence in Croatian internal affairs, however. The Croatian *ban* (viceroy) was appointed by the Habsburg monarch on the nomination of the Hungarian minister-president. Since the *ban* appointed the eight county prefects (*veliki župani*), the Hungarian government could manipulate the internal administration. The *ban* could also prorogue the *Sabor* and govern by decree until the next election. The Croatian port city of Rijeka (Fiume), which figured prominently in Croat national demands, was made *de jure* a *corpus separatum* of the Hungarian crown, completely outside the jurisdiction of the *Sabor*. And although the Magyar ruling oligarchy pledged to support the unification of both the Military Frontier and Dalmatia with Croatia-Slavonia, only the former was in fact amalgamated with Croatia (1881). The unification of Dalmatia with Croatia-Slavonia remained an elusive aim of all Croat political parties, save the so-called Magyarones.

The Hungarian government exercised a great deal of influence over Croatia-Slavonia's economy. Indeed, Croatian historiography has tended to stress the point that the *Nagodba* prescribed the limits of Croatia's economic development. Finance remained a joint Croato-Hungarian affair and this economic dependence on Hungary represented a steady drain on Croatia's resources. The issue of financial autonomy was one of the most dominant and vexing problems straining Zagreb's relations with Budapest. The financial terms of the *Nagodba* were to be renegotiated every ten years. According to the initial terms, Croatia-Slavonia was to contribute to the costs of joint Austro-Hungarian affairs: Hungary's share was 93.56 per cent and Croatia's 6.44 per cent. For its autonomous affairs, the so-called tangent (*tangenta*) of 45 per cent of all revenues collected within Croatia-Slavonia was allotted to Zagreb. The remainder went to Budapest to cover the costs of joint affairs in all of the Hungarian crown lands, including Croatia-Slavonia. The Croatian quota of 6.44 per cent for joint Austro-Hungarian affairs was unrealistic, however, for Zagreb could meet it only by contributing monies from its autonomous budget. The Hungarian government eventually agreed that the Croatian contribution to joint Austro-Hungarian affairs would be drawn from the 55 per cent alloted to Budapest; if that was not enough to meet Croatia's quota, Budapest agreed to cover the remaining amount.[17] After the 1889 revision of the financial terms of the *Nagodba*, Croatia-Slavonia retained only 44 per cent of total revenue collected. Clearly most of the revenues collected in Croatia-Slavonia did not remain in Croatia, particularly since little of the revenue allotted to joint affairs made its way back to Croatia-Slavonia.[18] Under the circumstances there was little state money to invest in industrial development. Thus, although the Kingdom of Croatia, Slavonia, and Dalmatia, as it was formally known, possessed some outward forms of statehood (defined borders, a legislature, and an administration), in terms of joint affairs it was made subordinate to Budapest both politically and economically.

As already noted, the *Nagodba* was greeted unfavourably in Croatia. In October 1871 Kvaternik, unbeknownst to Starčević, led an ill-fated insurrection in Rakovica in the Military Frontier and was killed. The Party of Right was consequently forced into retreat, and from then until 1878 it remained relatively inactive. The more moderate opposition around Strossmayer did not adopt such extreme methods, but was nevertheless vocal in its criticism. The anti-*Nagodba* sentiment eventually prompted the Hungarian government to negotiate in 1873 some minor alterations to the original clauses of the agreement, but the changes were insignificant and did not alter the substance of the Croato-Hungarian relationship. Coupled with Count Hohenwart's failure to accommodate Czech national demands (1871), this meant that the recently established dualist framework would not be altered in the immediate future. Disillusioned with the turn of events, Strossmayer withdrew from active political life.

Despite the prevailing disillusionment with the *Nagodba* and the despondency of the Croat opposition, the 1870s witnessed intensive reforms under *ban* Ivan Mažuranić (1873–80).[19] The first areas to be affected were the administration and judiciary. In November 1874 Croatia-Slavonia was divided into eight counties: Modruš-Rijeka, Zagreb, Varaždin, Križevci, Virovitica, Požega, Srijem, and Lika-Krbava, although the last one was not constituted until after the merger of the Military Frontier with Croatia-Slavonia in 1881. Three cities, Zagreb, Varaždin, and Zemun, acquired the same status as counties.[20] The counties were divided into administrative districts, which in turn were composed of communes. Each county had an assembly consisting of deputies elected by the district assemblies and *virilisti*, those individuals who by right of birth or membership in an ecclesiastical body automatically had the right to vote, and was headed by a prefect appointed by the king on the *ban*'s suggestion. Since the county prefects were simply the central government's commissioners, the administration was subordinated to the *ban* and the Hungarian government.

The judiciary was separated from the administration and modernized in a series of laws. The law of 10 January 1874 addressed the issue of the *ban*'s accountability to the *Sabor* and established the Royal Court which could in theory prosecute the *ban* for wilful transgression of the law. On 14 January 1875 a law was passed that recognized the right of assembly. The law of 19 September 1873 provided for the full political and civil equality of Croatia's Jews.[21] In 1874 a law regulating the medical and veterinary professions was passed, and in 1876 the first school for midwives was established. These were important reforms, for the standards of health care and of the medical profession were relatively poor. At the time there was only one doctor for every 989 people in the cities, and in rural districts only one for every 9,643 people. A total of 121 communes with over 600,000 people did not yet have any medical practitioners.[22]

There were also a series of important educational reforms. On 14 October 1874 a law was passed mandating six years of primary school for rural children and eight for urban children.[23] Education was removed from the control of ecclesiastical institutions, which invariably led to opposition from the ranks of both the Catholic and Orthodox hierarchies. Up to the 1860s ecclesiastical institutions had had control over primary and secondary schools. Communes paid the teachers' salaries and maintained the schools, but church consistories ran the upper administration. Under the new system, school committees were introduced that provided representation to teachers and parents.[24] In effect, a public school system was introduced in Croatia-Slavonia. From 1875 to 1885 the number of primary schools increased only from 673 to 719, but the quality of education undoubtedly improved. By the mid-1880s there were 242 settlements that did not have schools, and in 1880 about 75 per cent of the population of Croatia-Slavonia was still illiterate. Finally, on 19 October 1874 the University of Zagreb was officially established, with three faculties: law, theology, and philosophy.[25]

These and other laws laid the foundations of a modern civil society, and the intelligentsia, although still numerically small, acquired important new functions in education, cultural institutions and the administration, but not in economic life.[26] The relatively active 1873–5 period was followed, after the elections of 1875, by a period of legislative inactivity. Mažuranić's government came under increased pressure from both the Hungarian government and opposition groups in Croatia-Slavonia, who were critical of the National Party for abandoning its earlier federalist aspirations. Mažuranić finally resigned in 1880, partly because of frustrations regarding the inability to unify the Military Frontier with Croatia-Slavonia.

There was hardly any organized opposition at this time in the *Sabor*, especially since the Party of Right was only slowly being reconstituted in the wake of the 1871 uprising. A formal split did occur in the National Party in September 1880, however, when a group of prominent dissidents (Matija Mrazović, Kosta Vojnović, Fran Vrbanić, and eventually Franjo Rački) formed the Independent National Party (NNS, *Neodvisna Narodna Stranka*).[27] The NNS rejected some of the *Nagodba*'s terms, but otherwise demanded that the Hungarian regime abide strictly by its terms. This was also essentially the demand of the National Party; the difference was primarily in resoluteness. The NNS recognized the *Nagodba* as an unpleasant reality that had to be accepted, but with certain important revisions: the unification of all Croat lands (Croatia-Slavonia, the Military Frontier, and Dalmatia); that Croatia's sovereignty be fully respected; financial and administrative autonomy; and, that the *ban* be named without the counter-signature of the Hungarian minister-president. The NNS drew its support largely from the ranks of the moderate Strossmayerist intelligentsia and clergy, and its followers were known as the *obzoraši*, after their paper *Obzor* (Horizon).[28] With the creation of the NNS the original National Party eventually, by the late 1880s, became the regime's party, with the former unionists and opportunistic elements predominating.

Although the NNS still had the support of a large part of the intelligentsia, the main opposition party in the 1880s was Starčević's Party of Right, which garnered its support from students, the younger intelligentsia, and petit bourgeois elements. Beginning in 1878 the Party of Right's popularity began to grow. In that year it had only two deputies in the *Sabor* (Starčević and Fran Folnegović), but by 1881 it already had nine, and once elections were carried out in the former Military Frontier it had a total of fifteen deputies.[29] Starčević, or the Old Man, as he was known among his followers, who were known as the *pravaši*, led the hard opposition against both the regime and the magyaronized National Party at a time of growing Magyarization. His principled and uncompromising attitude on the issue of Croat rights, as well as his declared sympathy for the peasant masses, won him much sympathy in younger intellectual circles. Since Croat state right formed the basis of his political platform, social and economic issues were on the whole minimized, although not altogether ignored. While expressing sympathy for the difficult plight of the Croat masses, Starčević's program offered few solutions to the pressing socioeconomic problems of the village; he believed that until Croatia's state sovereignty was realized little could be done in the realm of social and economic reform. Like Croatia's other parties, the Party of Right remained relatively inactive *vis-à-vis* the village. Despite its popularity in the 1880s, the party was incapable of toppling the regime or establishing a democratic system, let alone unifying the Croat lands, which were always defined as Croatia-Slavonia, Istria, Dalmatia, Bosnia-Herzegovina, and the Slovene lands. Moreover, by refusing to cooperate with other parties and negating the existence of the Serbs, the Party of Right fell into political isolation. By the late 1880s it was forced to reassess many of its ideas.

The decline of the Party of Right's fortunes was closely tied to the appointment of Count Károly Khuen-Héderváry to the position of *ban* (1883–1903). Born in Nuštar near the town of Virovitica (Slavonia) to a German–Magyar magnate family, Khuen-Héderváry was familiar with Croatian conditions. Gradually he established a regime that acquired absolutist attributes and in the process broke the backbone of the Croat opposition. A relative of Kálman Tisza, the leader of the Liberal Party in Hungary, Khuen-Héderváry would become one of the Liberals' most prominent members and eventually, in 1903 and 1910–12, he served as Hungary's minister-president. Khuen-Héderváry ruled the country through bureaucratic and electoral corruption and by manipulating the growing differences between Croats and Serbs. Under Khuen-Héderváry the National Party ceased being a political party per se and became a clique of individuals tied to him. It included, *inter alia*, the *virilisti* and large landowners (especially in Virovitica, Srijem, and Požega counties), members of the bureaucracy, and the Serb minority of the former Military Frontier. Employing the entire bureaucratic apparatus, Khuen-Héderváry was able to ensure that his supporters were elected to the *Sabor* where they constituted an obedient and comfortable majority. His regime won successive elections, and by 1887 the Croat opposition had been effectively emasculated. From then until 1903 Khuen-Héderváry stood at the pinnacle of his power.

Under Khuen-Héderváry the judiciary was made more dependent on the government, which invariably gave his regime greater leverage in overtly political proceedings. County prefects were given greater authority in the counties and control over urban administrations. The opposition press was increasingly muzzled, and violations of the press law were now tried before a state judge. Most debilitating for the Croat opposition was the electoral law of July 1881, amended in September 1888 by Khuen-Héderváry's regime. The franchise was restricted to less than 2 per cent of the total population; in urban centres to men over twenty-four who paid 30 or more crowns in direct taxes, and in most rural areas to males who paid 100 crowns (60 crowns in poorer regions, like Lika and Gorski Kotar). Furthermore, all priests, retired army officers, members of the free professions, and government officials, including Magyar officials residing in Croatia-Slavonia, had the vote. By 1906 there were just over 45,000 voters in a total population of nearly 2.6 million.[30] Finally, the introduction of the so-called electoral geometry permitted the regime to gerrymander the electoral districts and, to make matters worse, voting was conducted in the open, as in Hungary.

The Croat opposition had been completely emasculated. The *pravaši* and the *obzoraši* struggled with little success in the late 1880s and 1890s, not least of all because of their lack of mutual cooperation. Although the NNS still commanded a large following in intellectual circles, the Party of Right was by far the more popular of the two. Starčević continued to proclaim that Croatia was an independent state, and he thus refused to recognize the *Nagodba*. Uncompromising in principle, in practice his ideas paid few concrete dividends, in spite of the fact that he shaped an entire generation of Croat youth in Croatia-Slavonia, Dalmatia, Istria, and Bosnia-Herzegovina. But refusing to recognize the *Nagodba* in no way altered the painful reality which that agreement's terms imposed on Croatia, any more than his non-recognition of the Serbs in Croatia prevented the Orthodox from adopting a Serb consciousness. The NNS remained more moderate, demanding a united autonomous Croatia within the Hungarian kingdom.[31] Although elements within both the NNS and Party of Right favoured a measure of cooperation against Khuen-Héderváry's regime, Starčević resisted all such moves.

In August 1881 the Croatian Serbs established their own party, the Serb Independent Party (SSS, *Srpska samostalna stranka*). This was not a fortuitous development. Hitherto the centre of Serb political activism in the Habsburg monarchy had been southern Hungary, especially the town of Novi Sad, and Srijem. But the merger of the Military Frontier, with its large Serb minority (47 per cent in 1880), with Croatia-Slavonia in 1881, prompted Croatian Serb leaders to create their own party. A proper understanding of Serb policies in Croatia, and the growing antagonisms between Croats and Serbs, is impossible without a comparison of the disparities between Serb and Croat national

TABLE 1.1
Population of Croatia–Slavonia by nationality, 1880 and 1910

Nationality	1880*	1910
Croats	ca. 1,250,000 (ca. 66.1%)	1,638,354 (62.5%)
Serbs	ca. 497,000 (ca. 26.3%)	644,955 (24.6%)
Others	ca. 145,499 (ca. 7.6%)	338,645 (12.9%)
Total	1,892,499	2,621,954

Sources: Mato Artuković, Ideologija srpsko-hrvatskih sporova: Srbobran, 1884–1902 (Zagreb, 1991), 12; Mirjana Gross and Agneza Szabo, Prema hrvatskome gradjanskom društvu (Zagreb, 1992), 40–3; and Adam Wandruszka and Peter Urbanitsch (eds.), Die Habsburgermonarchie 1848–1918, vol. 3, Die Völker des Reiches, pt. 1 (Vienna, 1980), 627–30.
*Although total population figures exist for 1880 (Civil Croatia–Slavonia and Military Frontier), precise figures by nationality do not. Nationality is defined here by religious affiliation and language.

TABLE 1.2
Population of Dalmatia by nationality, 1910

Nationality	1910*
Croats	ca. 488,000 (ca. 76.87%)
Serbs	ca. 122,000 (ca. 19.22%)
Others	24,186
Total	634,855

*According to the 1910 Austrian census, there were 610,669 'Serbo-Croats' in Dalmatia (96.19% of the population). Since approximately 80% of these were Catholic (i.e., Croat), I have calculated the above nationality breakdown.

ideologies. With the emergence of modern national ideologies at the beginning of the nineteenth century, Serb leaders in Croatia and Hungary gradually adopted the ideas of Vuk Stefanović Karadžić. Karadžić's role in shaping a modern Serb national ideology was critical, for he posited a linguistic definition of nationality. Borrowing from the works of contemporary Slavists, he insisted that all speakers of the Štokavian dialect, regardless of faith, were Serbs, whereas speakers of the Kajkavian dialect around Zagreb were defined as Slovenes, and speakers of Čakavian were Croats. For Karadžić a population

TABLE 1.3
Illiteracy rates in Croatia–Slavonia, 1869–1910 (%)

	1869	1890	1910
Male	74.4	60.1	38.2
Female	86.8	73.5	53.7
Total	80.6	66.9	46.2

Source: Rudolf Herceg et al., Pokret za pismenost
(Zagreb, 1938), 8.

that spoke three distinct dialects, like the Croats, could not constitute one nationality. This idea became firmly embedded in Serb national ideology.

In spite of encountering considerable resistance from the Serb intelligentsia and religious leaders of southern Hungary, Karadžić's ideas eventually gained broad acceptance among Serbs. His orthography was officially adopted by the Serbian principality in 1868. By the 1860s the Habsburg monarchy's most notable Serb leaders, like Mihailo Polit Desančić, Svetozar Miletić, and Patriarch Josif Rajačić, had essentially embraced Karadžić's theory of Serb nationality, although the old equation that Orthodoxy is synonymous with Serbdom had not disappeared entirely. In 1861 Rajačić declared that Serbs and Croats were two distinct peoples: Štokavians were Serbs, whereas Kajkavians (and Čakavians) were Croats. Orthodoxy was the foundation of Serb unity, but one part of the Serb people (Catholic Štokavians) had forcefully been placed under the control of the Catholic Church.[32] The unspoken assumption here was that Orthodox Štokavians had acquired a Serb consciousness, whereas their Catholic counterparts had not. In 1863 Miletić articulated the view, common to the majority of Serb leaders, that the Orthodox were all Serbs but that Catholic Štokavians had not yet developed a Serb consciousness. Rather, they employed regional names (Dalmatians, Slavonians), and he believed they would eventually acquire a Serb identity. Miletić strongly objected to the notion that both Kajkavians and Štokavians (not to mention Čakavians) could be Croats, which is why he rejected the application of the Croatian appellation to Slavonia and Dalmatia. It should therefore not be surprising that Miletić, like most Serb leaders, saw Strossmayer's Yugoslavism as an attempt to weaken Serb consciousness.[33]

By the 1870s the differences between Croat and Serb national ideologies were plainly evident. A number of specific issues worsened relations between the two groups in Croatia. That the Serbs possessed a measure of religious autonomy within Hungary and Croatia was crucial for the spread of Serb national consciousness among the Orthodox. The Hungarian Law IX of 1868 recognized Serb religious and educational autonomy, embodied in the Metropolitanate of Srijemski Karlovci, within Hungary and Croatia-Slavonia. This was critical for Croat-Serb relations, because the law was passed before the *Nagodba*. Under article 61 of the *Nagodba*, Croatia-Slavonia had complete autonomy in religious and educational affairs. But Law IX, signed by Franz Joseph only in 1887, made the Hungarian minister-president the ultimate arbiter of the religious and educational autonomy of Croatia's Serbs, which theoretically violated the terms of the *Nagodba*.[34] In most Croat circles this autonomy was seen as undermining Croatia's sovereignty, whereas the Serbs perceived Mažuranić's 1874 educational law as a threat to Serb interests.

After the merger of the Military Frontier and Croatia-Slavonia, Serbs constituted 26.3 per cent of Croatia-Slavonia's population and were concentrated in Srijem, Banija, Kordun, and Lika. The Serb Independents (members of the SSS) emerged that same year to preserve the Serbs' national identity, which meant safeguarding religious and educational autonomy, revising the 1874 educational law, and securing the use of the Cyrillic alphabet in areas where Serbs were in a majority. In October 1884 they began publishing *Srbobran* (*The Serb Defender*) in Zagreb. They were also active in the social and economic fields: in June 1895 they helped to found the Serb Bank and in January 1898 the Alliance of Cooperatives of the Serb Agrarian Workers.[35] The Serb Independents remained distinct from, and politically weaker than, the pro-regime Serbs, who constituted the Serb Club in the Croatian *Sabor* and subsequently merged with Khuen-Héderváry's National Party.

What is most significant for an understanding of Croat–Serb relations in Croatia is the Serb Independents' national ideology. By and large Independents adhered to Karadžić's linguistic theory of Serbdom, which is why their *Kalendar Srbobran* (1897) argued that there were no Croats in Croatia-Slavonia, only Serbs (Štokavians), Germans, Magyars, Slovenes (Kajkavians), and 'others.' Nevertheless, in essence there was a pronounced identification of Orthodoxy and Serbdom in their organ *Srbobran*; their nationalism possessed a distinct religious coloration.[36] But the tendency to equate Serbdom with Štokavian speakers led the Independents, as well as the Serb Radical Party in Hungary and the Serbian political establishment, to conclude that Bosnia-Herzegovina, Dalmatia, and most of Croatia-Slavonia (Slavonia, Srijem, Lika, Banija) were Serb lands. The Independents opposed the extension of the Croatian name to Dalmatia, and hence refused to support the unification of Dalmatia with Croatia-Slavonia. In the words of Dušan Baljak, a member of the Serb National Party (SNS, *Srpska narodna stranka*), which was formed in 1879 in Dalmatia and supported by the Serb Independents, if the Serbs supported the unification of Dalmatia with Croatia-Slavonia they would be committing 'the sin of suicide.' The ultimate objective of the Serb Independents was the unification of all Serb lands with Serbia.[37]

Given the significant anomalies between Serb and Croat national ideologies, it is not surprising that there was no cooperation between the Serb Independents and either of the Croat opposition parties. Starčević's non-recognition of the Serbs and insistence that there was only one Croat political nation on the territory of the Croatian state was an obvious obstacle to cooperation, but the Dual Monarchy's occupation of Bosnia-Herzegovina in 1878, which was, coincidentally, opposed by Starčević, brought to light important differences between the Croats and Serbs. The *obzoraši*, for example, hoped that Bosnia-Herzegovina would be unified at some point with Croatia, something that was anathema in Serb nationalist circles. Likewise, Serb demands for religious and educational autonomy engendered little sympathy in Croat circles. Finally, although the *obzoraši*, unlike the *pravaši*, were prepared to recognize the 'genetic distinctiveness' of the Croatian Serbs, they did not recognize a Serb political nation in Croatia. To do so would have meant acknowledging the Serbs' right to statehood in the Croat lands or to territorial autonomy within Croatia.[38] Since cooperation with the Croat opposition was difficult in principle, most of the Serb deputies (Serb Club) in the *Sabor* cooperated with Khuen-Héderváry's regime. After the September 1884 elections they formally joined the regime's National Party.[39]

Conversely, the fractured Croat opposition experienced one political setback after another. The 1887 elections proved catastrophic: the NNS temporarily ceased to exist, and the Party of Right experienced a crushing defeat. Over the next decade it would undergo important changes that would ultimately lead to a party rupture in October 1895. By 1887 the Croat opposition was weak and helpless to effect substantive political changes in Croatia-Slavonia. Khuen-Héderváry stood at the pinnacle of his power from then until 1903, when he was recalled to Budapest and appointed minister-president.

The reassessment of the Party of Right's ideas was initiated almost immediately after the disastrous 1887 elections. Among the more prominent individuals involved in this process was Josip Frank, a lawyer and from 1884 an independent deputy in the *Sabor*. Although he had few ties with the *pravaši* in the 1880s, and seemingly little sympathy for their ideas, he joined the Party of Right in 1890. Unpopular in some party circles, partly because of his Jewish origins, he nevertheless gained control of the party's organ *Hrvatska (Croatia)* because of his ability to finance it.[40] Thus began Frank's ascendancy within the party. Ironically, Starčević would side with Frank in the party's internal debate, even though Frank in turn substantially altered Starčević's original ideas. Frank emerged in 1895 as the leader of the Pure Party of Right (ČSP, *Čista stranka prava*). Gradually he reformulated Starčević's views in a number of important respects, most notably by expressing his willingness to solve the Croat Question within the confines of the monarchy, something that Starčević was never prepared to concede, and by extension asserting the party's Habsburg loyalism. These views and personal animosities within the party were bound to cause a split.

The *obzoraši*, seriously weakened in the 1887 elections, completely abstained from the 1892 elections. Yet in that same year they and the *pravaši* finally began cooperating. In 1894 a common program was achieved that called for the unification of all the Croat lands, which were defined as Croatia-Slavonia, Dalmatia, Istria, Bosnia-Herzegovina, Medjimurje, and Rijeka, and eventually the Slovene lands also, within the confines of the Habsburg monarchy, and ultimately the fusion of the two opposition groups. The rapprochement culminated in a public meeting between the two old foes and spiritual fathers of the two groups, Starčević and Strossmayer, in what was understandably a painful confrontation for both men. But just as the common program was adopted, Frank rejected the idea of fusion, even though the two groups now shared identical political platforms. In October 1895 Frank, Ante Starčević, his nephew Mile Starčević, and the writer Evgenij Kumičić broke from the Party of Right to form the ČSP. The following year Starčević died, and the two factions that claimed to follow his ideas, the Frankists and the *domovinaši*, named after their paper *Hrvatska domovina* (*Croatian Homeland*), would drift apart even further. In late 1896, however, the *domovinaši* and *obzoraši* formed a coalition. It was renamed the United Opposition in 1902 and merged to form the Croat Party of Right (HSP, *Hrvatska Stranka Prava*) in January 1903. This coalition would achieve some electoral gains in 1897, but in 1901 it again suffered a major defeat.[41]

The only other party to be formed in this period was the Social Democratic Party of Croatia-Slavonia (1894).[42] It demanded universal suffrage, the legalization of unions, and the gradual socialization of the means of production.[43] On the whole the party did not attract significant support in Croat intellectual circles. The Social Democrats attacked the growing nationalist hostilities between Croats and Serbs. They sought the unity of the South Slavs, for they were one people or 'one historical ethnic mass that is gradually constituting itself into one modern nation.'[44] The Social Democrats tried to establish a base in the countryside, but on the eve of the 1897 elections the regime arrested a number of socialist leaders, thereby smashing the party's nascent rural network. Among those arrested was Vitomir Korać, who would eventually come to play a prominent role in the movement.[45] The socialists did not do well in any of the pre-1914 elections; the first and only socialist candidate to be elected was Korać, in 1908.[46]

The crushing defeat of the Croat opposition in 1901 was followed shortly thereafter by increased Croat-Serb tensions, which had been growing steadily in the last quarter of the nineteenth century. The nadir of mutual relations was reached in the summer of 1902. In August *Srbobran* reprinted an article entitled 'Serbs and Croats' from a prominent Serbian literary journal. The author, Nikola Stojanović, articulated the view that Croats were not a nationality, nor did they stand a chance of ever becoming a nationality, for they did not possess their own language or other attributes of nationality. Stojanović suggested in conclusion that Croats were in the process of becoming Serbs, and insofar as this did not happen he envisaged a struggle 'to the extermination of us [Serbs] or you [Croats].'[47] The article initially provoked bitter polemics in the Croatian press and finally prompted serious anti-Serb riots in Zagreb, which lasted from 1 to 3 September and were instigated by the Frankists. On 3 September Khuen-Héderváry imposed martial law in Zagreb and about 100 people were arrested. Two days later the authorities banned the publication of *Srbobran*. The events of August–September 1902 marked an important political turning point in at least one regard: a new generation of Croatian Serbs, led by Svetozar Pribićević, Jovan Banjanin, and Bude Budisavljević, replaced the leadership of the Serb Independents and revived the party's organ under the name *Novi Srbobran*. Led by the ambitious and energetic Pribićević, the Serb Independents would solidify their hold over Croatia's Serbs between 1903 and 1905 and forge ties with the Croat opposition parties.[48] Together they would initiate the 'new course' in Croatian politics in 1905.

All of the Croat (and Serb) parties were active among a very small segment of society. Under Khuen-Héderváry the franchise was restricted to about 45,000 people, almost half of whom were government officials. In 1910 a new electoral law raised the number of eligible voters to approximately 190,000 people or 6 per cent of the total population. Because of the rural nature of Croatian society and the relative weakness of the bourgeoisie, the intelligentsia remained politically and culturally the most active and important group in society. But after 1868, and particularly under Khuen-Héderváry, the intelligentsia was dependent on the growing state bureaucracy for its very existence and was thus effectively co-opted. For many it was the only avenue of employment, and the authorities exerted a great deal of influence over officials, teachers, professors, and writers. The peasantry's influence on political and culture life was negligible at best. Although the politically active groups claimed to speak for 'the people' (*narod*), in reality they were separated from the peasantry by a wide social and cultural chasm.

This social divide, typical of most agrarian societies, along with the perpetuation of the division of the Croat lands after 1867, was one of the major obstacles to the completion of the process of national integration. Given the different political, social, and economic conditions in Croatia-Slavonia, Dalmatia, and Istria, a uniform process of national integration was virtually impossible. Moreover, the slow rate of social and economic modernization in Croatia proper and the growing divergence of interests between the city and the village meant that the peasantry had not yet been integrated into the national community by the end of the nineteenth century. Peasants had to be won over to the national movement for the process of national integration to be considered complete. The 'awakening' of the peasantry and its participation in the Croat national movement were necessary prerequisites for the transformation of that movement into its mass phase.[49]

The plight of the Croat peasantry was particularly difficult in the era of the Dual Monarchy,[50] for the European-wide Great Depression of 1873–95 had an especially harsh impact on the agrarian sector. The price of cereals declined steeply, while taxes increased substantially: from 10.1 million forints in 1872–4 to 20.5 million forints in 1883–5 to 22.9 million crowns in 1893–5.[51] The financial burden on the peasantry was exacerbated by the fact that the 1873–95 era was a deflationary period.[52] The average annual state income in direct and indirect taxes in Croatia-Slavonia rose 118 per cent between 1869–75 and 1880–5, and by a further 24 per cent between 1880–5 and 1890–5. This tremendous increase in taxation was the result of the growth of a Croatian state apparatus under Mažuranić in the 1870s: half of the budget went to the administration (officials, police), 30 per cent to the judiciary, and 18 per cent was spent on education and religion, mainly to cover teachers' and the clergy's salaries and pensions.[53] The cost of this growing bureaucracy was borne by the peasantry at a time of great economic distress. Moreover, this bureaucracy began to intrude into the daily lives of peasants in the form of various officials who were seen as outsiders in the village. It is hardly surprising that the peasantry now saw the state as a new and oppressive overlord.

The prolonged crisis in agriculture, combined with the considerable growth of the rural population, gave way to rapid social and economic differentiation in the village. In the 1870s the dissolution of the *zadruga* (plural, *zadruge*, extended households) increased under the operation of market forces. This trend began earlier, but after 1848 it became much more rapid and pronounced. Traditionally the *zadruga* was characterized by economic self-sufficiency; only a small part of the extended household's produce was sold to pay taxes and to purchase what it did not produce. Property was owned collectively by all members of the *zadruga*. This institution flourished in an economic system in which the market was not of paramount importance.[54] But during the nineteenth century the *zadruga* was increasingly replaced by the single family homestead and individual landownership. The most important reasons for this were the abolition of serfdom (1848), the introduction of the Austrian Civil Code in Croatia-Slavonia (1853), which was based on the principle of individual property, and, most importantly, the development of a market economy. The new bureaucratic state began to collect taxes in money, and this forced peasants to sell a greater share of their produce on the market and increased their need for credit. Increasingly drawn into the market, the tremendous increase in population and demand for land further induced dissolution of the *zadruge*.[55] The old subsistence rationale was destroyed and the process of dissolution was virtually completed by the First World War.

Under Mažuranić the regime attempted to quicken the pace of conversion of the *zadruge*. In March 1874 a law was passed to regulate this process which permitted any adult member of a *zadruga* whose parents were either dead or, if living, no longer members of a *zadruga*, to request its partition. The minimum land allotment was established at approximately three cadastral yokes (approximately 1.73 hectares).[56] The formation of new *zadruge* was expressly forbidden.[57] Khuen-Héderváry's regime passed a new law in 1889 that attempted to safeguard the *zadruge* in order to prevent the peasantry's proletarianization. The *zadruga* was thus officially retained, but in reality the process of dissolution continued, albeit secretly. In 1889 there were an estimated 39,000 secretly divided *zadruge*, representing about two-thirds of the total number in Croatia-Slavonia.[58]

These social and economic trends gave way, by the 1890s, to an uneven distribution of land ownership in Croatia-Slavonia. Latifundia still predominated in some parts of the country, particularly in those areas where the soil was fertile. In 1895 there were 209 estates exceeding 1,000 yokes (575.5 hectares) in Croatia-Slavonia, 118 of which were in Slavonia, particularly in Srijem and Virovitica counties.[59] Conversely, in western and northwestern Croatia (Lika, Croatian Littoral, Gorski Kotar, and Hrvatsko Zagorje) the land was often barren and the soil not as rich as in eastern Croatia. Consequently, small plots predominated in these regions. In 1895 estates of 100 cadastral yokes (57.55 hectares) or more made up only 0.27 per cent of all estates, but accounted for 27.68 per cent of all the land. Those between 20 and 100 yokes (11.51 to 57.55 hectares) accounted for 8.2 per cent of all estates and controlled 22.39 per cent of all the land. Farms of 5 yokes (2.88 hectares) or less, however, accounted for 44.22 per cent of all estates, but held only 8.47 per cent of the land.[60] Peasants were increasingly forced to obtain credit to maintain their livelihoods, but this often entailed paying usurious rates.[61] Tax arrears grew tremendously, and this was accompanied by a 60 per cent increase in the average annual mortgage debt between 1865–72 and 1879–83.[62] Indebtedness in the agrarian sector grew from 40.5 million crowns in 1880 to 171.1 million crowns in 1900, a 322 per cent increase.[63] There was a major growth in different credit institutions (banks, credit unions) and capital accumulation from the 1880s to 1914, which undoubtedly contributed to growing peasant indebtedness. In 1870 there were only fourteen such institutions, by 1890 ninety-four with 66.15 million crowns in capital, and by 1910 a total of 993 credit institutions possessed 312.25 million crowns in capital.[64] But a large part of this capital represented foreclosures on mortgages on peasant land, which was increasingly being taken from peasant hands.

By the turn of the twentieth century Croatia was still a predominantly agrarian and relatively backward society. The process of modernization had undeniably been initiated, but measured in terms of industrial growth and urbanization, its rate in Croatia was relatively slow. In 1890 Croatia-Slavonia had the second highest proportion of population deriving its livelihood from agriculture in the Dual Monarchy (84.64 per cent), and the lowest proportion in handicrafts, industry, and commerce. The bourgeoisie was numerically weak: in 1890 only 8.39 per cent of the population derived its livelihood from mining, handicrafts, and industry, and 2.35 per cent from commerce, banking, and related fields. Another 1.94 per cent derived its livelihood from intellectual endeavour, defined here as law, medicine, journalism, the teaching professions, and related fields.[65] In 1914 Croatia-Slavonia was still among the most agrarian and least industrialized of the Habsburg lands. As noted earlier, there was considerable population growth in the late nineteenth century: 15.5 per cent in the period 1880 to 1890, 10.5 per cent in the following decade, and 8.5 per cent between 1900 and 1910, for an overall increase of 38.6 per cent between 1880 and 1910.[66] Although the urban sector experienced growth, the ratio of urban to rural population was not altered drastically: in 1869, 6.2 per cent of the population lived in urban centres, and in 1910 this had grown only to 8.5 per cent.[67] In 1870 Croatia still did not have any urban centres with more than 20,000 inhabitants. Zagreb, the capital, grew rather slowly after 1870, from 19,857 to just under 40,000 in 1890. By 1910 it had a population of about 75,000.[68] Only a few other urban centres, such as Karlovac, Osijek, and Varaždin, experienced major growth.

Despite the slow rate of modernization, the traditional peasant way of life began to change. Burdened by heavy taxes, rural overpopulation, and indebtedness, many peasants could not sustain a viable economic existence in the village. What exacerbated the peasantry's plight even further was the persistence of outdated and unproductive agricultural techniques. In the late nineteenth century most Croat peasants still employed either the two- or three-field system. Under the two-field system peasants would sow cereals as a winter crop in one field and use the other field for spring crops like wheat, corn, and rye. The land was quickly exhausted because fertilizers were not yet commonly used. The only difference between the two- and three-field systems was that under the latter peasants would leave one field fallow (usually one-third of the land, often even more) in order not to exhaust the land too rapidly. Only on the larger estates were more productive techniques adopted in the 1870s and 1880s. Peasants rarely proved capable of improving their farming techniques, and hence their productivity, because of the low level of education, the paucity of information available to them, and the lack of capital to invest in land and modern equipment.[69]

The economic malaise of the Croatian village compelled many peasants to leave the countryside. They left for the city or, more often than not, emigrated because of the weak level of industrial growth in the urban centres.[70] In 1900 there were just under 19,000 workers, but very few were in heavy industry.[71] In the 1890s most workers in Croatia-Slavonia were employed in forestry and were peasants recently removed from, or still residing in, the village. By 1900, however, the lumber industry was in decline and being replaced by a variety of light industries, such as food processing, cement, glass, and other construction-related branches.[72] Working conditions were difficult, as unions were strictly forbidden by the regime in the 1890s. The slow pace of industrialization and rural overpopulation contributed to a rate of emigration that took on disastrous proportions. According to one estimate, between 1899 and 1913 close to 190,000 people emigrated from Croatia-Slavonia, accounting for about 6 per cent of the total population.[73]

In most cases, the best a peasant could hope for was to gain an education and enter government service or one of the free professions. But those who succeeded in leaving the village often treated the peasantry worse than the established urban élites did. Often despising their own meagre origins, these newly urbanized or embourgeoised peasants proved callous in their dealings with the village. The peasantry's struggle against exploitation and oppression, be it political, social, or economic, amounted to a struggle against the city.[74] This urban–rural or bourgeois–peasant divide, typical of agrarian societies, was one of the main features of Croatian life at the turn of the century. The former noble élite was now replaced by the government bureaucracy, staffed increasingly by the urban intelligentsia, which for the peasantry represented the city. The city was, in short, the tax collector, army recruiter, and manipulative market combined into one ominous and exploitative entity. Furthermore, it represented a virtually alien set of values and habits that were markedly different from those of the peasant sub-culture. The anger of the peasants was directed mainly at the *kaputaš*, the wearer of a *kaput* (city overcoat), who was the city incarnate. For peasants the expansion of the state after 1868 provided few, if any, benefits. Burdened by heavy taxation at a time of economic distress, peasants bore the brunt of the state-building process after 1868 and thus came to resent the new bureaucracy. Hence the growing animosity on the part of the peasantry towards the city (the bureaucrat, the *kaputaš*) and alienation from the state apparatus, as well as the immense chasm that separated peasants from the intellectual élite, regardless of their political or ideological affiliation.

This was demonstrated during the 'national movement' of the summer of 1883, provoked by the introduction of Magyar-language signs on government buildings in Croatia. Beginning in Zagreb, protests spread to small towns and eventually to the countryside, especially the region of Hrvatsko Zagorje and parts of the former Military Frontier. These peasant demonstrations exhibited an anti-Magyar character, showing that the national idea had begun to penetrate the village. But the underlying causes were social and economic in nature. The introduction of Magyar signs created fears in the countryside that the Magyars were about to impose new tax and other burdens. The Croat peasants of Blinjski Kut, Kinjačka, and Brdjani (Petrinja district) attacked the local teacher and priest and threatened all Croat officials with death for being in the pay of the Magyars. In Maja commune (Glina district) peasants attacked representatives of the local intelligentsia – the *kaputaši* – and killed a communal official. In Hrvatsko Zagorje, where the peasant disturbances began, peasants first attacked the local officials who collected the taxes and then all wealthier people, especially members of the National Party.[75] The disturbances were soon quelled, and in September 1883 a commissariat (absolutist regime) under General Hermann Ramberg was established, which lasted until December. A government official who investigated the peasant disturbances of 1883 succinctly summarized the peasant attitude towards his many new burdens: 'All of this feeds upon the wretched peasant and he therefore sees every civilized person as his enemy and torturing demon. That is why one heard the slogan during the disorders, all *kaputaši* should be killed.'[76] The events of 1883 demonstrated that the process of national integration had made important strides in the countryside,[77] and this can be attributed at least in part to the introduction of mandatory primary schooling and to the nationalist agitation of Starčević's followers. As the attacks against government officials, priests, teachers, and *kaputaši* in general showed, however, many, perhaps still most, peasants could not identify with the intelligentsia. Future peasant disturbances, such as those in 1918, would demonstrate the continued existence of an immense chasm between the peasantry and educated society.

This deep-seated antagonism was a major obstacle to the completion of the process of national integration. The peasantry for the most part could not identify with the urban élite (intelligentsia) that had hitherto dominated the national movement or the Croatian state that this élite was attempting to construct. In other words, the peasantry could not become the objective bearer of the national movement without first being won over to the national cause. The closely related issues of integrating the peasants into the nation and the proper relationship between the intelligentsia and the people, became the central questions that the younger generation of the Croat intelligentsia attempted to resolve in the 1890s. This was the generation of Stjepan Radić. He and his colleagues sought the means to remedy the social and economic ills that plagued Croatian society, and to bring to an end the growing nationalist antagonisms between Croats and Serbs. Central to their endeavours was the attempt to integrate the common people, the peasants, into the national organism.

2

Stjepan Radić: The Formative Years, 1871–1904

The truth be known, our wine is fiery, but that is why our intelligentsia is docile to the point of lethargy and cold to the point of iciness. They tell me everywhere that I will either smarten up or end up on the gallows or in a lunatic asylum.

Stjepan Radić, 1894

Stjepan Radić was born on 11 June 1871 in Trebarjevo Desno, a village on the banks of the Sava river to the southeast of Zagreb, near the provincial town of Sisak. Radić was near-sighted since birth, and of very limited material means; his future, like that of many other peasant children at the time, seemed far less than promising.[1] Yet, in spite of the imposing obstacles that lay in his path, he possessed a tremendous energy that would propel him through the most difficult of circumstances. His life is in many ways a testament to the important role that individuals can play in history and the ability of individuals to overcome and, to a certain extent, even to shape their environment.

It is especially important to analyse the various factors that shaped the character and contributed to the development of Stjepan Radić in his formative years. Influenced by a number of individuals, in most cases he synthesized their ideas into a world view that was later imparted to the party he co-founded. A number of ideological strains came together to form Radić's *Weltanschauung*, including, in varying degrees, Czech realism, Russian populism, and, most importantly, nineteenth century Croat political figures. One must also emphasize the role of Radić's, brother Antun, for he helped to mould Stjepan's character. In many respects Antun acted as a filter through which a number of Stjepan's views crystallized. Finally, it is impossible to ignore the obvious and determinant influence of his social milieu. Although individuals can often rise above the circumstances that confront them, they are seldom able completely to escape their environment. The Radić brothers came to maturity at a time when the Croat village was undergoing tumultuous social and economic changes. The hardships and misery that they experienced and later witnessed in their travels throughout the Croatian countryside undoubtedly had a profound impact on them.

Stjepan was the ninth of eleven children, three of whom died in infancy. Only he and his brother Antun, who was born on the same day as he was three years earlier, managed to leave the village. Their parents, Imbro and Jana (Ana) Radić, were illiterate and relatively poor. Imbro was a tall and physically imposing man, a serious and introverted type. It appears that Stjepan inherited his mother's personality characteristics, for Jana was a clever and spirited woman. Stjepan would exhibit these qualities from an early age, whereas Antun was much more like their father, reserved, introverted, and given over more to serious thought than to action. Moreover, unlike his father, Stjepan was shorter than average and physically weak, which provoked taunting and the occasional beating from his schoolmates. It was perhaps to compensate for his physical shortcomings that he demonstrated great energy and courage, and distinguished himself as a good student. Radić's parents were, according to him, religious, honest, and hard working, and all of this left an imprint on Stjepan. He was raised in a religious and loving environment; 'nourished on this love from my earliest years I did not fear anything or anyone.' 'God planted a feeling for justice in my father and mother like the rest of us,' he once wrote, 'and when this feeling is developed, from it must grow gentleness and kindness towards everything that is living, but especially towards people – God's children.'[2] Throughout his life Stjepan was a practising Christian, and this invariably shaped his political views.

Although Stjepan's parents were better off than many other peasant families in their village and surrounding region, the pervasive rural poverty of the time shaped the Radićes' existence. This was especially true after 1873 when the great economic crisis descended upon the village with a vengeance. This protracted economic crisis occurred during Stjepan's formative years, and it would have an important impact on his future views. He came to the conclusion at an early age that the struggle for Croat political and national rights had to be closely tied to social and economic work and reforms in the countryside.

Because of Stjepan's myopia and the family's limited financial resources, his parents were not keen on having him pursue his studies beyond the primary level. But the determined Stjepan had different ideas, and he decided to follow in his brother's footsteps. Antun had left in 1881 to study in the Zagreb gymnasium and, having shown himself to be an excellent student, was able to procure a modest scholarship. Stjepan wrote to his brother asking for his financial assistance, even though Antun's scholarship was barely enough to sustain his own existence. Antun was less than pleased by his brother's request, and only after Stjepan presented his brother with a *fait accompli* by appearing in Zagreb did Antun reluctantly agree to support him financially. Stjepan enrolled in the gymnasium in the fall of 1883.

During these years Stjepan lived a pauper's existence, regularly obtaining his daily meals from the public kitchens of Zagreb's charitable institutions. But what mattered to Stjepan was that he was continuing his studies. A good student, in his first year he resided with a Catholic priest before moving to the orphanage of the Zagreb archbishopric. There the general conditions were more tolerable and his hunger pangs not as frequent. There were problems, however. During his second year the gymnasium's doctor suggested that Stjepan be dismissed because he would probably be blind within a few years. On another occasion that same year he was struck by an older student who, appointed by the school administration to monitor the behaviour of the other pupils, had a proclivity to abuse physically the younger students. Stjepan returned the blow and was subsequently forced to leave the orphanage. Stjepan continued to encounter difficulties with the school administration. In his fourth year he nearly came to blows with an instructor, which led to his expulsion from the gymnasium. He was forced to complete his fourth year in the town of Karlovac. There his economic situation was even more deplorable, and he frequently experienced fainting spells brought on by hunger. His plight was remedied somewhat by the occasional package of food from his family in Trebarjevo Desno. Fortunately he was permitted to return to the Zagreb gymnasium to complete his next two academic years.

After his third year of study, in the summer of 1886, Radić left on foot to travel across northern and eastern Croatia, the first of many such travels. He left Zagreb for the northeastern town of Koprivnica, then going along the Drava river to the Danube he arrived in Zemun, and finally Belgrade. From there he returned along the Sava river to Sisak and eventually to Zagreb, but not before going to the town of Djakovo, where he met Bishop Strossmayer for the first time.[3] Strossmayer was evidently unimpressed by Radić, whereas Radić was clearly overwhelmed by the experience. Gradually the two would become better acquainted, and Strossmayer eventually became one of Radić's patrons. Radić travelled again in the summer of 1888. Retracing part of his earlier journey through Slavonia, he also passed through the Slovene lands (Styria, Carniola), Istria, and the Croatian Littoral. These trips proved to be an education in themselves, for he observed rural conditions throughout those areas of Croatia-Slavonia that he traversed. Antun urged his brother to observe 'the causes of the pains, wounds, and sufferings of the people, and also in short note what causes the people to grieve ... [and] wherefore are the people's ideals. More time and information is required for this; but do as much as you can.' 'Gather from around the world and collect,' Antun concluded, 'all that is the best! One more thing: be wary, discreet in everything; this you need.'[4] Stjepan would indeed observe and collect, but he refused to be discreet. He claimed that he was warmly greeted in virtually every village, be it Croat or Serb, and took notes about what the people thought about the government, the *gospoda* (gentlemen, educated élite), and how the people lived. Undoubtedly deeply impressed by the plight of the village, Radić claimed that it was after his first trip that he decided to enter politics and not the bureaucracy, the typical avenue of employment of most students upon graduation.[5] His travels brought him to the conclusion that the peasantry, in spite of its poverty, rampant illiteracy, and passivity, should be politically organized.

From his earliest days, Radić demonstrated tremendous vivacity, a personal trait that he never lost. The most probable explanation for this is that he was forced, from an early age, to confront his own physical shortcomings. Short, weak, and virtually half-blind, he overcompensated for these limitations, whether by being a good student or by refusing to be bullied by anyone. His brother Antun, who did not share these physical impairments, was not nearly as boisterous as his younger brother. What is more, when Stjepan Radić went off to school in Zagreb and Karlovac, he undoubtedly encountered a good deal of snobbery and had to confront an urban society that possessed a disparaging view of peasants and village life. His own sensitivities were undoubtedly heightened, as were his sense of defensiveness and need for affirmation. Consciously or not, being outspoken and diligent were ways of refuting the prevailing urban stereotypes of peasant sloth and ignorance.

Radić also demonstrated much courage in confronting established authority, be it an abusive schoolmaster, priest, district prefect, or Magyar railway official. In part this was undeniably connected to and a reflection of his own ebullient personality. More importantly, however, it may also have been an indication of his distrust of officialdom, a common trait in Croat villages at that time. Indeed, just as Radić was leaving in the fall of 1883 to study in Zagreb, a commissariat was established to quell the peasant disturbances that had rocked Croatia that summer. Although it does not appear that any of Radić's family were involved in the rebellions, some of the bloodiest scenes took place in the environs of the town of Petrinja, only a few kilometres from his native village. Radić may not have personally experienced the violence, but undoubtedly he was exposed to the rather customary peasant view that the state official was an exploiter. His brother's emotive 1888 letter, referring to 'the pains, wounds, and sufferings' of the peasant people, indicates well enough to what extent both of them believed that the villages were in torment. Confronting and standing up to authority may well have been not just another means of personal affirmation but, in a more profound sense, of peasant affirmation, the desire to be recognized and respected.

In 1888 Radić participated in his first political demonstration. During the 1880s Starčević's Party of Right was the most popular opposition party in Croatia, particularly among students. Starčević's uncompromising attitude on the inviolability of Croatia's historic rights, precisely at a time when those rights were being undermined by the rule of the *ban* Khuen-Héderváry, had a powerful sway over Radić. Possessed of a strong will for action, Radić's nationalist sentiments, which were awakened and nurtured in the Zagreb and Karlovac gymnasia, soon found expression. The catalyst for Radić's first political act was the last performance of Ivan Zajc's opera *Nikola Zrinski* at Zagreb's National Theatre. Khuen-Héderváry had ordered that the opera be closed. For Radić this was a provocative move, one which he could not let pass without incident. The opera's central character, Nikola Zrinski, a scion of one of Croatia's oldest noble families, died defending the town of Szeged in 1566 against Suleiman the Magnificent's janissaries. In spite of the over-whelming odds, Zrinski and his men held out for a considerable time, inflicting heavy losses on the Ottoman troops. The opera glorified Zrinski's sacrifice and clearly had nationalist overtones. During the third act of the performance Radić rose to his feet and shouted 'Glory to Zrinski, down with the tyrant Héderváry!' He was arrested but no serious penalty was imposed for his action, probably because Khuen-Héderváry did not want to turn Radić into a student martyr and preferred to let the matter pass.

Although soon released from custody, Radić was advised by one of his school instructors to remain voluntarily absent from the gymnasium, for this might spare him any formal penalties from the school administration. He did so but nevertheless received certification that he had completed the academic year successfully. Radić's last two years were beset with complications. In November 1889 he was disciplined by the school administration for agitating among his student colleagues, and in April 1890 he was sent to the mental infirmary of the Zagreb hospital. There he was held under observation for eight days, and once released was ordered to return to his native village. Ensconced in Trebarjevo Desno from then till the spring of 1891 he prepared for his final examinations.

Despite these problems, Radić continued his travels. In the summer of 1888, as Radić travelled through Slavonia, he again made his way to the town of Djakovo to meet with Strossmayer. Radić wished to go to Russia and hoped Strossmayer would provide him with a letter of introduction. But Strossmayer informed him that a letter from him, a Roman Catholic bishop, would be of little use in Russia and instead directed him to Mihajlo, the Metropolitan of the Serbian Orthodox Church in Belgrade, who in turn gave him a letter of introduction to the president of the Slavic Benevolent Society in Kiev.[6] While in Zagreb, Radić also met with the historian Canon Franjo Rački – 'the Croatian Palacký'[7] – in the hope that the latter would be able to provide some financial assistance for his trip. Rački did not and frankly told Radić that it was pointless to travel to Russia.

Disregarding Rački's advice, and with very little money, Radić set out for Kiev in the summer of 1889.[8] This was ostensibly to study Russian, but the trip was a pilgrimage of sorts, for Radić had demonstrated Russophile and Slavophile sympathies at an early age. Although it would seem that they were acquired through the influence of Strossmayer and Rački, it must be remembered that even Starčević's Party of Right went through a Russophile phase in the 1880s. Radić's early views about Russia were indeed excessively impressionistic and romantic, a fact which Antun pointed out.[9] In Kiev Radić stayed at the Monastery of Caves, where he was given Russian lessons by a resident monk and studied at the library of the local Slavic Benevolent Society. By the end of his two-month stay he had acquired a working knowledge of Russian. This was the first of a number of trips Radić would make to Russia. In 1889 he went there as a poor and impressionable student, in 1896 in the hope of enrolling at Moscow University, in 1908–9 as the leader of the peasant party to defend the Dual Monarchy's annexation of, and Croatia's claim to, Bosnia-Herzegovina, and finally in 1924 as the leader of the Croat peasant movement to win Soviet Russia's support for his cause.

Matriculating in 1891, Radić at once set out again to travel, this time to Dalmatia. Traversing the impoverished Dalmatian hinterland he made his way to Mostar, the capital of Herzegovina, where he was denounced to the police by some local Serbs for supposedly spreading Croat nationalist propaganda in the area.[10] He was briefly detained and forced to leave under police escort for Rijeka, where he was released. He finally made his circuitous way back to Zagreb where he enrolled in the faculty of law at the University of Zagreb.[11] In the city Radić actively sought out a number of political leaders and scholars, particularly Rački, Josip Frank, and Starčević, among others, and often met with them to discuss recent Croatian political history. It was through these contacts that Radić gained much of his knowledge of contemporary Croatian politics. At the university he became acquainted with other patriotically inclined students. It was this group of students that would participate in the anti-Magyar demonstrations of 16 October 1895 and subsequently, as a result of their expulsion from the University of Zagreb, move to Prague to pursue their education. They eventually constituted themselves as the Progressive Youth and would provide a new generation of Croat political leaders who would re-examine many of the assumptions at the root of Croat political life in the decade before the First World War.

Although both Rački and Strossmayer eventually exerted a considerable influence on Radić, in the late 1880s and early 1890s he was closer to Starčević. This is certainly not surprising, given the Party of Right's popularity among Croatia's students. Starčević's influence is revealed in an 1892 document in which Radić wrote that Croats had a 'native enemy' in their own land: 'They are those people, whom our people call Vlachs [Serbs] ... Their priests and teachers teach them, and have already taught them, that they are "Serbs" because they are of the same faith with those people in Serbia ... [and] that the Croats are merely a Serb race.' Assessing the Croat political parties of the day, he attacked both the so-called Magyarones (National Party) and the *obzoraši*, the political heirs of Strossmayer, for not defending Croat political rights. Of the *obzoraši* he wrote that 'you never know who they are,' for they 'began calling the Croats Illyrians, Yugoslavs, Serbo-Croats, and God knows what else, but not Croats.' He characterized the Party of Right, on the other hand, as a party 'that all Croats support,' especially the Croat peasants.[12] Starčević clearly exerted a considerable influence on the young Stjepan Radić.

Despite his initial devotion to Starčević, Radić broke with 'the Old Man' and increasingly came under the influence of the traditions of both Illyrianism and Yugoslavism, but with a pronounced emphasis on Croat state right. His split with Starčević was occasioned by a conversation the two men had in 1892 regarding a new paper the *pravaši* directed at the peasants. Radić was evidently dissatisfied with the content and layout of the paper and told Starčević that it was written in such a way as to be virtually incomprehensible to most peasants. 'Who will teach these people,' Radić frankly asked Starčević, 'if you, I, and the rest of us who are peasant children will not?' According to Radić, Starčević simply responded: 'Let the devil or God teach them, I will not. Whoever so wishes, here is [the Party of Right paper] *Hrvatska* [*Croatia*], from it he will recognize all of our enemies.'[13] With these words Radić's ties with Starčević came to an abrupt end, for they revealed a seemingly callous disregard for the interests and suffering of the peasantry.

Radić's disillusionment with 'the Old Man' and the Party of Right was certainly painful for him, for his early years had been shaped by an idealized vision of Starčević and the patriotic struggle of his party. But Radić already sensed the need to begin organized work among the ordinary people, yet neither the *pravaši* nor the *obzoraši* had a well established party network in the village or truly sensed the need for sustained political work among the masses. Nevertheless, in spite of the sense of disillusionment, Radić and his student colleagues supported the movement towards unification in 1893–4 between the two hitherto hostile opposition groups. Within two years, however, they would all relocate to different universities, most of them to Prague, some to Vienna, and Radić to Paris, from where they began a collective re-examination of the basic political tenets of the Croat opposition.

These patriotic students were dissatisfied with the prevailing state of affairs in Croatia and her subordination to Budapest. What they, and Radić in particular, wanted was action and results, and neither of the two Croat opposition parties could offer this. 'Our national misfortunes give you no respite,' Antun wrote to his brother in late 1891, 'this is a good sign, because you must have absorbed the desire for the greater glory of Croatia somewhere: you are therefore not alone, someone taught you this.'[14] But Antun was concerned about Stjepan's constant, almost intuitive, need to act and feared that his unbridled energy would do him more harm than good. It was necessary to channel this energy into constructive endeavours, and this is why he attempted to assuage Stjepan's restlessness. In early 1892 Antun wrote to Stjepan:

I often think about your whole manner of thinking – and in spite of the fact that you are my brother, in spite of the fact that I love you, I cannot approve of this manner of thinking. I talked to you much, but I believe that I have had little success. In one respect this heartens me: this is my guarantee that not everything that I thought about you is completely true, namely, that everyone's words win you over, only if they sound nice and if they say something grand ... But perhaps I have not succeeded with you because I did not talk to you of great things, on the contrary I spoke to you of the peaceful, legal development of things, and I did not fly to the heavens below the clouds or shatter mountains. Hear me, so that I can tell you something: Something about you terribly disturbs me – and that is why I beg you: think about this. Listen: you always have some kind of mission on your mind ... And because you have a mission on your mind you do not have peace, you cannot think about other things, not even a single thing, unless it is connected with this mission. This does you much harm: it disturbs your tranquility of judgment. I seek the roots, the causes: what could have provided the motive, but you have given yourself over exclusively, or at least overwhelmingly, to one idea: political. But why do you not contemplate ... God forbid that I should advise someone to abandon entirely their interest in political conditions, but I do not believe that agitation is a successful method ... My wish would be that you avoid every agitation among younger people – that you in general, as they say, not excel [as an agitator].[15]

This letter captures the essence of the fundamental differences between the two men and sheds important light on Stjepan Radić's character. Although Stjepan referred to Antun as 'my Mentor,'[16] for a good part of the 1890s, they would remain divided on a number of fundamental issues, not least the matter of political tactics.

Stjepan did not heed his brother's advice. In fact, he excelled as an agitator in attempting to organize his student colleagues and in manifesting their collective discontent. On 23 July 1893 Radić and a colleague acted as delegates of the university's student body at the commemoration in Sisak of the three-hundredth anniversary of the Croatian *ban* Tomo Bakač's victory over the Ottoman Turks. When one of the speakers used the occasion to praise Khuen-Hédervary, Radić shouted out in indignation: 'We are celebrating here the three-hundredth anniversary of the victory of a Croat *ban*, and not the tenth anniversary of the despotic rule of a Magyar hussar, who called himself this in the *Sabor* and added that he is proud of the title!'[17] He was arrested and sentenced to four months in prison (October 1893 to February 1894). He was also expelled from the University of Zagreb.

Before the trial took place, Radić travelled to Prague to make arrangements to continue his studies in Bohemia. A Prague associate, Oscar Plocar, was able to raise sufficient funds for Stjepan's tuition and the required books. 'I am completely happy like this,' Stjepan wrote from Prague, 'because I am according to the possibilities preparing myself one day to unify and liberate Croatia with the help of the just and eternal God and sincere and faithful friends.'[18] This was now Radić's mission, his crusade, and he already saw himself as a leader. He indicated that he was 'quickly winning over all of our younger men,' but regretted that he would have to spend time in prison just as this gathering process had begun.[19] Judging by a letter that he received from Frano Supilo, a Croat journalist in Dubrovnik who would become prominent in Croatian politics after 1905 as one of the architects of the 'new course,' Radić hoped to recruit Croat students to go to Prague to continue their studies.[20]

While in prison Radić worked on improving his Czech and occupied himself with what little literature he could get his hands on. But he seems to have been at odds with some of his former student colleagues, apparently because few of them would visit him in prison out of fear of reprisals.[21] 'It is not true that I do not have freedom,' he wrote to his brother Ivan in December 1893, 'I think freely about whatever I wish, and if I so desire I can say aloud whatever I think. My four walls will listen to me before our icy and wooden young Croats do.' The letter revealed profound bitterness, but in a sense his prison walls managed at least temporarily to temper his zeal for activism and forced him to contemplate his predicament. But the will to act could not be tempered for long. 'You know very well,' he wrote to an associate while still in prison, 'that no one would know of me unless our savage predicament forced me to react.'[22] Released in late February 1894, he was in Prague within two months.

In the 1890s Prague – 'this beautiful and great Slavic city'[23] – was the scene of a bitter German–Czech national struggle. In 1893 a wave of student riots led to the imposition of martial law. The growing radicalization and democratization of Czech society would force a reorientation of Czech politics in this period. Once there Radić adopted an immediate interest in Czech politics, joined the student society *Slavia*, and generally sympathized with the Young Czechs, the dominant party in the 1890s. Radić's Slavophile sympathies were immeasurably strengthened in Prague. Moreover, from these early years in Prague to the end of his life he would remain an admirer of the Czechs. In the process he acquired a Czech wife, Marija (Mařinka) Dvořák (1874–1954), a young schoolteacher whom he met in the village of Jistelnica near Tábor in 1894. Radić the activist and agitator could not avoid complications, despite his brother's earlier warnings. In the autumn of 1894 he again got into trouble during a student political meeting that was dispersed by the Prague police. Radić apparently accosted one of the policemen and cornered him near a window of the two-storey building, which led the officer to conclude, as he later reported to the court, that Radić was planning an act of defenestration. Radić denied this but still received a ten-day jail term, which he served from 15 to 25 November 1894, and was subsequently expelled from Prague University and the whole of Cisleithenia on 28 November.[24]

Expelled from yet another university, Radić initially contemplated going to the Polish university in Lwów (Galicia) and then travelling throughout Europe. This plan was dashed by his expulsion from the Austrian half of the monarchy. Once again his plans provoked a sharp rebuke from Antun. 'You dream too much,' he wrote to Stjepan in November 1894, 'you write that, if you are expelled [from Prague University], you will go to Lwów, after that you will travel, then to Paris, and finally to St Petersburg. When you become acquainted with the West, you will compare it with the East. These are big words. I advise you not to throw them around so lightly.' He added that 'decades are required for this kind of study.' Instead, he urged his brother to concentrate on his studies, for he would learn more this way than by his proposed meanderings throughout Europe. He advised him to enrol at the University of Vienna – this was before Stjepan's official expulsion from Cisleithenia – and to travel in his spare time. As before, Antun wanted Stjepan to curb his impulsiveness: 'You do not know how to observe quietly ... You also want to act. You promised me – but did not hold to your word. I would like to know how you justify your restlessness. To what end, and to whom, is your "work" of any benefit? I thought you would *study* and *observe*. At least if you were at home – but to pull the chestnuts [out of the fire] in such a faraway region [Bohemia] – for whom?'[25] Judging by Stjepan's subsequent actions, he disregarded this advice.

From Prague Stjepan returned to Zagreb in early 1895 with the intention of going to Budapest to enrol in the faculty of law for the spring semester. But it appears that in the autumn of 1895 he was thinking of again enrolling at Zagreb university 'so that I can better follow the development of political conditions [in Croatia] and work directly among the university youth.'[26] None of these plans came to pass, however. In the summer and autumn of 1895 preparations were under way for the official opening of the new National Theatre in Zagreb, scheduled for October 1895. As part of the celebrations the King-Emperor Franz Joseph was invited to Zagreb. Despite his brother's remonstrations, Radić intended to use the occasion to carry out another political demonstration. He was slowly gathering around himself 'a group of future workers for the complete awakening of the Croat people.' 'Today we have too many people in both Croatia and Bohemia,' he wrote in September 1895, 'who want to procure mercy from our oppressors through beggary.' He rejected this approach as 'unbecoming of a man'; his solution was action: 'Work, many-sided, little work saves peoples ... we love our people and not just the stones of our homeland, that is why we want to demonstrate with deeds that we want justice and freedom.'[27] Radić and his workers would shortly manifest these sentiments.

On 16 October 1895 Radić led a group of students to Jelačić Square in central Zagreb as Franz Joseph and his entourage, in the company of the Hungarian minister-president, toured the city's streets. After solemnly circling Jelačić's statue the students unfurled a Magyar flag and proceeded to burn it, shouting 'Long live the Croatian king!,' 'Glory to *ban* Jelačić!' and 'Down with the Magyars!' 'We did not trample on the Magyar flag,' he wrote shortly after the incident, 'we did not rip it up, but we only destroyed it, and this in front of the statue of that Croatian *ban* who knew how to combine loyalty and devotion to his Croat nation with a sincere devotion to the lawful dynasty.' The demonstrators hoped to impress upon Franz Joseph the level of Croat discontent and that the prevailing sentiment was decidedly anti-Magyar. Franz Joseph was not visiting just another Hungarian province.[28] There was a great deal of irony to the entire episode. Franz Joseph, who ascended the throne during the revolutionary upheavals of 1848–9 and almost lost his empire because of Lajos Kossuth's Hungarian revolution, had made his peace with Kossuth's heirs in 1867. Now the sons of Jelačić, a man who played a central role in the Habsburg counter-revolution, were impressing upon Franz Joseph the need to end the oppressive rule of the Magyars. Yesterday's counter-revolutionaries had now become revolutionaries, prepared and more than eager to carry out their own 'lawful revolution.'[29]

Radić and his colleagues, a total of fifty-one students, were arrested and charged with disturbing the public order. He wrote to Marija Dvořák a few weeks before his sentencing that he was 'ready for the maximum punishment, for five years of prison. I know that in politics and everywhere a man must suffer for his ideas, and I also know that only after a man suffers long and hard for them, does he completely and profoundly comprehend them.' Radić tried using the trial, which lasted from 11 to 16 November, as a platform to demonstrate Magyar abuse of Croat constitutional rights and delivered speeches to a packed courtroom. Although the students faced prison terms of up to five years, they all received reduced sentences. As the ringleader Radić received a six-month prison term (November 1895 to May 1896), but the flag-burning incident and the trial won Radić wider acclaim within Croat nationalist and student circles. Most of the students, having now been formally expelled from Zagreb University, decided to continue their studies in Prague after their release. This was actively encouraged by Radić, for he believed that the Czechs 'will still for a long time remain teachers to us Croats in everything, and especially in politics,' and that the Croat students would immeasurably broaden their intellectual horizons in Bohemia.[30] They already sensed that their horizons were too limited. To that end many of them began studying Czech (and Radić, French) and preoccupied themselves with what literature was provided to them by the prison administration. Radić was particularly impressed by Anatol Leroy-Beaulieu's *Das Reich der Zaren und die Russen*, for he believed that it presented him with an accurate assessment of conditions in Russia and the intelligentsia, as well as the works of the German scholar Johann K. Bluntschli. The latter's *Die Politik* 'explained to us the differences and obstacles between parties and nations [in Western and Central Europe] and informed us about the power of states, the projects of politicians, and the aspirations of rulers. How many times, having read a few pages, we looked at each other, telling ourselves, or at least thinking: we had no idea about all of these things, and yet we are almost at the end of our university studies.'[31] This was simultaneously an acknowledgment of the shortcomings of his own earlier education and a desire to broaden his intellectual horizons.

Radić also read and was evidently impressed by Tomáš Garrigue Masaryk's *Česká otázka* (*The Czech Question*, 1895). A prominent Czech scholar, Masaryk became increasingly vocal in Czech political life from the early 1890s as an exponent of 'realism.' Breaking with the dominant Young Czech party, Masaryk urged daily work among the common people, as opposed to the prevailing emphasis on high politics (Bohemian state right). Radić apparently met Masaryk briefly while in Prague in 1893 and became aware of his writings. Radić would eventually read a number of his works, including *Naše nynější krise* (*Our Present Crisis*, 1895). Commenting on this work to his Czech friend František Hlaváček, Radić wrote that he was pleased to see 'that I have already expressed the thoughts and views [outlined in *Naše nynější krise*] to my friends.' He claimed that Masaryk's *Sociální otázku* (*The Social Question*, 1900) had a profound impact on him.[32]

Indeed, Masaryk would greatly influence Radić and his colleagues, most of whom moved to Prague in 1896, although Radić himself would decide to pursue his studies in Russia. Once again Antun attempted to convince Stjepan that his complete devotion to political activism was altogether unhealthy. 'I do not mean to criticize you,' he wrote to Stjepan in December 1895, 'but I intend to repeat to you what I have already said and to add something. *Do not let politics entirely devour you!* There is life outside of politics – politics serves *life*.' Although he did not urge his brother to abandon politics, he wanted him to broaden his interests instead of sacrificing everything to politics.[33] It is unclear to what extent Radić heeded these words, but in the following few years Stjepan did place a much greater emphasis on his studies. Perhaps this was a result of his brother's admonitions, but it may also stem from the fact that between 1896 and 1899 he spent considerable time outside of Croatia and the Habsburg monarchy, and that most of his colleagues were also far removed from Croatia, having relocated to Prague.[34] They now placed a greater emphasis on their education, and by 1897 their political method changed. Instead of protests they would launch their own journal to win the hearts and minds of Croatia's students.

Released from prison in mid-May 1896, Radić was escorted by gendarmes to his home village of Trebarjevo Desno. With the financial support of a committee established to assist the jailed students and a number of patriotic Croats, Radić made his second journey to Russia.[35] He arrived in Moscow on 30 May and was to remain there until 25 August. He hoped to enrol as a law candidate at the university and to complete his studies in Moscow by June 1897. If this plan failed, he intended to go either to Paris or Cracow. He even entertained the idea of pursuing graduate studies in Moscow, but all of this hinged on being accepted as a regular student in the autumn of 1896. He was informed in July 1896, however, that he could not enrol as a regular student, although he was allowed to audit a number of courses. After one or two years of auditing courses he could petition the Ministry of Education to write the state exams and, if successful, receive the title of law candidate and then pursue graduate studies. This appealed to him, but since he was not accepted as a regular student, and because his poor financial predicament militated against a prolonged stay, Radić decided to pursue his studies elsewhere.[36]

In Moscow Radić read voraciously, and of the Russian works that he encountered, those of Vissarion Belinsky, the populist literary critic Aleksandr Skabichevsky, the nihilist writer Dmitry Pisarev, and the radical Nikolai Dobrolyubov, stand out.[37] It remains debatable to what extent any of this literature, especially the works of Russian literary populism, had an influence on the evolution of his political views. What is fairly certain, however, is that the abundant social criticism of Russian literature and the populists' portrayal of the sufferings of the common people, as well as the example they set in 'going to the people,' provided Radić with a useful comparative context from which he could make inferences about how the Croat intelligentsia should act towards its own people. Indeed, Antun Radić emphasized the importance of Russian literature because it provided guidance in the resolution of two critical issues: the problem of national culture and the proper relationship of the intelligentsia towards the people.[38] But in terms of cultural and economic work, Stjepan Radić was always more inclined to follow the Czech example. He consistently referred to Czechs as the most progressive of the Slavs and urged Croats to follow their lead in economic and cultural affairs.

While still in Moscow, Radić also read a Russian edition of John Stuart Mill's autobiography, which convinced him that his own intellectual horizons were still relatively limited. Mill knew more 'in his twelfth year than I do in my twenty-fifth,' and 'his knowledge was thorough and profound.' Radić sensed the shortcomings of his own hitherto erratic education and was determined to acquire a thorough and profound education of his own. He felt that hitherto he had only barely perceived the unclear framework of a proper education. Wanting to prepare himself for public life, he believed 'that politics in the true and broad sense of that word is the centre of modern education.'[39] Radić was determined to find a school that would provide him with a thorough education and prepare him for political life, and eventually found such a place in Paris in the form of the École Libre des Sciences Politiques.

Although his plans to stay in Russia proved unsuccessful, the trip evidently had an impact on him. Summarizing his work in Russia, Radić wrote that 'I watch, listen, study ... during the six months of my imprisonment [in Croatia] I had an opportunity to comprehend and to consider thoroughly everything that I need to accomplish what I have in mind. I am fortunate that I can learn much in Russia.' He asserted that his stay in Russia was 'reawakening' him.[40] What he now needed was to learn more. Evidently Antun's earlier remonstrations at last had some impact.

After a brief stay in Cracow in September 1896 Radić returned briefly to

Croatia in early October 1896. It is unclear whether he had decided to go to France at this stage. In his autobiography Radić writes that he learned of the École Libre while he was still in Moscow,[41] and he certainly raised the possibility of going to Paris while still there. In November 1896 he wrote that 'the foundation of my policy is the living homeland, the common people. That is why I enjoy living among the people, that is why I listen to every beat of the people's pulse ... I know that the Croats are only a branch of the great Slavic tree. That is why I sought and now still seek ties with all branches of this colossal, but still deeply slumbering tribe ... Hitherto Europe has been our stepmother, she has not recognized us as her children. In order for this not to remain so forever, we need people who will be able and know how to open Europe's eyes. That is why I must certainly go the West, especially to Paris.'[42] Yet it appears that he learned of the École Libre while in Prague in late December 1896 and January 1897.[43] Moreover, Radić indicated that he was informed of the school by the Czech politician Ladislav Pinkas, himself a graduate of the institution, and Radić obtained a copy of its program while in Prague.[44]

Armed with a letter of recommendation from Pinkas and barely enough money to get to France, Radić arrived in Paris on 22 February 1897 and settled at the Hôtel Saint-Pierre in the Latin Quarter. Radić could not have arrived at a more propitious time, for the Dreyfus Affair (1897–1906) would soon emerge as the central issue in French politics. This was a divisive and stimulating period in French politics. Yet judging by Radić's correspondence and private papers from this period, French politics seemingly provoked little interest in him, perhaps because of his low proficiency in French. Although he eventually acquired a number of French friends, and almost certainly discussed politics with them, he made few references to contemporary French political life in his published works or correspondence.

Lacking adequate funds and a good working knowledge of French to enrol immediately at the École Libre des Sciences Politiques, or 'Sciences Po,' as it was popularly known, Radić spent the summer in Lausanne studying French in a free summer course for foreign students. With financial support from his brother, friends, and various patrons, including Bishop Strossmayer,[45] Radić enrolled at the Sciences Po in October 1897.[46] There he studied diplomatic history, finance, comparative law, and ethnography, among other things.[47] He also met a number of prominent French academics and political figures, including Paul Deschanel, who in January 1920 was elected President of France. He passed his exams in June 1898 and began planning his marriage to Marija Dvořák. On 23 September 1898 they were wed in Prague and then left for Croatia, returning to Paris in February 1899. During the next five months he wrote his thesis, 'La Croatie actuelle et les Slaves du Sud.'[48] He completed his final examinations in June 1899 and, defending his thesis, received a bachelor's degree in political science.

It is difficult to ascertain precisely how significant Radić's Parisian experience was from an ideological perspective. To be sure, Radić became acquainted with the abundant French political and sociological literature and a number of English works in French translation, many of which he used subsequently in his scholarly works such as *Savremena Evropa* (*Contemporary Europe*, 1905) and *Savremena ustavnost* (*Contemporary Constitutionality*, 1911).[49] Radić attended the lectures of many prominent French academics, such as Anatol Leroy-Beaulieu, René Henry, Louis Léger, Ernest Denis, and Albert Sorel, most of whom had a scholarly interest in the Slavic peoples of Russia and East Central Europe.[50] This certainly broadened Radić's intellectual horizons. But besides acquainting himself with West European politics and international relations, as well as becoming a convinced Francophile (and probably more anti-German), it remains debatable to what extent he incorporated any of the ideas he acquired in Paris into his political philosophy or the peasantist ideology that formed the basis of his peasant party.

Yet the contours of Radić's political ideas were articulated precisely during his stay in France. In January 1897 Radić and his colleagues, most notably Živan Bertić, Milan Heimrl, and Milivoj Dežman-Ivanov, launched the first issue of their journal *Hrvatska misao* (*Croat Thought*), which they had been preparing since at least mid-1896.[51] It acted as the mouthpiece of the 'generation of 1895' or *mladi* (Young Men), as they called themselves at the time. Although it lasted only one year, it was succeeded by *Novo Doba* (*New Era*, 1898) and *Glas* (*The Voice*, 1899) and then resurrected in 1902 under its original name. Radić figured prominently in the pages of these journals and became the unofficial leader of the *mladi*.[52] In many ways this was completely natural, for Radić was, according to one of his first serious biographers, by far the most prominent and original of the *mladi*.[53] More importantly, Radić saw himself as a leader. In mid-June 1896 he noted in his diary: 'Because *I am* already a leader, I refuse to join any party. Whoever lets others carry out *his* ideas is a weakling, and he who plans on realizing them under the leadership of others is a fool.' He believed that he would remain a leader 'until I have a right to this. I will have a right until, according to the far-sightedness and profundity of my ideas, the resoluteness, adequacy and versatility of my *work*, I truly remain the first ... Leadership came into my hands naturally, by itself, and it will disappear naturally.'[54]

Radić's importance, and sense of self-importance, was clearly evident precisely at the time when the *mladi* were announcing themselves on the Croatian political scene. Their papers *Hrvatska misao* and *Novo Doba*, along with *Narodna misao* in Zagreb, the organ of the United Croat and Serb Youth who were led by the Croat Ivan Lorković and the Serb Svetozar Pribićević, were to herald new perspectives in Croatian political life; the policies of the existing Croat opposition, the *stari* (Old Men), were openly questioned and found lacking. Between 1897 and 1900 the *mladi* waged a campaign of sharp criticism of Croat politics and society. They would emerge within a decade as leading political and intellectual figures in Croatia, mainly within the Croat People's Progressive Party, which formed the core of the Croat wing of the Croato-Serb Coalition (HSK, *Hrvatsko-srpska koalicija*) in 1905. The Serb wing of the HSK, led by Pribićević, was recruited primarily from the Serbs of the United Croat and Serb Youth, who in 1903–5 displaced the old leadership of the Serb Independent Party.

These young intellectuals sought a remedy against what they perceived as the extreme despondency of Croatian politics, and they hoped to introduce new ideas to revitalize a decaying Croatian political, socioeconomic, and cultural edifice. Their task was 'to elaborate a correct methodology for the Croat political program,' and to find 'a path, manner, and tact which would enable the realization of our national demands.' Their starting point was to question and analyse a number of their own preconceptions. 'What is a nation?' was among the first questions they asked, as well as what the proper bases of national politics should be. In Bohemia – and Paris – they found a massive literature about these questions and became familiar with French and Russian intellectual trends through Czech works and in Czech translation, thus escaping the German cultural influence that permeated Croat intellectual endeavour in the second half of the nineteenth century. The *mladi* rejected the romantic concept of the nation as too sentimental and, critically analysing it using Auguste Comte's positivist philosophy, concluded that 'the nation is by no means that simple ideal and perfect being of the romantic world,' rather it was a 'complicated social organism, often very discordant, but certainly far from perfection.'[55] The masses were unenlightened, lived in poverty, and were for the most part apathetic. This was the painful reality that had to be addressed.

In many respects their endeavours represented a generational conflict, the Croat version of the struggle between the 'fathers' and 'sons.' The youth '*must* bring into life something new, something better,' the first issue of *Hrvatska misao* declared, 'because otherwise their accession in life would be superfluous.' 'That which is *new* among us,' the inaugural editorial continued, 'has since long ago been old elsewhere, that for which we might be stoned has elsewhere already become popular conviction.' They railed against the Magyarone regime in Croatia and at the same time criticized the Croat opposition,

for it did not 'methodically teach either the youth or the common people.'
Although there was 'integrity' and 'erudition' among the *stari*, there was
seemingly no love for the common people. 'We do not have either societies or
individuals who would go to the youth or to the people with love,' the *mladi*
cried, 'to instruct them by word, book, example; thus we are compelled to
help ourselves.'[56]

The *mladi* certainly did not intend to burn all of their bridges to the Croat
opposition. They hoped that it would be united into a single front and accept
their ideas. Radić indicated as much throughout 1897–8; he wanted firmer ties
between the *mladi* and *stari*, and for both the *pravaši* and the *obzoraši* to come
together on a common, populist platform. They remained bitterly opposed,
however, to the Frankist variant of the Starčevićist ideology. Radić referred to
Frank as a sectarian and 'a demagogue of the first order' because of his attitude towards the Serbs, his opposition to Slavic 'solidarity,' and his refusal to
accept any criticism of Starčević.[57] Despite their desire for firmer ties with the
older generation, this did not temper their angst. The *mladi* had to push the
intelligentsia and to expose the 'bareness' of Croatian society, in the hope that
this criticism would win over the intelligentsia.[58] The Croatian opposition
'does not have the will ... to teach us methodically and to lead us with love and
courage, rather it offers us a sad example of individual dissension, party intol-
erance, [and] political dogmatism.' To remedy this situation they wanted to
imbue Croat politics with new ideas.

The central notions that they promoted were realism and natural rights. This
gradually entailed a re-examination of the concept of a Croat political nation
and its concomitant, Croat state right. For the Croat opposition, Croatia was
simply 'a piece of land, and whoever thinks of an even greater piece of that
land [Great Croatia] is a greater patriot.' This the *mladi* rejected. 'Even the
concept of "nation" is not clear to us [Croats], because not even today do we
sincerely believe that the nation is composed of the peasant [*mužek*] of the
Zagorje [region] and the goatherd of the Lika [region], and it is especially
repulsive for us to hear that the "Vlach" [Serb] could be a member of this
nation ... The Croats and Serbs, therefore, are one nation. The lowest classes
in fact make up the core of this nation.'

If the common people – that is, the peasantry – constituted the core of the
nation, then in reality the intelligentsia had to be integrated into the peasantry.
At the same time, abandoning state right, the *mladi* could no longer regard the
Serbs as Orthodox Croats but as Serbs who formed one and the same people
with the Croats. Instead of phrase-mongering they wanted cautious, thought-
ful work in economic, cultural, and political life, and in place of political
romanticism 'we want political education and practical work.' The peasantry

could no longer be neglected; while the old patriots sang odes to the homeland the common people were being ruined materially. 'We delight in criticism, we are not afraid of struggle, we hope firmly in success.'[59] With these words the *mladi* announced themselves in Croatia, where they were initially denounced as socialists.

How were national politics to be conducted and how was the plight of the common people to be improved? Practical work became the slogan, but they soon recognized that it was easier to answer these questions in theory than in practice. Moreover, they did not all share the same answers. The first task was cultural enlightenment, that is, raising the people's cultural level, for there could be no radical change in social conditions without a 'revolution of the soul.' Closely tied to this cultural work was the need for economic work, sustained daily activity to improve the economic position of the people.[60] Under the influence of French positivism they wanted the socialization of culture. Moreover, they rejected revolution and adopted evolutionary means as the only viable method of political struggle.

Like Radić, the *mladi* were influenced by their Prague milieu in a number of ways. Not only were they exposed to Masaryk's realism and French and Russian literature, but their Slavic sensibilities were also strengthened. What was perhaps most important was their view of the Croat-Serb relationship. They attacked state right as unfruitful and adopted a belief in the *narodno jedinstvo* (national oneness) of the Croats and Serbs, that is, that they were one nation of two names. Their formula of *narodno jedinstvo* carried within it the implicit seeds of Yugoslav unitarism, particularly since many of them discarded Croat state right as a matter of principle. As one of their more prominent members wrote, demonstrating quite clearly the short leap from *narodno jedinstvo* to Yugoslavist unitarism: 'The national idea of the Croats and Serbs is therefore: a free and independent state on the entire territory on which the Serbs and Croats live in compact masses without consideration to historic and present state membership of individual parts of that territory.' The Croats and Serbs had to form one state in which both historical names would be cultivated, respected, and be completely equal.[61]

The *mladi* rejected 'the demons of tribal hatred' and tried to cooperate with the Serb youth. The declared task of *Novo doba*, which succeeded *Hrvatska misao* in 1898, was to establish the 'new spirit, new paths, new direction' among Serb and Slovene students in addition to Croats. Croat, Serb, and Slovene youth should act together for their 'common interests.' They employed the concept of *narodno jedinstvo* as a way of ending the growing Croat–Serb conflict in Croatia that had been exacerbated by the Khuen-Héderváry regime. They hoped to destroy the obstacles of hatred and fanaticism that lay in the path of mutual cooperation. But they did not want Croats and Serbs to renounce their individual names. In a healthily conceived *narodno jedinstvo* both Croats and Serbs were equal. To facilitate cultural oneness the *mladi* urged greater cultural interaction between Croats and Serbs, which would in turn promote the cultural integration of the 'Yugoslav tribes' (*jugoslovjenska plemena*), the end product being 'Yugoslav cultural federalism.' But this was only the first step, because 'these aspirations cannot remain without significant political repercussions. The aspiration for cultural oneness must awaken the aspiration for political amalgamation [*spojenjem političkim*], for Yugoslav political federalism.'[62]

These were pregnant words indeed, but this is to anticipate later developments. In the 1890s the possibility of such a common state was remote at best and few, if any, seriously thought in such terms at that time. The *mladi* were concerned with bringing immediate reform to Croatia. Furthermore, although they were held together by a common set of general principles and a desire to reform Croatian society, there remained important differences among them. For instance, state right was not abandoned by all of them, certainly not initially. The immediate task of the *mladi* was to 'broaden the national awakening to the broader masses of the people.' They saw the Illyrianist movement as an awakening of the Croat bourgeoisie that had done much to standardize the Croat literary language but had had little impact on the masses.[63] The youth had to 'prepare themselves for their future political work on a populist path ... [in order] to enrich politics with a social element.' They believed that a 'colossal power' lay dormant in the people; their task was to educate and raise the consciousness of the people in order to make them a political factor. Although they wanted the socialization of politics and culture, they distinguished between socialization and socialism. They were prepared to accept many aspects of the socialist critique of bourgeois society, as well as many of the demands of the socialists, but they rejected the Marxist dialectic and revolution and the collectivization of the means of production.[64]

The emphasis on realism was derived from Masaryk, whose role in shaping the *mladi* was very important.[65] This was particularly true in the case of state right, for he weaned them from this concept. Masaryk promoted realism and daily work and emphasized the need to labour among the lower classes. High politics was to give way to social and cultural work. Even though he rejected socialism, Masaryk saw in social democracy a useful ally in the struggle for political and social reforms. This view was imparted to many of the *mladi*, although Radić was an exception, as was Masaryk's anticlericalism. Furthermore, they concluded that the German *Drang* threatened Southern Slavs. In many ways the evolution of the *mladi* paralleled that of Masaryk, for just as he eventually broke with both the Old and Young Czechs and formed his own, Realist Party, the *mladi* would break with the traditional Croat parties and go their own way.

The *mladi* attacked the mixture of realism and romanticism in literature, as well as the ostentatious and solemn patriotic literature that did not deal with social issues. They came to represent a new literary current known as the *Moderna* that, generally speaking, had a cosmopolitan tone and emphasized the right to unfettered freedom of artistic expression and creation and rejected the idea that literature should have a didactic purpose.[66] Moreover, and more importantly, the existing Croat middle-class parties were criticized for neglecting the peasant masses. For the *mladi* the question of the proper relationship of the intelligentsia to the people was crucial and they invested some of their best intellectual endeavours in an attempt to resolve this issue.[67] It was precisely this question that would lead to a break not only between Radić and the traditional political élite (the *stari*) but also between himself and his former colleagues.

It was in the pages of the *mladi*-inspired journals that Radić began to articulate his political views. In his article about 'Croat ideals,' which represented the first coherent enunciation of his political ideas, he argued that national ideals were not the product of romantic dreams but of mature thought and strong character. Croats, and South Slavs in general, should not seek their ideals in the past: 'The past only divides us [South Slavs], and our greatest misfortune is that hitherto we have not had great politicians, economists, and philosophers, instead of great historians and philologists.' National greatness originated 'only from the soul,' whereas 'matter is the mother of terror and every type of savagery.' It was a 'great delusion,' Radić believed, that 'in our time there can exist "ideals" of territorial greatness [and] material supremacy.' That is why he attacked the concept of a political nation. 'There are Croats,' Radić wrote, 'whose "ideal" it is that Croatia should be as large as possible, but they do not think for a moment what kind of elements will make up this "Great" Croatia. We [*mladi*] do not fall into this group.'[68] This was a major departure from his earlier Starčevićist views.

Instead of state right, Radić espoused the *narodno jedinstvo* of Croats and Serbs. Indeed, this was the first ideal that Radić articulated. Although he recognized that historical circumstances had produced separate Croat and Serb identities, this did not diminish his belief in *narodno jedinstvo*. Simply stated, the Croats and Serbs were two tribes of one nation. Hence, 'total *narodno jedinstvo* is our ideal.' 'Our national soul is one,' Radić wrote, 'now it is necessary simply to manifest this oneness.' Slovenes and Bulgars, as 'the most similar peoples' to the 'Croat or Serb people,' must gradually draw nearer to

Croats and Serbs: '*Narodno jedinstvo* increases national strength a hundred-fold. It is the first condition to prevent the ruination of our people.' But according to Radić the ideal of *narodno jedinstvo* was not one of external form or of political autonomy, but a cultural phenomenon. 'For us a national state,' Radić wrote, 'is one in which the people are gathered and held together by a single, strong culture.' This is why, first of all, he urged that literature, music, and art, as well as national politics, be built and developed on Christian 'cultural principles,' and second, that Croats examine everything emanating from the West critically.

To do this meant sharpening their judgment and nourishing the Croat soul with the culture of the other Slavs. Slavic reciprocity was the second ideal that Radić articulated. By reciprocity he did not mean 'some kind of union of blood and history.' 'We are by blood only people,' he wrote, 'and our written history divides us [Slavs] like no other tribe [*pleme*]. But common traditions, entirely similar national character and language unite us, by which all Slavs are virtually one nation.' Slavs possessed a common soul, preserved through the ages by the common people: 'Instead of blindly praising the Slavic people, we will study its character, instead of threatening [others] with 100 million Slavs, we will study Slavic languages, *so that foreign interceders will disappear from among our midst.*' Radić believed that Croats had to learn from other Slavs, especially Czechs and Russians. Among the latter they would find a literature inspired with great ideas, 'an objective and extraordinarily abundant criticism,' particularly among the ranks of the intelligentsia, and an understanding of socioeconomic questions. Other Slavs should therefore be both a subject of study and a source of inspiration: 'Let us begin with Croat or Serb national oneness, continue with a healthily conceived Slavic reciprocity, and finish with an earnest and thorough study of the great West European culture.'

Closely tied to this notion of Slavic reciprocity was Radić's third ideal, that of religious oneness (*vjersko jedinstvo*). He was not implying a formal Catholic–Orthodox rapprochement, rather he urged unity on Christian principles, 'that unity which today exists, if rarely, in Christian hearts.'[69] This ideal reveals the important emphasis Radić placed on Christian ethics. What this amounted to was a call for Croats and Serbs to rise above religious denominationalism and nationalist particularism, two factors that had created much division between them since the 1870s. Radić's religious sentiments are important because they formed a central part of his political ideas. But even though he clung to Christian principles he remained an opponent of Catholic clericalism. 'We are and remain Christians,' he wrote in April 1901, 'but we do not want medieval one-sidedness which necessarily leads not only to the enslavement of free thought but also to the enslavement of healthy, *active*

Christianity.[70] Christian, as opposed to strictly Catholic, principles thus formed an important cornerstone of Radić's world-view, although for the *mladi* as a whole religious principles mattered little. Both Radić and his colleagues became opponents of clericalism, but he always maintained an emphasis on Christian ethics. The idea of an active Christianity was deeply embedded in Radić's mind and permeated all of his work and thought. All political actions had to possess an ethical basis and justification. Radić could not countenance a secular morality or a world devoid of Christian principles. Politics without a Christian moral framework would invariably degenerate into demagoguery. For Radić Christian principles and kindness represented the cornerstone of political character, and hence were essential to politics and social justice.[71] In this respect he was very close to Masaryk.

Having posited *narodno jedinstvo*, Slavic reciprocity, and religious oneness as national ideals, Radić therefore opposed all forms of (South) Slav nationalist megalomanias. In fact, as early as 1896 Radić had decried the miserable, overweening emphasis on Croat historicism.[72] He wrote in September 1901 that competing South Slav nationalisms and claims to different territories were 'the main reason of all the chaos and every weakness among the Southern Slavs.'[73] Earlier that year he spoke of 'our one nation,' whose intelligentsia had separated 'into four national [*narodnosne*] organizations, the Slovene, Croat, Serb and Bulgar.' It was both a great misfortune and a disgrace that Bosnia-Herzegovina and Macedonia had become battlefields where these intelligentsias struggled at cross-purposes employing the national principle.[74] Radić remained committed to these Slavophile sentiments throughout his life and consistently urged cooperation between South Slavs and indeed all of the Dual Monarchy's Slavs.

Radić produced another article on Croat national ideals in 1898 which essentially restated his earlier views in greater detail. Every political ideal needed three component parts: humanity, nationality, and personality or individuality, and should aim to develop, perfect, and improve the individual, enlighten the people, and move humanity forward. Croatian politics, he believed, did not yet possess such ideals. He again railed against the Starčevićist ideology. Starčević's Great Croatia was merely a copy of Great Hungary: 'Just as Hungary must stretch from the Carpathians to the [Adriatic] sea, so too must Croatia stretch from the Triglav to the Balkan [Mountains]. In both there will be room, enough land, and this is the most important thing; territorial form was the first thing – materialism of the worst kind – but no one thought about how the people would live, [and] what the political and social conditions would be.' Radić believed that Starčević's historicism and hatred for Austria were in large part derived from the Magyar ruling oligarchy. On the other hand, neither Illyrianism nor Strossmayer's Yugoslavism became true Croat political ideals, because they did not address the most pressing needs of the common people; the latter did not even win over the entire intelligentsia. Croatian politics were devoid of national political ideals and would not have any as long as Croat politicians 'continue to believe that the people do not have their own aspirations, their own ideals, but rather that these ideals must be created for them.'[75]

To remedy this situation Radić wrote of the need for social national oneness (*narodno jedinstvo društveno*). This was a reformulation of his views on Croato-Serb *narodno jedinstvo* that he had outlined in *Hrvatska misao*, but now with an added social dimension. 'Only from this internal social national oneness,' he wrote, 'will there develop an equality of all classes, the harmony of all social national powers.' When this social *narodno jedinstvo* was achieved it would result in substantive political reforms. 'Only on such a basis,' Radić continued, 'can the edifice of national sovereignty be built without illusion and irony.' Social *narodno jedinstvo* was needed because of the existing deplorable status of the common people, that is, the peasantry. 'Our soul becomes perplexed,' he wrote of the intelligentsia, 'when in such difficult times even the best "gentlemanly" sons of this people have only regret and excuses for the people.' He was convinced that 'the cause of all of this is the opinion of the gentlemen, that the people are below the gentlemen, that the "peasant is not a man."' That is why he concluded that the main national ideal of the Croats should be '*the social and political equality of the people, the "common" people with the "educated" gentlemen.*'[76] This was a direct attack against the 'gentlemen,' the term Radić employed to characterize Croatia's political and social élite, the intelligentsia, which was, he believed, to blame for the sorry plight of the common people. During the revolutions of 1848–9 the Croat intelligentsia demonstrated its strong national consciousness and willingness to defend the nation, but from that time the intelligentsia had become entirely despondent.[77]

Radić's espousal of Croat–Serb and social *narodno jedinstvo* was intended to remedy two of the prevailing problems in Croatian politics and society. By calling for *narodno jedinstvo* Radić wanted Croats and Serbs to overcome their mutual differences and to unite to bring about their national emancipation from the oppressive rule of, and subordination to, the Magyars. Since Khuen-Hedérváry had exploited these differences to perpetuate Magyar rule in Croatia, Radić believed that only through Croat–Serb cooperation could this domination be brought to an end. Of course, to cooperate with the Serbs it was necessary first to recognize them as a people who were one with the Croats. This necessarily meant reformulating, and in effect abandoning, the Starčevićist notion of a single Croat political nation. For Radić and the *mladi* the concept of *narodno jedinstvo* was to serve as a means of ending Croat and Serb rivalry and eliminating the incongruities between Croat and Serb national ideologies, thereby establishing the basis for joint cooperation against the Magyars. Social *narodno jedinstvo*, was to serve as the basis for a rapprochement between the intelligentsia and the people and was intended as a means of overcoming the growing social divide that separated the village and the city, the peasants and the bourgeois élite, the gentlemen.

Underlying this sentiment of social *narodno jedinstvo* was an idealistic assumption that the people, that is, the peasantry, represented the true national spirit. A political program that did not address the interests and needs of the common people could not form the basis of a truly national or democratic policy. According to Radić neither Croats nor Serbs had a truly national policy, and they would not as long as foreigners 'create our ideals or we construct them on their example.' Croats did not have to go to Vienna, Budapest, or Paris to acquire their political ideals. Rather they had to go to the people: 'We seek ideas, knowledge abroad; there we develop and acquire our intellectual abilities. But we must seek our political *ideas, a political directive* in the people. From these national ideas let us conceive our national ideals. On these national ideals let us develop national programs.' This was the basis, as Radić conceived it, on which a healthy national policy was to be conducted. Since he viewed politics as a social dynamic, it was inconceivable to him that political principles or ideals be devoid of social content or divorced from the most preponderant social group in Croatian society, the peasantry, which he believed formed the core of, if not the entire, nation.

If the peasantry was the core of the nation, then it was only natural that the intelligentsia should have a proper relationship towards it. On this matter Radić was unequivocal. It was not good enough simply to mourn the sorry plight of the common people. Radić argued that it was necessary 'to march along with the people.' What the people wanted, so he surmised, was national justice, that is, their own autonomous homeland, a people's legislature and government, as well as social justice and equality.[78] The ideals of social justice and national autonomy could be realized only if they were pursued with consistency and political aptitude, qualities that were, he seemed to imply, lacking among the contemporary Croat intelligentsia.[79] Radić rejected a passive political policy, which was characteristic of the existing Croat political parties, as unbecoming of a people's politician; a politician must always be active. Opportunism suggested weakness and meant sacrificing or compromising one's political ideals, and these should never be compromised. Radicalism was the only viable method of political struggle, but this did not imply revolutionary or violent tactics. What it did mean was pursuing one's ideals with determination and perseverance; to be a radical meant possessing an unwavering conviction in one's ideals and their realization.[80]

These were the broad contours of Stjepan Radić's political ideas in the late 1890s. He simply called on the Croat intelligentsia to go to the people, to set aside nationalist and religious differences with Serbs in order to manifest unity with them, and to place all of this within a broader context of Slavic reciprocity. But these views were refined through the influence of his brother Antun. Nevertheless, for most of the 1890s he was closer to the *mladi* than to his brother, particularly with respect to the issues of Croat state right and Croat–Serb relations. He would eventually break with his colleagues, however, because of his belief, one that was not, as will be shown, shared by them, that 'there already exists a firm social foundation and that this foundation must be preserved and expanded for the sake of constructing economic well-being and national autonomy.'[81] This foundation was the peasantry. This assessment was shared by Antun, for he believed that the peasants had preserved, through their national dress, customs, and folk songs, a national culture. National politics had to be based on the dormant strength that lay in the Croat countryside. As long as the people did not have an active role in politics and society, the principle of democracy would have little meaning in Croatia.

As Stjepan's ideational framework gradually shifted closer to Antun's, he distanced himself from Masaryk, despite the obvious influence that the Czech intellectual exerted on Stjepan. For instance, he objected to Masaryk's 'German,' as opposed to 'Russian,' orientation.[82] What he meant by this is not entirely certain, but what can be said with some assurance is that Radić's view of Russian autocracy was much more benign than Masaryk's. The latter, though a Russophile, always distinguished between autocracy and the Russian people, whereas Radić tended to overlook the political shortcomings of autocracy for reasons of Realpolitik. He believed that the German *Drang* was the main threat to all the Slavs and that, consequently, a strong Russia was needed as an effective counterbalance to the German Reich. That is why Radić defended the Russian regime during the 1905 revolution.[83] Furthermore, Radić would eventually return to the principle of state right as a powerful legitimizing weapon in the national cause, and he objected to Masaryk's abandonment of Bohemian state right. Radić also believed, and seemed to resent that Masaryk, although of Slovak background, had done little for the Slovak cause in Hungary, an issue that needed to be addressed in light of Magyar policy towards the Slovaks. He contrasted negatively Masaryk's neglect of the Slovaks with his defence of the Bohemian Jews and his campaign against anti-Semitism. This did not sit well with Radić's own anti-Semitic views; he would later claim that Masaryk had the support of 'the Jewish international financial organization.'[84]

Radić's anti-Semitism, which first manifested itself during his student days, has received virtually no attention in Croatian historiography.[85] It must be emphasized, however, that anti-Semitism never formed a major part of his platform, despite his occasional anti-Semitic remarks. Radić's negative characterization of Jews stemmed primarily from his Christian views, as opposed to racial doctrines, as is plainly evident from his first and only explicitly anti-Semitic tract.[86] Jews, he argued, lacked an appreciation 'for the fundamentals of every civilization: property and state.' Under the circumstances, he insisted, it was not surprising that Jews often tended to be outspoken supporters of socialism, because this ideology emphasized collective ownership of property and internationalism. Jews were simply 'amoral, materialistic, and irreligious.'[87] Most of his early anti-Semitic remarks were directed almost entirely at Josip Frank, a Croatian Jewish convert to Catholicism and the leader of the Pure Party of Right. Radić remarked in 1906 that 'we cannot and must not allow any Jew, whether a Semite or Aryan, to be our national representative and leader.'[88] Critical of the Frankists because of their neglect of the peasantry and their anti-Serb national ideology, he was also opposed to them because they were headed by a 'foreign Jew.'[89] In 1901 Antun Radić decried, much like his brother, the Frankists' liberal and irreligious political platform. Frank's liberalism was, he claimed, alien to the Croat peasantry and essentially the ideology of the monarchy's Jews.[90] 'As real Christians,' Stjepan Radić commented, 'we cannot be anti-Semites like the Germans.' 'Instead of anti-Semitism,' he concluded, 'we should therefore most rigidly pursue asemitism: instead of an unbecoming struggle against the Jews, most strenuous work without the Jews.'[91] The Radićes' anti-Semitism, although largely latent, resurfaced on various occasions, as will be seen, especially in the context of their campaign against the new course in Croatia after 1905.

Antun Radić influenced Stjepan's views in a number of respects. Antun Radić received a doctorate in 1893 from the University of Zagreb in philology and literature,[92] and he then spent a number of years teaching at various gymnasia in Croatia. In 1897 he became the editor of the Yugoslav Academy's *Zbornik za narodni život i običaje južnih Slavena* (*Journal for the National Life and Customs of Southern Slavs*). This position enabled him to travel extensively and to collect information about local customs and folklore. Eventually he initiated his own newspaper *Dom* (*Home*, 1899–1904) aimed specifically at the Croat peasant, and in 1902 he became the secretary of Matica Hrvatska (Croat Literary-Cultural Foundation), where he remained until 1909.

For Antun Radić the chasm that existed between the intelligentsia and the people was not the product of social and economic factors, but of two different cultures. He defined culture as the product of the collective labour of people, everything that they created to make their lives better.[93] The development of culture was closely tied to labour and the land. Surveying the history of Europe since the fall of the Roman Empire, he argued that a Greco–Judeo– Roman culture had been transmitted to all of the European peoples, who in turn developed it even further. But this European civilization was limited to the feudal and urban élites. The peasants, on the other hand, were largely untouched by this élite culture; they preserved, although unconsciously, a national culture in the form of customs, folklore, and a native language, whereas the élites preserved a cosmopolitan civilization based on the traditions of Roman–Christian universalism.

It was the existence of these two cultural spheres, an urban civilization and a peasant culture, which to his mind caused the chasm between the peasants and the intelligentsia: 'Civilization and the already mentioned cosmopolitanism tears man from his nation and homeland ... a civilized man rejects everything that was his and distinct.' Although he acknowledged some positive aspects of civilization (technical progress, learning), Antun Radić's words reveal a latent animus towards the city and its 'civilization.' Only the village and the peasant represented the true national culture. For Antun alienation was a concomitant of urbanization, for it divorced the individual from his home and native culture; in short, civilization destroyed culture.[94] The chasm between the *gospoda* (the gentlemen) and *narod* (the people), he explained, could be overcome only if the intelligentsia abandoned its disdain of the peasant and went to the people. 'Our intelligentsia is very far from the people,' he wrote in 1891, 'and one could say that we do not yet understand the true relationship of the intelligentsia towards the people.' Citing the case of the Russian intelligentsia, particularly the populists (*narodniki*), he concluded: 'No one is demanding this of our intelligentsia, but that it too will repent, this is certain.'[95] In actual fact, Stjepan Radić and the *mladi* were demanding a new commitment from the intelligentsia.

There were important differences, however, between Antun and the *mladi*, including Stjepan, in the late 1890s and early 1900s. Antun railed against the appearance of Croat literary modernism (the *Moderna*) with its call for the unfettered freedom of artistic expression.[96] Although he regarded the struggle between the *mladi* and the *stari* as in many ways natural, and believed it to be a product of the Croat opposition's complete political failure, he felt that literary modernism was becoming increasingly abnormal and chaotic, for it was divorced from national and patriotic ideals.[97] Stjepan Radić initially did not share his brother's concerns about the 'anational' character of Croat modernism, but he too eventually concluded that the movement was 'distancing itself from life' and Croat national ideals purely for the sake of artistic expression.[98]

Much more important, however, was the fact that Stjepan moved closer to his brother on the issue of Croat state right and thus distanced himself from many of his colleagues. Antun cautioned his brother in March 1900 that his commitment to Czech 'practicalism' (realism) would 'give birth to something discordant' in Stjepan, and urged him to return to 'Croat idealism.'[99] 'We will, I hope, agree,' Antun wrote to his brother in September 1901, but 'there is one thing to avoid: *idée fixe*. Do not misunderstand me, but I believe that the "Serbs" (and Bulgars) are your *idée fixe*: if you were to change this idea – we would agree.' This was an implicit reference to Stjepan's views about *narodno jedinstvo*. It was not that Antun disagreed with this concept as such, but he objected to Stjepan's abandonment of Croat state right. He wrote to Stjepan in 1901:

Question: Why and how did a *sharp, strong*, and *national* opposition emerge against the old (Illyrianist) National Party? Why did the Party of Right paralyze the work of the awakeners? – Answer: It is true that the history of the Croat people, its cultural history, cannot be imagined without the idea of Slavdom (Palmotić, Gundulić, Kačić). And that is why A. Starčević seriously erred when he held Slavdom to be a foreign (Austrian) plant. We cannot excuse him, but we can understand him. (1) "Austria" knew how to use the Slavic idea – hence his hatred of Slavdom; (2) he was not a man of the awakening ... He simply went from the eighteenth to the nineteenth century with that *political* ideal [state right], which our grandfathers created for themselves from the sixteenth to the eighteenth centuries ... If the (old) National Party, alongside its national-cultural ideal, firmly stood by the *concrete* Croat state right instead of the *politically impossible* Yugoslavism ... that *uncultured* man from Lika [Starčević] would never have been able to win over the people. I would be surprised if this was not clear to you. That is why I will not explain any more to you. I do not know why we (the two of us) cannot agree on this. I see and feel that the Croat state idea is *too old* for it to fade away.[100]

Thus, although sharing his brother's views about *narodno jedinstvo* and Slavic reciprocity, Antun emphasized the need to remain politically within the framework of Croat state right. In this respect he was successful, for Stjepan became a proponent of both Croat state right and *narodno jedinstvo*. Gradually Stjepan moved away from his colleagues and closer to his brother. Hence the process of the growing alienation of the *mladi* from the *stari* was simultaneously accompanied by the distancing of the Radićes from both the *mladi* and *stari*.

The differences between Stjepan and his colleagues were becoming apparent in the late 1890s,[101] although the final rupture did not occur until 1904 with the creation of the Radićes' peasant party. Many of Stjepan's associates concluded that his views about the peasantry were overly romantic and hence flawed. His friend and former cell-mate Živan Bertić wrote to him in March 1898 that his article 'about preparing for work in politics was not liked by anyone; on the contrary, the entire editorial staff [of *Novo doba*] believes that it cannot be published at all as it now stands.' What Bertić and the others objected to was Radić's tendency to draw conclusions, and to propose the contours of proper national policy, purely on the basis of 'the people's comprehension and thoughts:' '[You write that] "our people think such and such – therefore, that is how the intelligentsia must be" – but this appears to be the crudest speculation, that is, you took some verses from national poetry, some adages from the people's talk, and on the basis of these you deduce everything else ... No one agrees with you. You idealize excessively the [peasant] people.'[102] Writing four years later about Antun Radić's peasant newspaper *Dom*, Bertić welcomed its appearance as long overdue. But he detected a 'sick sentimentalism' in Antun's writings about the people, which at times created the impression that he was a reactionary and 'a small demagogue as opposed to a just teacher.'[103]

It is evident that the *mladi* differed with the Radićes with respect to the intelligentsia's proper role *vis-à-vis* the people. Indeed, Stjepan Radić contributed virtually nothing to the Vienna-based journal *Glas*, which succeeded *Novo doba* in 1899, and he claimed that it was during his stay in Paris that his influence over his colleagues began to wane.[104] What is more, many of Radić's colleagues resented, and in the event refused to take seriously, his claim to leadership. That Radić possessed a heightened sense of self-importance, expressed as early as the mid-1890s when he was only in his early twenties, is undeniable. This in turn certainly made it difficult for him to make compromises and to tolerate different views. But in this respect, Radić was very much a product of Croatia's contemporary political culture, which placed a premium on personalities as opposed to parties (hence Starčevićists and Frankists) and spawned intellectuals and politicians who placed an exaggerated emphasis on the purity of ideas as opposed to pragmatism. Many of his associates undoubtedly shared Frano Supilo's assessment that Radić 'is a very learned young man, but he is very eccentric and confused.' Radić could 'be used under good instruction – if he wanted to listen. He himself has no criteria [to become], nor is he, a politician.'[105]

There was, of course, an element of truth in these criticisms. His travels and Parisian experience notwithstanding, Radić was never able completely to leave the village either emotionally or intellectually. Despite his emphasis on realism, he tended generally to idealize the peasantry. This romanticized vision of the village in turn led him grossly to exaggerate the peasantry's potential and actual political strength. Radić was certainly sincere and eager, one might say impatient, in his desire to help the peasants, but at times emotion overruled reason, which lent the impression that he was temperamental and even impulsive.

Whatever differences did exist between Stjepan and his student colleagues in the late 1890s, they were not yet of a profound nature, or at least did not appear as such, for they continued to collaborate. After completing his studies in Paris, Radić and his wife settled in Prague in August 1899, where their first daughter, Milica, was born late that year. They remained in Prague until July 1900, and during that time Radić began a brief career as a freelance journalist. He met regularly with a number of Czech politicians, such as Antonín Hajn of the Czech progressivist movement, and Václav Klofáč, the leader of the National Socialist Party, and claimed also to have attended the founding congress of Masaryk's Realist Party.[106] Radić's days in Prague in the 1890s were clearly important for his ideological development, even more important than his days in Paris. He was deeply impressed by Czech political life and Czech economic and cultural organizations. Moreover, the Czech-German national struggle left an indelible imprint on Radić. He believed that the German *Drang* threatened not only Czechs, but Southern Slavs as well. He referred to Bohemia as the centre of 'the struggle between Slavdom and Germandom' and was convinced that the fate of South Slavs would be determined there. He also referred to the Slovene capital Ljubljana as 'the first and strongest defence of Zagreb against the flood of Germanization.'[107] This reinforced his belief that the Habsburg monarchy's Slavs should act as a united political force.

Returning to Croatia in August 1900, Radić and his wife settled in the town of Zemun, where they remained until December 1901. Their second daughter, Miroslava (Mira), was born in Zemun in 1900; they would have two more children, Vladimir (born 1905) and Branko (born 1912). In Zemun Radić continued his work as a journalist, writing for a number of Czech and French newspapers, and he began to take a more active role in political life. He claimed that he chose to live in Zemun rather than Zagreb because most of his colleagues, who had by now returned to Croatia, had abandoned him,[108] even though they would continue to cooperate. Until 1901 the *mladi* did not organize themselves as a distinct political group. But with the crushing defeat of Croat opposition in the elections of that year they formally constituted themselves as the Progressive Youth (*napredna omladina*) and became part of the United Croat opposition, which was formed on 15 January 1902 and encompassed all opposition elements except the Frankists. In February 1902 Stjepan

Radić became the secretary of the Executive Committee of the Croat Opposition. At this stage he was clearly not yet thinking of forming a new political party, although in September 1901 Antun Radić considered creating the 'People's Progressive Party,' which would, breaking completely with the older intelligentsia, work for the cultural and economic improvement of the peasants and organize them politically, and stand on the platform of Croat state right, the *narodno jedinstvo* of the South Slavs, and cooperation with the other Slavs.[109] Nor were Stjepan's progressivist colleagues yet thinking of a new party. In 1902 they still attempted to achieve the concentration of all opposition political forces. Stjepan Radić wished to impart a populist political agenda to the program of a united opposition that would include the old political élite, save the Frankists.

In early 1901 Radić had written to a colleague that it was necessary immediately to begin organized political work on a populist, national (Croat and South Slavic), and broad cultural basis. The intelligentsia had to be won over to a populist policy, one that would rise above the partisan politics that plagued Croat politics. He cited Antun's paper *Dom* as working on this basis, but planned to organize his own paper (*Živa Domovina – The Living Homeland*).[110] Radić never established this paper, probably because his colleagues decided to revive *Hrvatska misao*, which reappeared in early 1902 and of which he became the editor in the autumn of 1903. Radić therefore joined the progressives, in spite of their differences, in converting the older intelligentsia to their ideas. In late 1901 he urged 'that the *entire Croat intelligentsia* gather into one national and progressive group, that it move closer to its own [peasant] people, [and] to Slavdom.'[111] The central objective of Progressive Youth, according to Radić, was 'to complete the Illyrianist awakening in both the economic and social fields and to strengthen it in a national and political direction.'[112]

These were Radić's guiding principles during his tenure as secretary of the united opposition. He was of the opinion that 'our very national existence is in danger' because of the Magyar political and economic domination of Croatia, and he urged immediate political and economic work among the peasantry and unity between Croats and Serbs. When the intelligentsia adopted a populist platform and committed itself to the political and economic organization of the peasantry, the national cause would be strengthened immeasurably. This would set the stage, he believed, for a successful struggle against the Magyars.[113]

His efforts to place the opposition on a populist platform proved futile, however, even though they were reinforced by two significant developments. The most significant was the so-called national movement (*narodni pokret*) of 1903, which began with a rally for Croatian financial autonomy in early

March in Zagreb. Anti-Magyar demonstrations spread to other towns and even to the countryside, but by August the movement dissipated, largely because it lacked political leadership and coordination. The Croat opposition essentially remained inactive during the events of 1903. But Radić, who was arrested in late April 1903 and jailed for two months, was clearly impressed by these demonstrations and came to the conclusion that the people had acted 'almost completely without the leadership of their intelligentsia.'[114] He wondered aloud why this 'magnificent national army,' that is, the peasantry, was still without political leadership; with the proper leadership, the peasantry could become the core of the Croat national movement, which would then, he believed, be unconquerable.[115] Thus, 1903 marked an important turning point in Croatian politics. Radić and the progressives were coming to the realization that it was futile to work within the united opposition's ranks.[116]

The other important development was the early September 1902 anti-Serb riots in Zagreb, provoked by the publication of an anti-Croat article in the Croatian Serb paper *Srbobran*. Radić's repeated calls for Croat-Serb cooperation in Croatia were seriously undermined. On 2 September, the second day of the riots, Radić noticed that the store of his Serb neighbour was being vandalized, which prompted him finally to act. Radić confronted the violent mob, which nearly turned against him, and tried to convince it that the real villains behind Croatia's national misfortunes were the Magyars, not Serbs. If the mob wished to protest, it should march to Zagreb's central railway station and tear down the illegal Magyar-language inscriptions, and Radić even offered to lead the mob. What followed was not an anti-Magyar riot, but Radić's arrest and a short prison term (September 1902 to January 1903) for disturbing the public peace.[117] Unlike Radić, most of his progressivist colleagues and the older intelligentsia did little other than to observe the riots.

The final break between Radić and both the *mladi* and *stari* came in 1904. On 10 March 1904 Radić was ousted from his post of secretary of the Executive Committee of the Croat Opposition. What provoked this was Radić's continued hostility towards some of the leading personalities within the opposition and their refusal to place the new Croat Party of Right (HSP, *Hrvatska stranka prava*) – as the united opposition was called after its formal merger in January 1903 – on an explicitly peasant foundation. Radić refused to compromise on this issue; in January 1903 he had at last called for the creation of a Croat Peasant Party.[118] To be sure, these differences had been brewing from the moment that Radić assumed his position as secretary.[119] As early as 1899 Antun Radić had told Stjepan that it would be impossible to compromise with the old élite.[120] Many of the older politicians believed that Radić was too critical and uncompromising, or as the leader of the united opposition told Radić, he was 'too fiery and too copious in fervent talk,' in his criticism of the *stari*.[121] Radić's hopes of forming a peasant party together with Croatia's older intelligentsia were now dashed. The Radićes finally decided to establish their own party. But their wish that the Progressive Youth would join them was also shattered.

In spite of sharing a number of common principles, Radić and his erstwhile colleagues were separated by many fundamental issues. Although both saw politics as a social dynamic, the progressives largely dealt with urban social issues and were not prepared in theory to place an emphasis on one particular social group. They regarded the Radićes' views about the peasantry as overly romantic and sentimental. But Stjepan and Antun Radić viewed the problems of the village as the paramount social issue in Croatia. Whereas the progressives were generally sympathetic to social democracy, the Radić brothers remained hostile to socialism as a matter of principle. Because there was hardly a Croatian proletariat to speak of in this period, and what did exist was drawn from the village, it was inconceivable to the Radićes that the village be sacrificed to urban concerns, however pressing they might be. And although they shared a common animus towards Catholic clericalism, Stjepan and Antun Radić remained committed to Christian ethics. Finally, even though they were united by a common criticism of the old opposition's overemphasis on state right, Stjepan Radić never completely abandoned the framework of Croat state right. To be sure, Radić remained a proponent of *narodno jedinstvo*, but his variant differed substantially from that of the progressives, as will be demonstrated. One might also add that there was a personal dimension to all of this, for many of Radić's associates resented his claim to intellectual and political leadership.

These differences proved insurmountable. Stjepan Radić certainly hoped that many of his colleagues would join him in creating the peasant party. Some, like Svetimir Korporić and Milan Krištof, did, but the majority did not. Even Korporić and Krištof would eventually break with the Radićes, in December 1905 and September 1908, respectively. Stjepan and Antun Radić went their own way. They believed that the intelligentsia had to commit itself to organized and sustained daily work among the peasantry. Through this work the peasantry would be educated and mobilized to secure its political, social, and economic rights in society. On 5 December 1904 the Radićes and some associates decided to establish the Croat People's Peasant Party (HPSS, *Hrvatska pučka seljačka stranka*), and later that month, on 22 December, they formulated a party program. The HPSS was thus formed, but neither the older (*stari*) nor the younger (*mladi*) elements of the intelligentsia answered its call to action. The former constituted themselves politically as the Croat Party of Right (HSP), and the majority of the latter formed the Progressive Party (later renamed the Croat People's Progressive Party) in the same month that the Radićes founded the HPSS. For the Radićes this represented the failure of the Croat intelligentsia, and in this regard 1904 marked a turning point, for the differences that separated Stjepan Radić from his colleagues, not to mention the old élite, now materialized in more concrete party-political terms. The HPSS would herald a new type of politics: people's, or peasant. It was on this basis that the party sought to revitalize Croatian politics, address the problems of the village, and to integrate the peasantry into the Croat national organism.

3

Agrarianism and National Integration: The Ideology and Organization of Croat Peasantism

In Croatia even a foreigner notices at first glance that there are two peoples here: the gentlemen and the common people ... Everyone who wears a black coat has the right to the title of 'gentleman,' and only with this title can one in practice, in life, have any worth as a man. All of the others ... are 'peasants,' 'thick-headed,' 'cattle,' 'vulgar people,' or simply slaves, subjects. Neither the property, nor the personal honour, nor the individual freedom of any man from among the common people is secure ... Whoever says a single harsh word already sits in prison. A true reign of terror. In short: In Croatia only the *kaputaš*, the 'gentleman,' and more recently only the bureaucrat, is a man, a person.

Stjepan Radić, 1896

By the first years of the twentieth century a number of agrarian parties had been established in East Central Europe, which was part of a broader European process of the emergence of mass political parties since the 1890s. These parties shared a number of common characteristics, including the belief that society should be remodelled to reflect the peasant majority's values and interests, a social and economic program that emphasized peasant needs, and the belief that the peasantry's numeric preponderance necessitated a greater political role for that social group. That peasantist parties were formed at all demonstrated that a wide chasm separated the peasantry from the urban élites who dominated these societies. This urban–rural, or bourgeois–peasant, divide was typical of most predominantly agrarian societies. Disillusioned with, and distrustful of, the traditional political parties, peasants turned to the emerging agrarian or peasantist parties.[1]

The establishment in December 1904 of the Croat People's Peasant Party (HPSS, *Hrvatska pučka seljačka stranka*) was part of this process and marked the appearance of one of the most important agrarian parties in the entire region.[2] It also represented an important turning point in Croatian politics, although its full impact would not be felt until after the First World War. A relatively minor party during the Habsburg period because of the highly restrictive electoral franchise in the kingdom of Croatia-Slavonia, its prewar articulation of a peasantist ideology enabled it to become a national mass movement in the post-1918 era. It thereby played the central role in the completion of the process of national integration.

The HPSS certainly shared a number of principles with other Croat political parties, namely, an emphasis on state right derived from the Party of (Croat State) Right and a socioeconomic program similar to that of the Progressive Party, but it was the first party in Croatian history seriously to attempt to interpret the social and economic needs of the Croat peasantry and articulate them into a coherent program. To understand the HPSS's agrarianism requires an analysis of the central concepts elaborated by the Radićes: peasant politics, peasant right, and peasant state. It is also important to examine the HPSS's organizational structure and activism, particularly in its early years, for the HPSS was the only Croat party to develop a grassroots village organization that provided it with a firm hold over the countryside after 1918. For the Radić brothers Croatia's contemporary social, economic, and political malaise stemmed from the fact that the peasantry had been neglected in all respects by the intelligentsia. Croatian society could not progress if this neglect continued. Stjepan Radić's 1896 reference to two peoples in Croatia was the background against which the Radić brothers set out to establish an agrarian party that sought to elevate the peasant to a pre-eminent status in society.

The Radićes were keenly aware of the need to legitimize the formation of the HPSS, and thus to justify their assertion of the peasantry's right to a leading role in Croatian politics. This they did by elaborating the concept of people's politics. In their view, shaped as it was by Croatian realities, there existed only two types of politics: gentlemanly (*gospodska politika*) and people's. Defined in the simplest terms, the former represented the privileged rights and rule of a few, whereas the latter was based on the participation of the masses. Gentlemanly politics was essentially undemocratic because it treated the people as an object as opposed to a subject of politics and society.[3] Although the Radić brothers and the HPSS were quick to distinguish between aristocratic and liberal or bourgeois politics, and viewed the French Revolution as marking the turning point between the two, they regarded them as essentially the same because the chasm that separated the liberal intelligentsia from the people was in practice just as wide as the earlier gulf between noble and peasant.[4] People's politics was democratic in essence and in operation.[5] It was a negation of the principle of minority or élite rule, and it did not recognize any separate rights or privileges for the *gospoda*; it stood for the rights and equality of all with power vested in the majority. For Antun Radić people's politics simply meant a form of politics that the people conducted against a privileged élite to secure their political and other rights.[6] But the people could only do this successfully insofar as they were politically enlightened and organized.[7] Predicated on the notion that all authority ultimately resides with the people, the aim of people's politics was to construct a new political order based on the people's will.

Surveying the contemporary Croatian political landscape the Radićes asserted that there were no substantive differences between the existing parties in their political methods, which explains their use of the word *gospoda* to describe Croatia's intellectual élite, which was in fact very diverse. Although all parties paid homage to the *narod* and claimed that they had its support, this was a fiction. The phrase 'the people' was a mere slogan, Stjepan Radić claimed, because the contemporary political parties made no concrete efforts to work among the people or to organize them. They merely employed meaningless phrases and had no real program or plan of action to offer the peasants.[8] They believed that the masses were malleable and existed merely to serve interests which they knew nothing about and did not understand.[9] The traditional Croat political élites were incapable of altering their political tactics or devoting more effort to political action among the peasantry.[10] That was primarily because of the Croat intelligentsia's traditional emphasis on high politics (state right), which was in itself insufficient for political work because the social and economic needs of the peasantry were as a consequence completely neglected.[11] This had to end and, according to Stjepan Radić, 'our national organism must finally begin to be systemically strengthened.'[12] It had to be strengthened because 'we Croats still are not a real nation,' a result of the divide between the intelligentsia and the peasantry.[13] Bridging the divide required social, economic, and political work among the peasantry.

Since Croatia was a predominantly agrarian society, it was only natural that people's politics would be associated with the peasantry, which made up the majority of the population and was identified by the Radićes as 'the only true representative of Croatdom.'[14] Indeed, at times the Radić brothers made reference to the peasantry as the nation, a tendency much more pronounced in the postwar era when the HPSS acquired the attributes of a mass movement. 'The truth is,' Antun Radić wrote, 'the peasants alone are not the nation; but it is also true that besides the peasant there are very few [other] people, so that when we say "nation," we think foremost of the peasantry.'[15] Without the active participation of the peasantry there could be no people's politics. The intelligentsia formed but an insignificant minority of the population. Without the peasantry, which constituted over 80 per cent of the population, Croats would never become a serious political factor.[16] It was wrong even to consider the existing Croat parties as genuine since they were mere coteries and cliques.[17]

The absence of a numerically significant Croatian bourgeoisie, working class, or native nobility meant that the identification of peasantry with the nation seemed justified. As Stjepan Radić noted, 'Not one of our old parties has, nor can it have, a class nucleus, because aside from the peasantry there are no true classes among us.' A political party that lacked a class nucleus had no real basis.[18] In fact, the Radićes believed that the peasantry was already like a party, albeit an unorganized one.[19] All peasants were united by common needs and sufferings, but they lacked organization and a strong political consciousness. In spite of their tendency to equate the peasantry with the nation, the Radićes and HPSS viewed the nation as supra-class. This was reflected in their semantics. They tended to regard the *narod* as being composed of two groups: the *gospoda* and the *puk* (common people), and the peasantry made up the majority of the common people, among whom were included the urban workers.[20] Nevertheless, the numeric preponderance of the peasantry in Croatian society meant that the terms 'national,' 'people's,' and 'peasant politics' became virtually identical. And under the rubric of people's politics lay the Radić brothers' insistence on the peasantry's leading role in society in general and in politics specifically.

The Radićes thus treated peasants as a single group or class, a view common virtually to all of East Central Europe's agrarian politicians. But it is precisely this assumption on the part of the region's peasantists that has come under a great deal of criticism, not least from Marxist scholars.[21] Marxists have emphasized the operation of market forces in the countryside and the growing economic differentiation of rural society, leading to the emergence of wealthy peasants – a rural (petite) bourgeoisie – on the one hand, and, on the other, a middle stratum and a landless proletariat, whose class interests would invariably lead them into a joint struggle with the urban workers against the bourgeois order. Peasantist leaders, by attracting the wealthier peasants and operating within the existing political order, acquired a decidedly (petit) bourgeois character. Yet this interpretation is much too simplistic. The Radićes were certainly cognizant of the economic differences that existed in the Croat countryside, but believed that the culture of the village acted as a unifying force. This was an idealistic view, yet it must be emphasized that, even though economic differentiation was occurring, peasants were motivated by a complex and variegated set of factors. Moreover, peasants could and did demonstrate the strength and resilience of traditional rural ties, especially in and after 1918, when the external pressures of the new monarchical Yugoslav state led to greater social and political cohesion among peasants. To reduce peasant motives to economic interest alone is to sacrifice nuance.

Although insisting on the peasantry's right to political predominance, the Radićes always down-played the class nature of the HPSS. The party sought to organize the entire agrarian population, but it logically followed, according to the Radićes and the HPSS program, that all of those classes that could not survive without the peasantry, namely, the rural artisans, the merchants, and even the clergy, teachers, rural officials, and large landowners – in effect, everyone – should join or at least support the HPSS.[22] Since no social group could survive without the productive labour of the peasantry, it followed that what was good for the peasantry had to be beneficial for everyone in society.[23] According to the Radićes the peasantry would therefore eventually come to represent and assure the rights and interests of the whole of society.

Far from working along determinist and exclusivist class lines, the HPSS was animated by the idea of social consonance and sought the harmonization of class interests. The priest Fran Škrinjar, one of the HPSS's co-founders, noted: 'We do not exclude anyone, we invite all to organize themselves into one circle with their peasant brothers on a peasant foundation,' for if the HPSS were 'to exclude the gentlemen, as they have excluded 90 per cent of the nation, then we would be a class party.'[24] Social harmony was thus one of the aims of peasant politics; the goal was not merely to take power away from the *gospoda* but to ensure that it was broadened to include the peasantry. The HPSS wanted to elevate the peasantry to the level of the *gospoda*, but to achieve this would mean overcoming the existing gulf separating the two. 'If therefore we want people's politics,' Antun Radić wrote, 'we must ... bridge that chasm that separates the *gospoda* from the peasants, the *gospoda* must begin to feel that they are one with the peasants,' or in other words, the objective was 'that from the *gospoda* and peasants we finally form a *nation*.'[25] The aim of people's politics, thus formulated, was no less than the completion of the process of national integration begun nearly a century earlier by the Illyrianist movement. All Croats had to be integrated into the national community. Josip Predavec, the party's economic specialist, asserted that the HPSS, continuing the work of the Illyrianist movement, was spearheading a 'third, economic awakening,' that would in the end 'preserve and defend the entire nation, and thereby liberate and glorify the homeland.' But in order for this to occur, the Croat intelligentsia had to accept the idea 'that it must first of all work for the life's needs of the peasant people.'[26]

Despite the party's desire for social harmony, there was nevertheless a latent, and at times a pronounced, class component to its ideology and in the rhetoric of its leaders. This is certainly not surprising, for even the party's nomenclature reveals its class nature. At the HPSS's third annual main assembly (1907) Stjepan Radić was particularly critical of Croatia's urban élites and reminded the party's delegates that 'there is greater strength in the villages than in the cities,' because in the city 'everything is hard and unproductive, far from God and mother nature,' whereas in the village a peasant 'lives in union with mother earth, which he toils with God's blessing.'[27] One of the party's prominent figures, Djuro Basariček, insisted that the HPSS was working for the interests of everyone in Croatian society, but added that the existing laws represented nothing other than the vested class interests of the dominant groups within that society. The peasantry too possessed a right to shape the state and society according to its own class interests.[28] There was evidently much bitterness within the HPSS's ranks after the party's fourth main assembly. Held in Zagreb in August 1909, the assembly was greeted with indifference and even derision by the urban populace. This led one party delegate to propose that in future the main assembly no longer be held in Zagreb, which he called a rubbish-heap. Stjepan Radić believed that this bitterness was completely justified and castigated the urban élites for their snobbism and callousness, although he insisted that such a step was too harsh.[29] The HPSS often railed against the bourgeois élite but it denied accusations that it was attempting to widen the chasm between the intelligentsia and peasantry, and insisted that it 'does not see a [class] enemy in every *kaputaš*, but only in the one who wishes to live without beneficial work, at the expense of the people and to oppress them.'[30] Its criticisms of the 'corrupt' and 'wretched' intelligentsia and bourgeois order notwithstanding, the ultimate goal of the HPSS remained the integration of all Croats into the nation by bringing peasants into the political process and bridging the social divide that separated the city and village.

To achieve this and to elevate the peasantry to the level of the gentlemen, the Radićes elaborated the concept of 'peasant right.' Peasant right fundamentally meant the right of the peasantry to economic security, political participation, and, in general, respect in society from other social groups. Peasant right was subdivided into three specific categories: economic right, political right, and social right. In the first category the HPSS included the right of peasants to a homestead, land, forests, economic freedom, which in effect meant liberating peasants from indebtedness, and state support against natural disasters and livestock diseases. In the second category, that of political right, the HPSS included universal suffrage, peasant participation in institutions of government at all levels (commune, district, county), strict bureaucratic accountability, and the introduction of referenda for all major political questions. This was the basis of constitutionality (*ustavnost*), one of the HPSS's ideological pillars, which in principle meant that the people stood above the government. This presupposed a general improvement in cultural and educational standards among the peasantry, for 'the people, to whom electoral rights are granted and who are not even conscious of their rights, will always remain everyone's toy at elections to their own detriment.' The call for political right was thus linked to the third category of peasant right: social right. As the most numerous social element in Croatia the peasantry needed to acquire a corresponding level of respect. It would gain this respect once it overcame its parochialism and organized itself for economic, cultural, and political work. By organizing and educating the peasantry the HPSS wanted to elevate peasants to the same level of respect as *gospoda* and demonstrate that the peasantry could be a mature political actor.[31] This was as much a statement of the peasantry's collective rights as it was an imperative call to action. Just as the principle of state right legitimized a nation's claim to sovereignty in relation to other states, peasant rights legitimized the peasantry's claims to political, social, and economic sovereignty within the state, and also included all of the substantive demands of the peasant movement. In the Radićes' minds, peasant right was the conceptual mechanism through which the HPSS would elevate the peasants to the level of the gentlemen.

To reconstruct the HPSS's program and to determine the essence of its agrarianism, it is crucial to turn to a closer examination of the demands it formulated. As noted, by economic right the HPSS meant primarily the peasant's right to land, security against debt for the peasant homestead, and state financial assistance. At the turn of the century there was an uneven distribution of landownership in Croatia-Slavonia. A total of 44.24 per cent of all farms were below 5 yokes (2.87 hectares), and these constituted only 8.47 per cent of all the land. Farms ranging in size from 5 to 20 yokes (2.87 to 11.51 hectares) accounted for 47.29 per cent of the total, representing 41.46 per cent of the land. In other words, 91.53 per cent of the total number of farms held just under half of the land in Croatia-Slavonia. On the other hand, 326 latifundia, located largely in Slavonia and Srijem, which accounted for 0.08 per cent of all farms, controlled 24.29 per cent of the land.[32] To remedy this situation the HPSS proposed that estates exceeding 500 yokes (287.75 hectares) be broken up and parcelled out among the peasantry, and that the original landowners be compensated at fair market prices.[33] Collectivization and nationalization were never entertained by the HPSS because the very idea of confiscating land went against its belief in the sanctity of private property.[34] Furthermore, the HPSS insisted that all state-owned forests be sold to village cooperatives or the local administrative communes.

The HPSS also recognized the peasantry's need for money and the problem of its growing indebtedness. The parcelization of large estates would be completely untenable if the peasants were not provided with adequate financial resources to pay for this land. That was why the HPSS identified the local lending institutions as the main source of peasant indebtedness; these institutions often lent money at exorbitant rates of interest, in some cases exceeding 20 per cent.[35] The HPSS blamed these usurious lending institutions and the middle-class politicians who defended them, for the mass emigration of the Croat peasantry.[36] To solve this problem the HPSS proposed the creation of a state-sponsored Peasant Bank that would not only take over these debts, but in future provide low interest loans not exceeding 6 per cent.[37] Indeed, the HPSS identified such a Peasant Bank as one of the four most pressing needs of the peasantry, along with the reform of the administration and judiciary, and improved standards of education.[38] The HPSS's call for the parcelization of latifundia and the creation of a Peasant Bank was motivated by its view of the peasantry's relationship to the land. The peasant was organically tied to the land; without land the peasant could not survive.[39] That was why the HPSS's sought to stabilize the peasantry's economic position and reverse the pauperization trend of the previous half-century. Without land the peasantry had no future, with land its position in society would be secured. Hence, in the HPSS's opinion, peasant land ownership was the basis of social security and political stability. Although the HPSS's plan to establish a Croat Peasant Union (*Hrvatski seljački savez*), which would have acted as a peasant-based economic association, proved unsuccessful, in large part because of its inability to raise enough capital, the party placed great emphasis on the need to bring about immediate economic relief to the Croat village.[40]

The HPSS wanted the administrative communes to cease being arms of the central administration, dealing only with tax collection and military recruitment. Since the commune was the closest administrative unit to the peasants, it had to be reorganized to serve the peasants and aid in agricultural development. The communes were to take the lead in local economic projects, care for the unemployable, and find work for the unemployed; they would be self-financing, although they would receive state funding for schools and other projects.[41] Commune officials would be trained in agricultural techniques. Combined with this reform of the commune, the HPSS proposed the creation of regional, elected agricultural councils, the task of which would be to examine agricultural needs and advise the government of what reforms to implement in agriculture. A state committee would be created to centralize and coordinate all regional affairs. The HPSS also wanted the state to establish an insurance fund, based on tax income and peasant contributions, to assist peasants against natural disasters, fires, and livestock diseases.

Furthermore, the HPSS demanded the creation of specialized economic cooperatives that would produce a range of goods from clothing and leather products to sugar and spirits. It realized that if left to themselves such cooperatives would have little chance of success against cheaper, mass-produced foreign products. But the HPSS believed that the state, by freeing these cooperatives from taxation and providing them with low-interest loans, could stimulate local production and the domestic market. Millions of Austro-Hungarian crowns would thus remain in Croatia; they could then be reinvested in domestic economic production.[42] These economic cooperatives held an important place in the HPSS's program, for they were intended not only as a method of pooling the peasantry's existing resources, but also of strengthening the village's hand in the marketplace. The HPSS also called for the introduction of protective tariffs.[43]

Clearly then the HPSS wanted the state to play an active, but limited, role in economic life. According to Antun Radić, the state had only two tasks: order and assistance. It had to uphold the rule of law and provide economic and social assistance. The call for limited state intervention in economic life in turn raised the issue of taxation and finances. The HPSS program made no explicit demands for the reduction of existing levels of taxation, although it demanded an elimination or reduction of indirect taxes on certain peasant necessities, such as salt and kerosene. It advocated a more equitable redistribution of the tax burden, in effect calling for the implementation of a progressive tax system. What concerned the party more than the level of direct taxation was how these monies were being spent. It insisted that a large share of state taxes be reinvested in the agrarian sector to stimulate agricultural growth.[44] Coupled with this was the HPSS's demand that Croatia have complete financial autonomy vis-à-vis Budapest, for as long as Croatian monies went to Budapest, Croatia's economic well-being could not be fully achieved.[45]

Under the term 'political right' the HPSS meant first and foremost the rights of the peasantry to political participation and representation at all levels of government. The first step towards achieving this was the introduction of universal manhood suffrage, which would necessarily change the nature and role of every level of government.[46] The HPSS sought local self-government, for it believed that the central government had destroyed the administrative communes by reducing their officials to the status of overseers of the activities of the rural population and mere tax collectors. To complicate matters, these officials often agitated and voted for the regime's candidate during elections. It was no wonder, the HPSS argued, that the communes were in such dire straits. Three major problems were identified at the commune level: a few wealthy individuals had special voting privileges that enabled them to dominate communal committees, the unequal tax distribution that made the poorest peasant carry the same financial burden as a wealthy landowner, and the fact that all commune officials were appointed by the district prefect rather than the communal committees that paid their salaries. The communes had to receive greater autonomy and become 'the first and true school of political freedom, and the first and main hearth of peasant education and peasant economic freedom.'[47]

The communes would, under the HPSS's program, be run by popularly elected committees that would elect all commune officials. These committees would then be divided into subcommittees of three to five people to look after specific issues. Under the existing system commune committees could not elect officials; candidates were chosen on the recommendation of district officials, and ultimately the county could dismiss any commune official. Consequently the communes had only a very prescribed autonomy. The HPSS further proposed the creation of advisory national councils at every administrative level to hold officials accountable for major questions and to ensure that the peasantry would not suffer from bureaucratic arbitrariness.[48] Moreover, peasants in each commune would elect two district councillors to whom the district prefects would have to submit monthly reports about their activities, thus placing certain checks and balances on administrative officials. Similarly the eight county prefects would be accountable to county assemblies and not just the *ban* in Zagreb, who had appointed them. The county assemblies, in which peasants elected approximately half of the deputies, had to be reformed so that the peasantry gained a majority representation.[49] All communal officials would be trained in economic matters, and communes had to concern themselves primarily with economic issues. To ensure that committee members had sufficient training to perform their duties, the HPSS proposed the creation of annual courses, lasting two to three weeks, to instruct them in administrative and economic affairs.[50] The HPSS believed that such a system was the only guarantee that the communes and counties would become true organs of peasant self-government. The HPSS's emphasis on administrative decentralization reflected and was intended to remedy the peasantry's intense animosity towards the existing bureaucracy and state order.

At the national level the HPSS demanded universal manhood suffrage – and after 1918 it also sought the vote for women – so that the *Sabor* reflected the popular will. That mean that the so-called *virilisti*, who held their seats by right of birth or position, had to be eliminated from the *Sabor*. Moreover, the *ban* would no longer be nominated by the Hungarian minister-president but by

the *Sabor*. The HPSS demanded a reorganization of the three existing government ministries (internal affairs, justice, and religion and education) to reflect
better national needs, and the creation of new ministries to a total of eight:
agriculture, administration, justice, education and religion, commerce and
communications, finance, militia, and one for cultural ties with Croats outside
Croatia-Slavonia and with other Slav nations.[51]

Behind the third cornerstone of peasant right, social right, lay the HPSS's
insistence that the peasantry have the same respect as the other classes in
society. The existing disrespect was manifested in the misconceptions of city
folk and rural officials about the peasantry as being quintessentially stupid
and vulgar. It was further demonstrated in the countryside and smaller towns
where inns often segregated their clientele; one room existed for *gospoda* and
another for peasants.[52] More disturbing to the Radićes and the HPSS was the
process of embourgeoisement, whereby peasant children, once educated,
became gentlemen. Staffing the bureaucracy, they often treated peasants
more callously than the established urban élites. For the HPSS this was
symptomatic of the general level of contempt in which bourgeois society
held the peasant.[53] 'Even if the Croat peasant had all of his political rights,'
the HPSS program declared, 'and enjoyed his complete peasant rights in economic terms ... the contempt of the gentlemen towards him would be reason
enough to establish a peasant party.' Given the peasantry's numerical preponderance and importance as the bearer of the national culture, it was only logical to the Radićes that the peasantry have a corresponding measure of social
respect.[54]

Respect cannot be legislated, however, which is why the HPSS placed particular emphasis on peasant education and cultural enlightenment. The emphasis on education was not intended simply to reduce peasant illiteracy. To be
sure, the HPSS insisted on the establishment of primary schools in all villages
as the best way to attack illiteracy, and in 1913 called for the creation of 2,000
new primary schools across Croatia-Slavonia.[55] It also insisted that education
be practical. To that end, at the local level programs needed to be instituted to
teach peasants how to improve agricultural techniques. The *gymnasia* should
also be practical and teach students about pressing national and social issues,
and introduce the study of other Slavic languages, especially Czech and Russian, in place of Latin and Greek. The university should exist for those who
wished to pursue scientific and scholastic vocations. The HPSS bemoaned the
fact that the university and *gymnasia* had become factories for the mass production of bureaucrats and 'useless officials.'[56] Once education was reformed
and illiteracy reduced, the HPSS argued, peasants would increase their own
social standing. But the surest way of gaining respect, according to the HPSS,

was for peasants to organize themselves within the HPSS to demonstrate that they were capable of being a political force.[57]

As a concept people's politics legitimized the need for a peasant party. The other ideas which the Radićes formulated all stemmed from this concept. Peasant right legitimized the peasantry's right to a leading role in society and was simultaneously the economic, social, and political program of the peasant movement. In other words, peasant right encapsulated the HPSS's entire agrarian policy and program.[58] It was from these two concepts that the idea of the peasant state emerged, which represented the ultimate aim of the HPSS.[59] In their interpretation of history, the Radićes saw the evolution of estates, or classes, as central to society and social development. Each period of historical development was normally dominated by a single estate (clergy, nobility, bourgeoisie, proletariat, and peasantry), and history represented the transition from one to another of the five different periods, during which each one of the estates shaped the state structure according to its own particular interests.[60] With the advent of democratic principles and people's politics the era of the 'fifth estate,' that is, the peasantry, had arrived, and it logically followed, at least in the opinion of the Radićes, that the peasantry too would shape the state to suit its own interests, at least in those societies where it was socially dominant. The resultant entity would be the peasant state.

The peasant state, however, was not merely an end in itself. Like peasant right, it was, in fact, a critically important concept needed to mobilize the Croat peasantry behind the national cause. To bring peasants over to the national cause, the Radićes had to make the state reflect peasant interests. Peasants needed a state with which they could identify and that was truly their own, as opposed to the existing state, which they increasingly identified with the *kaputaš* and the bureaucrat. Peasant alienation from the existing state was demonstrated rather markedly by the peasant's intense animosity towards the bureaucrat. For the Radićes, the existing Croatian state structure had to be altered fundamentally. The peasant state would thus be a Croatian state, but one organized to reflect the social, economic, and political interests of the peasantry. The peasant state was of critical importance for the process of Croat national integration and peasant mobilization.

Thus, the fundamental postulate of the HPSS's ideology was that the peasantry, employing the principles of people's politics and peasant right, was entitled to take state power into its hands. Once this was achieved the peasantry would organize the state, from the national to the local level, to suit its interests on the basis of peasant right. The peasant state would only be achieved when the *Sabor* was dominated by peasants and when the entire state apparatus, from commune to county, was controlled by peasants.[61] Once the peasantry had achieved all that it was entitled to on the basis of peasant rights, the peasant state would be realized. Although the concept of the peasant state was most fully articulated in the party's constitution of 1921,[62] it took shape in the pre-1914 era under different circumstances than those of the 1920s. It remained the party's ultimate ideal, in both the Habsburg and Yugoslav periods.

This conceptual framework and program, which bore much resemblance to other agrarian movements in East Central Europe, formed the essence of Croat peasantism. It is often asserted that peasantist movements, and the HPSS is no exception, resisted and even tried to reverse the process of modernization. Yet this view is rather simplistic, or at the very least needs to be qualified. The HPSS was itself a response to the modernization impulse and offered its own path to modernity, one intended to address the interests of the social group in Croatian society that was most traumatized by this process. The Radićes and the HPSS attempted to mediate the peasantry's transition to modernity. Moreover, by asserting the rights of the peasant majority, the HPSS had a powerfully democratic impact on Croatian society and politics, especially after 1918. In this regard, it was very much an agent of modernization. Conversely, the Radićes did possess a rather static view of society in that they believed that the peasant way of life could be preserved, one is forced to conclude, indefinitely. Herein lay the Achilles' heel of their peasantist ideology, for modernization, however sluggish its pace in Croatia, was slowly yet irrefutably altering Croatia's socially dominant countryside, and eroding the peasantry's numerical preponderance. But to the Radićes, the agrarian nature of society was never in itself the problem, rather it was the existing constraints in that society, such as large estates, usurious middlemen, the lack of capital, and inadequate education, that posed a problem. When these constraints were removed the peasant's economic problems would be solved. This presupposition is debatable, and in the event flawed. To be sure, the HPSS's program of securing for all peasants an education, land, and capital, among other things, offered tangible benefits to the peasantry and would have strengthened their position in society. But the wider issue of what was going on around Croatia, and the forces of change that were fundamentally altering European society as a whole, was never truly confronted by the Radićes in a satisfactory manner.

This was demonstrated most acutely in the HPSS's attitude to industrialization. The HPSS never adopted a clear-cut stand on the issue of industrialization. Based on its tendency to rail against urban society and bourgeois culture, one might be tempted to conclude that the HPSS opposed industrialization. In fact, one HPSS sympathizer urged a return to the fields and claimed that industrialism was experiencing a crisis in the West. Yet this same author, responding to criticisms in the Croatian press, clarified his views and asserted that the HPSS did not categorically reject industrialization, but that Croatia's subordinate political and economic status *vis-à-vis* Hungary meant that, under the circumstances, one could not develop Croatian industry.[63] Stjepan Radić insisted that the Croats had to follow closely economic developments in Europe and be contemporary and progressive in economic affairs. Industry could be developed to facilitate the creation of a prosperous and modernized agrarian economy, but one needed capital and trained workers.[64] In effect, the agrarian economy first had to be 'stabilized' by the implementation of reforms along the lines of the HPSS's program. When that was achieved, and Croatia obtained political and economic emancipation from Hungary, it might be possible to pursue industrial development for the sake of modernizing the agrarian economy. Antun Radić, who gave the matter more careful thought, asserted that agriculture provided the most secure existence both to individuals and entire nations, but he acknowledged that industry would come to Croatia sooner or later, and that it was necessary to prepare for this. A nation that had no industry would continue to be exploited by others, and he noted the growing penetration of foreign goods in to the Croatian market. He concluded that Croatia had to develop at least some industry, and if this did not occur then it would continue to be subjected to foreign economic domination.[65] But how much industry was enough? And once the process had been initiated, how was the dynamic of industrialization to be controlled, if at all? The Radićes never offered any real solutions in this matter. This was yet another of the discrepant premises of the HPSS's ideology. It is also paradoxical that the Radićes (and especially Stjepan) were impressed by the Czechs and saw them as the most progressive of the Slav nations, and yet seemingly failed to note some of the objective circumstances that had contributed to Czech national progress. Bohemia was one of the most industrialized – and industrializing – Habsburg lands, and Czech progress was undoubtedly connected to this fact. Though aware of the need for some industry, the Radićes and the HPSS never supported industrialization as an end in itself, nor did they see it as a panacea to remedy Croatia's relative socioeconomic backwardness. The reason for this was simple enough. The HPSS viewed the peasantry as the bearer of national culture, and it could not commit itself to any policy, such as industrialization, that eroded the status of the peasantry in society, for such a policy would invariably facilitate the peasants' transformation into urbanized workers. To promote industry meant undermining Croat national culture.

The HPSS's ideology represented an eclectic synthesis of sorts of liberal and socialist principles. The party's emphasis on private property, democratic principles, and limited state intervention in society were common traits of

European liberalism, although the last point was much more rooted in specific Croatian conditions. The peasant viewed the state as a new and oppressive lord, and this animus towards the existing state structure was so deeply entrenched in the countryside that it compelled the Radićes to articulate the concept of the peasant state. But the HPSS's ideology differed from liberalism in its emphasis on the whole peasant community as opposed to the individual and in its opposition to the economic principle of *laissez-faire*. The notion of unfettered economic competition of individuals within society was incompatible with the Radićes' and the HPSS's understanding of social justice. Land did not exist as a means of accumulating greater wealth, but was an intrinsic element needed for the peasantry's socioeconomic security. The party program explicitly declared that the HPSS was against 'capitalist insatiability,' for this went against the most basic tenets of social justice.[66] The ideology of Croat peasantism had a decidedly anticapitalist dimension.

What is more, in the Radićes' minds capitalism and liberalism were closely tied to Jewry. There were clearly economic and political considerations to the Radićes' anti-Semitism, which was only reinforced by the fact that Croatian Jews were highly urbanized and formed, by 1910, Zagreb's largest non-Catholic minority. Jews were successful capitalists and financiers, the HPSS argued, because they lacked a homeland. The Jew 'is nowhere among his own – he is everywhere a foreigner.' The lack of a homeland motivated Jews to acquire money rather than immovable property. 'It must be recognized to the Jewish tribe, that with its keen intellect it long ago foresaw,' Antun Radić wrote, 'the following: One day our empire will also come, our emperor will one day rule, that is, today the glorious ruling emperor of emperors His Majesty Money. They have received their saviour!' The Jew was, simply stated, an economic exploiter and the main beneficiary of capitalism, for he 'almost exclusively spends what others have earned.'[67] Based on their rhetoric, it is undeniable that the Radićes viewed Jewry as an agent of economic modernization.

The Radićes also tended to associate Croatia's and the monarchy's Jews with liberalism. In their opinion, the most salient characteristic of liberal ideology was the state's disassociation from society. In other words, the state had 'no obligation to help its citizens, and Jewish liberals also teach that it is not in the state's interest to help the poor people, the peasant or pauper, but that everyone must be left to his fate.' This was a serious problem for the Radićes, as was liberalism's clash with religion. Jews and liberals were promoting the view, the HPSS argued, that 'not a single intelligent, especially a learned man should have any faith in religion, in God, because religion is only for the common people.'[68] This was clearly a major problem for a party that emphasized Christian principles in its political platform. As early as 1901 Antun Radić alluded to Stjepan of the threat posed to the Croats by Germandom and 'Judeo-liberalism.'[69]

On the issue of Jewish assimilation, the Radićes seemed adamant that Croatia's Jews were quintessentially alien and therefore virtually impossible to assimilate. One of the most perplexing issues for Antun Radić was that the Jews seemed to his mind unwilling to assimilate into the societies in which they lived. Yet in 1904 he observed that many Jews in Hungary and Croatia had begun changing their surnames. He urged caution: 'The [Croatian] government should, I believe, be careful when Jews change their surnames, and not permit them to adopt nice, old, and honourable Croatian names.'[70] The Radićes interpreted the emergence of Zionism as a natural development, since 'there is no way that they [the Jews] can blend and accommodate themselves with the people, because they have neither a lineage ... nor friends in the [Croat] nation. That is why I too do not understand, how a Jew could be a Croat.'[71] A year earlier Antun had written that it was simply 'no good if a Jew is christened: to the people ... a Jew remains a Jew,' although he quickly added that 'that is not entirely correct, and it is not necessary to judge each Jew according to the way all of them are, nor all of them according to one [Jew].'[72] That helps partly to explain why the Radićes always maintained a disparaging view of Josip Frank, a Jewish convert to Catholicism. His conversion was merely one of form, an act of Jewish 'cunning.'[73]

To the extent that the Jews wished to assimilate, this was seen by the HPSS as primarily a ploy. That is why the HPSS was critical of those middle-class Croat politicians who supported assimilation; when someone complained about Jews, they 'begin wisely to explain that the Jews are our co-citizens, that we must not reject them.' Croatia's intellectuals and newspapers 'write more about our 20,000 Jews than our 2 million peasants. Every year they can write against the peasantry whatever they wish ... and no one will complain, but if only one newspaper writes something against the Jews, entire studies would be written, how this is unworthy of enlightened people, how it is criminal to hate someone because of their faith (as if anyone complains about the Jews because of their faith).' This situation was unacceptable to the HPSS. 'We [HPSS] are not anti-Semites,' wrote one party activist, 'that is, we are not in favour of a struggle and fight against the Jews.' What the HPSS wanted was for the Croats to 'work alone, and without the Jews ... That is our anti-Semitism.'[74] In the rhetoric of the HPSS, supporting Jewish assimilation would have meant bolstering capitalism and liberal ideology, both of which undermined the vital interests of the Croat peasantry.

The HPSS opposed the excessive accumulation of wealth, emphasized the rights of one social group, and urged cooperative economic organizations. In this regard the HPSS had a socialistic strain. But in the minds of the Radićes, Croat peasantism was equidistant from both socialism and capitalism. The roots of the Radićes' hostility to socialism were varied. The cornerstone of their ideology was the assumption that the peasantry, based both on its numerical preponderance and its role as the bearer of the national spirit, formed the core of the nation, which in turn legitimated its claim to national leadership. The absence of a significant Croat proletariat meant that that class could not assume the leading role in society. The working class, like the intelligentsia, had to recognize the leadership of the peasantry. Any movement or ideology which subjected the peasantry to a subordinate status in society, in this case the socialists with their claim of the proletariat's leadership, was invariably treated by the HPSS with hostility. Furthermore, the socialist emphasis on class struggle contradicted the Radićes' pacifism and, they believed, the interests of peasants. Admittedly, the Croatian Social Democrats geared their activism towards the trade unions and reformist tactics, not revolutionary struggle, but the postwar communist emphasis on revolution brought out this difference in much starker terms.

Neither Stjepan nor Antun Radić possessed a thorough knowledge of Marxist theory, and their understanding of the European socialism was negligible.[75] This did not, however, make them an exception, for socialism made little headway in Croat intellectual circles before the Great War.[76] To a certain extent this was merely a reflection of Croatia's lack of an industrial base and its overwhelming agrarian nature. The Radićes interpreted the appearance of socialism as a by-product of the wretched conditions of the workers in the industrial centres of Europe.

In addition to opposing the socialist claim to the proletariat's leading role in society and the class struggle, the Radićes essentially feared that the socialists wished to create a powerful state that would control all wealth. For instance, they interpreted some aspects of the socialists' social reformist objectives, such as legislating a minimum wage, as invariably contributing to the increase of the power of the state. It was one thing, they believed, for the state to ban child labour or to regulate daily or weekly working hours, but an entirely different matter for the state to determine a worker's wage, that is, the value of labour. If the state set the value of labour, this could potentially undermine the worth of a proprietor's property and other possessions, for it was impossible to acquire wealth without labour. If the state controlled labour, it would invariably control property and wealth. That is why the HPSS repeatedly referred to socialism as 'the apostle of state omnipotence.'[77] The socialist emphasis on collectivization only heightened the Radićes' fears about the socialists' intention to create a powerful state. But collectivization, they insisted, would never eliminate poverty or social inequality, for it fundamentally went against human nature. To be accomplished it would necessarily have to be forced, and as such nothing positive could be accrued from collectivization.[78] Finally, if one adds to all this the Radićes' firm belief that socialists wanted the proletarianization of the peasantry, which was bound to undermine Croat national culture, it is not difficult to understand why they remained opposed to socialism, whether before or after 1918.[79] In their own minds, the Radićes saw themselves as charting a distinct, 'third-way' ideology.

Perhaps most important was the question of how this program was to be achieved. Legality, or the rule of law, was one of the HPSS's key ideological pillars. The HPSS never sought to overthrow the existing order or to abolish its political and economic institutions. It remained staunchly antirevolutionary and pacifist in its orientation, both before and after 1918. The HPSS sought to enact new laws to improve the peasantry's plight by employing the existing channels to gain political power and reform society.[80] The peasant state, once established, would be governed by the rule of law. The Radićes believed that conditions in Croatia were sufficient for a successful political struggle by legal means.[81] Revolution was rejected not only because it went against their Christian beliefs, but because, quite simply, they believed revolutions always ended in tyranny.[82] The HPSS wished to instil a commitment to legality in the peasantry's political consciousness, as well as what it called a 'constitutional consciousness,' that is, a respect for the rule of law. This involved converting peasants to the conviction that they had a right to determine all matters relating to state organization, and that they adopt legal means to achieve their rights. But this required political enlightenment, or what might be termed 'political acculturation,' as well as firm organization.[83]

The HPSS also rejected revolutionary means for the very practical reason that such uprisings had failed in the past and were bound to fail in future. The failure and brutal suppression of the Croat peasant disturbances of 1883 and 1903 undoubtedly factored into the Radićes' thinking. The HPSS's opposition to violence always remained a principled one, however. Revolutionary outbursts tended only to widen the already immense chasm that existed between the peasantry and *gospoda*.[84] Commenting on the outbreak of the peasant revolt in Romania in 1907, Stjepan Radić wrote that 'such a bloody warning to the government and *Sabor* is not only too costly, but goes against our Christian spirit and conscience.' The only path for peasants to take was to mobilize themselves behind the HPSS and eventually to send deputies to the *Sabor* to create a 'true Christian and people's government.'[85] The HPSS's aims determined its method of struggle. Because it aspired to attain social justice and political freedom, and not domination over other classes, the HPSS could only employ 'just' means of political struggle, which in the eyes of the Radićes meant legality.[86] Legality, constitutionalism, and pacifism remained fundamental postulates of the HPSS's ideology throughout its existence, although in the aftermath of the First World War many of the party's younger and more radical members, who saw the party primarily as a social–militant movement, were not as devoted to these tenets as Stjepan Radić and the central leadership.

Radić's reference to 'our Christian spirit and conscience' reveals an important characteristic of the HPSS. Its commitment to social justice, which in turn prescribed a commitment to pacifism and legality, was strongly influenced by the Radić brothers' own religious and ethical principles, as well as their exaggerated belief in the supposedly deeply religious nature of the peasantry. A proper understanding of the Radićes' political ideas is impossible without reference to their views on Christian morality. For the Radićes there could be no separation of Christian ethics and politics. Religion was a necessary prerequisite of morality, and morality was equally necessary to politics. The notion of a secular morality was completely alien to them. Once politics was divorced from Christian morality, the political process ceased having a moral frame of reference. Within the context of such a moral vacuum, politics would invariably degenerate into exploitation, manipulation, demagoguery, and even violence. That is why the HPSS's program of 1905 declared that the 'first foundation' of the party was faith in God.[87]

For the HPSS democracy and a Christian world-view went hand in hand, for 'democratism is an integral part of the Christian understanding of the world and life.' A political party had to base its program on a synthesis of the intellect and faith, that is, reason enlightened by Christian ethics, which is what the HPSS had claimed to achieve. This synthesis is not only an important one in understanding the political philosophy of the HPSS, but it helps also to explain why the party opposed both clericalism and liberalism, which the Radićes interpreted as a political credo resting purely on rationalism. The problem with clericalism was that it disregarded this synthesis and sought to subordinate society to the tenets of the Catholic Church.[88] Liberalism disregarded this synthesis, but in the opposite direction. Stjepan Radić, writing in late 1918, reaffirmed the party's commitment to this synthesis of Christian morality and the intellect: 'Christianity without enlightenment is too submissive and too meek and provides an opportunity to tyrants to impose, broaden, and strengthen the worst slavery with their violence. Enlightenment without Christianity is too arrogant and too selfish and provides the best opportunity to all kinds of speculators and heartless people to incite to struggle class against class, nation against nation, and to create a true hell on earth, as is now seen in

Russia. A state without religion becomes therefore a slaughterhouse, and without enlightenment a prison.'[89]

The HPSS's anticlericalism was based primarily on its opposition to 'gentlemanly politics.' In the eyes of the Radićes, clericalist elements almost without exception translated the submission of the people to God in religious terms to mean submission to the Church in politics. Although the HPSS 'holds faith in God to be the source of every justice,' it could not 'mix religion with politics, but on the contrary, strictly differentiates between the two and teaches that it is not proper to employ either religion or "atheism" in politics.'[90] The HPSS contested clericalism because people's politics opposed the submission of the peasantry to any élite, including the clergy.[91] A clericalist party was nothing other than a small clique of individuals that could only work against the interests of the people, for it merely represented the interests of priests who were placing 'their own will and benefit above the well-being of the entire nation.'[92] Perhaps even more importantly, the fact that clericalist circles in Croatia gradually gravitated towards, and ultimately fused with, the Pure Party of Right, with its anti-Serb ideology, and increasingly tended to identify Croatdom with Catholicism, went against the HPSS's belief in the *narodno jedinstvo* of the Croats and Serbs. A Catholic party, in a country such as Croatia, which was divided among different faiths (Catholic, Orthodox), could never be a national party.[93] This was why the HPSS was equally hostile towards the political activism of the Serb Orthodox clergy.[94] The Radićes' emphasis on Christian religious principles also invariably led them into a confrontation with those political elements in Croatia that were, at least in their minds, excessively liberal in their political philosophy, like the intellectuals of the Progressive Party and the Young Croats (*mladohrvati*), a student group that was formally under the tutelage of Josip Frank and his Pure Party of Right. The HPSS's commitment to Christian ethics hardly endeared it to clericalist elements in Croatia, for the obvious reason that the Radićes railed against the appearance of Croat clericalism.

Croatian historiography has tended to date the appearance of clericalism in Croatian politics from 1897, when clericalist elements emerged within the framework of the Croat opposition coalition aiming to erect a workers' organization to counteract the activism of the socialists. In actual fact, however, Croat political clericalism made its real appearance in 1904 with the establishment of the paper *Hrvatstvo* (Croatdom). What is important to note is that the growing activism of clericalist elements presented the HPSS with a formidable obstacle in its attempts to establish itself politically in the countryside. 'The task of our paper,' wrote the editor of *Hrvatstvo*, 'is to defend the Catholic faith and Croatian homeland against all attacks, from whatever direction they might come.' Citing the recent appearance of supposedly antireligious political parties in Croatia, *Hrvatstvo* appealed 'to all friends of the Catholic faith and the Croatian homeland to assist us in this struggle.'[95] Since the clericalists unequivocally interpreted the HPSS as an anti-Catholic party, they directed many of their polemics against the Radićes.

In July 1905 all Catholics were invited to join a Catholic political organization. The clericalists believed that such a political organization was needed in light of developments in Croatia over the previous decade. All Croat Catholics were cautioned that there had appeared in Croatia 'a society ... [that] seeks to destroy and pull down the Christian faith of the Croat nation.' This was a reference to the socialists and the Progressive Youth; indeed, the progressivist papers *Pokret* (*Movement*) and *Novi list* (*New Paper*) and Antun Radić's *Dom* (1899–1904) were singled out as agents of anti-Catholicism.[96] *Hrvatstvo* concluded that all of the attacks directed at the Catholic Church were merely means by which various demagogues, among whom it identified Stjepan Radić as one of the most prominent, sought to achieve their own ends.[97] The clericalists refused idly to observe these supposedly anti-Catholic currents. They wanted Catholic ideals to be 'the standard for our public and private life,' and the Croatian *Sabor*, public institutions, judiciary, schools, families, and individuals to act according to these principles: 'Whoever does not want this is not a Christian Catholic.' Christian ideals 'do not help, do not save [anyone] if they are not enacted into life. On the contrary, they bind individuals, society, and the state – they should therefore be enacted into life by the state, society, and individuals. Christianity must be practical.'[98] This became the rallying call of Croatia's clericalists. Although the clericalists, or *furtimaši* as they were pejoratively known,[99] did not possess the support of the majority of Croatia's Catholic clergy, they nevertheless wielded considerable influence.

The clericalists viewed the HPSS as a seditious party. Stjepan Radić's writings and activism amounted to 'unconscionable demagoguery,' for he was attempting to discredit the intelligentsia in the eyes of the people and to portray himself as the saviour of the peasantry. He was propagating the notion that 'the broad masses should look after themselves and at the same time lead a bloody [*sic*] struggle against the intelligentsia.' The HPSS's demand for the introduction of referenda for all major political questions and laws was seen as its most seditious trait. 'A referendum in a monarchical state!! To take away from the king the right of ratification, and to place it instead on the people!! Gentlemen, do you intend to lead our peasant into this kind of endeavour, into this kind of struggle against the monarchical principle, and still to pretend that you are his sincere friends?! We ask every rational man, can there any longer be any doubt about the normality of the mind of the "president" of the peasant party?' The

HPSS's program was otherwise characterized as 'murky' and 'nebulous.'[100] The consistent theme that the clericalists addressed in their attacks against the Radićes and the HPSS was demagoguery and sedition.

When, in the spring of 1905, over 6,000 copies of the HPSS's program were confiscated by the authorities, *Hrvatstvo* was elated: the Radićes were 'so unjust that they present only themselves as saviours and friends to the peasantry.' And for this to succeed 'they slander on the one hand the entire older generation [of the intelligentsia] with indolence to the peasant population, while on the other hand their unconscionable demagoguery is so blatant, that they keep telling the peasants all kinds of theories which could, be they either properly or incorrectly understood, mislead the peasantry to the wildest practices.' To advocate referenda in a monarchical state 'is the most heartless demagogic speculation or madness.'[101] One clericalist author, writing about Stjepan Radić's motives, argued that 'like the French Jacobins he wishes to shatter and destroy everything in Croatia which has hitherto existed, so that on the ruins of all of this he can promote himself as the only promised Messiah of the Croat people.'[102] Since the clericalists interpreted the HPSS as seditious, they repeatedly directed some of their bitterest invective against the Radićes. Their hostility to the HPSS was symptomatic of the fear that most conservative elements had of any rural political organization as a potential source of instability and social radicalism.

What truly separates the HPSS from the mainstream Croat political parties in the Habsburg era was its organization, which was constructed at the village level, although before 1918 the party's organization revealed important regional variations. This grassroots organization paid few concrete dividends in the pre-1918 era. But the prewar organizational base, coupled with the new conditions after 1918, assisted the transformation of the HPSS into a national mass movement. The party organization had three aims: social, political and 'national–political.' The social aim was to break down the existing prejudices and parochialism of the peasants by bringing them together through meetings and rallies. By joining the party and attending rallies the peasants could become acquainted, realize their similar needs and, eventually, their collective strength. Conscious of this strength they would no longer fear the *gospoda*. The political aim of party organization was to use these gatherings to educate peasants about political problems and for the purposes of political indoctrination. In principle, although not necessarily in practice, the HPSS recognized that it had to provide a forum for the exchange of opinions and be attentive to its membership's desires. Through its organization the HPSS wished to instil its program firmly in the collective consciousness of the peasantry. The national–political aim of party organization was to create a party cadre at both the local and national levels that would remain accountable to the entire membership, possess a firm grasp of basic political issues, and actively work at the local level to keep the membership informed. The HPSS placed firm emphasis on the need for organization and proclaimed the principle of 'peasant concord' to be one of its objectives, for there could be no successful work without unity.[103]

The HPSS program of 1905 laid down the basic procedure of party organization. In January 1905 the temporary executive committee of the HPSS recommended that local meetings of thirty to forty people be held in private homes or dwellings to inform people about the aims and objectives of the HPSS, and to recruit a membership and a local party cadre. An annual Main Assembly (*Glavna skupština*), attended by delegates from all parts of Croatia-Slavonia, would elect a Main Committee (*Glavni odbor*) that would oversee all party affairs and act as the executive until the subsequent Main Assembly, when it had to be re-elected. Membership was open to all adults who understood and agreed with the HPSS's program. After registering with the local HPSS commissioner (*povjerenik*), an individual was formally admitted to the party. To become a party commissioner, one needed to have an active interest in party affairs and subscribe to one of the party-affiliated papers.[104] Moreover, one had to find two other subscribers to join the party or, if they were already members, they had to back the proposed commissioner's candidacy. If in a given region there were a number of subscribers who aspired to the position of commissioner, they were to inform a member of the Main Committee, who would then meet with the concerned parties to mediate the selection of a commissioner. Local initiative was tolerated and even encouraged at the village level, although the Main Committee could and certainly did influence the selection of local party leaders. Once a membership had been established at the commune level the local commissioners would meet with either the president (Stjepan Radić) or another member of the Main Committee to choose a confidant (*pouzdanik*) for the entire administrative commune. The party's regional confidants and commissioners would attend the HPSS Main Assembly to elect the Main Committee and vote on party policy, although attendance was open to all members.[105]

The impediments to establishing a local party organization were immense. Croatia was organized into eight counties which were subdivided into eighty-eight electoral districts and hundreds of administrative communes. Any party hoping to establish a national network at the village level faced the immediate physical problem of poor communications, such as the lack of good roads and railways. But this was by no means the only or even the biggest problem, although it should not be minimized. The HPSS, which originated as a party of a few intellectuals, was plagued by financial hardship from the outset. Stjepan Radić recognized as early as February 1905 that the HPSS's organizational work was being hampered by the fact that there were too few educated people to carry out organizational tasks. He admitted that this was a problem and would mean that the peasants themselves would have to take the lead. The party was also confronted with government interference. On 22 April 1905 the authorities seized 6,600 of the original 10,000 copies of the party's program, one month after it had been published, and censored it in thirty-two places. Although the case was successfully challenged on 21 June 1905 in the Zagreb district court by Stjepan Radić, and the confiscated copies returned to the HPSS, the incident inflicted serious financial losses on the HPSS.[106]

The number of incidents of official interference intensified as the HPSS's organizational activism proceeded. One of the first incidents occurred on 6 August 1905 in the district of Gornja Stubica (Zagorje), when Stjepan Radić and an associate tried holding a meeting in a local village. They were confronted by a number of gendarmes and three soldiers who informed them that the prefect had banned the meeting on the basis of an Imperial patent from 1852. Although Radić initially resisted, he and his associate were eventually escorted to the local police station and fined for resisting the orders of the prefect.[107] Just over a week later two other prearranged HPSS meetings in the Zagorje region were banned for no apparent reason, which led the party to conclude that in this particular area of Croatia all 'fundamental constitutional laws' had been suspended.[108] On 20 August another planned meeting in the village of Komarevo, in Petrinja district, was also banned.[109] There were other such incidents throughout 1905 which certainly complicated the progress of the HPSS's organizational work, but did not prevent its growth.

This problem was accentuated when the HPSS came under attack from the Catholic Church hierarchy. The Archbishop of Zagreb, Juraj Posilović, issued a circular to the parish clergy on the eve of the May 1906 elections instructing them and their parishioners not to vote for any party against the Catholic faith, including the HPSS. The HPSS countered such accusations by denying that it was against religion. 'If our Archbishop had studied the program of the HPSS more closely,' one of the HPSS papers commented, 'if he had the opportunity of attending just one of our meetings, we are convinced that he would not consider us to be enemies of the faith.' The HPSS was not against religion, but it sternly denounced those priests 'who under the chimera of religion pursue political spite and who preach one thing but live and work something else.'[110] The Church hierarchy's policy towards the HPSS, combined with the constant criticism of the clericalist paper *Hrvatstvo*, created a formidable obstacle that the HPSS had to overcome. The HPSS leadership was acutely aware of the problem of the clergy and was kept apprised of the activities of local priests who denounced the HPSS as antireligious. In a typical example, Stjepan Hrastovec, an HPSS activist from the village of Dubrava, near Zagreb, informed Stjepan Radić that a local priest was actively agitating among the peasants to convince them not to vote for the HPSS, while his assistant spread rumours about the HPSS leadership. Another HPSS activist, also from Dubrava, informed Radić that a priest had told him that the Archbishop of Zagreb had expressly forbidden all clergy from joining the HPSS because of its 'antireligious policy.'[111] To penetrate the village, the HPSS had to break the rural clergy's hold over the minds of the Croat peasantry. In addition to this formidable obstacle, it must also be emphasized that virtually all of Croatia's existing parties came out against the HPSS. For some it was a seditious party, while others interpreted the Radićes' populist platform and their frequent tendency to invoke religious tenets as pure demagoguery. From 1904 to 1918 the HPSS retained its status as a political outsider.

Perhaps the greatest obstacle, however, was the peasants themselves. In many cases illiterate, passive, and parochial, peasants were plagued by a sense of social inferiority, a fact of which the HPSS leadership was painfully aware. Even Stjepan Radić was troubled by this phenomenon. He observed in these early years that when it came to defending the rights of his village, his commune, or his entire homeland, the Croat peasant was a 'coward.' At rural assemblies, he added, 'it is enough for a "state official" to show up ... and no one dares to speak up. And how afraid he is when a district prefect or inspector shows up in the company of gendarmes.'[112] This was a major hindrance to peasant mobilization and one of the reasons why the party's main organizational aim became to instil in the peasantry a perception of their collective strength as a means of ending this sense of inferiority.

In spite of these obstacles, the HPSS made slow but steady progress in organizing itself at the village level. Most other Croat parties worked in the villages only during election campaigns or neglected them altogether, but the HPSS sank deep roots in villages. Stjepan Radić's organizational efforts were remarkable; he traversed much of the Croatian countryside consulting with local party workers and, in areas where none existed, actively recruiting them. Indeed, one could legitimately compare the zeal of this organizational activism with the Russian populists' 'going to the people.' In 1905 alone, Radić spent 169 days outside of Zagreb working to build a party organization in the countryside.[113] Upon entering a village that did not have any HPSS workers Radić sought out individuals who, in his eyes, were morally fit to work in the party. If a man was not a drunkard, did not fear either the local government officials or priest, and treated his wife with respect, he would try to recruit him as a local party worker. According to Radić, it was with the assistance of such local peasant leaders that he was able, by early 1909, to organize over 10,000 peasants behind the HPSS.[114]

In attempting to reconstruct the early years of the HPSS's activism and recruiting, one is confronted with the problem of the absence of party membership rolls. It is therefore difficult to determine precisely how many party workers the HPSS had in these years or how many people joined the party. This problem is accentuated by what appear to be inconsistent assertions in the contemporary HPSS press regarding organizational activities and membership. For example, the party's main organ claimed that by the eve of the HPSS's first annual general assembly, held 17–18 September 1905, 242 commissioners indicated that they would attend, of whom only 185 actually attended the assembly. It was claimed that the 174 commissioners in attendance at the opening session of the assembly had hitherto organized 157 private meetings and had recruited 1,945 members.[115] The total number of party commissioners was not indicated. Another HPSS paper insisted that by the eve of the first assembly up to 150 meetings had been held with 30,000 participants, and that over 400 commissioners had been chosen.[116] But Stjepan Radić, reviewing the party's work and achievements in its first year, claimed in December 1905 that by the time of the HPSS's first main assembly, only 376 commissioners had been elected and that the party had 1,945 registered members. According to him, by the end of that year the HPSS had 565 commissioners and just over 14,000 registered members.[117] At the second main assembly, held on 15 September 1906, the party leadership claimed that 215 commissioners had attended the first assembly, a clear contradiction of its earlier claims.[118] If these contradictions reveal anything, it is almost certainly that the party's early organizational work was accompanied by a great deal of chaos.

Even the regional distribution of the party workers is not entirely certain, although the available sources enable a fairly accurate assessment. For instance, both of the party's newspapers claimed that there were party workers from twenty-six of Croatia's eighty-eight electoral districts at the first party assembly, the inference being that the HPSS had established itself only in those districts.[119] But at the second main assembly in 1906 the party leadership claimed that commissioners from thirty-two electoral districts had attended the first assembly.[120] In spite of the contradictory numbers, however, what can be asserted with some certainty is that the majority of party workers came from Zagreb and Bjelovar-Križevci counties and that the HPSS was strongest there. The only county in which the HPSS did not have any commissioners was Lika-Krbava, and it did not run any candidates there before the First World War. If the party's own data from September 1905 regarding the regional distribution of 241 of its commissioners are analysed, then the following picture emerges: 137 commissioners came from the county of Bjelovar–Križevci, 62 from Zagreb county, 19 from Požega county, 11 from Modruš-Rijeka, 7 from Varaždin county, 3 from Srijem county, and 2 from Osijek county.[121] Although similar data for the following years are lacking, it appears that the party generally strengthened its existing regional base and did not expand tremendously beyond the two counties where it was strongest. Stjepan Radić claimed in late 1905 that the HPSS was active in virtually all areas of Croatia-Slavonia, but he acknowledged that its real strength was in the northern part of the county of Bjelovar-Križevci and the southern part of Zagreb county near Sisak and the Radićes' home village of Trebarjevo Desno.[122]

Subsequent party assemblies reveal a gradual growth in party membership, although the HPSS's regional expansion did not seem to follow the same pattern. The second annual assembly was attended by approximately 1,500 members, a third of whom were party workers, from thirty-eight electoral districts. The third assembly, held 24–5 August 1907, was attended by about 2,000 members, approximately 600 of whom were party workers, from a total of twenty-seven electoral constituencies.[123] Between the first and third assemblies the party's central leadership organized forty-two public rallies and 123 large meetings, whereas the local party workers organized hundreds of smaller meetings. The party claimed that up to 100,000 people had attended all of these meetings and that it had just over 1,000 party workers by late 1907.[124] The sixth assembly (2 February 1912), the HPSS's last prewar assembly, was attended by just over 400 party workers, but it took place on the eve of the introduction of a commissariat in Croatia and with Stjepan Radić in prison.[125] As the earlier contradictions point out, these figures must be treated with caution.

The local party workers were almost exclusively peasants. Moreover, the HPSS's executive body, the Main Committee, eventually came to have a peasant majority. In March 1905 the professional-social distribution of the twenty-one members of the Main Committee was as follows: twelve (57.1 per cent) were intellectuals, defined here as writers, journalists, priests, and lawyers; five (23.8 per cent) were classified as peasants; the others were largely artisans and shopkeepers.[126] In mid-July 1905 the Main Committee was expanded, so that by the time of the first Main Assembly in September the HPSS's Main Committee had thirty-six members: 17 (47.2 per cent) peasants, 12 (33.3 per cent) intellectuals, with artisans and shopkeepers again accounting for the majority of the remaining members.[127] By the third Main Assembly in 1907 the party's Main Committee had sixty-eight members, 44 (64.7 per cent) of whom were peasants and 13 (19.1 per cent) of whom were intellectuals.[128] By

1912 the HPSS's Main Committee had the following professional–social breakdown: 83 per cent were peasants and 9 per cent were intellectuals.[129] The HPSS ran twenty-nine candidates in the December 1911 elections, nineteen (65.5 per cent) of whom were peasants, seven (24.1 per cent) of whom were intellectuals, with three (10.3 per cent) proprietors.[130] In terms of the professional–social composition of its local activists and Main Committee, the HPSS came to reflect the existing social structure of Croat society.

Despite the gradual growth in party membership, difficulties remained. In July 1911 Antun Radić bemoaned the lack of party unity; the HPSS's central leadership subsequently placed greater emphasis on strengthening the local party organization and fostering party cohesiveness.[131] By the eve of the First World War the HPSS had established a party cadre and a membership that probably ranged in size from 10,000 to 15,000 people, although, of course, the number of its sympathizers was much greater. It nevertheless remained a political outsider because of the restrictive franchise and because it was not seen as a respectable party in middle-class and intellectual circles, which effectively meant that it had virtually no support in Croatia's urban centres. The HPSS ran candidates in five prewar elections (1906, 1908, 1910, 1911, 1913), gaining no seats in the first and two, nine, eight, and three of eighty-eight seats, respectively, in the subsequent campaigns (see Table 4.1).

The First World War would bring about increased radicalization among peasants, which facilitated the party's transformation into a national, peasant-based mass movement. The party's grassroots organizational work before 1914 paid dividends in the postwar era, but neither the strength of the HPSS's organizational machinery nor the importance of local party functionaries should be exaggerated. The party devoted great attention to organization in its first years and held regular main assemblies (1905, 1906, 1907, 1909, 1910, 1912), but these became biennial in 1907 and then ceased during the First World War, only to be recommenced in 1919. Although the party encouraged peasant participation at the local level, in terms of policy formulation and initiative, the central leadership and Stjepan Radić assumed the dominant role. The simple fact remains that the HPSS was not able to establish effective machinery that would enable its local leaders to voice their concerns about general policy. But this was certainly not at variance in any way with the party's populist nature: Radić saw himself as an interpreter of the people's will, and his charismatic and dominant personality meant that he shaped the contours of the HPSS's policy. The importance of the HPSS's organizational work should not be underestimated, however. In those regions where it had already established itself by 1914 the party's transformation into a mass movement after 1918 was much more rapid. Conversely, in those regions of prewar Croatia-Slavonia where it was weaker, and in Dalmatia and Bosnia-Herzegovina, where it had no commissioners before the early 1920s, it took longer for the party to capitalize on the new radicalism of the peasants.

It was that radicalism, particularly the republican sentiments of the Croat countryside after 1918, that would transform the HPSS into a mass movement. The First World War was clearly the fundamental turning-point. Peasant radicalism was most markedly manifested in the context of the Habsburg dénouement in the form of the Green Cadre movement.[132] The party's central leadership would be able to claim by the early 1920s, as will be seen, that it had over a million organized members.[133] With an agrarian ideology and organization already in place, the HPSS was much better situated to capitalize on the peasantry's new radicalism than any other Croat party and gradually penetrated virtually every Croat village, not just in Croatia-Slavonia, but in Dalmatia and Bosnia-Herzegovina as well.

With the exception of republicanism, the HPSS's peasantist ideology would not change in any substantive way in the postwar era. Its basic tenets, such as peasant right and peasant state, remained at the core of the party's ideology. Nor did the party's tactics change. It remained committed to legality and pacifism. The important point that needs to be emphasized is that the HPSS, through the Radićes' elaboration of the concepts of peasant right and peasant state, was able to offer the peasants, first of all, an ideology that asserted their right to a leading role in Croatian politics and society and, second, a program for their political, economic, and social emancipation. It is tempting to dismiss as unconvincing the Radićes' attempt to create for their party a veneer of ideological sophistication. The temptation should be resisted, however; the party ideology's obvious lack of sophistication did not detract from the manifest appeal and resonance that ideology possessed in the Croat village. Even the Radićes' Marxist critics acknowledged the powerful allure of the HPSS's ideas, especially that of peasant right. It was conceptually provocative enough in the context of prewar Croatia, that it prompted a storm of denunciations from Croatia's political élite.[134] More importantly, it was simple enough for all peasants to understand. By enacting this program the HPSS wanted not only to emancipate the peasantry but also to complete the process of Croat national integration. After 1918, however, the HPSS program, and its central aim of a peasant state, could only be achieved at the expense of the new Yugoslav monarchy, a state that denied the national individuality of the Croats. National and social aspirations thus became inextricably intertwined, and by galvanizing peasant opinion the party came to play the most important role in the completion of the process of national integration that took place in the 1920s.

4

Stjepan Radić, Croatianism, Yugoslavism, and the Habsburg Monarchy

In one form or another, the notion of Slavic reciprocity and the corresponding idea that the South Slavs constituted a single historical or linguistic–national community has long received considerable support in Croat intellectual circles. Ljudevit Gaj's Illyrianist movement (1836–48), which represented the initial stage of the Croat national awakening, recognized this idea and attempted to construct a common culture for all South Slavs under the neutral Illyrian name while operating within the political framework of the kingdom of Croatia. Illyrianism was succeeded in the 1860s by the Yugoslavism of Bishop Josip Juraj Strossmayer and Canon Franjo Rački, both of whom were committed to forming a common South Slav culture. Moreover, like the Illyrianists, they operated within the Habsburg framework and sought a federalized monarchy, although they emphasized the kingdom of Croatia's historic state right more than the Illyrianists had.

The Yugoslav idea reached its nadir in the late 1870s and 1880s, as Ante Starčević's movement grew in popularity. It was revived only in the mid-1890s by the Progressive Youth who preached the *narodno jedinstvo* of Croats and Serbs. Although in many respects continuing in the traditions of both Illyrianism and Yugoslavism, the intellectuals of the Progressive Youth, unlike their ideological predecessors, Gaj and Strossmayer, increasingly looked to the creation of a Yugoslav state as a solution to the South Slavs' political problems within the Habsburg monarchy. Implicit within their formula of *narodno jedinstvo* was unitarist Yugoslavism. This was especially true of the prewar Nationalist Youth (1908–14). Thus, the Yugoslav idea ultimately raised the question of whether Croatia's future was best secured within the monarchy or in some kind of Yugoslav state.

Consequently, Yugoslavism became one of the most important issues in Croatian politics, particularly in the immediate pre–First World War period.

The widespread dissatisfaction in Croatia with the prevailing state of affairs in the decade before 1914 prompted many adherents of Yugoslavism to consider the possibility of solving the Croatian or 'South Slav' question through the creation of a Yugoslav state. This idea was not exclusively limited to the supporters of integral, unitaristic Yugoslavism, who remained in a minority, but was also supported by advocates of other variants of Yugoslavism. By 1914 even some former advocates of integral Croat nationalism had adopted Yugoslavism. The 'South Slav' question was also of dire significance for the monarchy itself, especially with the ascent to power in 1903 of the Karadjordjević dynasty in Serbia. Serbia's territorial aggrandizement during the Balkan wars (1912–13) confronted the Habsburg monarchy with an enlarged, pro-Russian state that seemingly harboured territorial ambitions towards its South Slav lands. Indeed, in 1908 a British observer remarked that 'the key to the whole Balkan question lies among the Serbo-Croatian race [*sic*],' and that 'the future of Bosnia and Servia [*sic*] depends upon the situation in Hungary and Croatia.' What he was referring to was the national question in Hungary, the solution of which 'will exercise a decisive influence upon the [European] Balance of Power.' If the House of Habsburg abandoned its 'historic mission' of 'the vindication of equal rights and liberties for all the races committed to its charge,' the very existence of historic Hungary and the Habsburg monarchy would be endangered.[1]

Five years later this same observer claimed that Croat and Serb political unity was simply a matter of time. The Habsburg monarchy had the choice 'of delaying its attainment for a generation and reaping the fruits of so fatal a policy,' but this alternative was 'an especial concern of Germany, for she might find herself paying the political debts of Austria.'[2] The following year, on 28 June 1914, the heir to the Habsburg throne, Archduke Franz Ferdinand, was assassinated by a Serb nationalist in Sarajevo and within five weeks the armies of Europe were on the march in what was to become the greatest war in human history to that day.

Stjepan Radić wrote extensively in the prewar era about Yugoslavism, Croat–Serb relations, and the question of Croatia's status within the Habsburg monarchy.[3] Because Radić emerged after 1918 as the only significant leader of the Croats and had a profound impact on the evolution of the first Yugoslav state, it is critical to examine his national ideology. This has to be done particularly in the context of the growing Yugoslav movement within the monarchy and Serbia's emergence as a major Balkan power. An analysis of Radić's national ideology reveals that it was significantly different from that of the prevailing intellectual mainstream in Croatia, and will enable a clearer understanding of his actions in the context of Yugoslav unification in 1918 and during the 1920s. Although Radić was a proponent of *narodno jedinstvo*, his variant differed substantially from that of the contemporary Croat intelligentsia, primarily in its political implications. The idea of creating a single Yugoslav state, encompassing the Habsburg monarchy's South Slavs and the kingdoms of Serbia and Montenegro, was politically anathema to Radić. He simultaneously emphasized Croatia's state right and the unity of Croats and Serbs within Croatia's historic borders. Reduced to its bare essence, Radić's *narodno jedinstvo* was operative within, and politically confined to, the borders of Croatia and the Habsburg monarchy.

The most important political grouping in Croatia in the decade before 1914 was the Croato-Serb Coalition (HSK, *Hrvatsko-srpska koalicija*). The HSK was essentially the product of the Progressive Youth. Because most of the Progressives studied in Bohemia, they were indelibly influenced by their Prague milieu and the intensification of the German-Czech struggle in the 1890s. They saw the German *Drang nach Osten* as the greatest national danger to Serbs and Croats. In the face of this threat, national unity was an absolute necessity, as was cooperation with other small nations in East Central Europe. The intellectuals of the Progressive Youth, among whom Radić initially played a leading role, sought national autonomy and the democratization of society, and provided the impetus for a fundamental change in Serb–Croat relations, epitomized by the New Course in Croatian politics after 1905.[4] Although shaped by wider European developments, the new course, which was largely the work of the Croat politicians Ante Trumbić and Frano Supilo,[5] essentially represented a reaction against the traditional Croat opposition's lack of concrete political results.

The fundamental postulates of the new course were as follows: the aim of an independent Yugoslav state was too distant to be realized in the near future. Such a state could only be formed by gradual means, by the exploitation of the monarchy's internal crisis or crises, with Serbo–Croat cooperation, and with the assistance of all forces threatened by the German *Drang*. Under the circumstances, the proponents of the New Course concluded that they had to support the Magyar opposition led by Ferenc Kossuth. Although the Magyar opposition was even more nationalistic than the ruling Liberal Party, the proponents of the new course associated the contemporary Magyarone regime in Croatia with the Magyar Liberals. By providing support for the Magyar opposition against Vienna in its struggle for economic independence and a national army, they hoped to gain the former's assistance and thereby achieve their minimal aims, namely, the collapse of the Magyarone regime in Croatia and the implementation of constitutional and economic reforms and ultimately Dalmatia's unification with Croatia.[6] Although few deputies implicitly trusted the Magyar opposition, the political situation led them to a pro-Magyar position, especially since few believed that Vienna would solve the Croatian question. In many Croat political circles Vienna was seen as the main source of Croatia's ills.

As one of the main architects of the new course, Trumbić believed that Croats had to cooperate with the Serbs and Italians in Dalmatia and that the Croats and Serbs in Croatia had to support Budapest. The constitutional crisis opened new perspectives in Croatia and some saw the opportunity of bringing about a fundamental change in Croatia's status by exploiting the crisis, particularly since the Magyars, hitherto one of the pillars of the dualist order, began to undermine the very foundations of dualism. The essence of the new course in Croatia was summed up by a contemporary slogan: 'Against Austria certainly, for the Magyar opposition in principle, along with our demands.'[7] Realizing that they were too weak to change Croatia's status through their own limited forces, they chose the lesser of two evils, which they perceived to be the Magyar opposition coalition. Moreover, an autonomous Hungary without Austria's support would not be as dangerous *vis-à-vis* the South Slavs as Austria backed by Germany. The Rijeka Resolution was announced on 3 October 1905 and its Serb counterpart, the Zadar Resolution, on 17 October 1905. These memoranda, which formally initiated the new course, shaped the contours of Croatian politics until the First World War. The Croat and Serb deputies pledged to support the Magyars in their struggle for the gradual attainment of full autonomy; Serb support for Croatian unification was further made conditional on Croat recognition of the complete civil equality of Croats and Serbs.[8]

The new course found expression in the formation on 11 December 1905 of the Croato-Serb Coalition. The HSK was initially made up of the Croat Party of Right, the Croat People's Progressive Party, the Serb Independent Party, the Serb Radical Party, the Social Democratic Party, and a number of independent deputies, although in 1907 the Serb Radicals and the Social Democrats left the coalition. By 1910 there were only two parties within the HSK: Svetozar Pribićević's Serb Independent Party and Ivan Lorković's Croat Independent Party, formed that year by the merger of the Progressive Party and the Croat Party of Right. The HSK's inaugural declaration stated that it stood for the equality of Croats and Serbs, constitutional rule, and civil freedoms, such as universal manhood suffrage, local administrative autonomy, and the reform of the worst violations of the *Nagodba*, especially in the realm of finance.[9] The HSK's ultimate goal was unification with Serbia, but in the meantime it wished to prepare the people for this.[10]

The new course was quickly undermined when in April 1906 a compromise

TABLE 4.1
Election results in Croatia–Slavonia, 1906–1913

	May 1906	Feb. 1908	Oct. 1910	Dec. 1911	Dec. 1913
HSK*	43	57	35	25	48
National Party**	25	0	18	22	12
Frankists	20	24	15	27†	9
SSP†	–	–	9	–	12
HPSS	0	2	9	8	3
Serb Radical Party	–	2	1	3	0
Non-Party et al.	–	3	1	3	4†
Total	88	88	88	88	88

Sources: *Dom*, 29 Feb. 1908, p. 2; 3 Nov. 1910, pp. 1, 3; 10 Jan. 1912, pp. 2–3; 31 Dec. 1913, p. 3; Milan Marjanović, *Savremena Hrvatska* (Belgrade, 1913), pp. 329–32.
*HSK (Croato-Serb Coalition): In 1906 it consisted of the Croat Party of Right (14), the Serb Independent Party (16), Croat Progressive Party (3), Serb Radical Party (3), and non-party/independents (7). In 1908 its parliamentary breakdown was as follows: Croat Party of Right (26), Serb Independent Party (19), Croat Progressives (4), and Autonomous Club (8). After 1910, with the merger of the Croat Party of Right and the Progressives, the HSK consisted of only two parties, the Croat Independents and Serb Independents. In 1910 the Croat Independents received 20 seats and the Serb Independents 14, with one non-party member. In 1913 the Croat Independents gained 31 and the Serb Independents 17 seats.
**National Party: Used here to refer to deputies who supported the regime of the Croatian *ban* (prorex).
†SSP (Starčević's Party of Right): Split from the Frankists in April 1908, ran jointly with them in 1911, but not in 1913. In 1913 two of the "non-party et al." deputies were elected on the united Frankist–SSP platform.

was struck between Franz Joseph and the Magyar opposition, on the basis of which the latter came to power in Hungary; the *raison d'être* of cooperation between the HSK and Magyar opposition collapsed. Despite this fact, new elections were called in Croatia for May 1906, which led to a victory by the HSK and made it the leading factor in the *Sabor*; it remained the most important political grouping within Croatia until 1918 and represented the interests of the majority of Croatia's intelligentsia, both Croat and Serb.[11] Neither the Serbs nor the Croats of the HSK sought the 'hybridization' of the South Slavs, although elements of an integral, unitarist Yugoslavism were implicit in the HSK's formula of *narodno jedinstvo*.[12] The policies of the HSK were essentially 'national–revolutionary' in character because they were designed to assist all forces that sought to weaken the monarchy, and this became a major issue of division between Radić and the intellectuals of the HSK. Its means were at times certainly openly opportunistic, but the HSK's long-range goal remained the monarchy's demise, although many of its followers were prepared to accept a reorganization to form a triple monarchy.[13]

The new course was doomed to fail, however, especially after the Magyar opposition came to terms with Vienna. The definitive break between the HSK and the new Magyar regime – the so-called ministry of all the talents – of Sándor Wekerle, which was dominated by the nationalist Independence Party, occurred in May 1907 when Ferenc Kossuth proposed the railroad pragmatic. These regulations made knowledge of Hungarian obligatory for all employees of the Royal Hungarian railroads. Although knowledge of Croatian was required for employees in Croatia-Slavonia, the official language was specified as Hungarian. The HSK saw this legislation as a violation of the *Nagodba*, and its forty deputies in the lower house of the Budapest parliament conducted a month-long, and ultimately unsuccessful, obstructionist campaign. The new course was dead.

The collapse of the new course was followed in 1908 by a confrontation between the HSK and the Croatian regime of *ban* Pavao Rauch (1908–10). Appointed in January 1908, Rauch's aim was to break the HSK by resorting to Khuen-Héderváry's tactic of *divide et impera*. He was instructed in the spring of 1908 by the Austro-Hungarian foreign minister, Alois Aehrenthal, to collect documentation implicating the HSK's Serb leaders of high treason, that is, of maintaining clandestine and subversive ties with Serbia. The purpose of the investigation was to prove Serbia's intention to annex Bosnia-Herzegovina, which the Austro-Hungarian government (Ministerial Council), at its session of 1 December 1907, had decided to annex.[14] In August 1908 fifty-three Croatian Serbs, members of the HSK's Serb Independent Party, were arrested and the charges against them announced on 12 January 1909. The Zagreb high treason trial, which began on 3 March 1909, was supposed to justify the Habsburg monarchy's annexation of Bosnia–Herzegovina of October 1908. The Serbs were accused of spreading the idea of a Great Serbian state and preparing a revolution with the aid of the Serbian and Montenegrin armies in order to annex the monarchy's South Slav lands. The charges lacked substance, and the state prosecutor had little evidence, but the trial ended on 5 October 1909 with thirty-three of the accused being sentenced to prison terms of varied duration, although they were subsequently amnestied.[15] In the aftermath of the high treason trial, the HSK was gradually forced into a policy of opportunism and cooperation with the regime, in part because of its fears of renewed persecution. It thus found itself in the position of its erstwhile nemesis, the Magyarone National Party.

The HSK's policies regarding the monarchy and Croat-Serb relations differed substantially from those of the Starčevićist currents in Croatia. Josip Frank, the leader of the Pure Party of Right, had substantially altered Starčević's original views regarding Austria since the original split within the state right movement in October 1895. Frank emerged as one of the most outspoken opponents of the new course. Eventually Frank linked his party's fortunes to the Great Austrian circle around the Archduke Franz Ferdinand, which sought to transform the monarchy into a centralized, German Great Austria, which necessarily meant diminishing or abolishing the political power of the Magyar ruling élite. For allies they looked to Hungary's non-Magyars, especially the Croats and Romanians, and they were prepared to permit wider local autonomy as an incentive for cooperation. But the enthusiasm of the Frankists for a triple monarchy went against the basic concept of this program, for the Great Austrian circle never seriously entertained the idea of a triple regime, and insofar as it did it saw in it three administrative units of a single state and not three sovereign states of a larger confederation, as many Croat advocates understood the concept. Nevertheless, Frank tied his fortunes to Franz Ferdinand and his circle (military officers, Austrian Christian Socialists). Under the rule of *ban* Pavao Rauch, he lent his services to the regime against the Serbs, in effect becoming the regime's party.[16] Frank's Great Croatia, had it been realized, would merely have been an administrative unit as opposed to a truly sovereign state. Hence, by September 1910, when his party merged with Catholic clericalist elements to form the Christian Social Party of Right, Frank's 'pure Croatism' had two basic characteristics: Austrianism and militant anti-Serbianism.[17] Although theoretically committed to Starčević's ideals, he represented the interests of a unitary monarchy in the hope of securing his party's political fortunes. In spite of his party's lackey status, Frank still commanded a following in some intellectual, petit bourgeois, clericalist, and student circles.

Frank's overt opportunism caused a fracture within his party in April 1908. The leader of the break-away faction, Mile Starčević, formed the Starčević's Party of Right (SSP, *Starčevićeva stranka prava*), which became the most popular current among the state right factions in the immediate prewar years. Claiming that Frank had distorted Ante Starčević's tenets, the *milinovci*, as the SSP's followers were known, sought to return to his original ideals. In the process they modified Starčević's argument on the need for establishing an independent Croatian state outside of the monarchy's confines, although they did not reject this out of hand. To strengthen their own influence they increasingly expressed an interest in cooperation with the HSK and the Serbs, but this cooperation was made conditional on Serb acceptance, in principle, of the unification of Bosnia with Croatia.[18]

The Starčevićists believed that Serbs should be guaranteed cultural and religious autonomy. They thereby recognized the Serbs as a distinct ethno-religious community within Croatia and Bosnia, although linguistically and politically the SSP still considered them to be 'Croats.'[19] The Starčevićists continued to maintain a position of conditional loyalty to the monarchy and advocated a middle course between the two extremes: expectations that Serbia might make possible the liberation of Croatia, on the one hand, and, on the other, loyalty to the Habsburg dynasty. The 'true' Starčevićist policy must remain between these extremes. They were equally aware that neither Serbia nor the Habsburg dynasty would help to realize Croatian autonomy; only Croats could achieve this. True to their Starčevićist tradition, they proclaimed: Neither for Austria nor against her, neither for Hungary nor against her, neither for Serbia nor against her, but rather only for Croatia.[20] During the First World War, however, the *milinovci* emerged as leading proponents of the creation of a Yugoslav state.

The establishment of a commissariat under *ban* Slavko Cuvaj (1912–13) in the spring of 1912 – and its perpetuation under *ban* Ivan Skerlecz (1913–17) – largely as a reaction to the agreement struck between the HSK and the Starčevićists, which united the major opposition forces in Croatia, and to the Balkan wars, marked a turning point in Croatian politics and led to the emergence of new ideological trends.[21] A new Starčevićist current had emerged known as the Young Croats, after their paper *Mlada Hrvatska* (*Young Croatia*). Although ostensibly under the leadership of Frank, the Young Croats were alienated from his party because of its fusion with clericalist elements, and they gradually drew closer to the youth of the Progressive Party.[22] Their significance lies in the fact that in the immediate prewar period many of these young intellectuals adopted unitarist Yugoslavism.

Two new ideological currents appeared: radical progressivism and Yugoslav nationalism, both of which were variations of the same Yugoslav unitarist theme. For the radical progressives, Croats and Serbs (Slovenes and Bulgars were rarely mentioned) were either one nation or elements that must develop into a single Yugoslav nation. Their task was to quicken and direct this fusion towards the creation of a common Yugoslav state through the cultural and economic elevation of the people. The other Yugoslav nationalist current rejected gradualism in favour of the revolutionary creation of a Yugoslav state. Towards this end it was necessary to raise the collective consciousness of the people and to revolutionize them through individual acts of sacrifice by the young intellectual élite.[23] Frustrated by the absolutist regime in Croatia and the failure of the opposition to achieve substantive gains in the national struggle, the Nationalist Youth turned to desperate and violent means, such as the

attempted assassination of Cuvaj in June 1912 and of his successor Ivan Skerlecz in August 1913.

To these young intellectuals the road from Croat exclusivism to unitarist
Yugoslavism was not as circuitous as it might seem, although the reasoning
they used to justify this leap was indeed flawed. For the leaders of the Young
Croats, the evolution of the Starčevićist ideology would be completed when it
was melded with unitarist Yugoslavism. Had not Starčević argued that all
South Slavs were really Croats? If this were the case, then the only difference
between the Croat and Yugoslav unitarist ideologies was not one of substance
but one of name. And these young intellectuals did not struggle too long over
the issue of the name of this nation; for them the name was not as important as
the nation's individuality and soul. This was of course illusory, but nevertheless many Young Croats adopted this line of thinking. Thus, they easily
bridged what otherwise was the wide chasm separating Starčević's Croat
exclusivism and Yugoslav unitarism. It is clear, therefore, that by the eve of the
Great War an important segment of Croat youth had adopted Yugoslav unitarism, while the HSK's formula of *narodno jedinstvo* also carried within it the
seeds of Yugoslav unitarism. The Starčevićists, although not formally recognizing the Serbs as a people within Croatia, held open the possibility of solving
the Croat question outside of the monarchy. This at least implicitly opened the
door to a future confederated state with Serbia. The significant point that needs
to be emphasized is that the idea of a common South Slavic state gained support among many in Croat middle-class and intellectual circles.

The views of Stjepan Radić on *narodno jedinstvo* and the monarchy differed
from the prevailing intellectual mainstream as outlined above. Radić's espousal
of the principle of *narodno jedinstvo* dated from the mid-1890s when he
emerged as one of the central leaders of the Progressive Youth. The variant of
narodno jedinstvo that he espoused did not carry within it unitarist tendencies,
however. Unlike many of his colleagues, Radić never abandoned the framework of Croat state right, and this would have important political repercussions
in terms of their subsequent mutual relations. Consequently, the national ideology that he articulated, and the national program that the HPSS pursued, represented a synthesis of political Croatism and cultural Yugoslavism. Radić
argued that any objective observer who examined the customs and traditions of
the South Slavs must be absolutely convinced of their *narodno jedinstvo*; there
was not a nation in Europe that was 'so identical from the ethnographic viewpoint in general, and from the linguistic [viewpoint] specifically, as are the
southern Slavs.'[24] That neither a collective national consciousness nor a common national name existed was not a hindrance, since a common name, he
argued, did not necessarily denote a common national consciousness, just as the

lack of a common name did not preclude a common national consciousness among the South Slavs. The main obstacles to *narodno jedinstvo* were the competing megalomanias that were limited to segments of the respective intelligentsias of the Croats and Serbs; it was fortunately absent, he believed, among the peasantry, which represented the true and uncorrupted national spirit. 'The [peasant] people hate no one because of their name,' he wrote in 1898, 'the people do not force names on others; the people condemn every proselytism, religious and political.'[25] This nation, broadly conceived along cultural and particularly linguistic criteria, thus 'can only be weakened by its intelligentsia, if it steadfastly continues in its particularistic policies on the basis of narrow Slovene, Croat, Serb, and Bulgar patriotism.'[26] At a time when social, economic, and cultural factors were drawing disparate nations closer together, 'only a cretinous mind or criminal soul can preach about divisive medieval tribal hatred.'[27]

National unity and political cooperation between Croats and Serbs was crucial for Radić because it was one of the preconditions for solving Croatia's and the South Slavs' national ills.[28] Croats and Serbs would not be able to secure their political position in the Habsburg monarchy, that is, to defend themselves against the threat posed by Magyarization and the German *Drang*, or tackle the problems of economic backwardness unless the intelligentsia began to work for the people and Croats and Serbs in Croatia embraced each other. Radić's distinction between the *gospoda* (intelligentsia; 'gentlemen') and the peasantry is an important one for an understanding of his national ideology. The *gospoda*, 'who are to our whole nation what the soul is to a man,' were essentially ignorant and quarrelsome, they 'mislead more than lead our whole nation, they spoil it more than direct it, strangle it more than raise it.'[29] For Radić, then, the national and social questions clearly intersected; to solve the Serb-Croat dispute first necessitated a resolution of the *gospoda*–peasant relationship.

Radić was convinced that all small Slavic nations owed their 'national resurrections' to the idea of Slavic reciprocity, and that their future depended on it, as well. But unfortunately neither the Croat nor the Serb intelligentsia was sufficiently committed to Slavic reciprocity. For Radić, Croat political individuality could be permanently secured only 'by our common cultural work with the other South Slavs and with even closer cultural and economic reciprocity with them,' as well as with the other Slavs of the monarchy. Radić blamed Croatia's precarious political status on the 'political superficiality' and 'sectarian biases' of the traditional political élites. That is why he was so critical of those elements in Croatia propagating an exclusivist Croat national program. It was inconceivable to him that anyone could believe 'that Croatian conditions could be significantly changed *only by our Croat strength.*' If the Croats were not 'a part of our whole nation from the Triglav to the Balkan [Mountains],' he wrote, 'we would have already perished in this isolation.' Radić thus called for a return to a democratically based, populist cultural Yugoslavism, 'but this time [we must] take this position with a developed and highly raised Croatian flag.' It naturally followed, then, that Croats '*externally* must meld with the Serbs, so that for the outside world there will only be Croatia from Rijeka to Zemun, and further beyond Serbia, but only *two forms of one and the same national–cultural idea,* as two representatives of one and the same most justified and most natural cultural and economic community.'[30] This in no way meant that Radić wanted to meld Croats and Serbs into a hybrid nationality, or that he advocated the formation of a Yugoslav state. Only one great stumbling block lay on the path to the realization of national– cultural unity: those segments of the Croat and Serb intelligentsias that pursued exclusivist national programs.

For Radić, then, Serbs and Croats were 'one indivisible ethnic whole,' and his patriotism was Croatian 'because it is most understandable and most natural that I attest to this through my deeds in the Croatian part of this whole,' and because, second, 'as a Croat I already have an inherited frame [of reference] for my patriotic work: *the state of Croatia.*' And a Serb, working within this frame of reference, was for Radić a Croatian patriot with a Serb name, that is a Croatian citizen, 'a worker on the Croatian part of the national field.' Croats and Serbs were no longer two tribes, but rather two indivisible parts of one and the same nation. Attempts by one at eliminating the other 'means destroying or extraordinarily weakening the whole national force.'[31]

Although Radić argued that Croats and Serbs were two equal parts of one nation, which meant that their national–cultural interests were identical, he realized that their different historical experiences under the Habsburgs and Ottomans had contributed to the creation of two distinct political and state conceptions and traditions. He was prepared to recognize the 'national–cultural oneness' of Serbs and Croats, but he called for 'state–political dualism.' Croats, like Serbs, had a separate state, 'but not only are the interests of this Croatian state unopposed to the interests of the Serbian state, rather they are tied to and complement them, especially from the national–economic standpoint.' Consequently Croats could recognize the Serb name in Croatia only as a subjective feeling of individuals, but not at all 'as evidence of a separate Serb national consciousness different from the Croat national consciousness, *or even opposed to it,*' and even less so could they recognize this name 'as a sign of separate Serb political aspirations, different from *or even opposed to* Croat [aspirations].' From the standpoint of *narodno jedinstvo* and political dualism the Serb in Croatia was both a Croatian citizen and a Croatian patriot. That is why Croatian Serbs should not oppose outward forms of Croatian statehood, such as the flag, since these symbols were mutual national symbols. Nor should they oppose the Latin script in favour of Cyrillic, since both were merely different forms used to convey one and the same language.[32] Similarly, Radić recognized the need to spread the use of Cyrillic among Croats and Slovenes to facilitate easier literary contacts with Serbs and other Orthodox Slavs. He also believed that it is unnecessary and even harmful to equate Orthodoxy with Serbdom, especially in Croatia; there is no reason why an Orthodox cannot be a Croat, just as there is no reason why a Catholic cannot be a Serb. 'I bitterly regret,' Radić wrote, 'that we have so narrowly tied national consciousness, or rather, this national christening, to the Catholic [faith] on the one hand and to the Orthodox faith on the other.' It would have been better, he believed, had Belgrade and Zagreb 'worked on a purely national foundation, and there would today be a few hundred thousand Catholic Serbs and roughly the same number of Orthodox Croats.'[33]

What all of this meant, at least in Radić's mind, was that Croats and Serbs had to respect their political traditions and existing state borders. Just as all Croats recognized the kingdoms of Serbia and Montenegro as indisputable Serbian state territory, similarly all Serbs had to recognize the Triune Kingdom as indisputable Croatian state territory. But this necessitated a resolution of the existing territorial disputes between Croats and Serbs. On the divisive issue of Bosnia–Herzegovina Radić initially argued that both Croats and Serbs in principle had an equal right to Bosnia–Herzegovina. Radić was equally critical of both Croat and Serb attitudes towards Bosnia; he saw their mutual competition there as resembling a form of medieval tribalism. Croats and Serbs had shamed themselves the most in their agitation *vis-à-vis* the Bosnian Muslims and in their attempts to win the latter's loyalty. How could they hope to attract the Muslims when they could not cooperate among themselves? What was needed first and foremost was for Croats and Serbs to work together for the cultural enlightenment and economic progress of their masses. Once this had begun they should unite to gain political dominance in Bosnia, enlisting the support of the Bosnian Muslims on the basis of *narodno jedinstvo*.[34] Although Radić had a tendency to refer to the Bosnian Muslims as Muslim Croats, he admitted in May 1910 that, based on his travels through Bosnia, he was convinced that they were neither Croats nor Serbs. Croat and Serb policy in Bosnia had experienced 'complete failure' because of the Croat–Serb national struggle and the fact that national consciousness was too closely tied to religion.[35] Nonetheless, initially Radić argued that if a solution to Bosnia's status depended solely on the Croats and Serbs, which at that time seemed inconceivable, both would have to work towards an equitable division of Bosnia-Herzegovina between Croatia and Serbia.[36]

After the annexation of Bosnia by the Dual Monarchy in 1908, however, Radić altered his position and unequivocally argued that the whole of Bosnia–Herzegovina historically belonged to Croatia on the basis of state right. His support for the annexation was further motivated by the belief that with the infusion of even more Slavs into the Habsburg monarchy, the position of the Croats and the other Habsburg Slavs would be strengthened in relation to the Germans and Magyars.[37] As to territorial disputes in eastern Croatia (Srijem and Slavonia) Radić insisted that all Serbs had to recognize that area as historic Croatian state territory; they had to choose between Croatia and Hungary. Budapest's assimilationist Magyar policies had in fact made the Croat–Serb dispute there academic; the question was no longer whether the area was Croatian or Serbian but whether it would remain Croatian or become Hungarian.[38] Serbs had to unite with Croats to ensure that it remained a part of Croatia.

Based on the state–political dualism that he outlined, Radić insisted that Croatia's Serbs recognize the Croatian flag as their state flag and also as a common national flag; they should genuinely recognize their Croatian political citizenship. In return he recognized the Serb right to their name, religion, and Cyrillic script but added that 'we Croats are in Croatia the older brothers, we founded and defended the most our Croatian home, and therefore our common home [must be] led in the name of the elder brother, hence as Croatia.' The flag and other state symbols, as well as the language, were to be Croatian. Since Radić considered the Serb question in Croatia 'as in fact a Croatian question, that is: the future of us Croats, much more so than that of the Serbs outside of Croatia, depends on how it is resolved,' he argued that the Croats should pursue a policy towards the Serbs 'from the standpoint of a general national, South Slavic consciousness,' that is, respecting their full equality and rights but insisting that they recognize Croatia as their political homeland.[39] 'A border cannot be drawn between us anywhere,' he wrote, 'on the contrary, we cannot "cleanse" individual regions even by a civil war, unless we are going to exterminate each other, to destroy each other completely.' The reconciliation of the Croats and Serbs 'is therefore unavoidable ... And as soon as not only Croatia and Serbia, but the Croats and Serbs, unite it will be possible to work for our national right.'[40] Through cooperation they would assure their collective political and national rights.

This was a point that the Radićes and the HPSS continuously emphasized: the Croats had to work united with the Serbs, but the Serbs in turn 'must respect, love and defend our common Croatian homeland.'[41] They were opposed, however, to a separate 'Serb policy' in Croatia, that is, any and all

Serb demands that they perceived as undermining the integrity and interests of the Croatian state. Antun Radić wrote that in the HPSS's opinion, 'We [Croats and Serbs] are one nation, but we have two states: the Serbs the Serbian and the Croats the Croatian state. In our opinion, only a Croatian policy can be conducted in Croatia, that is, such a policy that works for [the interests of] the Croatian state, so that the Serbs in Croatia must work for this Croatian state, for our common homeland.'[42] Stjepan Radić denied the accusations of Croatian Serb leaders that the HPSS was anti-Serb; the Serbs had a right to their name and freely to practise their Orthodox faith and customs, but there could be only a Croatian policy in Croatia, which the Serbs had to support.[43]

The HPSS not only promoted Croat–Serb unity, it also urged the Serb peasants to join its ranks, for its agrarian ideology would secure the social, economic, and political position of both the Croat and Serb peasants. In October 1905 Antun Radić claimed that the HPSS was accepting Serb members.[44] Indeed, the HPSS press asserted that Serbs were attending its organizational meetings in early 1905; one party rally near the town of Petrinja was apparently attended by about 200 Serb peasants.[45] One of the party's activists in Slunj (Petrinja district) was Kosta Obradović, a Serb, and in the village of Gornja Sredica in the Podravina region, two Serbs, Nikola Radelić and Vaso Brković, organized HPSS rallies.[46] There is no evidence to suggest, however, that a significant number of Serbs actually joined the HPSS, or that those who did join remained members beyond the party's initial organizational drive in 1905–6. The majority of Croatia's Serbs were organized behind Pribićević's Serb Independent Party, while some, largely those of Srijem county, were committed to the Serb Radical Party. Therefore, from the outset the HPSS was overwhelmingly Croat, and this was especially true after 1918. Despite the party's claims that Serbs were attending its rallies, one HPSS activist, countering the repeated assertions of Croatian Serb leaders that the party's program was too vague on the matter of Serb rights, admitted that 'our program is written for Croats.'[47] Nevertheless, unity and cooperation with the Serbs remained one of the central objectives in the HPSS's political platform.

Stjepan Radić's variant of *narodno jedinstvo* had clearly defined political borders and limits: those of Croatia and the Dual Monarchy. He recognized the national–cultural oneness of Croats and Serbs, but stridently believed that their different historical experiences necessitated mutual recognition of their respective state traditions. And since he believed that Croatia's rights could best be defended within a restructured monarchy he naturally opposed any and all variants of *narodno jedinstvo* that either explicitly or implicitly sought the creation of a common South Slavic state built upon the ruins, or territorial amputation, of the monarchy. Such views invariably led him into confrontation with the most significant prewar political group in Croatia, the HSK, as well as the different splinter groups of the Starčevićist tradition.

An analysis of Radić's views on the monarchy reveals that they differed substantially from the prevailing political and intellectual currents in Croatia. Radić devoted considerable time and effort to this issue and outlined a broad vision of a federalized monarchy.[48] This was one of the fundamental tenets of his and the HPSS's political ideology. It was also one of the critical issues over which Radić and the intelligentsia disagreed; indeed, the final split between Radić and a considerable segment of the intelligentsia came in 1905 over the Rijeka Resolution. Since the HSK's politics were predicated in the short term on weakening the monarchy and ultimately on its very destruction, they were bound to conflict with Radić's own belief that Austria was a necessity not only for the European balance of power but also as a guarantor of the national interests of its small nations.[49] Radić's views also differed from those of the state right parties, although he generally tended to be closer to them on the issue of the monarchy.

It must be emphasized that when Radić spoke of 'Austria' he thought first and foremost of the Austrian Slavs (Czechs, Poles, Ruthenians, Slovenes, and Dalmatian Croats). He once told a Serb cell-mate in one of Khuen-Héderváry's prisons that 'I have already said on a number of occasions, if there were no Czechs, Poles, and Little Russians [*sic*] under Vienna, and over a million Slovenes, finally half a million Croats, I too would speak differently [about Austria]. Thus, I am in favour of the closest political union with them, particularly since I became convinced that, in comparing Prague, [Buda-]Pest, Zagreb, and Belgrade, the Germans would quite easily inundate and swallow the Danubian region if they succeeded in conquering the Poles, Czechs, and Slovenes.'[50] These words capture the essence of Radić's Austro-Slavism.

Radić elaborated a vision of a democratic and internally reorganized monarchy that would respect not only historic state rights but also the national rights of the so-called non-historic nations. The monarchy was neither German nor Magyar, although its dualist structure lent those two nations a predominant political and socioeconomic position. It comprised in fact three hitherto historically preserved Slavic states (Bohemia, Croatia, Galicia) and nationally conscious Slavic peoples (Czechs, Slovaks, Poles, Ruthenians, Croats, Serbs, and Slovenes). Although Radić blamed the German and Magyar politicians for many of the monarchy's ills, he was particularly critical of the Slav politicians in the monarchy for their lack of unity.[51] This disunity prevented them from realizing their common ideal: federalism. According to Radić, the 'cultural ideal' of Slavic politics in general, and in the monarchy particularly, 'is the reconciliation between East and West, because this is the singularly fundamental condition of the very survival of Slavdom.'[52]

The struggle between East and West, Constantinople and Rome, has historically shaped the destinies of the Slavs and this fact lay at the root of the Polish–Russian, Polish–Ruthenian, and Croat–Serb antagonisms. The Slav intelligentsias had to free themselves from these respective traditions and adopt cooperation and reciprocity as their common ideal. Only then, he believed, would they achieve significant political progress. Reconciliation was central to Radić's program: 'We [the monarchy's Slavs] do not want to be the West's bridge to the East, or a fortress of the West against Russia; on the contrary ... We want to create a great home of national equality, where it will be easy for the Slav and German, Magyar and Romanian ... to join the great flame of enlightenment and freedom.'[53] It naturally followed from this that the ultimate political ideal of the East Central European Slavs would be a great federation of nations of Central and Southeastern Europe.

This 'Danubian Union of States and Nations,' as Radić called it, would comprise five components: Hungary, Bohemia, Galicia, the Alpine lands (German-speaking hereditary crown lands with Lower Austria), and Croatia. They would be constitutionally equal and mutually independent; they would be bound together by the monarchy, as well as by certain common diplomatic, military, and civil political interests.[54] Hungary would become a confederation of nations, that is, a state with a common political organization but with wide-ranging national freedoms. Although the Magyars would be the leading political element in this Hungarian state, Hungary's national minorities would have complete autonomy in cultural and religious affairs. Imperial laws and control would be needed to regulate these rights and would apply to all of the federal units.[55] The Bohemian crown lands (Bohemia-Moravia-Silesia) would remain whole but become a bilingual state. The Czech-German issue could not be solved by partition. Although the Czechs should predominate, the German minority would enjoy complete cultural autonomy. Its rights would, as in the case of all minorities, be protected by Imperial laws and inspection. Similarly, Galicia would be enlarged through the inclusion of an autonomous Bukovina and would become a bilingual state, providing equal treatment and representation to Poles and Ruthenians. The Croatian unit of this federation would be made up of the monarchy's South Slav lands and would have a common political administration; Croats, Serbs, and Slovenes would be completely equal.[56] The German Alpine hereditary lands and the Italian part of the Tyrol would form the fifth unit. The Alpine diet would be based in Vienna; the Tyrolian Italians, enjoying cultural autonomy, would have the right to use Italian in the diet. Vienna, the capital of the federation, would be excluded from this unit and would have its own administration.[57]

Czech would become one of the three official federal languages, along with German and Magyar, and the common language in political discourse for all of the monarchy's Slavs. Radić chose Czech since the Czechs and Slovaks combined were the most numerous of the monarchy's Slavs and all of them lived within its borders. Moreover, Prague was a major cultural and economic centre and the Czechs were the most progressive Slav nation; their public life had reached a level of sophistication surpassing that of the other Slavs. The Slavs would furthermore have to insist that the monarch know Czech and address the Slavs in this language, and that every diplomatic representative and all higher ranking army officers know Czech.[58]

All common affairs would be decided by the 'Imperial delegation,' which would be composed of elected delegates from the five units. It would be made up of three subdelegations: state, nationality and economic–financial. The first subdelegation would have an equal number of popularly elected delegates from each of the parliaments of the five federal units and would deal with all matters relating to public law and the mutual relations of the units. The economic–financial subdelegation would be an expert committee representing all five units and would have the task of formulating common economic policy; it would deal with, *inter alia*, commerce, trade, and agriculture. The third, the nationality subdelegation, would represent all national groups within the federal monarchy and would implement all political and socioeconomic reforms. Radić did not specify precisely how many delegates would be sent to each subdelegation and for how long, or how often the Imperial delegation and its subcommittees would meet. Nor were the roles of the three subdelegations explained in any great detail. Moreover, Radić failed to explain precisely how the delegations would work to satisfy all the nationalities and how a decision would be reached in the likelihood of disagreement, or who, if anyone, would possess the right of veto. Radić seemed to assume that consensus politics would prevail, a rather fantastic assumption given the monarchy's complicated national make-up.

Perhaps most important, however, Radić never fully explained how the transformation from dualism to federalism would be accomplished. He appealed to the Slavic intelligentsias to overcome their particularisms and unite behind a common cause and political front. It follows, then, that the first step towards federalism, at least in Radić's mind, was Slavic cooperation and a common political program based on a broad Slav consciousness, the lack of which was the main cause of their collective national ills. According to Radić, mutual Slavic hostilities would cease as '*Slavic* consciousness gradually develops, as a higher idea, above the particular Czech, Croat, Polish consciousness,' just as the idea of humanity remained 'the highest ideal and above such a general idea as Slavic reciprocity.'[59] Slavdom should be to Slavic nations what national identity is to the individual. The political disorganization of the Habsburg Slavs was the main cause, in Radić's opinion, 'of the depravity and tyranny of so many German politicians and the entire Magyar aristocratic policy.' When the Slavic peoples ended their quarrelling, there would be in the monarchy 'a cultural factor of more than twenty million people with a single political, national, economic, and social program,' it would no longer 'be possible further to strengthen the dualist feudalism and the Germano-Magyar-Jewish [sic] hierarchy, which is already undermining the very Slavic cultural foundations which survived the assaults and slavery of the Avars, the Tatars and the Ottomans.'[60] United by a common political program and over twenty million strong, the monarchy's Slavs would prevail. Just as he urged *narodno jedinstvo* between Croats and Serbs as a *means* to unify Croatia and bring about complete political autonomy with respect to Hungary, so too did he urge Slav political cooperation as a means of strengthening their collective position within the monarchy. Under such conditions it would be impossible to perpetuate the dualist order.

Even assuming that such cooperation could ever have been achieved, it does not of course follow that dualism would have been destroyed. Beyond the call for Slavic reciprocity and cooperation Radić did not elaborate on the means by which federalism would be realized. In practice, however, and in party-political terms, Radić placed considerable hope on the Habsburgs and a royal-imperial initiative that would alter the dualist order to the advantage of the Slavs. That is why he placed his faith in the heir to the throne, Archduke Franz Ferdinand, and his supposed intention to change the Croato-Hungarian relationship in the Croats' favour. And that is why, furthermore, Radić did not categorically reject a triple monarchy, at least as a transitional stage on the path to federalism.[61] He wrote in October 1907 that 'our future sovereign [Franz Ferdinand] is a determined proponent *of the equality of all peoples in the monarchy,*' and that he was especially in favour of '*complete national equality* in Hungary and for *the state equality* of the kingdom of Croatia towards the kingdom of Hungary.'[62] Two years later Radić wrote, with little evidence to support his assertion, that Franz Ferdinand's first official act as king-emperor would be to end Croatia's subordinate status *vis-à-vis* Hungary.[63] Radić's deep-seated commitment to an Austrian or Austro-Slav orientation naturally brought him into open conflict with the proponents of the new course in Croatian politics. It is easy to dismiss Radić's Austro-Slavism as naïve and unrealistic, as many have indeed done, yet it is important to keep in mind that at the time when he formulated these views the monarchy was undergoing a period of serious political crisis that brought into question the continuation of the dualist order. Radić's views, however unrealistic or unworkable they may have been, should be viewed against the background of this crisis and similar such reform ideas it provoked, rather than against the background of the failure of Austro-Slavism in 1848–9, as many of Radić's contemporary and later critics did.[64]

Although in theory both Radić and the intellectuals of the HSK stood on the traditions of Illyrianism and Yugoslavism, in practice they were consistently at odds. There were essentially two reasons for this: the HSK's support for the Magyar opposition in the monarchy's constitutional struggle, and the significant anomalies between the HSK's and HPSS's conceptions of *narodno jedinstvo*. The Radićes and HPSS voiced their opinion about the constitutional crisis well before the proclamation of the Rijeka Resolution and the formation of the HSK. The HPSS believed that all the parties in the Hungarian parliament, with the exception of the Social Democrats and national minority parties, were undemocratic. These parties wished above all to protect Hungary's 'medieval constitutionalism,' but in order to accomplish this they had to perpetuate the social privileges of the Magyar ruling oligarchy and Magyarize the non-Magyars.[65] Furthermore, the Magyar opposition was even more nationalistic, and hence dangerous for the non-Magyars, than the Liberal Party. 'How the Magyar opposition gained the love of some Croat oppositionists,' the bewildered Antun Radić pondered, 'this we truly do not understand.' He concluded that 'not a single party that is for freedom and justice can honourably stand alongside the Magyar opposition.'[66]

The assault by the Radićes and the HPSS on the Rijeka Resolution becomes comprehensible in this light, for it was predicated on the belief that the new course would only serve the interests of Croatia's most immediate national enemy, the Magyar ruling oligarchy.[67] Stjepan Radić suspected that all Magyar politicians had two fundamental aims: to Magyarize the non-Magyar minorities, including the Croats; and, gradually to distance the kingdom of Hungary from the rest of the monarchy.[68] Shortly after the Rijeka Resolution was proclaimed the HPSS's main committee issued a statement condemning the memorandum as 'a political betrayal and humiliation of the Croat nation,' as well as a 'great evil, a calamity.' How could it be, the HPSS statement declared, that the Magyars were fighting for freedom when they were oppressing all of Hungary's non-Magyars, who formed a majority of the population? Croat politicians who signed the memorandum betrayed their nation because they had abandoned the idea of Croat state right, and dared not make any reference to the city of Rijeka, which was Croat in character but under the direct rule of Budapest and not Zagreb.

The memorandum was also a betrayal of Croat national interests because it made no reference to the plight of the Croats in the region of Medjimurje, which was also overwhelmingly Croat in national character but part of the kingdom of Hungary proper, or southern Hungary, let alone those of Istria and Bosnia–Herzegovina. The memorandum was also a betrayal of the Slavic idea, for instead of working to strengthen ties with the Austrian Slavs, or drawing attention to the sorry plight of the Slovaks in Hungary, the Croat politicians were promising to assist the Magyar opposition in its goal of greater autonomy, to distance Hungary from the rest of the monarchy. Finally, the memorandum was a betrayal of the Croat peasant people, who were at no point consulted about the document. This was a grievous error, for instead of working among the people to gain power in Croatia, they were hoping to receive political power from the Magyar opposition.[69]

The Radićes' anti-Semitism resurfaced during their assault on the new course. They repeatedly expressed the view that the Jews lay behind the policies of the Magyar ruling oligarchy. Such an opinion was not uncommon on the peripheries of the Hungarian kingdom, including Croatia, since most non-Magyars regarded the Hungarian Jews as agents of Magyarization.[70] Commenting on rampant electoral corruption and the persecution of non-Magyars in Hungary, Stjepan Radić referred to Hungary as a 'political garbage heap' that was ruled by a numerically insignificant Magyar-Jewish oligarchy. He added that Budapest's Jews were financing Magyar policy, particularly the assimilationist policy towards the non-Magyars.[71] Writing about the constitutional struggle between Vienna and Budapest, and the latter's demand for a Hungarian army, Antun Radić asserted that Hungary's Jews were ardent Magyar nationalists because they wished to conceal their exploitative role in Hungarian society. Simply stated, 'The entire Magyar policy is led by Jews.' The ordinary Magyar did not know that Vienna was merely a scapegoat for the country's problems; 'the real oppressors are at home [in Hungary].'[72] As part of the Hungarian kingdom, Croatia was exposed to a system of government that was, the HPSS ideologues argued, an exception in Europe: 'The Magyaro-Jewish rule is in many ways Asiatic, that is, barbaric, despotic ... shameless, deceitful.' The only way for Croats to secure their national rights from this regime of 'Asiatic-Jewish terror' was to seek the support of the dynasty and the monarchy's other Slavs.[73] That naturally entailed opposing the HSK and new course.

The other persistent theme in the Radićes' attacks on the HSK was that the Croat deputies were too compliant in relation to the Serbs and that they downplayed and consistently minimized Croat rights to placate their Serb colleagues. The Croat Progressives of the HSK, in particular, were seen as being anational whereas the Serbs were viewed as being stridently nationalistic and thus as more determined to pursue their own interests. Stjepan Radić suspected that the coalition's Serb deputies had their own agenda that was inimical to Croat interests.[74] That was precisely why Radić was so critical of the HSK after the monarchy's annexation of Bosnia-Herzegovina in October 1908. Basing his arguments on state right, Radić saw the HSK's refusal to recognize the annexation, and its lack of support for Croat claims in Bosnia, as a sign that Serbs controlled the HSK's policies and that the Croat parties had tied their own hands. The HSK was, simply put, behaving as if it had no Croats.[75] Although acknowledging the need to work with the Serbs, Radić bluntly stated that 'there is no room for [a separate] Serb policy on the territory of the Croatian state – because the Croats have their state, and the Serbs theirs. Bosnia is nationally and historically Croatian, and political circumstances have brought it under the same ruler as the rest of Croatia.'[76] The HPSS insisted that the HSK recognize and then openly proclaim Bosnia as Croatian territory and that Bosnia belonged within the monarchy.[77]

Radić's criticisms were not limited to the HSK. Although the Frankists had enthusiastically recognized the annexation, Frank's decision, with the tacit approval of official circles in Vienna, to establish a Croat National Legion supposedly to defend Croat claims against Serbian expansionism was condemned by the Radićes and the HPSS. Undoubtedly recalling in their own minds the 1902 anti-Serb riots in Zagreb, in which the Frankists played an important role, the Radićes interpreted this move as another attack against the idea of Croat-Serb unity and cooperation and as a clear provocation intended further to deepen Croat-Serb hostilities.[78] They also rejected Frank's claim that Serbs, especially Croatia's Serbs, were the Croats' most dangerous enemies. Disunity was the biggest misfortune of the Croats and Serbs and threatened to ruin both; without unity the Germans and Magyars would easily dispense with both the Croats and Serbs.[79] That is why some of Stjepan Radić's harshest criticisms were reserved for the Frankists, for 'under the chimera of Great Croatianism they serve our enemies to the detriment of our entire nation.'[80]

Radić continuously stressed the need to cooperate with Serbs in the areas of culture, education, and economic work, but acknowledged that this was increasingly difficult politically. He pointed to the refusal of Serbia's political élite to recognize in principle the kingdom of Croatia, as well as the Bosnian Serbs' hostility to their Croat counterparts. Radić was particularly suspicious and critical of the Serb Orthodox clergy, whom he suspected of working along exclusivist Serb lines. Despite the sense of frustration, the Radićes seemingly never contemplated abandoning the Illyrian-Yugoslav traditions, for as Antun

Radić commented, 'Today there would likely be neither a Croatia nor Croats if our awakeners, with Ljudevit Gaj at their head, did not enthusiastically and steadfastly proclaim the idea that between Trieste and Constantinople there exists one nation.' In spite of the conflicting state and political aspirations of the Croats and Serbs, the HPSS remained committed to its belief in the *narodno jedinstvo* of Croats and Serbs, but stressed that 'the struggle between Croats and Serbs cannot be solved unless national politics in Croatia are conducted under the Croatian name, just as they are conducted in Serbia under the Serbian name. Our Orthodox can therefore call themselves Serbs insofar as the Serb name is for them a term for the Orthodox faith, or a memory of their old homeland Serbia; but the Serb name cannot have a political meaning [in Croatia].'[81]

The HPSS's Main Committee agreed in December 1908 that Croatian Serb policy should be judged by the Serb attitude regarding Bosnia-Herzegovina's unification with the monarchy, and eventually with Croatia. Serb opposition was for Stjepan Radić a clear sign that they were pursuing their own separate Serb agenda to the detriment of what he perceived to be common national interests. He repeated this during the Zagreb treason trial. The HPSS's opinion was that if it could be shown that these Serbs were actively working to undermine the monarchy then they should be punished. Radić suspected that the Serbs were pursuing the interests of Serbdom against Croat interests, which prompted him to declare openly that 'we [HPSS] are opposed to Serb policies in Croatia because these policies do not have reasonable ends.' Serbs were completely equal citizens in Croatia, but 'whatever goes beyond this is unreasonable, since the spread of Serbdom and the Serbianization of that which is Croatian, does not have ... reasonable ends in Croatia.'[82] This was a point the Radićes stressed repeatedly.

Stjepan Radić clearly believed that Serb aspirations were dangerous for both Croatia and the monarchy, which explains why he perceived the HSK's policies to be detrimental to Croat national interests. He voiced these concerns openly and unequivocally. It was not enough simply to say that Serbs and Croats were one people. The HSK had 'enabled Serb policy to predominate,' but the HPSS had wanted 'to achieve an agreement [between Croats and Serbs] in the sense and on the foundation of Croat state right.' Only those Serbs who recognized that Croatia was their homeland and the monarchy their only 'shelter,' 'will understand that it is preposterous to separate themselves from us Croats in everything.'[83] He always suspected, however, that there was not a single Croatian Serb politician who would defend the Croat and Imperial view that he had laid out. Indeed, he argued that Serbs were hostile to Croat rights.[84]

Antun Radić also reiterated that all Croats had to oppose a separate Serb policy, 'which at every turn leads us astray and into misfortunes.' Unfortunately, however, the Serbs 'are united as one, but not even three Croats within the [Croato-Serb] Coalition are united about what we Croats should do and what we should hold to in this Empire.'[85] The HSK was, simply stated, accommodating Serb policy and interests, which was best demonstrated by its opposition to the annexation of Bosnia-Herzegovina.[86] The Radićes portrayed the Croat deputies of the HSK as virtual hostages of their Serb colleagues. Since the Croats of the HSK feared that the Serbs might potentially go over to the Magyars in the event of the HSK's demise, as they had done during the rule of Khuen-Héderváry, they placated the Serbs at every turn. The HSK was guilty of increasingly being less Croat and more Serb in nature, such that 'this is no longer unity with the Serbs but shameful and dangerous servitude to Serb policy.'[87] Stjepan Radić could not escape the conclusion that the HSK 'can do nothing without the Croatian Serbs, and there is not a single Serb who would be for an Imperial policy, that is, for our Empire to be strong.' Croats of the HSK had to follow the Serbs in this matter, and 'that is why they are against an Imperial policy.'[88]

The Radićes' fears were not unfounded. In the aftermath of the Zagreb high treason affair (1909–10) and the political departure of Frano Supilo, the HSK was dominated by Svetozar Pribićević and his Serb Independents. Pribićević was one of Radić's student associates and the most prominent Serb of the united Croat–Serb youth of the late 1890s. Like the Croat Progressives he was an outspoken proponent of *narodno jedinstvo*. In 1897 he first publicly articulated the view that 'Serbs and Croats are parts of one nation.' He was quick to point out, however, that 'the concept of nation is not a historical, political concept.'[89] That he rejected the political concept of nation, and had a deep-seated aversion to Croat state right, is hardly surprising, for there could be only one, namely, a Croatian, political nation in Croatia. By resorting to unitarist Yugoslavism the incongruities of Croat and Serb national ideologies could be minimized and, in Pribićević's mind, the security of the Croatian Serbs thereby confirmed.[90] Although many of Pribićević's pronouncements in the 1890s on *narodno jedinstvo* were not unlike Radić's, the two men drew radically different conclusions with respect to the political significance of this theory.

For Pribićević the logic of *narodno jedinstvo*, and the interests of his Croatian Serb constituency, entailed the unification of the monarchy's South Slavs with Serbia. As such, his policies were well attuned to the interests of Belgrade. As the leader of the HSK he adopted an opportunistic policy *vis-à-vis* Budapest partly in order to spare Croatian Serbs any further persecution by the Habsburg authorities. Through his brothers Adam and Valerijan in Belgrade, who met in 1913 with the Serbian minister-president, Nikola Pašić, Pribićević was informed that Serbia was not prepared for a war with the monarchy, and that it desired the normalization of political conditions in Croatia.[91] This simply reinforced his policy of accommodation with Budapest, which would last to 1918. But Pribićević's real objective remained unification with Serbia and the destruction of the monarchy.

The Croat half of the HSK, which by 1910 meant the Croat Independent Party, lacked in Supilo's absence a dynamic personality who could act as a counterbalance to Pribićević. The leader of the Croat Independents, Ivan Lorković, was a reticent intellectual who was never able to stand up to Pribićević. But the Croat Independents suffered from a more profound problem. As one of them later indicated, although they realized that Pribićević's wing 'demonstrated a tendency to complete the process of *narodno jedinstvo* with the victory of the Serb name,' many Croats of the HSK manifested a marked 'indifference towards the Croat name, Croat traditions, and the demand for Croatian statehood.' For instance, when the monarchy annexed Bosnia, some of the HSK's Croats wanted to support this move. But the dissension within Croat ranks, combined with the strong Croatian Serb opposition to the annexation, led the HSK to oppose the monarchy's diplomatic manœuvre. Lorković, who tried remaining loyal both to Croatdom and the idea of Croat–Serb *narodno jedinstvo*, increasingly believed that the HSK's political line was leading to Serb domination. He hoped initially to change the HSK's political course, but was eventually compelled to defect.[92] By 1913–14 the HSK had abandoned its earlier defence of Croatia's rights and become a docile political force in relation to Budapest.

The HSK's accommodation with Budapest incensed the Radićes, who stood adamantly on the basis of an Imperial policy. In early 1909 Stjepan Radić called for a return to the policies of Croatia's former *ban*, Baron Josip Jelačić, who led the Imperial armies against the Magyar revolutionaries in 1848–9. Indeed, he argued that the HPSS was the only Croat party that could be considered a successor to Jelačić, for their common platform was 'loyalty to the King and to the whole Empire; loyalty to our Croatian homeland, that is, the struggle against Magyar power ... [and] loyalty to the Croat nation, that is, justice towards the peasantry, loyalty to the other Slavs, [and] particularly unity with the Serbs on the basis of Croat peasant and state right.'[93] Although the Radićes repeatedly stressed the point that they had adopted all that was beneficial from the old Croat parties, that is, Strossmayer's National Party and Starčević's Party of Right,[94] they claimed that the HPSS 'is continuing the awakening work of our illustrious leaders Gaj, Jelačić, and Strossmayer.'[95] Despite their emphasis on Croat state right, which was adopted from the Party of Right, the Radićes and the HPSS regarded themselves as the successors of Gaj, Jelačić, and Strossmayer, but not necessarily Starčević. At the fourth Main Assembly of the HPSS in late August 1909 the party leadership decided to amend its program explicitly to include loyalty to the Habsburg dynasty and fidelity to the 'Austrian' – as opposed to the Austro-Hungarian – Empire. At the same time, and to mark the centenary of Gaj's birth and the fiftieth anniversary of Jelačić's death, the HPSS declared its commitment to adhere to the main principles of these two 'great Croats': unlimited devotion towards the Croat nation and homeland; loyalty to the dynasty; faithfulness to Slavdom; and, devotion to the Croat people, that is, the peasants.[96]

The Radićes thus were ideologically closer to the traditions of Gaj and Strossmayer, than to Starčević, although the reverse is asserted at times in the literature.[97] This should not be surprising, for apart from their shared commitment to state right the Radićes and Starčević were bound together by little else. Unlike Gaj, who was prepared to rely on Habsburg support to counteract the threat of Magyar domination, Starčević saw the Habsburgs and Austria as the greater threat to Croat interests. Nor did Starčević devote much attention to the monarchy's remaining Slavs, apart from the Slovenes and Serbs, whom he regarded as Highland and Orthodox 'Croats,' respectively. The Radićes, like Gaj and Strossmayer before them, wanted the federalization of the monarchy as the best guaranty for Croatia's national interests. For the Radićes, co-operation with the Serbs and loyalty to the dynasty were intended as means to this end.

This helps to explain why they distanced themselves from, and in fact at times railed against, Starčević and the pravaši. Antun wrote in 1909 that Starčević was by nature 'a surly man, indifferent to education, an arrogant Roman, without a bit of feeling in general, and in particular without a trace of basic Christian direction: love and sympathy towards the small and weak ... This is madness!' He had advanced 'the accursed doctrine about a free homeland – without a free people ... This blindness has lasted for decades – and pravaštvo is still a holy thing, their [state right] program – the Croat gospel!'[98] Stjepan Radić was even more candid. Starčević was 'the biggest reviler and blasphemer of everything that was good and magnanimous in Croatia.' He had reviled and blasphemed especially 'the great and immortal bishop of Djakovo, Strossmayer.' Radić characterized Starčević as irreligious and uncultured, whereas Strossmayer was 'a man of great intellect and noble heart,' who wanted to reform the monarchy so that its Slavic majority would attain equality in relation to the Germans and Magyars. He cared for and took a great interest in both the Slavs and enlightenment, but Starčević hated both. Radić asserted that the contemporary pravaši inherited their founder's insolence, which is why they considered themselves to be the only true Croats.[99] It was inconceivable to the Radićes that the *pravaši* could ever attain their program and unite the Croat lands, for they could not even manage to unite themselves. Commenting on the rapprochement between the Frankists and the *milinovci* – which proved to be only temporary – the HPSS's main organ declared that 'unfortunately we do not expect anything from this, because we see the same people, for whom we know that they are incapable of achieving anything.'[100] Finally, it should be emphasized that the Radićes and HPSS believed that none of the Starčevićist factions paid sufficient attention to peasant social and economic needs, and dismissed their claim that little could be done to improve the plight of the peasantry until Croatia was united and completely free.[101] Despite their overly critical characterization of Starčević and his contemporary followers, the fact remains that the Radićes saw themselves as continuing the work of Strossmayer, under the banner of 'a developed and highly raised Croatian flag.'

The Radićes always devoted much greater attention to the Croato-Serb Coalition than the various state right factions, however, for the former remained politically more important throughout this period. And since the Radićes equated Croatia's interests with those of a reformed monarchy, they interpreted the Coalition's anti-Imperial stand as detrimental to Croat state interests and thus naturally opposed its policies. Moreover, Stjepan Radić believed that even the most intelligent and moderate Serbian politicians were hostile to Croat national aspirations and would pursue their own exclusive interests in both Bosnia-Herzegovina and Dalmatia to the detriment of the Croats. Serbian politicians were concerned only with expanding Serbia's borders, which made Radić an avowed opponent of Serbian state policy.[102] During the Balkan wars Radić railed against Serbian policy. Initially he welcomed the Balkan allies' victories against the Ottoman Turks because he hoped that the Croatian Serbs, seeing that Serbia had realized her historic territorial aims (Kosovo and Macedonia) would now support Croat efforts at unification.[103] His hopes were grossly misplaced, and Radić's early enthusiasm soured as the erstwhile Balkan allies turned against each other. He attacked the shortsightedness of both Serbia's and Bulgaria's politicians, who sought only to enlarge their respective state territories. In his view, these élites stressed only their Serbdom and Bulgardom, each at the expense of the other, and they were digging each others' graves.[104]

Radić's assessment of the Serbian state élite only reinforced his commitment to a solution of the South Slav question within the monarchy. Unification with Serbia was fraught with danger for Croatia, because in line with 'what the Serbs are doing in Macedonia to the Bulgars [*sic*], who are all Orthodox ...

in the event of a Serbian advance [at the monarchy's expense] we Croats must fear something even worse.'[105] Moreover, Serbia had no historic justification for expanding into either Bosnia-Herzegovina or Dalmatia, areas that he considered historically Croatian.[106] For Radić the idea of creating a Yugoslav state was illogical and dangerous for the Croats, for Serbia's expansion all the way to Trieste would mean the end of the old Croatian kingdom. Whoever, therefore, sought the destruction of the monarchy worked against Croat interests because this 'certainly could and would end up only with the complete destruction of Croatia and the Croats.' Any policy 'that must first divide our four-hundred-year-old Empire, thereafter destroy the thousand-year-old kingdom of Croatia, that is, first provoke a flood of blood and the real hell of a world war, so that after all of this our entire Croat nation can supposedly be united and liberated [under Serbia],' was perilous and criminal.[107]

Radić's critique of Serbian state policy, the Croatian Serb leadership, and Croat intellectuals of the coalition who, he believed, pandered to Serb interests, is comprehensible only if understood as part of his broader vision of Croatia's status within a federalized monarchy. That was why the HSK's claim to have created *narodno jedinstvo* was consistently berated. For the HPSS, *narodno jedinstvo* 'should be a *means* by which higher goals, Croat unification and the defence of Croatia against foreigners, must be fulfilled.' The purpose of this *narodno jedinstvo* was 'to give us the strength, power, and resistance first to defend ourselves from all Magyar assaults and attacks and especially to defend ourselves against [Magyar] financial slavery.' What the coalition had hitherto created was not *narodno jedinstvo*, but rather Croat servitude. *Narodno jedinstvo* should 'have the effect of ending every struggle between Croats and Serbs, and Serbs *together with us Croats* should work for economic and cultural progress, for our Croat unification within the monarchy.' To win the people over to *narodno jedinstvo* 'is therefore only possible if they are shown good results and economic and political successes on this basis, and if their national feeling is not offended. If a party of *narodno jedinstvo* such as the Croato-Serb Coalition in advance renounces the struggle for great economic aims, such as financial autonomy, and the culmination of political success is for them gaining power at the price of suffering and sanctioning violations of our legal rights, and if the Coalition along with this erases the Croatian name for us Croats, then this *narodno jedinstvo* and the like is true national traitorousness.'[108]

The Radićes and the HPSS thus continuously opposed the HSK's formula of *narodno jedinstvo*, which they saw as a front under which the Serbs were pursuing their own policy and national interests. *Narodno jedinstvo* should be used as a means to strengthen 'our national home, our Croatian state,'[109] and to strengthen it required the unification of all Croat lands as well as concrete reforms to improve the plight of the peasantry. In these two respects the HSK had singularly failed.[110] Radić's opposition was only reinforced after 1910, when Pribićević assumed the leadership of the HSK and achieved a *modus vivendi* with the Magyarone regime.

Increasingly at odds with the HSK and disturbed by the Yugoslav unitarist trends among the revolutionary youth, the Radićes' hopes were delivered a crushing blow with the news of Franz Ferdinand's assassination in Sarajevo on 28 June 1914. Convinced that Franz Ferdinand intended to reorganize the monarchy and unify Bosnia and Dalmatia with Croatia, Stjepan Radić immediately identified the Serbian political élite with the assassination. 'The greatest hope of Croatia,' he wrote, 'and the whole Empire has been destroyed, and now iron-clad Croat unity, determination, and steadfastness is needed, so that this perfidious and criminal Serb policy is forever repelled on Croatian territory.' Antun Radić added that the Serbian politicians 'in their all-too-great desire for Bosnia and in their even greater hatred against everything that is Croatian, Catholic, and Austrian, conceived of and ordered the villainous and malicious crime that unfortunately succeeded for them, because these politicians are true masters of such crimes.'[111]

As the Great War began there could be no doubt as to where Stjepan Radić and the HPSS stood. His hostility to the formation of a Yugoslav state in 1918 becomes comprehensible in this light, as does his jettisoning of *narodno jedinstvo*. To be sure, Radić's *narodno jedinstvo* differed from that of the contemporary Croat and Serb intelligentsia, primarily in its political implications. Implicit in the HSK's and Nationalist Youth's formula of *narodno jedinstvo* was unitarist Yugoslavism. Indeed, when the Habsburg dénouement finally came in 1918, most Croat politicians and intellectuals were committed to Yugoslavist unitarism. Radić, however, was simultaneously a proponent of *narodno jedinstvo* and Croat state right. Like the Croat national ideologists of the nineteenth century (Gaj and Strossmayer, but not Starčević), Radić struck a delicate balance between political Croatism and cultural Yugoslavism. Consequently Croat state right remained one of the pillars of the HPSS's national program, for this was an overwhelmingly powerful legitimizing tool in the Habsburg era. So firmly embedded was state right in the Radićes' thinking that they believed that without (Croat) state right there could be no (Croatian) state.[112]

This synthesis of political Croatism (Croat state right) and *narodno jedinstvo*, with the latter always intended to strengthen the former, won the HPSS few sympathizers among the intelligentsia. For the state right parties, particularly the Frankists, Stjepan Radić's frequent references to 'oneness' and unity with the Serbs prompted derision and accusations that he was a *posrbica* ('Serb proselyte'). Radić's talk of an Imperial policy and loyalty to the dynasty led intellectuals of the HSK and the Nationalist Youth to conclude that he was a Habsburg lackey. But what is perhaps most significant to note is that since his variant of *narodno jedinstvo* was a means to an end, the unification of all Croat lands within a federated Habsburg monarchy, it is not difficult to see why Radić abandoned the idea with the collapse of the monarchy. He would emerge after 1918 as the leader of a peasant-based mass movement that not only eclipsed the prewar intellectual and political élite (the *gospoda*), including the intellectuals of the HSK and the state right parties, but also posed a severe challenge to the new state based in Belgrade. The Croat intelligentsia would be discredited in the eyes of the peasantry because of its support of Yugoslav unification, and this fact, coupled with Radić's opposition to this process, enabled him to lead a veritable national revolution after 1918.

5

The Revolt of the Masses:
Stjepan Radić, the HPSS, and the
Great War, 1914–1918

The First World War, or Great War as it was called until its more infamous successor, was a major turning-point for European society, including the South Slav lands and peoples. The attendant costs of this massive struggle, the human toll in dead and wounded, the economic dislocation, and the political turmoil contributed to tremendous changes in the postwar era. Of these changes 'the revolt of the masses,' to borrow José Ortega y Gasset's phrase, was among the most significant. 'The mass crushes beneath it everything that is different,' Ortega wrote, 'everything that is excellent, individual, qualified and select. Anybody who is not like everybody, who does not think like everybody, runs the risk of being eliminated ... Nowadays, "everybody" is the mass alone.'[1] The ascent of the masses was a phenomenon common to the political and social landscape of the whole of Europe. But the revolt which Ortega observed with such dread, and it should be emphasized that he was primarily referring to the cultural ramifications of this revolt, was perceived by millions as liberation, a new awareness, a consciousness borne through the privations of war. This new consciousness would lead to an assault on the remaining institutions of prewar Europe.

In the South Slav lands this revolt was as readily observable as in other parts of Europe. The peasantry, particularly in Croatia, was radicalized during the conflict. The number of soldiers from Croatia–Slavonia who were killed during the war may have been as high as 100,000.[2] The introduction of a system of obligatory delivery of food production and inflationary pressures all took their toll on the economic position of the peasantry. Furthermore, the Austro-Hungarian military authorities suspected the Slavs of treachery for the simple reason that they were not German or Magyar.[2] The anti-Slav chauvinism contributed to the stirrings of the non-dominant nationalities. By 1918 the Croat peasantry was in open revolt against the city, for it had come to the conclusion that the old political and social order was no longer worth fighting for. This radicalization would in no uncertain terms contribute to the HPSS's transformation from a minor party into a national mass movement. It is therefore critical to examine the policy of the HPSS during the war against the background of the growing radicalization of the rural population. Croatia's bourgeois and intellectual élite would, as a consequence of the peasantry's open revolt against the city in 1918, be cast aside into a position of political impotence, insofar, of course, as it did not become like 'everybody' and acknowledge the leadership of the peasantry. But before it was cast aside in the heady days of 1918, this élite, which was at the time overwhelmingly committed to Yugoslavist unitarism, would work to bring about the formation of a new state, known formally as the Kingdom of Serbs, Croats, and Slovenes. The Great War thus also produced another form of liberation, namely national, although this in reality proved to be ephemeral and problematic because the substance of that liberation remained to be determined at the time of the unification on 1 December 1918. It is necessary to examine the policy of the HPSS against the background of two related processes: the Yugoslav movement abroad as embodied in the Yugoslav Committee (*JO, Jugoslavenski odbor*) and its relations with the Serbian government; and, the Yugoslav movement within the Habsburg monarchy.

At the outset of the war the dominant group in the Croatian *Sabor* was the Croato-Serb Coalition (HSK).[4] From that point to October 1918 the HSK, dominated by Pribićević's Serb wing, pursued a policy of accommodation *vis-à-vis* Budapest in order to spare any reprisals against the Serbs. Its ultimate objective, however, remained unification with Serbia. But the HSK was hardly as united as it appeared at the time. The leader of the HSK's Croat wing, Lorković, was thinking of defecting as early as July 1914 because of its general political course. He feared that if Austria–Hungary won the war, she would squash the Croats because of their cooperation with the Croatian Serbs. Conversely, the Croatian Serbs had Serbia, which in turn had Western diplomatic support, and if Serbia won the war, the Croats would 'completely collapse.'[5] The Croat opposition parties, the Frankists, Starčević's Party of Right (SSP), and Radić's HPSS, openly favoured a reorganization into a triple monarchy, although Radić continued to view federalism as his ultimate goal.[6] But that goal had been seriously undermined, at least in Radić's mind, by the assassination of the Archduke Franz Ferdinand. His bitter reaction to the latter's death, and his willingness to associate that crime with the Serbian political establishment, meant in practice support for the Habsburg war cause and the hope that Serbia's plans, which he assumed to be aggrandizement at the expense of the monarchy, would be crushed. The enlargement of Serbia, he believed, would invariably pose a severe danger to Croat national interests.

As a result, for the better part of the war Radić collaborated with the Frankists and SSP, and together they pursued what came to be known as the 'Croatian course.' For Radić the objective of the Croatian course was to emancipate Croatia from Hungary, remove all Magyar officials from Croatia and, ultimately, unify all Croat lands, by which he meant Croatia–Slavonia, Dalmatia, Istria, and Bosnia–Herzegovina.[7] The Croat nation had entered the war, according to Radić, with the aim of securing its rights within the monarchy. The Croat Question could only be solved within the monarchy, Radić indicated in June 1915, for the Croats did not want Serbia to turn the Croat lands into another Macedonia. Neither such views nor his cooperation with the state right parties should be taken to mean that Radić had yet abandoned his belief in the *narodno jedinstvo* of South Slavs. In fact, he argued that the HPSS still supported 'the position of the complete national oneness of Slovenes, Croats, and Serbs,' as well as 'the position of a single Croatian state unity.' As in the prewar period, Radić believed that *narodno jedinstvo* should be the basis on which Croats and Serbs would cooperate to bring an end to Magyar domination and to protect their national interests. Radić still remained committed to a synthesis of cultural Yugoslavism and political Croatism: *narodno jedinstvo* should serve as a means to achieve national unification and emancipation, all of course within the Habsburg framework. He in fact believed that the war was uniting Croats and Serbs: 'After the war there will be only Croats or Serbs, or Serbo–Croats or Croato–Serbs [*sic*] – however you prefer – but we will be one [*jedno*], and on Croatian territory the Serbs will declare themselves as Croats.'[8] The unity of Croats and Serbs, on the basis of Croat state right and *narodno jedinstvo*, would ultimately lead to the unification of all Croat lands within the Dual Monarchy. But in addition to calling for unity between Croats and Serbs, Radić insisted on Croat unity and to that end cooperated with the state right parties.[9]

Although Radić's successor, Vladko Maček, claimed that he secretly wanted the monarchy to lose the war in order to bring about its internal reorganization, his public statements in the *Sabor* and press gave an entirely different impression. Of course, to a certain extent it could not be otherwise, for all parties had to express loyalty to the Habsburg dynasty and support the war effort or else risk the consequences. But Radić's commitment to the reorganization of the monarchy and fear of Serbian aggrandizement led him to support the war effort, in spite of his Russophilism and apprehension of Germany's growing might. The Great War would gradually challenge many of his loyalties, but in the early years of the war he could not bring himself to envisage a solution to the Croat Question outside of the borders of the monarchy. That was why he openly declared, shortly after hostilities were initiated, that Serbia, Russia, and France had provoked the war and that the monarchy could not lose, for its peoples were united behind the war cause.[10] After this victory conditions would improve, for it seemed only logical that, as Radić put it in late June 1915, 'for our spilt blood, of which there is much,' the Croats would achieve their national rights.[11]

The events of 1917–18 were to have an important impact on Radić and consequently on the HPSS's policies, although this was not immediately apparent. The first of these were the Russian revolutions of 1917 and the overthrow of autocracy. In spite of his long-standing opposition to socialism, Radić generally tended to view developments in Russia after 1917 with great interest and hope mixed with trepidation. After the February Revolution the HPSS weekly paper followed events in Russia very closely. Radić believed that Russia was transforming itself into a republic such as did not exist anywhere in the world, a republic that was liberating the 'spiritual' forces of the Russian nation.[12] He declared in the *Sabor* that the catastrophic war had transformed Russia into 'a source for the awakening of all nations,' and at the same time he made positive reference to the Entente: it was fighting for 'great principles' and wanted 'a lasting peace with the gradual limitation of armaments and the self-determination of nations,' principles which were not being supported in either Berlin or Vienna, and certainly not in Budapest.[13] The February Revolution was evidently contributing to his reassessment of the policies of both the Central and Entente powers, but he still remained committed to the Habsburg framework, for he believed that the implementation of democratic reform in Russia would invariably force the Habsburg monarchy to adopt similar reforms.

The February Revolution was according to Radić neither a bourgeois nor an intellectual phenomenon, but combined elements of all social strata behind the cause of political and social justice. That is undoubtedly why Russian developments captivated him so, and why he believed that the February Revolution represented 'an absolute and unmitigated gain for the whole of humanity.'[14] Radić's enthusiasm for the developments in Russia began to wane somewhat after the October Revolution and when, in January 1918, the Bolshevik regime dispersed the Constituent Assembly. By late January he was comparing developments in Russia with the French Terror and attacked the Bolsheviks for their policy *vis-à-vis* the other Russian parties.[15] In spite of his reservations, however, he could still write in February 1918 that the greatest achievement of the revolutions, and especially the October Revolution, was that they completely destroyed 'the largest barracks in the world,' and thus put an end to Russian militarism and imperialism.[16] That revolutionary Russia had seemingly renounced Imperial Russia's claims to Poland, Constantinople, and other areas, and had proclaimed the right of national self-determination for its peoples, clearly impressed Radić. This was why he concluded that the revolutions had 'changed all of the foundations of international law,' and 'struck the foundation of a sincere and honourable international law, which will guarantee freedom, justice, and happiness to every conscious and able nation.'[17]

Radić was also clearly impressed by the fact that Russia's large estates were being partitioned and that the Imperial bureaucracy had seemingly given way to a workers' and peasants' administration.[18] Just as important was his belief that the Russian revolutions, whatever their eventual outcome, were helping to bring the war closer to an end.[19] That the revolutions had an impact on Radić's thinking, and that he viewed developments in Russia with some sympathy, is beyond doubt, but there always remained an underlying fear in his words about the true intentions of the Bolsheviks. He certainly acknowledged that Russia could not return to the pre-1917 days, but he correctly suspected that Lenin and the Bolsheviks were inimical to the interests of the Russian peasantry. What is important to emphasize is that the revolutions, coupled with the American entry into the war in April 1917 and the growing influence of Woodrow Wilson, would have a powerful impact on Radić's thinking and the HPSS's policies. This should not be surprising, for by 1917–18 the war had acquired an ideological character. The revolutions and Wilson's proclamations in support of national self-determination would reverberate throughout Europe.

Of more immediate concern to Radić was the emerging Yugoslav movement within the monarchy as embodied in the 'Yugoslav Club' in the Austrian *Reichsrat*, called to session on 30 May 1917 for the first time since the outbreak of hostilities. On that day the Yugoslav Club, composed of South Slavic politicians from the Slovene lands, Istria, and Dalmatia, issued the May Declaration, a manifesto calling for the unification of all of the monarchy's Slovenes, Croats, and Serbs into a single autonomous administrative unit on the basis of the national principle and Croat state right.[20] Of the Croatian parties only the SSP publicly supported the May Declaration and thereafter became increasingly willing to entertain the idea of unification with Serbia. It emerged as one of the most outspoken proponents of this course of action and by mid-1917 distanced itself from both the Frankists and the HPSS.[21] Radić's initial comments regarding the May Declaration seemed to lend support to the general principles enunciated in the manifesto. He welcomed the Yugoslav Club's recognition of what he termed 'the historic importance of Croatdom,' that is, its explicit reference to Croat state right. The manifesto was 'the most felicitous and most complete formula of our Croatian, national, state right, [and] democratic program,' for it represented the unification of the monarchy's South Slavs in what was to be a united Croatian state. In many respects the May Declaration encapsulated his own objectives; after all, as part of his call for the reorganization of the monarchy, Croatia was to become the political centre of the South Slavs. The manifesto, he believed, had recognized that the Croats were 'the state and national foundation of all the South Slavs in the monarchy.'

Radić's support for the emerging Yugoslav movement within the monarchy was qualified, which he made abundantly clear. The May Declaration was very brief and hence had many ambiguities. What was unclear to Radić was whether the politicians of the Yugoslav Club wanted this autonomous South Slavic unit to be called Croatia, on the basis of Croat state right, or 'Yugoslavia,' on the basis of *narodno jedinstvo*. That is why, in spite of his initial favourable reaction, Radić did not wholeheartedly support the manifesto. In fact, he stressed in July 1917 that

> if the war ends without any large, or perhaps any, territorial changes, the lands that are inhabited by the Slovenes, Serbs, and Croats will be the Kingdom of Croatia. If the war ends with the complete alteration of state borders, which is impossible, then Yugoslavia may come about, but a Yugoslavia that would include all Yugoslavs, Bulgars, Serbs, and Croats. Where Serbia will be, this we do not know, but that she will be larger and stronger than she was, this is certain. But alongside a free Bulgaria and a free Serbia there will not be here among us a mixture called Yugoslavia. This would be an absurdity and an injustice from the Croatian standpoint, this would be an impossibility and treason. If others would like to betray us, we must not betray ourselves. There can only be a Croatian state here while the monarchy remains, and we will defend it to the end.[22]

Radić thus essentially remained committed to his earlier synthesis of Croat state right and Yugoslavism: the principle of *narodno jedinstvo* had to serve as a means for the unification of the Croat lands. He still believed that after the war the Croat lands would be united, and all existing ties between Croatia and Hungary – but not between Croatia and Austria – would be severed. The monarchy would become, next to Russia, the leading state in Europe.[23]

Radić therefore continued to press the monarchy's case throughout 1917 and even into 1918. It should be emphasized that the question of the Habsburg monarchy's fate, as far as the Western powers were concerned, was not decided until the last months of the war. Woodrow Wilson's famous Fourteen Points (18 January 1918) promised only autonomy for the peoples of Austria–Hungary and not outright independence. Many Western policy makers continued to hope that a separate peace with Austria–Hungary was possible. Only in June 1918 did the Entente finally agree to support the creation of Czechoslovak and Polish states, thereby sanctioning the dissolution of the Dual Monarchy.

Radić was initially critical of the Entente for treating the South Slavic question as essentially a Serbian problem, thereby neglecting Croat interests. He believed that after the war one of two things would happen in Central Europe. Either the territorial status quo would be preserved, in which case the kingdom of Croatia 'will be free and united within the monarchy,' alongside 'a united, resurrected Serbia and a strong Bulgaria,' or in the event of a 'radical solution,' by which he meant the monarchy's collapse, the situation would be resolved by the Slovenes, Croats, Serbs, and Bulgars themselves. In the latter case, the South Slavs would have to recognize their respective state traditions: the Croats were the only historic political nation in the monarchy's South Slav regions, and the Serbs and Bulgars were political nations on their respective state territories. Radić's aim still remained Croatian unification within the Habsburg monarchy.[24] Although the Serbs of Serbia 'are our brothers not only by language and spirit, but also in every social respect,' this did not logically entail unification with Serbia, 'because we have our thousand-year-old state and we want to remain in the monarchy.'[25] These remarks were made in August 1917 and should not be taken to mean that Radić was satisfied with the existing situation in the monarchy, for his frustration with the new Emperor Karl I (Karl IV in Hungary), who succeeded Franz Joseph in November 1916, gradually became evident. According to Maček, who met with Radić a few months after Karl I's accession, Radić was still optimistic because he hoped that the new monarch would negotiate a separate peace with the Entente and then reorganize the monarchy along federalized lines.[26] By the end of 1917 Radić was becoming increasingly disillusioned, but his repeated references to a Habsburg solution to the Croat Question were undoubtedly motivated by his fear that, without the monarchy, that question would have a decidedly Serbian solution.

There was certainly cause for such concern, and in the event it was legitimate. Soon after the war began a number of influential Croat and other politicians and intellectuals, such as Ante Trumbić, Frano Supilo, and Ivan Meštrović, fled the Dual Monarchy to carry on their political activities abroad. In April 1915 they formed the Yugoslav Committee, which was based in London.[27] Trumbić and Supilo were the main architects of the new course in Croatian politics after 1905, the objective of which was to weaken the monarchy. Now that war had erupted, they carried on their anti-Habsburg campaign abroad. During the war the Yugoslav Committee formulated a political program calling for the unification of all Croats, Serbs, and Slovenes. In this sense, it continued the work of the new course in exile by calling for the destruction of the Dual Monarchy. Although the Yugoslav Committee from its inception suffered from a lack of legitimacy, it received the active support of a number of British intellectuals, such as R.W. Seton-Watson, H.W. Steed, and Sir Arthur Evans, as well as certain émigré, largely Croat, communities in the United States and South America. But the Yugoslav Committee remained without official recognition by the Entente throughout the war, a fact that constantly hindered its work.[28]

The Yugoslav Committee attempted to come to terms with the Serbian government. The latter articulated its war aims in the form of the so-called Niš Declaration of 7 December 1914, which represented the first official program of the wartime Serbian coalition government regarding the unification of the Serbs, Croats and Slovenes.[29] In the Niš Declaration the Serbian government affirmed as its objective the liberation and unification of all Serbs, Croats, and Slovenes, although no mention was made of the internal organization of this future state.[30] From the outset the Serbian government had two general war aims: the maximalist aim was the unification of all Serbs, Croats, and Slovenes within an enlarged Serbian state; the minimalist aim was to incorporate only those territories which it regarded as predominantly Serb, namely, Bosnia–Herzegovina, although the Vojvodina and Dalmatia were also factored into these plans. The realization of the former necessarily meant the realization of the latter, although the reverse was obviously not the case. What can be determined fairly accurately is that the government of Nikola Pašić sought to preserve Serbia's predominance in the event that the maximalist aim was obtained.

Pašić resolved from the outset that Serbia had to play the leading role in the process of unification. He was prepared to countenance the activities of the Yugoslav Committee insofar as they served to propagandize the Serbian war effort and aims. At no time did he view the Yugoslav Committee as an equal. The latter, on the other hand, desired unification with Serbia, but resisted Serbia's self-assumed role as a South Slav Piedmont. It wanted unification on equal terms. Both Trumbić and Supilo feared that the real intent of the Serbian political élite was not the liberation but conquest of the Habsburg South Slav areas.[31] Nevertheless, they were encouraged by the Niš Declaration.[32] However, it became increasingly evident to the members of the Yugoslav Committee and its sympathizers that Pašić and the Serbian government saw Serbia as a liberator of the South Slavs, with all that this implied.

The position of Supilo, Trumbić, and their associates was further undermined by the secret Treaty of London, which was signed by the three Entente powers (Britain, France, Russia) and Italy on 26 April 1915. In exchange for her entry into the war within a month of signing the treaty, Italy was promised, among other things, Gorica and a part of Carniola, which were overwhelmingly Slovene, as well as Istria and northern Dalmatia, which were predominantly Croat. The members of the Yugoslav Committee soon got wind of the treaty. In fact, the Yugoslav Committee was formally established only days after the London pact had been signed. Italy's entry into the war seriously complicated matters for the Yugoslav Committee.[33] Formed to propagate the cause of South Slavic unification among the Western powers, the Yugoslav Committee was now confronted by a new partner of the Entente whose territorial interests were diametrically opposed to its own. On the other hand, even though the Serbian government was not pleased with the treaty, this document did not seriously jeopardize the minimalist option of Serbia's war aims.

Relations between the Serbian government and Yugoslav Committee remained strained during 1915. In an effort to bring Bulgaria into the war, the Entente tried to convince Serbia to grant territorial concessions to Sofia in Macedonia in exchange for parts of northern Albania and some Habsburg lands, namely, Bosnia–Herzegovina, those parts of Dalmatia not already promised to Italy, as well as Slavonia. When the Yugoslav Committee heard of these negotiations it began seriously to doubt the intentions of the Serbian government. Supilo in particular believed that the Croat lands were being partitioned, and he subsequently endorsed a compromise solution to Sir Edward Grey, the British foreign secretary: Bosnia–Herzegovina, southern Dalmatia, and Croatia–Slavonia should decide their future by plebiscite. This move was interpreted by the Serbian government as an attempt by Supilo to create an independent Croatian state. Supilo met with disagreement within the Yugoslav Committee, however. Although Trumbić shared Supilo's fears, he nevertheless believed that Italian ambitions posed a greater danger and that cooperation with the Serbian government had to continue. But Supilo left the Yugoslav Committee in 1916 and from then until his death the following year increasingly looked to secure a separate deal for Croatia that would safeguard her national rights. His disillusionment with Yugoslav unitarism was complete, and in this sense he represented the first of many Croat intellectuals, indeed a generation of unitarist Croat intelligentsia, who would become disillusioned with, and eventually abandon, *narodno jedinstvo* and its implication: Yugoslavist integralism.[34]

Even after Supilo's departure relations between the Serbian government and the Yugoslav Committee did not improve appreciably. The question of how to organize the Croat, Slovene, and Serb prisoners of war in Russia remained problematic. The Yugoslav Committee wanted to create 'Yugoslav' legions from these POWs, but Pašić interpreted this as an attempt to create a

Croat army. Consequently he insisted that they be under strict Serbian military control, even though the majority of the POWs were Croats and Slovenes.[35] The course of the war turned against Serbia in late 1915, however, which obliged Pašić to adopt a seemingly more conciliatory policy *vis-à-vis* the Yugoslav Committee. Confronted with a renewed offensive by the Central Powers, this time with the assistance of Bulgaria, the Serbian army was forced to beat a quick retreat across Albania to the Adriatic and was subsequently transferred to the Salonika front while the Serbian government established itself on the island of Corfu. Its position was further weakened in 1917 by the February Revolution in Russia, hitherto Serbia's most outspoken supporter, as well as growing criticism within its own ranks about its inactive foreign policy. Pašić was therefore forced to come to terms with the Yugoslav Committee, itself plagued by internal dissension and undermined by the loyalty of the domestic parties to the Habsburg war cause. A conference on the island of Corfu 15–20 July 1917 produced the fourteen-point Corfu Declaration (20 July 1917).[36]

This document proclaimed the determination of Serbs, Croats, and Slovenes to form a united state that would be a constitutional, democratic, and parliamentary monarchy headed by the Serbian Karadjordjević dynasty. The constitution of the new state would be drawn up by a Constituent Assembly and accepted by a 'numerically qualified majority.' The document made no provisions for the continuation of existing historical territorial units or their legislative bodies, such as the Croatian *Sabor*. The Corfu Declaration was in principle a compromise between Pašić and Trumbić: it recognized the equality of the three South Slavic *tribal* names, three flags, two religions, and two alphabets. In practice, however, and as events would demonstrate, Pašić had not conceded anything to the Yugoslav Committee. That the declaration included no provisions for the internal form of government, and that the issue of centralism versus federalism was not addressed, did not bode well for the future. To the extent that local autonomy was envisaged in this document, it was to be based on non-historical territorial entities. Whatever the shortcomings of the declaration, the Yugoslav Committee thought it had reached a basic agreement with Serbia. But Pašić virtually ignored the agreement and considered it as an expedient measure to allay the concerns of his Western critics and some within his government, and not as a binding agreement. He clung to the view that Serbia was a liberating power, the South Slavic Piedmont; he made no promises that might hinder his, and consequently Serbia's, ability to organize the postwar state. In October 1918 Pašić told one British supporter of Yugoslav unification that the Corfu Declaration 'had merely been issued by him in order to make an impression on European public opinion,' and he dismissed federalist and other decentralist schemes as 'impossible' because 'the Yugoslav people were very mixed.'[37] Nevertheless, the movement towards a Yugoslav state had seemingly achieved an important success with this document.

The shortcomings of the Corfu Declaration were all too apparent to Radić. His position towards the Yugoslav movement, both within and outside of the monarchy, was articulated most comprehensively in September 1917, as a response to the recent Corfu Declaration. Restating his earlier view that South Slavs were, in linguistic and social terms, one nation, he argued that the Serb proponents of *narodno jedinstvo* were employing this principle for their own particularist objectives. Paradoxically, he identified Nikola Pašić as the most 'energetic representative of trinomial Yugoslavism,' but believed that Pašić was prepared to countenance Italian territorial ambitions in Dalmatia at the expense of Croat interests. For Radić this demonstrated that the Serb variant of *narodno jedinstvo* was merely a chimera that Serbia's politicians were using to further their own national interests. This was equally true, he believed, of the Pribićević-led HSK. Radić was adamant that if a reorganization of the Dual Monarchy occurred Croatia had to be the centre of this unit, based on its historic state right.

In Radić's mind the prevailing variant of *narodno jedinstvo* was merely being employed as a cover for Great Serbianism, as embodied in the policies of both Pašić's government and some elements within the HSK. He did not conceal his fear that these policies were essentially anti-Croat, 'because for our [Croatian] Serb politicians there never existed, nor does there exist, a Croatian state,' and because Serb politicians 'have always easily come to terms with Italian policy in the whole of coastal Croatia [Dalmatia].' In other words, all Serb politicians were inimical to Croat national rights: Pašić because he was prepared to barter Dalmatia to Italy – even though, of course, it was the Entente that did the bartering – as long as Serbia's rights were secured in the area, and the HSK's Serbs because they were pursuing an opportunistic and subservient policy towards Budapest at the expense of Croatia's interests. Consequently, Radić concluded that Croatian interests were being threatened from within (by the HSK) and by developments abroad (by the Serbian government, and the Yugoslav Committee), and this perception only reconfirmed his view that the Croat (or South Slav) Question had to be resolved within the framework of the Habsburg monarchy.[38]

Radić kept repeating these criticisms of Serbian state policy and the HSK in early 1918, even as he began gradually distancing himself from his Frankist allies. The HPSS and Frankists had always been divided on important matters of principle, and their alliance, formed in 1913, was in actual fact a marriage of convenience, directed above all against the HSK. It is therefore not surprising that Radić became increasingly critical of the Frankists, particularly the Catholic clericalist elements within their ranks. He believed that their anti-Serb views would invariably further antagonize Croatia's Serbs and undermine *narodno jedinstvo*.[39] But most of Radić's criticisms were directed against the HSK, particularly its Serb wing. For Radić the Croatian Serb leadership had, since the adoption of the new course, pursued an anti-Croat policy under the rubric of *narodno jedinstvo*. But because of their espousal of that concept they managed to win over the greater part of the Croat intelligentsia. The HSK's policies were certainly not motivated by a concern for Croat national interests, because the HSK had done nothing, either before or after 1914, to achieve the unification of the Croat lands. It was, for its own expedient reasons, formally committed to perpetuating Croatia–Slavonia's subordinate status within the Hungarian crown lands.[40]

Radić eventually adopted a more negative view of the May Declaration and its supporters in Croatia, Starčević's Party of Right (SSP). Radić believed that this manifesto did not strike a proper balance between the principle of *narodno jedinstvo* and Croat state right, and laid the blame on the Croatian Serb politicians. They were quite simply inimical to Croatia's state individuality: 'Our Croatian state is being rejected first by our Serbs, [and] because of them our most natural allies, the Slovenes, are rejecting it, and because of both many Croats are rejecting it in the belief and hope that with the *narodno jedinstvo* of the Slovenes, Croats and Serbs we will more easily build a completely new state,' rather than strengthening the existing Croatian state. But this Radić was not prepared to accept. He proposed a different course of action. Together with the Slovenes, the Croats 'want to construct our national democratic state of Croatia. In this Croatian state our Serb brothers will have all of those rights that we have. If the Serbs oppose this Croatian state, we will employ all means at our disposal to create it without them, even against them, because we are convinced that without unity with all Slovenes and without the integrity of the historic Croato–Bosnian–Dalmatian Triune Kingdom [*sic*] there can be no existence, let alone progress, for the Croat people.'[41] Radić still remained consistent with respect to his view that *narodno jedinstvo* had to serve as a means of bringing about Croatia's liberation from Magyar rule and the unification of all Croat lands. Croatia's historic rights could not be compromised for the principle of *narodno jedinstvo*. The latter had to serve as the basis for the realization of the former. This was why Radić railed against the HSK and was critical of those politicians who supported the May Declaration.

The events of 1918 would bring about a change in Radić's thinking. Radić's plan for the federalization of the monarchy gradually lost all meaning in the course of 1918, particularly after he realized that the Czechs, whom he had always regarded as the most progressive of the Slav nations, were increasingly becoming radicalized and might seek the creation of a Czechoslovak state. Indeed, the Epiphany (6 January) 1918 declaration of Czech deputies for self-determination and Czechoslovak participation at a future peace conference appeared to indicate that the Czechs were moving towards a break with the Dual Monarchy. In early April 1918 Radić was approached by an intermediary of the Czech agrarian leader, Antonín Švehla, and invited to Prague for discussions with the latter. Radić was informed that Czech leaders were in contact with émigré groups (Masaryk's National Council) and were losing all hope that the monarchy could be reorganized along democratic lines.[42]

Radić left for Prague and on 13 April attended a meeting of Czech and South Slav politicians. He now began urging a coordinated Czech–Polish–Yugoslav policy within the monarchy as a *sine qua non* for its successful reorganization,[43] and thus it seems that he was still thinking in terms of a restructured monarchy. The political manifestations in Prague had a profound impact on Radić. He supported the unity of the Czech parties which had existed since May 1917 and the Epiphany Declaration which called for Czech and Slovak unification. He also began referring to a new union between the Czechs, Slovaks, and South Slavs. Moreover, he now increasingly emphasized the importance of the principle of national self-determination that had emerged as a consequence of the Russian revolutions and the American involvement in the war. The future peace settlement, and the new European political order, 'will not be imposed on peoples and states.' Rather the future peace settlement 'will be formed by a true world international congress, in which the leading, and perhaps even determining, word will be had by the three great republics: America, France, and Russia.'[44]

After April 1918 Radić's policy finally underwent a change. He now argued that of the political groups in Croatia, the HPSS belonged to 'the camp of Yugoslav democracy,' which in his mind also included Starčević's Party of Right. This was the same party that he had recently criticized for its public endorsement of the May Declaration. Nonetheless, the HPSS and SSP had to create a common political organization on an agrarian foundation, modelled on the unity of the Czech political parties. After the events in Prague 'the direction of Croat and Yugoslav policy in the Banate [Croatia–Slavonia] is clear: the organization of the Croat and Serb peasantry on an agraro-economic, Yugoslav national, and a Croat state right foundation.'[45] This was a subtle although not yet serious departure from his earlier views. On 13 May Radić again travelled to Prague for the celebration of the fiftieth anniversary of the National Theatre in an effort further to strengthen the new 'union' between the Czechs and South Slavs that he believed had been established the previous April.[46] At the same time he continued his attacks against both the HSK and the Frankists. He condemned the former for its refusal explicitly to support the spirit of the manifestations in Prague, and to defend Croatia's political rights within the monarchy. He also bitterly rebuked the anti-Serb attitude of the Frankists and their 'spiritual dependence' on Vienna.[47] He no longer had much use for the Frankists, in large part because of their continued willingness to rely on official circles in Vienna to achieve their party's state right program and their belief that the Serbs were the Croats' greatest enemy. Their policy 'goes against healthy reason and our entire war experience.'[48]

What Radić was now insisting upon was that the Croats, Slovenes, and Serbs of the monarchy cooperate to achieve their unification on the basis of Croatia's state right, and at the same time coordinate their policy with those of the Czechs and Poles. By May 1918 there was virtually no mention in Radić's writings of Austria or a reorganized Habsburg monarchy. In fact, it was now the HPSS's 'holiest duty' to support 'that world policy [the Entente's] that gives and recognizes the complete and unconditional right to national self-determination to every nation.'[49] But even though his old faith in the Habsburgs had disappeared, Radić's vision of a broad Central European union had not. 'A lasting and honourable peace,' Radić wrote in early June, 'can come into being if all nations on the border of the former Russian Empire, in the Danubian area, and in the Balkans receive the complete right to national self-determination in such a way that, first, each will unite, liberate, and organize itself, and then together that they create a great union of equal national people's states in that part of Europe that was in this war the main battlefield and because of which this war began in the first place.' This union would not be directed against any other state, but would be 'a strong and lasting guarantee against possible German, Italian, and Russian imperialism or military conquest.'[50]

It is evident that Radić still believed in mid-1918 that some kind of Danubian federation or union could be formed out of the decaying Habsburg monarchy and its neighbouring territories. This point is important for an understanding of his thinking at this time, particularly in relation to the Yugoslav movement. The Yugoslav movement had hitherto been on the wrong path for 'it was led only by the Serbs,' that is, the Serbian government, and the émigrés (Yugoslav Committee). But with the creation of the Czech–Polish–Yugoslav 'triumvirate,' as Radić called it, in Prague in April 1918, the Yugoslav movement was on a proper course and based on a Slavic, European, and democratic foundation. At this stage Radić was primarily concerned with maintaining firm political cooperation and ties with the Czechs and Poles, and believed that with their coordinated effort 'there stands here a force of fifty million people, around which ... will gather all of the others in the Danubian basin and the

Balkans, and even on the borders of Russia.' His old vision of Habsburg federalism now gave way to an even more grandiose vision of an East Central European union. He envisaged the possibility of Bulgaria and Ukraine joining this
'Czecho–Polish–Yugoslav connection,' in which case 'we will have 100 million!' 'We are looking before us,' he wrote, 'at a magnificent scene: the emancipation, liberation, and organization of the greater part of Europe,' such as
humanity had never before seen.[51]

Radić's idea of a broader Slavic union or conglomeration, however unrealistic and grandiose, should not be minimized, if only because it clearly formed
a central part of his thinking at the time. The central tenet of his earlier
espousal of Habsburg federalism was the fact that the Slavs were a majority of
the monarchy's population. Now that the monarchy was on its last legs he
envisaged a new, perhaps much broader, union which was essentially a reformulation of his earlier federalist views. Croats would achieve national unification and liberation within this new union. Radić insisted that Croats wanted
peace 'on the basis of such an international agreement, by which in future
there will be neither permanent armies nor wars, and by which we Croats, as a
thousand-year-old state and enlightened nation, will finally achieve our complete state independence and our total national unification.'[52] Radić was prepared to see a free and united Croatia join a broader union that would act as an
important instrument of European peace and stability. That is why he was so
critical of those Croat politicians who were thinking only of unity with the
Serbs and Slovenes. The task at hand was much greater. As long as twenty-
five million Poles remained divided and oppressed and as long as Czechs and
Slovaks were not truly free, then neither Croats nor the other South Slavs
would be able to achieve unification and liberation. 'The Croat, rather the
Yugoslav, Question,' he wrote, 'is only a part of the question of all of the non-
Russian Slavs.'[53]

That is how Radić was thinking in the summer of 1918. On 19 July the
Croatian *Sabor* held its last summer session and it would not meet again until
late October 1918 under very different political circumstances. In the interim,
and in order to maintain close ties with Czech political leaders, Radić again
travelled to Prague in August, while at the same time working to establish a
'national concentration' of all Croat parties that had gone to Prague in April,
that is, the HPSS, Starčević's Party of Right, and some HSK dissidents. On
25 August the HPSS Main Committee held a session in Zagreb to determine
party policy with respect to the Yugoslav movement, the Czech–Polish–Yugoslav union and the issue of the establishment of a Croatian National Council.
After a four-hour meeting, the HPSS's Main Committee adopted a number of
important resolutions recognizing the principle of national self-determination

and supporting the process of the unification of the monarchy's South Slavs *alongside* a new Czech–Polish–Yugoslav union.[54]

It is important to clarify Radić's thinking about the gradual movement towards Yugoslav unification at this time. In August 1918 Radić wrote that 'Yugoslavism has only true objectives,' and these were: '(1) complete liberation from [censored, the Magyars]; (2) the complete attachment of the Slovenes to the Croats, [and] other South Slavs; [and,] (3) the political unification of the entire Adriatic coast [Dalmatia] to the Croatian, respectively the Yugoslav, state.' The South Slav Question would be resolved only when 'all of the [monarchy's] South Slavs *are unified in the Croatian state* [emphasis added].'[55] It is evident that Radić, while looking to rally the monarchy's South Slavs around the Croatian state, which is what he meant by the Yugoslav movement, was at the same time looking north, to the Czechs, Slovaks, and Poles, in the hope of some form of association or union with them. But political and military developments would shortly bring about a radically new situation which would dash all of Radić's hopes.

The movement towards Yugoslavs unification took on added momentum in the autumn of 1918. A National Council (*Narodni Svet*) was established in Ljubljana on 16 August 1918 for the South Slav political parties in the monarchy's Austrian half for the purpose of uniting the South Slavs within an independent state.[56] On 6 October 1918, with the military situation rapidly deteriorating for the Central Powers, the delegates of the Croat, Serb, and Slovene parties that favoured South Slav unification created the National Council of Slovenes, Croats, and Serbs (*Narodno vijeće Slovenaca, Hrvata i Srba*) in Zagreb as their supreme political body. On 8 October the HSK, which had hitherto pursued a subservient policy towards Budapest, joined the National Council. The Slovene priest Anton Korošec became its president and Pribićević (HSK) and Ante Pavelić[57] (Starčević's Party of Right) its vice-presidents. Radić entered the working committee of the National Council on 7 October. This committee was formed to conduct the affairs of the National Council's presidium until a non-partisan Central Committee was formed.

Radić welcomed the formation of the National Council because it represented the concentration of national political forces that he had been urging since the spring. He argued that its main task was to liberate and unify all the monarchy's South Slavs into an independent state with a representative national government. The hour had finally come for all Slovenes, Croats, and Serbs 'to achieve their totally free and independent national state,' and the HPSS would work to organize this national state according to West European and American political standards and the peasantry's needs, that is, on the basis of peasant right. Though some were already calling this state Yugoslavia, Radić believed that 'how it will in fact be called is not an issue now, because the name is easy, when you have the thing.' What had to be emphasized and announced to the Croat people was that '*all three of our old, purely national names*: Slovene, Croat, and Serb, will have in our whole state entirely equal right and the same respect.' This was certainly a departure from the position he had outlined in the summer of 1917, when he refused to countenance the creation of a Yugoslav 'mixture' on the monarchy's South Slav territories. Radić did not abandon his central belief that the integrity and independence of the Croatian state, which would be proclaimed shortly, should be respected. The common state of Croats, Slovenes, and Serbs, which was in the process of being formed, would in Radić's opinion be an independent national state, in which all three religions (Catholicism, Orthodoxy, Islam) would be equally respected and tolerated, and in which the peasants and workers would achieve their social aims. But Radić was adamant that the National Council had to seek a closer union with the western Slavs and work to eliminate the last vestiges of militarism, capitalism, bureaucratism and feudalism, which he identified as the causes of the Great War.[58]

On 19 October the National Council announced that, having been authorized to do so by all parties, it would take the lead in national politics and assume formal control on the former Habsburg territories of the South Slavs. It also announced its intention of seeking unification with the kingdom of Serbia. On 21 October, the National Council formed sections for specific affairs and Radić became the head of the agrarian section. Even though Radić continued to participate in the National Council after it made known its intention to seek unification with Serbia, on 28 October he argued that it was imperative for the interests of both Croats and Serbs that the state sovereignty and individuality of both Croatia and Serbia be respected.[59]

On 29 October 1918 the Croatian *Sabor*, in a historic session, broke all ties with Hungary and the other Habsburg lands and declared the Triune Kingdom (Croatia–Slavonia–Dalmatia) with Rijeka to be an independent state. It also transferred executive powers to the National Council, which two days later decided that the newly constituted State of the Slovenes, Croats, and Serbs (*Država Slovenaca, Hrvata i Srba*),[60] composed of all of the South Slav territories of the monarchy, was prepared to enter into a common state with the kingdoms of Serbia and Montenegro. The National Council became the de facto government of this state and a new factor in the Yugoslav equation. Pašić now became troubled by the events in Zagreb, however, because he feared the emergence of a potentially rival institution in the former Habsburg territories. On 1 November 1918, on the same day that the Serbian army entered Belgrade, the National Council informed the Yugoslav Committee in

London that it should act as the former's representative abroad and inform the Allies of its desire to unify with Serbia and Montenegro. At the same time a mission of the National Council, headed by Korošec, arrived in Geneva and immediately learned of the Yugoslav Committee's troubled relations with the Serbian government.

In an attempt to settle matters with the Yugoslav Committee and the National Council, Pašić went to Geneva to meet with Korošec and Trumbić. What resulted was the Geneva Conference of 6–9 November 1918, which was attended by representatives of the Yugoslav Committee, the Serbian government, Serbian opposition parties, and Korošec.[61] Pašić recognized the National Council as the legitimate government of the South Slavs of the former Habsburg monarchy. To pave the way towards unification, a compromise agreement was struck in the form of the Geneva Declaration which stated that a twelve-member joint ministry would be established with six ministers each from the Serbian government and the National Council, and that a Constituent Assembly would eventually be created to work out the constitution of the new state which was in the process of being formed. A common state was agreed upon, and the kingdom of Montenegro was invited to join. The agreement was in effect supposed to supersede the Corfu Declaration and was definitely a political defeat for Pašić's centralist philosophy and seemingly a victory for Trumbić and the Yugoslav Committee. The Geneva Declaration was quickly made null and void, however, as resentment to it mounted within the Serbian cabinet. Serbia's vice-premier, Stojan Protić, submitted his resignation over the issue of the declaration and Pašić, because of the opposition to the declaration within his government, followed suit. But the prince-regent offered Pašić a mandate to form a new cabinet, which he did on 16 November. The new government rejected the Geneva Declaration. So too did Pribićević in Zagreb.

The Serbian government felt that it had good reason to reject this agreement, primarily because its position was much stronger than that of the Yugoslav Committee and, more importantly, the politicians of the National Council. In fact, the final decision to rush headlong into unification occurred in Zagreb. Colonel Dušan Simović, a representative of the Serbian military who had been sent to Zagreb to work with those elements of the National Council who supported a speedy unification with Serbia, reported to his superiors on 14 November that Zagreb was overwhelmingly 'taken by the idea of Yugoslav solidarity,' even though it 'represents an irresolute element.' The republican idea was gaining ground in the countryside, and this fact, combined with the growing peasant disturbances, which will be discussed below, would only force the pace of unification. Simović advised the Serbian government that it tell the Yugoslav Committee that it was clearly not informed about the situation in Zagreb.[62] On 23 November the National Council's Central Committee debated the issue of how best to enact unification with Serbia and decided to send a twenty-eight-member delegation to Belgrade to discuss the terms of immediate unification. The situation appeared desperate. With Italian troops now occupying parts of Dalmatia, Istria, and Slovenia, and rural unrest growing under the 'Green Cadre' (*zeleni kader*), even the Yugoslav Committee became convinced of the need for immediate union with Serbia to protect existing frontiers.

On the night of 24 November, at a session of the National Council's Central Committee, Radić opposed the decision of that body to send a delegation to Belgrade, although he was one of the individuals selected to make the journey. It was at this session of the Central Committee that Radić delivered his final warning to the politicians of the National Council in what later came to be regarded as one of his most famous speeches. 'Your mouths are full of words like *narodno jedinstvo* – a single unitary state, one kingdom under the Karadjordjević dynasty,' Radić said, 'and you think that it is enough to say that we Croats, Serbs, and Slovenes are one people because we speak one language, and that because of this we must have a single centralist state.' This was not only foolish and dangerous, but undemocratic and unconstitutional. He accused the National Council's politicians of being indifferent towards the peasantry and attacked their futile efforts to restore order in the countryside. The peasants, Radić argued, believed that the intellectuals were no better than their former German and Magyar oppressors. 'You are consequently scaring our people like little children [with the Italian threat],' Radić added, 'and think that you will in this way be able to win over the people for your policy. Perhaps you will win over the Slovenes, I do not know; perhaps you will temporarily win over the Serbs; but I firmly know that you will not win over the Croats, and you will not win them over because the entire Croat peasant people are as opposed to your centralism as against militarism, equally in favour of a republic as they are for a national agreement with the Serbs.' If the Serbs of Serbia and Montenegro wanted a centralized state, so be it, but the Croat peasantry wanted an independent peasant republic that might eventually (con)federate with Serbia. 'Our Croat peasant,' Radić went on, reminding them that the peasantry composed the overwhelming majority of the population, 'has become a complete person in this war, and this means that he will no longer serve anyone, be a slave to anyone, neither to a foreigner nor to his brother, neither to a foreign state nor his own, but he wants the state to be organized, at this great time, on a free republican and a just, humane (social) foundation. And you, a handful of gentlemen, are opposed to this!' By opposing this republican desire of the peasantry the intellectuals were committing a 'terrible injustice' and an act of 'enormous stupidity.'[63] But Radić's warnings had little effect on the subsequent decisions of the National Council. On 1 December 1918 the National Council's delegation presented its Address to the Throne in Belgrade, calling for unification with Serbia. The Prince-Regent Aleksandar formally accepted it, and the new Yugoslav state, the Kingdom of Serbs, Croats, and Slovenes, became a reality. The great issue that would plague this state for the rest of its existence, the question of federalism versus centralism, had not, however, been resolved.

The formal act of unification was a severe blow to Radić. He had supported the break with the Habsburg monarchy of 29 October, but his attitude towards Yugoslav unification differed markedly from that of the intellectuals of the National Council. It is critical to pay close attention to Radić's views at this point, for he would emerge after 1 December 1918 as the most determined opponent of unification. Some of his comments at this time left contradictory impressions. For example, in early November he wrote that 'we are uniting and liberating ourselves as citizens of the common national state of the Slovenes, Croats, and Serbs,' and that it was certain 'that our state frontiers will [extend] ... as far as our national language reaches.' The new state was being built from two ends: 'From the south it is being restored and built *by the Serbian army* with the military assistance of the Entente. From the centre we Croats are building it in our Croatian state *Sabor* with the diplomatic (political) assistance of America and the Entente.' These words lend the impression that Radić was thinking of a broader Yugoslav state, including Serbia and Montenegro. He was quick to emphasize, however, that with the *Sabor*'s decision of 29 October, Croatia (Croatia–Slavonia–Dalmatia with Rijeka) was now 'a completely free and independent state' that had 'voluntarily limited its independence' within the context of the State of the Slovenes, Croats, and Serbs. Radić added that this independent Croatian state 'is entering into a common Yugoslav state in such a way, that this common state should be organized by a constituent assembly of all of the Slovenes, Croats, and Serbs, *who live in the former Austria-Hungary* [emphasis added].'[64] This was an important qualifier, for Radić insisted, and would keep insisting throughout the following year, that a constituent assembly, elected on the basis of universal suffrage and deciding not by a simple majority vote but a qualified one, had to decide whether this Croatian and Yugoslav state would be a monarchy or republic, and what its relation to Serbia and Montenegro would be. Radić was prepared to recognize the authority of the National Council in the interim, that is, until this constituent assembly determined the nature of the new state. The 'Yugoslav' state of which Radić spoke only encompassed the lands of the former monarchy's South Slavs. Unification with Serbia and Montenegro could only be sanctioned by a popularly elected constituent assembly.

The demand for a constituent assembly would place Radić at odds with the politicians of the National Council. When independence was proclaimed on 29 October, the National Council began immediately to prepare for unification with Serbia without any set preconditions for the terms of that unification. Radić, sensing that the peasants were opposed to the stated policy of the National Council to unify the former monarchy's South Slav lands with Serbia, became increasingly vocal in his criticism of the politicians of the council, the majority of whom were by now committed to Yugoslavist unitarism. On the same day that the Croatian *Sabor* broke all ties with the Dual Monarchy, the HPSS Main Committee met in Zagreb to clarify the party's policy towards the National Council. When Radić arrived at the meeting he was greeted with shouts of 'Long live the first republican.' National liberation had been achieved, now it was necessary to realize the goals of social justice and peasant rights. The surest way of achieving this was through the creation of a republic. Radić expressed at this meeting his belief that 'a spirit of republican freedom and peasant democracy' would eventually prevail in the National Council.[65] This may well have been an implicit reference to future elections on the basis of universal suffrage, which would, he was convinced, assuredly result in an overwhelming victory for the HPSS.

Clearly by the eve of Yugoslav unification, along with the immense chasm between the intellectuals and the peasant masses, the differences between Radić and the intellectuals were growing. At a public rally on 10 November in Ivanićgrad, Radić made reference to the need for a republic; he was in favour of a 'Yugoslav people's federal republic' modelled after the United States.[66] Radić began to chart a new course; republicanism would form the mast of the HPSS ship over the next six years. By November Radić was viewed by many as the main opponent to the National Council's headlong rush to unification with Serbia. On 20 November a group of students, officers, and sailors, predominantly Dalmatian Croats, demonstrated in front of the *Sabor* demanding that Radić be tried as a traitor for opposing unification. It has even been suggested that Pribićević, one of the National Council's vice-presidents, wanted to have Radić killed.[67]

Radić stood his ground in the face of growing enthusiasm for unification among Croatia's intellectuals. He remained true to his conviction that, although all Croats, Serbs, and Slovenes were one people from a linguistic and social perspective, Croatia's historic state right and political individuality had to be retained. The politicians of the National Council could 'work for a single state of Slovenes, Croats, and Serbs, but these people may do this insofar and inasmuch as this does not destroy our thousand-year-old Croatian state.' At a time when the Slovenes, Croats, and Serbs of the former Habsburg monarchy were finally achieving liberation 'in the Yugoslav framework and on the basis of Yugoslav *narodno jedinstvo*,' it would be 'a true scandal' for the Croats, 'supposedly for the sake of that framework and for the sake of that unity, to destroy our Croatian state.' If the Serbs of Serbia and Montenegro wanted to erase their state identities in order to unify with the remaining Serbs and the Croats and Slovenes, and thus to create a new state without internal frontiers, Radić argued that the Croats could not and should not agree to such a move. What the Croats wanted, he argued, was 'to have a single Yugoslav or Sloveno–Croato–Serb state for the outside world [*prema vani*], but at the same time we want further to maintain our internal Croatian state border.' This Croatian state would be organized on the basis of peasant right and Wilsonian principles, that is, on the right of national self-determination.

Radić clearly feared that the Serbs, having emerged as victors in the conflict, would come to dominate a unitary Yugoslav state. Radić also alluded to Serbia's prewar political instability and the lack of constitutionalism, most clearly epitomized by the 1903 coup in Belgrade. That is why 'in the name of *narodno jedinstvo* and brotherhood, in the name of humane and Christian justice and freedom, and in the name of healthy reason, and on the foundation of the thousand-year-old Croatian national and state right we say: We Croats want our own Croatian state within the Yugoslav unity.'[68] Since Radić always saw *narodno jedinstvo* as a means for the liberation and unification of the Croat lands, it was only natural that he would oppose any trend that undermined that liberty and unity. After Croatia–Slavonia's official break with the Habsburg monarchy, liberation was achieved and Magyar domination was ended, and it was criminal, at least in Radić's eyes, for Croatia's intellectuals to sacrifice this achievement in a thoughtless and speedy unification with Serbia.

Radić's criticisms and warnings went unheeded. On 24–25 November the HPSS held a session of its Main Assembly, attended by over 2,800 party workers, to discuss the party's policies in light of the rapidly changing situation.[69] The HPSS called for the implementation of peasant right and demanded that Croatian state individuality be preserved. Croatia had to become a people's republic, and there was little doubt that the peasants wanted anything other than a republic. This Croatian republican peasant state could eventually join a wider, loosely organized Yugoslav union. The HPSS even spoke in grandiose terms of the need to create 'a great Slavic republican union' with the Czechs and Poles. Radić railed against the politicians of the National Council in uncompromising terms, for they 'are fanatics, fools, and selfish people.' Croat politicians should have worked 'to gather the Slovenes here, to reunite Dalmatia [with Croatia], they could have brought Bosnia and Herzegovina into a union with Zagreb, and we would have proclaimed a Croatian state that would form a union with brotherly Serbia.' But this new union had to be based on equality and not on the negation of national and political individualities. Radić again demanded a republic, for he believed that a republican wave was engulfing the Croat countryside, and raised the possibility of seeking the support of Woodrow Wilson to guaranty the Croats' right to a state. He believed that the HPSS would receive two-thirds of the vote to a Croatian constituent assembly and would then proclaim a republic.

The other speakers at the General Assembly merely restated Radić's views. One party delegate attacked the idea of a unitary state and opposed the invitation extended by the National Council to the Serbian army to restore order in the Croatian countryside, which was in an open revolt against the city. The Serbian army 'will be used for political ends on the orders of some of our domestic people, who have taken over policy in their hands.' Benjamin Šuperina, a member of the HPSS's Main Committee, was even more categorical. The politicians of the National Council 'say that the rifle-butt of the Serbian soldier has opened the doors to our freedom. Have not our people suffered through the centuries in the struggle for their freedom? How can they spit on their own people? The Croat gentlemen are spitting on the Croat name ... the Serbs are sufferers, the Serbs are conscious, the Serbs are everything, but we are nothing. This treatment is undeserving. Why bring forth shame on one's own people? And these people, who have contempt for their own nation, want to lead us? They invited the Serbian army and want to force a Serbian king on us. Even if the Serbian king is proclaimed, the Croat people will remain republicans.'[70]

This was the typical sentiment running through the party's ranks. The lines were now drawn. The HPSS issued a number of resolutions condemning the Italian penetration into the Croat lands (Istria, Dalmatia) and calling for the implementation of peasant rights according to the party's program. It also denounced the diminution of the Croatian state's independence at a time when it had just been achieved. It blamed the Croat political élite's 'fanaticism' for Yugoslav *narodno jedinstvo* for this state of affairs. The HPSS also issued a resolution calling for a 'Yugoslav people's federal republic' that would include the Bulgars. Finally, the HPSS called for closer cultural and economic cooperation with the Czechoslovak and Polish republics and expressed the hope that 'an entirely democratic and pacifistic Slavic Union' might eventually be created.[71] The party also decided to launch a new daily paper, *Republika (The Republic)*, but this never materialized.[72] Just days after this session of the HPSS's Main Assembly, Radić left again for Prague in a final attempt to win Czech politicians over to the idea that a new union should be created out of the defunct monarchy, but was rebuffed.[73] Nothing that the HPSS did could stem the tide of Yugoslav unitarist sentiment that prevailed among the politicians of the National Council.

The movement towards Yugoslav unification occurred against the background of growing rural disturbances from the end of October through to December 1918. These disturbances, which encompassed much of Croatia–Slavonia, were initiated by the local peasantry and armed bands of the so-called Green Cadre, military deserters who returned to their villages to work the land. Armed, and thus dangerous, they grew in number in the course of 1918, perhaps to as many as 200,000 men, to the point where they formed 'an incipient social movement.'[74] Attacking and pillaging smaller towns, manors, and estates, including those belonging to both the Catholic and Orthodox churches, these armed bands made the Croatian countryside virtually ungovernable for two months; a local official from Našice (Slavonia) spoke of 'great rebellions and terrible days.'[75] The authorities were almost completely helpless. Although many of these armed bands were simply interested in looting, the 'green' movement did manifest political overtones.

The peasant disturbances demonstrated all too well that the peasants believed that the politicians of the National Council did not represent their social and political interests. Just as important, the disturbances revealed that the peasantry did not share the Yugoslav unitarist ideals of Croatia's middle-class intellectuals.[76] For the peasantry the monarchy's collapse meant liberation, or in other words, freedom from the hated bureaucrats, landlords, and merchants, whom they saw as oppressors, and a redistribution of land, particularly in Slavonia with its many latifundia. A typical example of this peasant animosity was provided on 27 November, when peasants from around the town of Ogulin (Lika region) sent a message to the National Council in Zagreb demanding that their local national council be reorganized. They bluntly stated: 'We do not need capitalists and those people who always stood against the people's will, and who provoked the Green Cadre against themselves, to fight on our behalf,' for they did not have any faith in these politicians. They wanted representatives whom they could trust and who were from among the people. 'The gentlemen are separating themselves [from the people],' they concluded their message, 'and do not ask the people anything, they only command. Everyone says that this is the same violent regime as the one we had under the Magyars, hitherto we were slaves of Magyardom, and now we are slaves precisely of those [gentlemen] who oppressed the people even worse than the Magyars.' The peasants were being ignored 'because these gentlemen are thinking [to themselves] that they [the peasants] are our servants and rabble [*fukare*].'[77] But the politicians in Zagreb could not fulfil the peasantry's demands, nor did they intend to, for they were committed to maintaining the administration, and the bureaucrats who staffed it, to preserve order until unification was complete. The divergence of opinion between Croatia's middle-class intellectuals and the peasantry was painfully obvious. In 1918 the chasm that separated the two worlds was indeed great.

To the intellectuals in Zagreb and much of the provincial élite in the smaller towns, the rural disturbances were the result of peasant ignorance about 'the great task at hand,' which is to say, Yugoslav unification; they proposed 'iron discipline' to remedy the situation.[78] The problem was that they had no means of imposing, let alone enforcing, such discipline. One official from Vinkovci (Slavonia) wrote on 3 November that 'all around the sky is red from arson' and that 'the character of the revolution [*sic*] is social.' He noted that whenever some provocateur, 'particularly a prisoner [of war] from Russia,' appeared in a local village the peasants 'burn and loot.' An official in Donji Miholjac (Slavonia) reported that 'the Green Cadre has destroyed everything.' One of the desperate leaders of a local council in Okučani (Slavonia) reported to the National Council in Zagreb on 4 November that to restore order he would 'have to hang the whole locality.' Yet another official reported that same day that 'the peasants are saying that they can do as they please, because now there is freedom.' He pleaded with the authorities in Zagreb to send military assistance. On 5 November the same official spoke of 'frightful circumstances' in his district.[79]

The National Council could not even rely on the local militia (*Narodna straža*), which was organized by municipal and village committees, because in many areas the militias were composed of peasants who had taken part in the disturbances.[80] On 25 November an official from Garešnica (Slavonia) urged the authorities in Zagreb not to establish any more militias in his district 'because the populace here is infected by Bolshevism.' Four days later an official from Vrbanja (Slavonia) reported that the local militia had to be dispersed because 'it began to spread Bolshevism.'[81] Given the widespread disorder and the inability of the National Council or its local councils to stem the tide, Croatia's political élite came to see Serbian military intervention as the only solution. As one official of a local council in Slatina (Slavonia) noted on 6 November: 'The people are in revolt, total disorganization prevails. Only the Entente's army, moreover only the Serbian army, can restore order. The people are burning and destroying ... The mob is now looting the merchants, because all the landed estates have already been destroyed. Private fortunes are destroyed. The Serbian army is the only salvation.' This was repeated on 7 November by the prefect of Požega county, who urged that 'some Serbians come here as soon as possible to restore order. With respect to military assistance, the situation is very urgent and the quickest assistance is needed because everyone is afraid for their own safety.' The same official indicated two days later that he was 'gladly awaiting' the arrival of Serbian troops, which he repeated on 12 November.[82] The move towards unification was intensified under the impact of the rural unrest.

These disturbances continued throughout November and well into the next month. In mid-November the leader of the local council in Pregrada (Slavonia) reported to Zagreb that at a recent mass assembly the peasants began to deride and taunt the 'gentlemen.' They were in an uproar upon hearing of the imposition of martial law in the district, 'which the gentlemen devised in fear for their own skin and declared against the peasants.' It is not surprising that the worst devastation occurred in eastern Slavonia with its multitude of great estates. The prefect of Virovitica county reported to Zagreb on 14 November of the recent 'days of revolution.' The town of Osijek had just barely been saved from 'general pillaging.' The rebellion had 'encompassed the entire territory of Virovitica county, spreading partly from the county of Požega where a few days earlier there occurred very serious revolutionary events.' Virtually the entire county had fallen victim to peasant mobs and the Green Cadre. His colleague from Požega reported on 17 November that it would take much effort to bring the peasants 'to their senses,' and he noted the 'sad fact' that they 'refuse to till their fields, because they are saying "we have enough for ourselves, let the gentlemen die."'[83] These sentiments were typical in the Croat countryside of 1918, and they are hardly surprising. In early December 1918, just six days after Yugoslav unification, an official in Osijek ascertained 'that peace and order are being imposed most often by people who are either direct or indirect agents of great landlords.' Unfortunately, in the process of establishing order 'the peasant is beaten and robbed.' He concluded that the peasants 'are dreadfully agitated, and if these violent measures, in the name of the state, do not cease, things will soon be worse than they were.'[84]

The politicians in Zagreb eventually concluded that the disturbances were political and became anxious about the revolutionary character of the unrest. They also realized that their policies had little support in the countryside. The intelligentsia was, as one official in Daruvar (Slavonia) noted, 'the only foothold of our new state.'[85] Another official, from Donja Stubica (Slavonia), reported on 9 December that 'the whole populace, with honourable exceptions, is for a republic.'[86] Indeed, peasant 'republics' were proclaimed in a number of places in eastern Slavonia, such as Donji Miholjac, Petrijevci, and Feričanci. Many officials suspected that Radić and the HPSS had a hand in the disturbances. An official from Ludbreg (Zagorje) reported on 10 November that the local peasants were 'excited' by a recent speech Radić had given in the area. Soldiers were refusing to return to their units. Radić had held a mass rally in Koprivnica two weeks earlier and since then over 800 soldiers had deserted from the unit stationed in the district. 'In those places where there are followers of Radić,' the official concluded his report, 'there is noticeable a powerful animosity towards *kaputaši*.'[87] But there is little evidence to suggest that Radić and the HPSS central leadership had any involvement in promoting peasant disturbance. They would shortly benefit from the growing radicalism of the peasants, however.

In actual fact Radić initially defended the National Council and urged the peasants not to view this institution as the protector of war profiteers but as the defender of 'our young national freedom.'[88] This soon changed. By the end of November 1918 Radić was much more hostile to the National Council and its handling of the peasant disturbances. 'We protest against what is being said in the National Council,' Radić told the HPSS's Main Assembly on 25 November, 'that our peasant people are a herd, beasts, that the army should be sent against them from all sides ... remove the cause of the dissatisfaction and there will be peace.' The politicians of the National Council would achieve nothing by force: 'Violence will create fear and not peace. Do not keep the people in fear. They accuse me of provoking the disturbances. This is an insinuation ... [and] a shameful lie.' Stjepan Uroić, one of the party's local activists, investigated the causes of the rural unrest and informed the Main Assembly that innocent peasants had been killed because of their supposed involvement in the Green Cadre. He blamed the corrupt district bureaucrats and 'usurious Jews' for the disturbances and called for a purge of the administration, a 'just' land redistribution, and measures against war profiteers. He concluded that the peasants had no trust in the National Council and would not as long as the administration remained as it had hitherto been.[89]

In the autumn of 1918 Radić believed that the prevailing conditions would finally bring about the realization of the peasantry's right to social and economic freedom. Moreover, the collapse of the monarchy, although it was long a fixture in Radić's thinking, had seemingly paved the way to the realization of national liberation. National and social issues, always closely tied, became intricately interwoven in the context of Habsburg dénouement in 1918. When the peasants of Croatia manifested their preparedness to act on their realization that liberation was at hand, this was initially interpreted by Croatia's political élite as simple plundering. Even when the political ramifications of these peasant disturbances were acknowledged, republicanism was dismissed as inappropriate. One Croat member of the National Council, Fran Barac, suggested in early November that, with such a large population of rural illiterates, the South Slavs were not ready for a republic. In light of the rural unrest, what was needed immediately was 'a strong hand, a dictatorship,' and he cited the wartime role of the Karadjordjević dynasty, which had fought for the freedom of all Serbs, Croats, and Slovenes. Pribićević also spoke of the need for the National Council to assume 'the central authority with dictatorial powers.'[90] For Radić the growing rural republican tide of 1918 demonstrated not only the traditional peasant hostility towards the urban politicians and the bureaucrats, but also opposition to their unitarist Yugoslavism. This of course overlapped with his long-established views on this issue. In no way was Radić prepared to abandon Croat political individuality for the sake of unification. As Croatia's intellectuals rushed towards unification, Radić and the peasantry resisted the process. This was to set the stage for the political struggle of the next half-decade. In the process, Croatia's middle-class political and intellectual élite, confronted by 'the revolt of the (republican) masses,' was swept aside and relegated to a position of political impotence. The HPSS, or 'the party of Radić,' as many called it, would soon come of age.

Radić, who argued that he did not lead the peasants but merely listened to what peasants wanted and 'guessed the people's thoughts,' saw himself as an interpreter of the people's will. He was incontrovertibly closer to the Croat peasant than any other politician in Croatia in 1918. The 'gentlemen' had to recognize that the peasantry formed the overwhelming majority of the Croat nation. The spirit of the times demanded no less of them. 'Today a leader is not a ruler of the people,' Radić wrote weeks after the unification, 'but a herald of the people's wishes, an executor of the people's will.'[91]

At the time of unification the peasantry seemed to be decidedly republican, a result of the wartime economic exactions and the influence of the revolutionary events in Russia. This had a decisive impact on Radić's thinking, as did the fact that the new Czechoslovak and Polish states, not to mention Russia, were also republics. Opposed all along to the hastily conducted process of unification and the unitarist implications of the prevailing variant of *narodno jedinstvo*, the rural republican tide only strengthened and reaffirmed his opposition. National liberation had been achieved, and now the time had come for the peasant majority to create a peasant state and to implement peasant rights. That is why the HPSS demanded a Croatian constituent assembly at the end of December 1918 on the basis of the principle of national self-determination.[92] But as opposed as Radić and the HPSS were to the nature of unification, they did not exclude altogether the possibility of a Yugoslav state. In late December 1918 the HPSS called for the creation of a federal Yugoslav republic, but warned that 'violent centralism is against today's natural and social laws,

[and] could soon provoke dissatisfaction among the Croats and Slovenes.'[93] That is precisely what happened.

Just days after the unification, on 5 December 1918, a group of over 100 largely unarmed Croat soldiers from the 25th and 53rd infantry regiments of the former Austro-Hungarian army, stationed in Zagreb, marched through the streets. As they made their way to the centre of the city, they shouted 'Long live the Republic,' 'Long live Radić,' and 'Down with King Petar.' When they reached the city centre, they were confronted by a well-armed unit of mounted police. In the scuffle that ensued, over a dozen soldiers were killed and nearly twice as many wounded.[94] Almost immediately 'preventative' censorship was imposed and an investigation, followed by arrests, was launched against the participants. It was an inauspicious beginning to a seemingly auspicious enterprise.

6

The Neutral Croat Peasant Republic and the Politics of National Mobilization, 1918–1925

Yes, we enacted the Constitution without agreement with you [Croats], even against your will, but we did this for higher state need and necessity.

Lazar Marković, 1921

The Serbian Ministers realise at the back of their minds that Radic [*sic*] and the other Federalists are really right in esteeming that the Serbians intend to be the dominant partner in the Jugoslav concern. Dr Laza Markovic [*sic*], the Minister of Justice, was telling me how they have endeavoured to convince Radic of the power he would have, with his band of seventy followers (to whose docility M Markovic referred with envy), in the Parliament and the advantages which he would be able to extract for his constituencies. I asked him whether, if Radic with the other groups from the new provinces were to command a majority and claim the administrative power, the Serbs would really tolerate this subordination. M Markovic only smiled. The Serbians, in the last resort, refer to the Croats and Slovenes as being, in effect, defeated parties liberated by the Serbians, who, having paid the piper, are entitled to call the tune.

Sir Alban Young, British Minister to Belgrade, to Marquess Curzon, 1923

Nikola [Pašić] the Serbian, he never knew how to distinguish between the limits of his power and the limits of his luck; he never knew where one ended and the other began. Especially in the World War, the luck of Nikola Pašić far outran his power and that of his little statelet. He wanted to create a Great Serbian state but in the meantime fate, his luck, this is that element of tragedy, brought him something much greater, it brought him the Kingdom of Serbs, Croats and Slovenes, it brought him a work in front of which he paused, astounded, not understanding either this work or the new laws of its life.

Sekula Drljević, 1927

The Postwar Setting: Political Parties and National Ideologies

After the First World War the seemingly innocuous HPSS of Stjepan Radić became the only significant political party in Croatia. The introduction of universal manhood suffrage and the party's republican platform, which overlapped with the sentiments of the Croat village, helped to transform the HPSS from a relatively insignificant outsider into a national mass movement that gradually penetrated every village and eventually commanded the loyalty of 80 per cent of the Croat populace. In the process the peasant movement overwhelmed the dominant prewar Croat parties. The HPSS transformation into a mass movement made it, by 1923, the second largest party in the Kingdom of Serbs, Croats, and Slovenes, commonly referred to as Yugoslavia. The importance of 'the party of Radić,' as many called it, can in no way be doubted, nor can an understanding of the formative years of the first Yugoslav state be achieved without an analysis of Radić's policies. The cornerstone of his policy, at least until 1925, was peasant republicanism, a demand for a neutral Croat peasant republic. This necessarily meant opposing unification, which had taken a monarchical and unitarist form and thus violated the republican aspirations of the Croat peasant and the principle of national self-determination.

In the aftermath of the Great War, republicanism was an attractive idea for the peasantry. It represented freedom, above all liberation from conscription, taxation, usury, requisitioning – everything which the peasant associated with the city – from the bourgeois élite, the dreaded bureaucrats and the *kaputaši*. But this was only part of the attraction of republicanism. Liberation brought new empowerment: the 'Neutral Croat Peasant Republic' was to be a peasant state in every sense of that term, in which the peasant majority would determine and resolve all issues, a plebiscitary democracy that gave full voice to the village. In this sense it represented liberation from the city and the *kaputaš*. The people, that is, the peasantry, would be truly sovereign. They would have the right to determine the form of administration from the lowest level of state organization and exercise power directly. As the external pressures of the new monarchical state increased – a state that perpetuated many old, and imposed many new, burdens that the peasants detested, and that denied their national individuality – peasant social and political cohesion intensified and coalesced around Radić's party. It was in this context that Radić's central concepts of peasant state and peasant right came to acquire tremendous appeal in the Croat countryside, for they served not only as ends in themselves, but as powerful slogans that were used to mobilize the peasantry into a mass movement. Under the post-1918 circumstances, the peasant state could only be achieved at the expense of Belgrade; hence, social and national objectives became inextricably intertwined. In the context of its struggle against Belgrade between 1918 and 1925 for a Croatian peasant republic, the HPSS facilitated the completion of the process of Croat national integration.

The republican appeal was even more attractive in light of the fact that the first two years of the new kingdom's existence were disastrous in political terms.[1] The elections to the Constituent Assembly, which was to determine the form of government and draw up a constitution, did not occur until November 1920. From December 1918 until these elections the prewar Serbian bureaucratic system was implemented throughout the new state and rigorously enforced. A popular conviction soon arose among the Croat peasants that the new bureaucracy, and the state it served, were markedly worse than their predecessors. As part of the process of centralization of all authority in Belgrade it was necessary effectively to destroy the vestiges of Croat political individuality. This task fell to the Croatian Serb leader Svetozar Pribićević, who, as Minister of Internal Affairs from December 1918 to February 1920, implemented what at times appeared to be a dictatorial regime in Croatia and Bosnia–Herzegovina, but less so in Slovenia and Dalmatia, where support for the new state was stronger. In February 1919 Pribićević expanded the Serb gendarmerie, formed the previous month under the control of the Serbian military establishment, to 12,000, to enforce the central government's directives and maintain order.[2] In late October 1919 he proposed a further increase of 2,000 gendarmes which was approved by the government in Belgrade.[3] Since the Serbian army had a well-organized command and had been untouched by the revolutionary disturbances of 1918, it was increasingly relied upon by Belgrade to preserve order in the former Habsburg lands. In August 1919 French military intelligence reported that Belgrade 'believes the unification of the three nations [Serbs, Croats, Slovenes] can be achieved by employing the old diplomatic doctrine of the forceful elimination of [national] differences and the subjection of the Croats and Slovenes to the Serbian supreme authority.' 'Serbian troops are employed to maintain order in Croatia,' the report concluded, 'which would not be necessary if the project of Serbianization did not exist. The Serbian police serves only to enhance the oppression of the Croats, oppression which is little different from the former Hungarian oppression.' Citing a recent clash in Maribor (Slovenia) between Slovene deserters and Serbian troops, French military intelligence concluded that a larger and potentially bloodier crisis was looming in Croatia.[4]

The HPSS, which formally became the Croat Republican Peasant Party (henceforth referred to as HRSS, *Hrvatska republikanska seljačka stranka*) in December 1920, emerged after 1918 as both a rural social movement expressing the collective will of the Croat peasantry and a national movement predicated on the peasantry's desire to preserve and affirm its national individuality. Its national ideology differed considerably from that of the two major Serbian political parties, the National Radical Party (NRS, *Narodna radikalna stranka*) of Nikola Pašić and the Democratic Party (DS, *Demokratska stranka*) of Ljubomir (Ljuba) Davidović, although the Democrats attracted many non-Serb unitarists. The NRS was essentially the party of the Serbian establishment (middle class, bureaucracy, army) and pursued a Great Serbian policy: it wished to maintain Serbia's preeminence and to expunge non-Serb identities within the new state. State centralism was seen as the most effective way of doing this and of preserving the recently obtained unity of all Serbs. Although the Radicals' base was prewar Serbia, they had substantial support in Srijem and Vojvodina, where the Serb Radical Party of prewar Hungary and Croatia–Slavonia merged with the Serbian Radicals, and established a solid base of support among Bosnia–Herzegovina's Serbs.

In their national ideology the Radicals clung to Vuk Karadžić's notion of linguistic Serbianism, although they also assumed that, at least in Bosnia and Croatia, all Orthodox were Serbs. Most of their leaders, like Pašić, Stojan Protić, Ljuba Jovanović, and Lazar Marković, believed that the Štokavian dialect was Serbian alone. To the extent that Croats existed at all, they were confined to the Kajkavian-speaking regions of Zagreb, but once they too adopted Štokavian as their literary language, they would simply become Serbs. In this respect there was a powerful assimilationist strain in the Radical national ideology, for they believed that centralism would eventually result in the Serbianization of the non-Serbs, particularly the Croats and Bosnian Muslims. It is therefore not surprising that the Radicals, with few exceptions, rejected as artificial the historical provinces of the new Yugoslavia. When in 1918 one British supporter of Yugoslavia told Pašić that it would be best for Serbia to respect the historic individualities of the other constituent parts of the country, especially Croatia's, a visibly upset Pašić retorted that 'the Kingdom of Croatia–Slavonia–Dalmatia had been created by Austria against Serbia.'[5]

Even a cursory reading of the NRS press reveals that party's adulation of the state as an entity unto itself, and the need to protect it virtually at any cost. The NRS could not abandon centralist principles, because 'these principles are the postulate of our state strength.' Moreover, as a predominantly Serb party 'it cannot adopt a viewpoint that would be repugnant to the Serb part of our nation.'[6] The Serbs were, quite simply, 'centralists from conviction, centralists from experience.' The Serbian state's evolution was instructive, the NRS claimed, for before 1918 centralism gave Serbia 'that which is most important: one will and one strength.' The non-Serbs who opposed centralism were pursuing a path of 'individualist regional wishes and individualist tribal

TABLE 6.1
Main political parties in Yugoslavia (1918–1928), their national affiliation, and position on state organization

Party	Position on state organization	National affiliation
National Radical Party (NRS)	Centralist; Great Serbian	Serb
Democratic Party (DS)	Centralist; trinomial Yugoslav nation	Predominantly Serb; some Croat and Slovene unitarists
Independent Democratic Party (SDS), founded 1924	Centralist, after 1927 autonomist; trinomial Yugoslav nation	Croatian Serb; some Croat and Slovene unitarists
Alliance of Agrarian Workers (SZ)	Centralist	Predominantly Serb; some Slovenes
Croat (People's/Republican) Peasant Party (H(P/R)SS)	Anti-centralist; confederalism	Croat
Communist Party of Yugoslavia (KPJ)	Centralist; after 1924 federalism	All national groups
Slovene People's Party (SLS)	Autonomist; sought local autonomy	Slovene; cooperated with Croat clericalists (Croat People's Party)
Yugoslav Muslim Organization (JMO)	Autonomist; sought local autonomy	Bosnian Muslim
Croat Union (HZ)	Autonomist; confederalism after 1924	Croat, largely urban
Džemijet (Cemiyet)	Autonomist; sought local (cultural) autonomy	Slav Muslims (Sandžak region), Turkish minority, and Albanians

Note: Refer to Table 6.2 for electoral support in November 1920.

demands [that] do not lead to the true aim,' namely, the state's consolidation.[7] By contesting centralism the non-Serbs were also opposing 'healthy unity and a modern organization of our state.' The NRS would protect a strong central-ized state, because the state was 'costlier than everything else and dearer than everything else. It is the idol which we served, which we serve, and which we will serve to the last breath.'[8] These remarks obviously begged the question of whether the NRS regarded the new state merely as an extension of Serbia or as a new state requiring a markedly different system of governance. On this mat-ter the NRS left no doubt. Radić and other foes of centralism were cautioned that 'they cannot force us to forget our obligations to the state, in whose foun-dations are included mostly Serb blood, Serb bones, and Serb sweat.' Under a centralized state system Croats and Slovenes would be perfectly equal to Serbs before the law, and 'this must be enough for them.' Anything more than that would be 'unjustified.'[9]

The DS was a party of *narodno jedinstvo* (national oneness), but it too pur-sued a policy of state centralism. The DS was a heterogeneous party, com-posed of very diverse elements including Radical dissidents and others from Serbia, the Serb wing of the prewar HSK, and some Slovene and Croat uni-tarists. It argued that there was only one, trinomial Yugoslav nation composed of the Serb, Croat, and Slovene 'tribes.' Whereas the Radicals believed cen-tralism would lead to the assimilation of the non-Serbs, the Democrats were convinced that the end result would be a hybrid Yugoslav nationality. Like the Radicals they rejected Yugoslavia's historical provinces as artificial, but for different reasons. For the Radicals these provinces not only limited Serbia's borders but might hinder the assimilationist march of Serb national identity. The Democrats, conversely, believed these provinces only heightened the tribal divisions within the new Yugoslav nationality, instead of nurturing its 'oneness.' Consequently they opposed all political movements, such as Radić's, that aspired to preserve these political–historical divisions. Federal-ism was rejected as dangerous, for it would only weaken state unity and foment anarchy, thus opening the door to foreign intervention on the part of Yugoslavia's rapaciously revisionist neighbours.

That explains why the HRSS was immediately identified as the main anti-state political element in the country, although few unitarists realized the party's real strength until the 1920 elections. Radić was attacked in the uni-tarist press in violent and uncompromising terms. 'This old political adven-turer,' commented one unitarist paper, 'is working entirely according to the Italian plan for Italian interests ... That there can be no talk of some internal conviction, however mad, in his work is clear. His past and the complete unat-tainability of his supposed aims demonstrate this. "The Croat republic" is unrealizable because the Croats do not want it ... That is why the darkest elements are now gathering around him.'[10] Such attacks were not isolated: 'We knew him since long ago, the gypsy blood, which seethes in his veins, drove him in the early days to wild leaps, to acts of villainy, to the most perverse eccentricities. At that time we held him to be insane. We fooled ourselves: what he does – he does deliberately. He will today, with criminal intent, proclaim a republic, and tomorrow he will like a hyena slink back among the enemies of our freedom, show them all of our most sensitive places and invite them to destroy our kingdom and slaughter us alive.'[11] Another author argued that Radić had no program other than to become the dictator of Croatia by first 'hypnotizing' the peasants and then sowing 'old tribal hatreds' to further his own ends: 'His republicanism is a vulgar political manipulation. If this state were a republic, he would probably be a Habsburgist-monarchist.'[12]

These views were in keeping with those of the Democrats' two luminaries, Davidović and Pribićević, at least in the immediate postwar period (1919–1922). Gradually, however, Davidović's Serbian-based wing of the party indicated a willingness to consider some reform of the political system, whereas Pribićević's predominantly Croatian Serb wing resisted any change to the centralized state system. Whereas Davidović hoped to displace the NRS in Serbia, Pribićević was prepared to cooperate with the NRS to preserve the state system. Despite these internal fissures, the DS enjoyed the support of many intellectuals of Yugoslav unitarist persuasion, particularly those around the influential Zagreb-based journal *Nova Evropa* (*New Europe*) of Milan Čurčin and the newspaper *Slobodna tribuna* (*Free Tribune*).[13] Whatever the differences in principle between the NRS and DS in the early postwar period, in practice both sought a centralized state order, which is why they formed a coalition government in the state's critical early years, from January 1921 to December 1922.

The Communist Party of Yugoslavia (KPJ, *Komunistička partija Jugoslavije*) also supported a centralized state system in the immediate postwar years, which meant that with respect to the national question, the KPJ and HRSS stood at opposite poles.[14] The dedication of the KPJ's following to Yugoslav unitarism had diverse origins. Among the socialists of the former Habsburg lands this commitment was a product of their espousal of the formula of *narodno jedinstvo* in the pre-1918 period. Serbian socialists adopted *narodno jedinstvo* more out of expediency. Given prewar Serbia's homogeneous national character, these socialists saw no need to develop supranational formulas such as *narodno jedinstvo*. But since the socialists of the former Habsburg lands supported this principle, and because the unification of 1918 appeared to have won a broad acceptance, Serbian socialists came to accept it as well. In practice the *narodno jedinstvo* of Yugoslavia's socialists differed little, if at all, from the variant espoused by the 'bourgeois' Democratic Party; its common denominator was a disavowal of all national and historic individualities among the South Slavs. Socialists propagated the theory of a Yugoslav trinomial nation, and thus emerged as defenders of centralism in the immediate post-unification era. The KPJ's support of centralism was an important, although hardly the only, bone of contention between it and Radić's party.[15]

After the KPJ was banned in August 1921,[16] the party began to re-examine its position on the national question. This process engendered a series of factional disputes, with the left faction associated with federalism and the right with anti-federalism. In spite of these internal differences, there was a consensus among the Yugoslav communists that the HRSS was in essence a (petit) bourgeois party which, like other peasant parties, was formed 'to serve the bourgeoisie, its government and order.'[17] Nonetheless, the left faction, although hardly sympathetic to Radić's ideas and policies, was prepared to acknowledge that the HRSS had 'become the representative of the whole Croat people in the full sense of that word, because it expressed pronounced and sharp resistance to the policy of Serb centralism.'[18]

The KPJ's growing realization of the importance of the national question culminated in its Resolution on the National Question, issued at its Third Landed Conference (January 1924) in Belgrade. The document was an important victory for the left faction. Although it asserted that the 1918 unification was a step 'in the direction of historical progress and the interests of the class struggle of the proletariat,' it directed the KPJ to adopt federalism as part of its political platform. What is more, the resolution acknowledged the right of each nation to secession and the creation of its own state. For unification to fulfil its historical mission, the Yugoslav state had to be organized 'on the basis of a voluntary union and on the total equality of all of its parts, which hitherto was not the case.' Since unification had been carried out by the bourgeoisie in a monarchist form and for its own class interests, and then usurped by the Serbian bourgeoisie, the process of the formation of one Yugoslav nation was halted and national differences intensified. The KPJ argued, therefore, that the proletariat had to assist 'the struggle of the peasant masses and exploited nations,' and tie these movements to the general struggle against capitalism.[19]

The KPJ's resolution on the agrarian question in Yugoslavia, also issued at the January 1924 conference, was closely related to the resolution on the national question. Although the HRSS was denounced in this document as a bourgeois party and for weakening the revolutionary potential of the peasantry with its pacifist policy, the KPJ affirmed that the proletariat had to join its struggle against capitalism with the peasant-based national movements.[20] Taken together, the KPJ's resolutions on the national and agrarian questions represented a significant departure from the party's earlier espousal of *narodno jedinstvo*. The KPJ now had to forge ties with the likes of Radić's peasant movement, while at the same time working to liberate it from the influence of the bourgeoisie.

Censured by unitarist elements for his opposition to the new state, Radić was attacked also by the Yugoslav Left. For the Yugoslav Social Democrats and communists alike, Radić's peasantist program was bourgeois and reactionary to the core, offering no viable solutions to the ills that plagued Croatian (and Yugoslav) society. Conceptually his peasant republic, resting on the flawed notion that the peasantry constituted a unitary class, was no more than a copy of the existing social order. As such, this republic 'is like Noah's ark, in which Mr Radić and his assistants think that they can transport ... from the flood to more peaceful times all of the valuables that are a document of our smallness.'[21] The republic would be a museum, a repository of all that was odious and that the people held in contempt: the cross and the tricolour, the bureaucracy and private property. The HRSS's resistance to the nationalization of the large estates was ample proof of its bourgeois character and its perfunctory commitment to social justice.[22] Representing as it did the interests of the Croat kulaks, the HRSS's eventual alliance with the 'bourgeois' Croat Union, in the form of the Croat Bloc (1921–4), gave the party an even more decidedly bourgeois character. In this respect, Radić was becoming a major obstacle to the resolution of the national and peasant questions, both of which could ultimately only be solved through class revolution.[23] Be that as it may, between 1919 and 1924 the KPJ's views on the Yugoslav state underwent serious change.

In addition to the two major Serbian parties and the KPJ, the HRSS also opposed the policies of the Croat centralists, particularly the Croat Union (HZ, *Hrvatska zajednica*), formed in July 1919 and composed of the Croat segments of the prewar HSK and Starčević's Party of Right.[24] The spokesman of Croatia's middle classes and a significant segment of the Croat intelligentsia, the Croat Union supported 'the national and state oneness of all Serbs, Croats, and Slovenes,' as well as 'the gradual levelling of all tribal and confessional differences on the basis of equality.' It rejected 'any kind of privileges or authority for one tribe or tribal name at the expense of the others, or one region at the expense of another.' Though it recognized the principle of *narodno jedinstvo*, it sought respect of local tribal differences. Regional autonomies were in the interest of the new Yugoslav state because 'they enable a natural transition from the existing divisions into a new state community,' and would also make the state more comprehensible to the broader peasant masses. The Croat Union initially pledged to work in all important issues together with other Serb and Slovene parties that supported its ideal: 'that our new Yugoslav state be a free home to all three tribes: the Serb, Croat, and Slovene, on the basis of brotherhood and complete equality.'[25] The Croat Union's reference to the Croat 'tribe' prompted condemnation from the HRSS. Josip Predavec, one of its key leaders, noted with some justification in late 1920 that 'after the revolution [*prevrata*, 1 December 1918] everyone in the city of Zagreb became a Yugoslav. The peasant world has remained Croat. Croats have become for our gentlemen a tribe.'[26] For the proponents of *narodno jedinstvo* Croats, and to be sure Serbs and Slovenes also, were merely a tribe (*pleme*) of the trinomial Yugoslav nation. The natural consequence of this idea was centralism, which necessarily meant eliminating the remnants of any historical identities, although the Croat Union certainly differed markedly from the Democrats in this matter. To assert national individuality in the context of the post-unification period meant, at least as far as the exponents of Yugoslav unitarism and *narodno jedinstvo* were concerned, undermining the new state and the liberation of this supposed trinomial nation that had been achieved in 1918.

The Croat Union's middle-class base proved to be a political liability, as did its early support of the new state and references to the Croat tribe, for they compromised its standing among the Croat peasantry. After the 1920 elections to the Constituent Assembly it had little choice but to link its political fate to Radić's party. The Croat Union was painfully aware of the fact that, as one of its local leaders noted on the eve of the 1923 elections, 'only Radić with his personage can demolish everything and unite everyone.' What he was demolishing was his Croat political opponents and thereby uniting all Croats under his own banner. Another party member, reporting on conditions in his district, observed that Croatia's Serbs were divided between the Radicals and Democrats, but that 'all Croats and non-Serbs will vote for the HRSS.'[27] It is therefore not surprising that the Croat Union decided in 1923 not to run any candidates against Radić and in November 1924 adopted a republican platform in deference to Radić's Croat peasant movement.

Of all the political parties in the new state, the HRSS was seemingly closest to the Frankists, who now operated under the name Croat Party of Right (HSP, *Hrvatska stranka prava*). Like the HRSS, the Frankists were opposed to the new state on the grounds that the unification violated Croatia's state right. Unlike the HRSS, however, the Frankists had a long anti-Serb pedigree. Days after the unification their party organ *Hrvatska* (*Croatia*) was banned, and in

March 1919 two of their most important leaders, Vladimir Prebeg and Josip Pazman, were arrested. Although the Frankists still commanded a following in petit bourgeois and intellectual circles, the introduction of universal manhood suffrage showed all too well that they lacked mass support in Croatia's socially dominant countryside.

The Frankists conceded Radić's control of the countryside, but they would not admit that his movement was capable of achieving Croat statehood. As one émigré Frankist observed, they were waging a struggle against 'Serb policy which with unbending consistency is working to destroy Croatdom.' Faced with such a threat, Croats under the leadership of the feeble and 'inconstant' Radić could never hope to defend, let alone to achieve, their own national goals.[28] The Frankist leadership would briefly cooperate with Radić in 1921–2 (as it had between 1913 and 1918), but turned much of its attention to its émigré leaders, like Ivica Frank, and various Croat, formerly Habsburg officers (Baron Stjepan Sarkotić, Stevo Duić, and others) who were courting foreign support for the Croat cause. In May 1919 the émigrés established the Croat Comité in Austria, which moved to Hungary the following year, to fight for the independence of a Great Croatian state. Given their own electoral weakness in Croatia, to elicit foreign support they often pretended to be agents of Radić. In short, the Frankists remained on the fringe of the Croat national movement in the 1920s, with no mass support, and eager to court whomever seemed prepared to back their party's Great Croatian program.

The Struggle against Belgrade, 1918–1925

Closely in touch with the peasantry, Radić could gauge the people's mood more effectively than any other Croat political figure at the time. Indeed, Radić possessed a remarkable grasp of the peasantry's psyche, and this ability was reinforced by the party's rural organization, at least in those areas where it was strong before the war, which enabled him to gain information about rural sentiment. Yet in some instances Radić was prone to confusing reality with his own perceptions about what the peasants wanted. For example, Radić repeatedly asserted after 1918 that the Croat peasantry had undergone what he termed a 'spiritual revolution,' which was more than just a change in public mood.[29] For Radić the Great War was clearly the central turning-point in the disposition of the collective will of the Croat peasantry, and this was a claim that the party's press and local leadership consistently emphasized. Referring to the experiences of the Croat peasant–soldiers during the Great War, particularly on the Russian front, he argued that 'the Croat peasant soul was awakened completely.'[30] But awakened to what? Before the war Radić acknowledged the 'cowardly' and insular nature of the Croat peasantry, but he clearly (and correctly) saw the new consciousness of the peasantry as a by-product of the horrors of the Great War, as well as the influence of the Russian Revolution. They had been aroused, he believed, to the need decidedly to act on behalf of their own social and national rights. 'There were more than 100,000 of our people in Russia [during the war],' Radić once said, 'and they saw what the greatest world revolution really was. They understood its spirit, namely, that a free peasantry be created. They supported this spirit of freedom, but they condemned the methods.'[31] Radić believed that Croat peasants had ascertained that there was perhaps no other solution in Russia, where the peasantry could not achieve its rights by other means, but rejected the same approach in Croatia. This proposition is questionable, for the Croat peasant disturbances of 1918 demonstrated that not all peasants condemned Russian methods. Nonetheless, Radić argued that the Croat peasant–soldiers returning from Russia did so as committed pacifists and republicans in the hope that they would find in Croatia a republic. What they found, however, was that 'a handful of gentlemen, without any consultation of the people ... proclaimed the Karadjordjević dynasty [as rulers of the state].' The Croat peasant people were now continuing along their republican path for 'an absolutely pacifist (neutral) state,' and against the 'centralism of Belgrade.'[32]

It was this new consciousness, or 'spiritual revolution,' to use Radić's words, that helped to facilitate the HRSS's transformation into a national mass movement. The party's advocacy of republicanism and concepts such as peasant state and peasant right, certainly helped it to attract peasant support. On the eve of the war the party probably did not have more than 15,000 members, but by 1921 it could boast of having over 2,000 local party organizations with approximately one million followers.[33] The party leadership claimed at the end of 1922, apparently after an exhaustive examination of its membership rolls and local organizations, that it had 1.483 million organized members. This figure was certainly an exaggeration of the party's actual size, for it included all members and sympathizers who reported to the party that they were of a 'peasant republican spirit and thought.'[34] The size of the party's actual membership was clearly lower. Though an exaggeration, it is nevertheless indicative of the immense popularity that the party acquired in the countryside. This is not to say that the HRSS had an effective and centralized party machinery. The evidence seems to indicate that there was no efficient centralized party apparatus, least of all in those areas where it achieved its first major gains. Nonetheless, the HRSS central leadership attempted to ensure the predominance of peasants in a leadership capacity in its local organizations. In December 1922 the central leadership instructed its local organizations that the president of each local party branch should be a 'meritorious' peasant. A gentleman (non-peasant) could only head a local organization under exceptional circumstances and if he had demonstrated over at least a two-year period that he supported the aims and tactics of the peasant movement. The party's main committee urged its local organizations to meet at least once monthly to deliberate over political and other issues and then to inform the central leadership about its activities. It also suggested that each organization establish a library or reading room where peasants could read the party's literature.[35] Thus, the party clearly sought to keep peasants in leadership roles, and in this respect it was largely successful.

Whereas republicanism was the defining characteristic of the Croat peasant movement's political platform to 1925, Radić's views about Croatia's status underwent some important changes in the same period. Radić is often regarded as the most active exponent of federalism in the 1918–25 era, but a reading of his correspondence reveals that he was in fact committed to outright independence (a neutral Croatian peasant republic) in 1919–20 and only gradually moved towards Yugoslav (con)federalism. It should be noted, as was argued in the last chapter, that Radić did not dismiss altogether the possibility of a Yugoslav state in October–November 1918. Before such a state could be formally proclaimed, however, he insisted that Croats had to be given the freedom to express their wishes in a Croatian constituent assembly that would negotiate the terms of Croatia's status within any new Yugoslav state. Moreover, Radić believed that this constituent assembly would proclaim a Croatian republic, which in reality would have made unification with the Serbian kingdom exceedingly difficult, and probably impossible. But after the unification, and with the extension of the Serbian state apparatus to Croatia, even Radić's references to a union on more equal terms disappeared. The fact that he was imprisoned only radicalized his own thinking; union with Serbia was out of the question. In 1919–20 there was virtually no thought of keeping Croatia, even as a republic, within a Yugoslav (con)federal state. Only when Radić realized that the statesmen assembled at the Paris Peace Conference would not act on behalf of the Croats did the party adopt a (con)federalist Yugoslav platform.

For Radić the proclamation of unification, and thus the creation of the Kingdom of Serbs, Croats, and Slovenes, amounted to an unconstitutional and undemocratic act that had been carried out by a handful of intellectuals. It was unconstitutional because it was never ratified by the Croatian *Sabor*, undemocratic because it was never authorized or subsequently approved by the Croat people. The act of 1 December 1918 was, in short, an 'oligarchical proclamation.'[36] Before the war Radić viewed the Serbian political establishment with great circumspection, for he believed this élite to be quintessentially corrupt and concerned only with Serbian territorial aggrandizement. He was now directly confronted with this same élite that viewed the Kingdom of Serbs, Croats, and Slovenes not as a new state, but rather an extension of the prewar Serbian kingdom. 'We Croats – and all of this sad "Yugoslav" people,' Radić wrote in June 1919, 'are threatened by a purely Magyaro–Turkish worsened system of administration.' The state would be organized 'in such a way, that we Croats will not make decisions. All of this in the name of oneness [*jedinstva*]!' That was why it was necessary 'that we Croats employ *all* means – except revolution – to gain complete power in Croatia as soon as possible.'[37]

Radić consequently jettisoned his prewar commitment to *narodno jedinstvo*, although this did not necessarily entail an abandonment of his Slavophile sympathies. In January 1919 he and his brother Antun, who died unexpectedly on 10 February, still claimed that all of the Slavs were, in the broadest possible sense, one people, but they did not agree with the view that this presupposed a unitary Yugoslav state among the southern Slavs.[38] And in February 1921 the HRSS's deputies, in a message to the Prince-Regent Aleksandar, admitted that all Slavs 'are not only a linguistic but also a moral and spiritual whole.' They added, however, that the Croats and Serbs 'are not one people in the political sense of that word.'[39] 'Before the dissolution of the monarchy and the military collapse of Germany,' Radić wrote in August 1919, 'it was necessary to *swallow all of that* [about cooperation with Serbs] and to be patient, that is, to be apostolically ardent; there are *new* facts here today, and not only coercion, but the old Serbian military and bureaucratically corrupt and conspiratorial system, which was shameful before the war, but today is catastrophic.'[40] Radić repeatedly emphasized these points. In late 1922, for instance, he remarked: 'Through twenty years we said that we were one [*jedno*] with the Serbs. We did this because we had to defend ourselves against the Magyars, Italians, and Germans ... We were foreigners in our own land.' But now the situation had changed radically: 'Today we know that we are free from this foreign force. We have an opponent with whom we are equal and even stronger. We do not need to submit to a policy of coercion [*batinaška politika*].'[41]

Radić's variant of *narodno jedinstvo* never carried within it unitarist overtones, primarily because he never abandoned the framework of Croat state right. This was not the case with most other Croat proponents of *narodno jedinstvo*. Radić's prewar espousal of *narodno jedinstvo* was predicated on the notion that the Croats and Serbs had distinct political traditions. To distance himself from the unitarist implications of *narodno jedinstvo* after 1918, Radić emphasized Croat political individuality even more lest the Croats lose it within the new state. Before 1918 Radić distinguished between 'national–

cultural oneness,' which in essence meant that the Croats and Serbs – and all South Slavs – were linguistically, culturally, and in social terms, one people, and 'state-political dualism,' which meant that the Croats and Serbs had distinct state traditions and were, in effect, separate political nations. Radić's prewar espousal of *narodno jedinstvo* had been intended as a means to an end, the unification of the Croat lands within a reformed monarchy. After 1918 *narodno jedinstvo*, at least the variant espoused by Radić, made little sense. Oppressed under a highly centralized state system, Radić stated in 1925, 'we abandoned *narodno jedinstvo*.'[42] While many contemporary critics interpreted Radić's abandonment of *narodno jedinstvo* as another volte-face on his part, his attitude and policy with respect to Yugoslavism and Croat–Serb relations demonstrated great consistency. When Radić spoke of the Croat and Serbs *nations* after 1918, he did so in political terms: they were distinct political nations, and each possessed the right to determine its own political destiny.

In early February 1920, while in prison, Radić gave a declaration that he was for *narodno jedinstvo* towards the outside world, that is, 'for a *common* state *towards* the outside world,' as well as 'for brotherhood with *all* Slavs (therefore with the Bulgars also) and for an intellectual west-European orientation.'[43] Radić was in theory still prepared to recognize the cultural unity of the South Slavs, but he consistently emphasized that their distinct political traditions had to be recognized and respected. He wrote in May 1919 that before the war 'it was necessary unconditionally to defend nationality, therefore unity, oneness with the Serbs, because *foreign* brute force was over and around us; now that *foreign* force is gone; *now justice* (democracy, the peasantry) must be defended against *domestic force and injustice*.'[44] To challenge unitarism, *narodno jedinstvo* was effectively abandoned. After 1918 there was little talk of unity or 'oneness' with the Serbs; the emphasis now was on the right of the Croats to national self-determination, either in the form of an independent republic or a loose confederal state with Serbia.

Within months of the creation of the Yugoslav state, the Peasant Party publicly proclaimed its intention to seek Croat national self-determination and to internationalize the Croat Question. On 3 February 1919 it held an extraordinary session of its Main Assembly in Zagreb, attended by over 6,000 followers, to address developments in the new Kingdom of Serbs, Croats, and Slovenes since 1 December. Radić attacked the regime in Belgrade and the implementation of centralization in Croatia which, according to him, was tantamount to the introduction of foreign rule in Croatia. In the name of *narodno jedinstvo* the rights of the Croat peasantry were being trampled on by a monarchical system of government. Radić voiced his demand for a Croatian republic, national sovereignty, and a Croatian constituent assembly. Although he made reference to a federal Yugoslav republic, he insisted, much as he did in October and November 1918, that the Croat people first had to possess the right to determine their future in a Croatian constituent assembly before such a federation could even be considered.[45] This constituent assembly would determine Croatia's precise relationship to the rest of Yugoslavia.[46] The party also issued a memorandum to Wilson and the peacemakers, in which it declared that the Croats wanted the creation of a neutral republic and held open the possibility of joining a neutral federal republic of Yugoslavia, but only if the Slovenes, Serbs, and Bulgars wished to form their own republican states.[47] Demands were also raised for the removal of Serbian troops from Croatia. But the key demand at this party assembly, and throughout 1919, was for a Croatian constituent assembly.[48] To this end the party leadership initiated a drive to collect signatures for a petition to be sent to Paris demanding the right of self-determination for the Croat nation.

With the launching of this action, and Radić's continual criticism of Belgrade, on 26 February 1919 the authorities banned the publication of the party organ *Dom*. Although the party had been offered two seats in the Temporary National Representation (PNP, *Privremeno Narodno Predstavništvo*),[49] which began its deliberations on 1 March 1919 in Belgrade and was to lay the groundwork for the Constituent Assembly of the new South Slavic state, in late February Radić rejected participation. The policy of abstention was thus initiated. To participate in the PNP, or subsequently the Constituent Assembly or National Parliament, would have meant legitimizing the act of unification. This Radić would not countenance. For the Peasant Party abstention became a policy in itself until 1924, when it was finally abandoned. This is why, on 8 March 1919, the Peasant Party adopted a nine-point resolution in which it categorically refused to recognize the Serbian Karadjordjević dynasty or the work of the PNP as having any legitimacy in Croatia. It demanded, *inter alia*, a neutral Croat peasant republic and declared its intention to send a petition to Woodrow Wilson in Paris.[50] Alarmed by the Peasant Party's seditious activities and by the fact that Radić handed a copy of the 8 March resolution to the French military mission in Zagreb, the provisional government of Stojan Protić in Belgrade ordered his arrest, and on 25 March 1919 Radić was detained by the authorities.[51] He spent the following 339 days, until 27 February 1920, in detention.

In early 1919 Radić and the party thus effectively committed themselves to Croat independence. The party's petition to Paris was supposed to demonstrate and, in the absence of elections at that time, legitimize the Croat desire for an independent republic. By the end of March 1919 over 115,000 signatures had been collected.[52] At the end of April 1919 Radić indicated to his wife that on the basis of this petition he hoped to be invited to Paris to present his case. He wrote to his close associate Vladko Maček that in light of the fact that '*all* of our constitutional and elementary human rights have been trampled,' it was only natural 'that we now demand from the Entente, from Europe, from Wilson, from cultural humanity, our Croat republic without any regard to the Serbs, [and] Slovenes.' And again to his wife Radić wrote: 'All of our work and all of our endeavouring should be directed so that we Croats establish a *neutral* peasant republic of *Croatia.*'[53]

Radić seemed to believe that the Croat cause would win the sympathy of the Great Power statesmen assembled in Paris. 'Today I found out (a reliable source),' he wrote to his wife on 11 May 1919, 'that Croatia will become a *French protectorate.*' Five days later he wrote to her asking her to convince Rudolf Horvat, one of the party's leaders, to go to Vienna to see the French representative, Henry Allizé, and explain to him the party's position, specifically 'that *the social and cultural structure* of Croatia demands (a) complete independence, (b) agreement with socially and culturally similar Austria.' Days later Radić again wrote that Croats '*will not remain either under Serbia or with the Serbs*; we will become a French protectorate.' The existing situation could not be allowed to continue, for if it did it would end first in 'Serb domination, and then Serb and Croat ruin, because in Belgrade there are no capable men, and Pribićević, who alone is capable, is a vulgar tyrant of the Turkish type.' Radić insisted that Croats should seek the protection of a Great Power that would guarantee the independence of a Croat republic, but 'our relationship with that Great Power should be settled on the basis of an international agreement, which is agreed to by equals. Now – or never.'[54]

Assessing the situation at the Paris Peace Conference in mid-June 1919 Radić believed that Albania and Montenegro would become republics under Italian and French protectorates, respectively, and that 'the new "Rijeka" [Fiume] (in fact, *Croato*-Italian) republic,' would become an Italian protectorate. 'All of this means,' Radić concluded, '*Byzantium* (= Serbdom) repulsed from the Adriatic by Rome.' He repeated that 'the Croat peasant republic with Bosnia will be under a French protectorate.' He also believed that the Great Powers would recognize the new Yugoslav state only under three conditions: if a constituent assembly was called; if Croatia obtained autonomy; and if genuine political freedoms were introduced.[55] This constituent assembly had to be a Croatian assembly, the elections to which would ideally be held under international supervision, 'and if we do not get a *Croatian* constituent assembly, we will employ all other means,' though he did not specify what that meant. For the better part of 1919–20 Radić remained convinced – in all likelihood because of his faith in Woodrow Wilson and Wilsonian principles – that the

Great Powers would force Belgrade first to give Croatia autonomy and then the right to hold a plebiscite to determine its future. Radić hoped that all republicans elected in Croatia, Dalmatia, and Bosnia–Herzegovina would meet in Zagreb as a Croatian constituent assembly.[56]

Because Radić desired the creation of a Croatian constituent assembly, he emphatically and persistently urged one of the party's leading figures to take the party-sponsored petition to Allizé in Vienna. Radić even suggested in early July 1919 that the party deputy Mirko Neudörffer go to Paris to convince the assembled diplomats to invite him.[57] In fact, most of the party's leading figures were detained because of their attempts to smuggle the memorandum and petition out of the country. Maček and Josip Predavec co-signed the petition as the party's vice-presidents, and Ljudevit Kežman, who had established contacts with the Italian military mission in Ljubljana, evidently hoped to take the petition to Paris via Trieste with the assistance of the Italians. When the Yugoslav authorities got wind of this plan, they detained Predavec, Kežman, and Maček.[58] Predavec was released to his native village of Dugo Selo, whereas Maček and Kežman were placed, on 11 June 1919, in the same prison as Radić. There they would remain until early March 1920.

Given this turn of events, the sense of urgency tinged with exasperation in Radić's letters of the summer of 1919 is not surprising. There was clearly an underlying fear that his pleas and the petition would come to nothing, for he believed that the Paris peacemakers were making a settlement that might well last for centuries.[59] 'I have written enough articles,' he again wrote to his wife. 'To these [articles] add those signatures – this must have an impact, if at this moment in Paris there are not just merchants, or short-sighted "realists" (practicalists).' If the Paris peacemakers recognized the new Yugoslav kingdom – which they did by June 1919 – 'we will nevertheless go along our way prudently, but with determination and implacability.' Recognizing that this could be 'a long path, perhaps a path of years and years,' Radić nevertheless believed that 'even this is better, than a revolution, blood. According to my soul and intellect I cannot be for any kind of revolution, and especially for a peasant [revolution]. Blood begets blood.' Radić remained true to his prewar pacifist and Christian sentiments, and he even indicated that after his release from prison he planned to revive the party press, establish a new monthly called 'World Peace' and rename the party the 'Croat Pacifistic Peasant Party.'[60]

Any party that amassed such a broad following was bound to encompass within its own ranks a divergence of opinion on both aims and tactics. Despite his own pacifist inclinations, one of the major problems with which Radić and the party leadership were confronted was the issue of maintaining a firm hold over local party functionaries, particularly the younger and more radical elements. During his imprisonment Radić wrote to his wife that 'our *old* followers, who are imbued with an entirely Christian spirit of *kindness* and forgiveness, will at most only pray to God for me, and send Prib[ićević] to the devil; but those *fanatical* younger followers, who were in the war, and perhaps even in Russian captivity, and who interpreted the peasant party as a *social militant* party, are capable of conceiving and enacting a conspiracy.'[61] Radić was clearly concerned with the possibility of such a 'conspiracy.'

In September 1920, while Radić was still in prison, a rebellion occurred in the environs of Zagreb that was provoked by the government's policy of draft-animal registration, which involved branding oxen and horses.[62] Since branding was a novelty in Croatia, peasant misunderstanding of this procedure resulted first in resentment and then rebellion. What is important to note here is that some of the party's local leaders were involved in the rebellion, and it appears that they may have enjoyed some backing from the central leadership. Radić's long-standing commitment to non-violent tactics meant that the party never seriously entertained such a course of action. As the 1920 rebellion demonstrated, however, not all of the party's members shared this view. Radić remained cognizant of this fact. He once noted that he was committed to a peaceful resolution of the country's political crisis, but added that he had to use all of his influence 'to prevent a revolution that others wanted to initiate, believing it to be possible and successful.'[63] In this matter he was certainly correct, and he accurately argued that the peasant party 'regulated' the republican movement among the Croats after 1918, which was no easy task for it was 'a movement which was elementary, terribly fierce.' By 'regulating' the republican sentiment the party had thereby prevented an internecine conflict between Croats and Serbs.[64] It is not surprising that some of the party's militants, like Stjepan Uroić, who participated in the 1920 rebellion and was subsequently elected as one of the party's deputies, broke with Radić after the latter's abandonment of the republican platform in 1925.

In 1919–20 there was certainly no indication that republicanism would be abandoned any time soon. Radić continued to believe in 1919 and early 1920 that a 'Danubian federation' of some kind was still possible, though it appears that he saw such a federation as being largely an economic association. On 28 May 1919 Radić wrote that 'Austria' would be revived, 'except I fear that the whole of "Yugoslavia," therefore Serbia too will enter into it.' It is clearly evident that he wanted Serbia to be excluded from such an association. In a series of letters to his wife between 6 and 8 August, Radić argued that Yugoslav federalism might have worked in the autumn of 1918, but that it was now too late for such a federation. Insofar as Radić was thinking of federalism at all at this time, it was in the hope that a 'Danubian federation,' encompassing Austria, Hungary, and Croatia, would be formed. This was merely a reformulation of his broader vision of an East Central European union that he had advocated in the summer and fall of 1918. In December 1919 Radić wrote that 'the main thing for us (*and the people*) is a republic and [Yugoslav] federalism, because republic = self-determination, and federalism = Norway towards Sweden and at the opportune moment Norway from Sweden (1907).'[65] Radić evidently perceived the discussions about federalism within the country as a by-product of the Entente's pressure against Belgrade, and thus he gradually moved towards the idea. This was an important step in Radić's thinking. Nevertheless, in December 1919 Radić was still not committed fully to the idea of Yugoslav (con)federalism.[66]

Radić remained so opposed to any association with Serbia at the time that he even entertained the idea of carrying on his struggle from some adjoining territory. He wrote in June 1919 that 'if by some misfortune our cause here in Croatia should truly end in evil (for now), I think it would be best for us to go to Rijeka and that **we create a Croatian** *Piedmont* [*sic*] from the "Rijeka state" [Free State of Rijeka (Fiume)].' Days later he again wrote that if the peacemakers did not address the Croat question 'and if everything turns for the worse, *we* will make the Rijeka state a *Croatian* Piedmont.' In July he even considered the possibility of creating a Croatian 'Piedmont' in Sopron (Hungary), especially if a territorial corridor were established between the Czechoslovak and Yugoslav states.[67]

Just as significant for an understanding of Radić's tactics is the fact that he believed in the likelihood of political and social instability in Serbia. He seemed convinced that Serbia was on the verge of social revolution: 'This spring [1919], but certainly this year, Serbia will become a bolshevik republic. *Then our time will come.*'[68] In mid-June 1919 Radić wrote that 'our signatures have achieved the *main purpose* completely: *Croat peasant democracy* has become an international question.' He was convinced that the party's petition had 'fortified the Entente [in the view] that Croatia must not be *handed over to Serbia* ... For the first time we Croats have placed our question in a modern contemporary form. This will be seen especially then, *when a bolshevik revolution explodes* (I do not say, if it explodes) *in Serbia.*' Radić noted on 15 June that bolshevism was spreading in Serbia like a fire. Just two weeks later he observed that, given the lack of support from the Paris Peace Conference, 'we [Peasant Party] will have to create a republic by our own strength and in connection with the neighbouring socialist republican movement.' What precisely Radić meant by 'the neighbouring socialist republican movement' is not certain. It may have been an implicit reference to the Béla Kun episode (March–

August 1919) in Hungary and his belief that communist-inspired revolution would engulf Serbia, thereby creating favourable international circumstances for Croatia. Only days later Radić added that an imprisoned communist from Budapest had said that a communist insurgency was being planned in Serbia and that the Serbian monarchy would collapse. 'I do not, of course, believe all of this, but I read in *Temps* that Bela Kuhn [*sic*] has 200,000 soldiers, of whom half are well armed.'[69] This particular expectation, like many others at the time, never materialized, although Radić continued to believe into 1922 that social revolution would undermine the Serbian establishment. This conviction had an important influence on his policies *vis-à-vis* Belgrade.

Though he believed Serbia would likely succumb to a social revolution, Radić made sure that his party pre-empt the communist threat in the Croatian countryside. Radić certainly viewed the Russian revolutions of 1917 as a major turning-point in world history and as a necessary evil, since he believed that the revolutions might have been the only solution to Russia's internal crisis. But he regarded Bolshevism as 'a purely social *negative* movement,' and remained implacably opposed to the Yugoslav communists.[70] In its anti-communist propaganda, the Peasant Party railed against the communists for their support for Yugoslav unification, but it was also careful in pointing out the essentially anti-rural bias in communist ideology. It reminded the Croat peasants that the communists' opposition to agrarian parties, and their negation of the peasantry as a single class, demonstrated their deeply rooted hostility to peasant interests.[71] The simplicity of the Peasant Party's message to the peasants explains its great effectiveness: the communists wanted to 'requisition' everything from them, above all their land.

That is why the HRSS urged its followers not to be deceived by communist propaganda on land reform, for even the smallest peasant landholder was a capitalist, and hence a class enemy, in communist eyes.[72] Communist talk of land reform was merely a tactic, for the communists 'never think anything good about the village or peasants.' They intended only to destroy the peasant 'because everywhere in their program they emphasize that private ownership has to be abolished.' If they ever came to power 'this would be a new peasant slavery, comparable in every respect to the old serfdom.'[73] The communists would not only collectivize all land, they would create a powerful state with a highly centralized bureaucracy. These new bureaucrats would over time become 'new lords, even worse than barons and nobles.'[74] In light of the peasantry's traditional distrust and even hatred of the bureaucracy, which was only reinforced after 1918 by the actions of the new Yugoslav state, this line of argumentation could not but have powerful resonance in the Croat village.

What is more, the Peasant Party tactfully exploited the Yugoslav communists' early espousal of *narodno jedinstvo*. By repeatedly reminding Croat peasants that the communists supported Yugoslav unitarism (and thus denied Croat national individuality) and were in practice no different from the bourgeois Democrats, the Peasant Party associated the KPJ with the Yugoslav state and all the new burdens it had imposed on the countryside. Radić urged the Croat peasantry in March 1920 to be wary of the communists 'who are without exception in agreement with Pribićević's party of the big stick.'[75] This was not merely good propaganda, it was conviction. The participation of many prominent socialists in government, like the Croatian Serb Vitomir Korać, the prewar leader of the Croatian Social Democrats, heightened Radić's fears that they were closely cooperating with the middle-class centralists, such as Pribićević, to construct a unitary state. He believed that the split between the so-called ministerialists, like Korać, who were prepared to work within the established system, and the more radical pro-Bolshevik socialists, was merely a ploy so as not to lose the workers' support by cooperating with the existing ruling élite.[76] So convinced was Radić of the confluence of interests between the communists and Democratic centralists, that he suspected that if Pribićević and his associates were unsuccessful in implementing their centralist schemes, they would in effect wilfully hand everything over to the communists: 'Then this same thing (centralism = Great Serbianism) would exist under a Bolshevik firm.'[77] By aligning the communists in the same camp with the bourgeois unitarist parties, the Peasant Party reaped significant benefits in the village. In the national as in the social sphere, it had a decided advantage over the Yugoslav Marxist Left.

Radić was freed on 27 February 1920. On 22 March he was rearrested and charged with crimes against the fatherland. Radić used the trial, which began in early July, to justify his earlier political activity. With regard to unification and Croatia's status the position that Radić adopted during the proceedings would form the basis of his policy for the next half decade. He interpreted the right of self-determination to mean two things: every nation possessed the right to live in its own national state, and he added that 'the essence of that right lay in the fact that the people can create a government of their own choosing, that they can organize the state as they wish.' This meant that the right of self-determination had two faces, 'one purely international with respect to the determination of frontiers, and the other internal ... with regard to the organization and creation of the state.'[78] In other words, although the new Yugoslav state received international recognition, this did not mean that the powers that recognized her supported centralism or absolutist methods. Radić pointed out that only the existence of the state's frontiers had been recognized, but not its internal organization; that had to be determined by the free will of the people: 'But to recognize the kingdom today means providing one's seal, one's approval to violent centralism, and I will not and must not do this, because I am not convinced that this is good and because I am at the head of thousands of people who do not want this.' Radić refused to recognize the monarchy as a legal institution because 'the Croat peasant people do not recognize it.' He also raised the possibility of non-recognition of the system determined by the Constituent Assembly in Belgrade.[79]

By this point Radić was willing to entertain the idea of a Yugoslav (con)federation, although he did not commit himself to this idea entirely until after the elections to the Constituent Assembly (November 1920), when he was finally forced to recognize that no immediate assistance would be forthcoming from the Great Powers. Radić was prepared to accept the principle of *narodno jedinstvo vis-à-vis* the outside world, that is, he recognized the international frontiers of the new state, but he emphasized that this term did not necessarily have to imply a centralized state order. He reiterated his prewar view that in Croatia, 'Croat and Serb unity had to strengthen Croatian statehood, not destroy it.'[80] Radić could thus state without equivocation that a Croatian state already existed, based on the 29 October 1918 decision of the Croatian *Sabor*, and that Croats could not join the new state as 'inferiors.' Their state-political individuality had to be respected.[81] Radić was willing to accept a 'historical federation' in Yugoslavia, but openly opposed Serbian hegemony. In other words, what Radić clearly wanted was a Croatian republic within the framework of a South Slavic confederation, that might evolve into a federation, a union that preserved the historic political individuality of all the South Slavs and allowed each of them to determine their own fate.

Radić's confederalist conception and the terms for a resolution of the country's political instability were most clearly outlined in the summer of 1922. Radić expressed his willingness to come to terms with Belgrade, but the preconditions he enunciated were bound to be rejected by the Serbian political establishment, which invariably interpreted such schemes as contributing to the destabilization of the state. In an interview with an American journalist in July 1922, Radić argued that the Peasant Party would not send its deputies to the Belgrade parliament in light of all that had occurred since unification. Belgrade had to recognize the Croatian state as sovereign within the international frontiers of the Yugoslav community. Once the Croatian state was recognized by Belgrade, and its sovereignty guaranteed by the League of Nations, a delegation of the Croatian *Sabor* would go to Belgrade to participate in a common legislature that would determine the joint affairs of the Croatian–Serbian confederation. Radić did not envisage one executive branch of government for this confederation, but insisted that the executive would rest with the constitu-

TABLE 6.2
Elections to Constituent Assembly, 28 November 1920, major parties, 419 seats

Party	Votes	Percentage	Seats
Democratic Party	319,448	19.8	92
NRS	284,575	17.7	91
Communist Party	198,736	12.3	58
HPSS	230,590	14.3	50
Serbian Agrarians	151,603	9.4	39
Slovenes (SLS)*	111,274	6.9	27
Bosnian Muslims (JMO)	110,895	6.8	24
Social Democrats	46,792	2.9	10
Džemijet	30,029	1.8	8
Croat Husbandmen	38,400	2.3	7
Croat Union	25,867	1.6	4
Others	–	4.2	9

*The SLS's (Slovene People's Party) total numbers in the Constituent Assembly
include the votes of the clericalist Croat People's Party.
Sources: Branislav Gligorijević, *Parlament i političke stranke u Jugoslaviji,
1919–1929* (Belgrade, 1979), 86, 89; Ferdo Čulinović, *Jugoslavija izmedju dva
rata* (Zagreb, 1961), 1: 312–13.

ent parts of this confederation. 'With such a confederation – and only with it –
can the rapprochement between Croatia and Serbia, between the Croat and
Serb peoples, begin anew,' although he held out the possibility that such a
confederation might eventually evolve into a federation.[82]

In spite of a brilliant defence, on 4 August 1920, Radić was found guilty
and sentenced to two years plus six months in prison. To add insult to injury
he was ordered to fast on each 1 December, the date of Yugoslav unification.
But Radić remained in prison only until 28 November 1920, when he was
amnestied by the regent.[83] His release coincided with the elections to the Belgrade Constituent Assembly in which the Peasant Party received 230,590
votes and fifty seats. This amounted to a resounding victory for the party and
confirmed its new status as the only major Croat party. The results were a sur-
prise not only for Belgrade, but also for the established Croat political élite.
The other Croat parties, namely, the Croat Union, the Croat Party of Right,
and the clericalist Croat People's Party (HPS, *Hrvatska pučka stranka*), were
reduced to insignificance. The Peasant Party's votes were mainly rural and it
made few inroads in the towns, however. The rural nature of the party's vote is
best demonstrated by a comparison of its results in Zagreb county, where it
received 67.35 per cent of the popular vote, and the city itself, where it gained

TABLE 6.3
Election returns in Croatia (prewar Croatia–Slavonia), 93 seats

Party	Votes	Percentage	Seats
HPSS	230,590	37	50
Democratic Party	78,406	12	19
NRS	39,050	6	9
Communist Party	31,281	5	7
Croat Union	22,950	4	3
Croat People's Party	11,871	2	3
Croat Party of Right	10,880	2	2

Sources: Branislav Gligorijević, *Parlament i političke stranke u Jugoslaviji,*
1919–1929 (Belgrade, 1979), 86, 89; Ferdo Čulinović, *Jugoslavija izmedju dva*
rata (Zagreb, 1961), 1: 312–13.

only 6.77 per cent. Thus, although it commanded the loyalty of Zagreb's peasant environs, the Peasant Party was only the fifth largest party in the city of Zagreb.[84] In the Constituent Assembly the Peasant Party was the fourth largest party.

Radić and the party interpreted this electoral victory in Croatia as a national plebiscite for a Croatian republic, and whereas the party refused formally to proclaim the existence of this republic, it nevertheless considered the vote as the right to do so. Assessing the situation after the vote, Radić argued that it was necessary for Croatia and Serbia to come to an agreement, but 'in such a way so that neither will be above or beneath the other.'[85] On 8 December 1920, at an extraordinary session of the Peasant Party's Main Assembly in Zagreb, the HPSS was formally renamed the Croat Republican Peasant Party (HRSS). In justifying the new name, the HRSS leadership argued that the party was from its very creation republican in spirit and that since the end of the Great War its public activities were entirely republican. With its republican platform it rejected participation in the Constituent Assembly, a policy it would maintain until 1924.

The vote of 28 November was an affirmation of the decidedly republican aspirations of the Croat village and legitimized the formal adoption of a republican platform. The HRSS's newly elected deputies took an oath to the Croat peasant people whereby they pledged to organize Croatia, on the basis of the right of national self-determination and in agreement with the other southern Slavs, as a neutral peasant republic within the existing international borders of the Yugoslav state.[86] Painfully cognizant after the elections to the Constituent Assembly that no assistance would be forthcoming from the

Western statesmen, Radić and the HRSS were now committed to a 'just' agreement with Belgrade that would enable Croats to form their republican state within a Yugoslav confederation.

The HRSS also articulated its policy towards the Constituent Assembly at this session of its Main Assembly, and made it clear that it rejected participation. The HRSS resolution, adopted at this assembly, considered the decision of the Croatian *Sabor* of 29 October 1918 to break all ties with the Habsburg monarchy as forming the basis of Croatia's *de jure* independence. In light of the party's November 1920 electoral victory on the territory of prewar Croatia–Slavonia (fifty of ninety-three seats), the HRSS considered this independent Croatian state to be a republic, for the vote was nothing other than 'an incontrovertible plebiscite for a neutral peasant republic of Croatia within today's international frontiers of the southern Slavs.' The HRSS could participate 'only in such a true Constituent Assembly of the majority of the southern Slavs – Slovenes, Croats, and Serbs – in which there will be no majorization.' Resolutions had to be reached by reciprocal agreement. The HRSS added that it considered the demand of the provisional government in Belgrade that all deputies in the Constituent Assembly swear an oath of allegiance to the regent to go against the very idea of such an assembly, for the regime was pressuring the deputies to work according to its wishes.[87] If the Constituent Assembly was genuinely to determine the form of government, the oath of fealty to the regent precluded the possibility of anything other than a monarchical system. The HRSS also declared that it possessed the right to take over all government authority in Croatia–Slavonia.

All of this was restated in the HRSS's memorandum to Prince-Regent Aleksandar in February 1921, drafted on 11 February by the HRSS's deputies at a session attended by six delegates of the (Serbian) Republican Democratic Party (RDS, *Republikanska demokratska stranka*) of Milovan Lazarević. The HRSS again asserted that its deputies were elected on Croatian state territory and were, as a majority, the legal representatives of the Croat nation. In the name of both the Croatian state and Croat people the HRSS declared null and void the proclamation of unification of 1 December 1918. Unification went against the Croatian *Sabor*'s act of 29 October 1918 that severed all ties with the Habsburg monarchy; more importantly, the nearly 160,000 signatures of 1919 and the elections of November 1920 further made unification null and void, for the peasantry was decidedly republican. The HRSS again demanded a neutral peasant republic and a Croatian constituent assembly. Although the Paris Peace Conference had determined the international frontiers of the Slovenes, Croats, and Serbs, it did not attempt 'to impose a monarchy in general, and a Serbian monarchy in particular, on the independent Croatian state and

Croat people on this internationally recognized territory.'[88] The policy of administrative centralization was condemned as illegal.

The February memorandum also cast aspersions on the Belgrade Constituent Assembly, for its decisions could not be considered legal and binding in Croatia as long as Croatia's legally elected deputies did not participate. The rights of the Serb minority in Croatia were also recognized, and it was asserted that the HRSS's program of social justice and republicanism would ensure the equality of all, regardless of nationality. The HRSS restated its desire for a peaceful agreement with the kingdom of Serbia. The South Slavs were linguistically 'one whole'; they were not, however, one nation politically, and this had to be recognized.[89] The central argument in this memorandum was that the Croat people had never renounced their national individuality. The memorandum concluded with an appeal to the regent to permit the HRSS, 'executing the complete and unlimited right of national self-determination, to take over the complete state authority and administration in Croatia,' which would then negotiate a confederal agreement with Serbia.[90] Unsurprisingly the message failed to elicit any response from Belgrade.

The position enunciated in the February 1921 memorandum would form the cornerstone of the HRSS's policy until 1924–5. It was perfectly clear that the HRSS did not recognize the new state, with the implication that such recognition would not be forthcoming in the near future. There was no suggestion that the HRSS's deputies would go to Belgrade, and the policy of abstention was thus implicitly reaffirmed. Both Jovan (Joca) Jovanović-Pižon of the (Serbian) Alliance of Agrarian Workers (SZ, *Savez zemljoradnika*) and Lazarević of the Republicans had come to Zagreb in February to convince Radić to come to Belgrade, but their plea was rejected.[91] Radić continued to believe that the process of state formation would be robbed of legitimacy by his party's absence.

As the HRSS's memorandum produced no result, and as the Belgrade Constituent Assembly worked to form a constitution for the Yugoslav state, Radić and the HRSS began formulating their own constitution for a neutral Croat peasant republic. A draft constitution was discussed by the HRSS's deputies on 5–6 March and 9 April 1921, and formally adopted on 14 May 1921 as the 'Constitution or State Organization of the Neutral Peasant Republic of Croatia.' In the following six weeks the constitution was disseminated by local party workers throughout the Croatian countryside where, according to Radić, it was overwhelmingly accepted and approved.[92] On 26 June the party's constitution was formally proclaimed.

This document was as much a constitution for a Croatian republic as it was a statement of the HRSS's demands, for it was subsequently published in 1922 as the fourth edition of the party's program. It was also the final expression of Radić's conception of a peasant state. The document enshrined, among other things, the principles of administrative decentralization and peasant participation at all levels of state organization. Croatian state territory was defined as the eight counties that comprised prewar Croatia–Slavonia. Asserting the principle of national self-determination, the constitution proclaimed that this territory, in addition to possessing the attributes of statehood as embodied in prewar Croatia's state right and the popular will of the people, could only be expanded on the basis of self-determination by plebiscite. In other words, Dalmatia, Bosnia–Herzegovina, or even Slovenia could join this state if they wished.[93] This neutral Croat peasant plebiscitary republic was to be founded on the pacifist inclinations of the Croat people. But the constitution also declared that this peasant republic could enter into 'a freely agreed community of states (confederation) on our present common territory recognized by international right, which the whole world already calls Yugoslavia.'[94] The constitution did not envisage the need for the Neutral Peasant Republic of Croatia to have a standing army, and it also guaranteed human and civil rights (personal security, no death penalty, freedom of speech, freedom of assembly, and the franchise for women).[95]

When the authorities in Belgrade got wind of the HRSS's intentions to draft its own constitution they became alarmed that an uprising was being prepared, particularly because many HRSS local activists seemed to be carrying on their agitation and holding meetings at night-time. The head of Croatia's regional administration noted in early March 1921 that even though the HRSS was only in the first stages of drafting its constitution, the peasants 'do not know that only a constitutional *draft* and the *adoption* of one of a number of drafts is planned, but believe that on the respective day [5 or 8 March] their, that is, a republican, constitution will be proclaimed.' If, contrary to the peasants' expectations, the HRSS constitution was not proclaimed on that date, 'there will be even greater bewilderment among the [Croat] peasant people,' for they are 'imbued through and through with the republican idea,' even though he concluded that 'they are carrying on peacefully and doing their work.'[96]

In late May 1921, as the HRSS's constitution was being disseminated in the countryside, the Croatian regional administration was instructed by Minister of Internal Affairs Milorad Drašković temporarily to ban all HRSS rallies: 'Since I see from all official reports sent here by the [Croatian] Landed Government about the rallies of Radić's party, that this party consistently propagates a system and plan for the creation of an independent Croat peasant republic, which in the final analysis contains treasonous tendencies directed against the integrity of our state,' Drašković considered it necessary to ban all future HRSS assemblies, and any party activists who tried circumventing this ban were to be severely dealt with.[97] Just three days before the HRSS constitution was proclaimed, the head of the regional administration, acting on instructions from Belgrade, informed the county prefects that all representatives of the HRSS 'who are caught in anti-state agitation,' that is, holding unauthorized assemblies, should receive the same treatment as the communists, whose local organizations had been suppressed earlier that year.[98] The authorities even suspected that Radić was in touch with the Croat Comité in Hungary and had despatched two agents to meet with Ivica Frank in early 1921, presumably to organize an insurrection against the Yugoslav state.[99]

The central government in Belgrade was clearly overwhelmed and alarmed by the imposing size of the peasant republican movement. In the first years of the new state it associated all forms of rebellion in the Croat lands, real or imagined, with the HRSS and hence viewed it with great suspicion. The head of Croatia's regional administration, Ernest Čimić, reported to the Ministry of Internal Affairs in Belgrade that the state was confronted by a 'party movement of great proportions [u velikom stilu] that has won over to itself the overwhelming majority of peasants and intellectuals ... of the Croat tribe [sic].' It was a movement of 'hundreds of thousands of citizens, distributed over an extraordinarily broad territory, and organized into the firm and extraordinarily disciplined organization of the HRSS, so that the authorities are in many ways impotent towards it.'[100] The administration felt powerless to determine what the HRSS's local organizations were up to, for it was incapable of penetrating the party organization or successfully bribing individual members of the party, especially in the village. Čimić added that 'I have already stressed in my earlier reports, as is known, that peasants assemble in and outside of the villages, but that it cannot be determined what they are discussing ... because it is impossible to induce a single one of them to inform us for any sum of money or profit. The psychology of the masses has a particularly great role in this and from it stems the fear that he [informant] will be considered a "national traitor," so that this is stronger than the desire for profit.' The inability of the administration or gendarmerie to determine the ulterior motives of the HRSS forced the government to rely largely on the party's public declarations and the actions of its regional and central leadership. By 1923 the regional administration seemed to believe that the HRSS's activities were confined purely to legal avenues, and that Radić's popularity was primarily a function of the postwar hardships as well as, interestingly enough, the shortcomings of the administration.[101]

Such reports did little to satisfy the central authorities in Belgrade or to alleviate their fears about the HRSS's subversive anti-state activities. For instance, in the autumn of 1923 Minister of Internal Affairs, Milorad Vujičić noted 'the sad fact that the administrative authorities are not in a position to monitor the activities of such a numerous organization;' this was 'an entirely unhealthy situation.' Vujičić added: 'Keeping in mind that this party [HRSS] carries out all of its actions behind the back of the authorities, I must seriously question its work, because what end would all of this secrecy serve when it could have enacted its organization completely in the open?!'[102] Vujičić was implicitly referring to the nocturnal work of some HRSS activists, and his statement clearly indicates that the authorities in Belgrade continued to believe that the HRSS was committed to subversive anti-state activities. That is why they demanded 'the most serious attention' from the regional administration pertaining to the peasant party's activism.

The call for increased vigilance had few substantive results. In an all-too-typical example of the administration's powerlessness, the prefect of Novi Marof (Hrvatsko Zagorje) reported with alarm that he believed that 99 per cent of the district's population supported the HRSS and that it was consequently impossible effectively to monitor the activities of the party and to determine with any degree of certainty its real intentions in that area.[103] The prefect of Varaždin district, echoing the alarm of his colleague from Novi Marof, reported that the HRSS's followers 'have a blind faith in the leadership' and were prepared to follow its every lead. He was evidently impressed by the discipline of the party, which he likened to that of a religious movement.[104]

The coinciding proclamations of the HRSS and Yugoslav (Vidovdan) constitutions were symptomatic of the immense political differences that separated the HRSS and the centralist parties. The latter document, named after the date of its promulgation (St Vitus's day – Vidovdan – 28 June), was passed by a small majority (223 for, 35 against, 161 boycotted). The popular conviction soon arose that the constitution was a Serbian document and represented a victory for Serb interests, for it was a product of centralist principles. It was adopted without the approval and against the will of most of the non-Serb parties.[105] Adoption of the Vidovdan constitution was clearly a defeat for the HRSS, as it was for most non-Serb parties, but nevertheless the HRSS's stand was buttressed by the growing disillusionment of the other Croat parties. In early May 1921 the Croat Union and its Bosnian ally, the Croat Husbandmen's Party (HTS, *Hrvatska težačka stranka*), left the Constituent Assembly. In June they were followed by the Slovene People's Party and its ally, the Croat People's Party, and by the communists. Radić, referring to the 12 May 1921 vote in the Constituent Assembly on the acceptance of the government's constitutional proposal in general, remarked that 'only the Serbs voted for this constitution [constitutional proposal]. *It follows, therefore, that the constitution is Serbian.*'[106]

In addition to confirming state centralism and Serbian dominance, the Vidovdan constitution gave far-reaching powers to the monarch. Theoretically the constitution recognized the parliament as a sovereign organ of authority, and thus established the new kingdom as a parliamentary monarchy. The constitution did not obligate King Aleksandar to name ministers from the parliament or even to respect the will of parliamentary majorities. Legislative authority was vested in both the parliament and the king, but the latter was actually the more important factor. In fact, he was above the parliament, possessing the right to sanction or reject parliamentary bills and to call to session or dissolve the parliament at any time. Moreover, the king controlled the army and conducted foreign policy. He could also make administrative appointments and wielded considerable authority over the judiciary. In short, King Aleksandar was answerable to no one. These facts seriously threatened parliamentarism and its institutions from the very outset. Between 1921 and 1928 governments were formed not in parliament but at Aleksandar's court. As will be seen, the king brought down governments with majorities and sustained those lacking them. His right to call to session or dissolve the parliament at any time made him the ultimate arbiter of the Yugoslav political system.[107]

From mid-1921 on the lines were drawn. The HRSS's constitution set the party on a course diametrically opposed to that of Belgrade and the unitarist parties. Until 1924–5 Radić's position did not waver: independence for a Croatian republic within the international frontiers of the new state, that is, in a confederation with Serbia on the basis of a mutual agreement. After 1921 the only solution to the existing political crisis, as far as Radić was concerned, was for the Serbian political establishment to recognize Croat political and state individuality. He told as much to Stojan Protić, the only Serbian politician, aside from the representatives of the Republicans and Agrarians, to approach Radić at this time (July–August 1921). A prominent NRS dissident, Protić broke with Pašić over the constitutional issue. Unlike Pašić, Protić was prepared to allow greater local autonomy and proposed the creation of nine provinces along quasi-historical lines. He was willing to make greater concessions to the non-Serbs and feared that the imposition of centralism, in addition to causing greater resistance from the non-Serbs, might also jeopardize Serbian liberties. This is why he approached Radić in the summer of 1921, although their meetings proved to be unsuccessful. Radić told Protić that the Croat nation's political individuality had to be respected because Croats 'are not and will not be *anyone's tribe*, nor are we just *a part* of some [trinomial Yugoslav] nation.'[108] Radić and the HRSS could not be assuaged by talk of greater local autonomy.

The HRSS's political position was buttressed by the formation of the Croat

Bloc (*Hrvatski blok*), an alliance between the HRSS, the Croat Union, the Croat Party of Right and, eventually, the HRSS-sponsored Croat Workers' Union (HRS, *Hrvatski radnički savez*).[109] The Croat Bloc first took shape in late May 1921 when its constituent parties issued a message to the Croat people, but it was not formally inaugurated until the following October. The Croat Bloc stood on the principles of Croat national individuality and state sovereignty as well as a 'humane' social policy as articulated in the HRSS's program. According to Radić it represented the 'supreme national and social leadership of the Croat people,' with the HRSS as its core.[110] As the only significant force in the Croat lands the HRSS emerged as the leading element in the Croat Bloc and set the tempo and direction of its policies, although important differences continued to exist between its constituent parts. Its policy was therefore essentially the policy of the HRSS.

The creation of the Croat Bloc was important for a number of reasons. Radić now stressed that the HRSS stood in the vanguard of a supra-class national movement that represented all elements of Croat society: the peasantry, bourgeoisie, intelligentsia, and workers. In Radić's eyes this was truly a national front under the peasantry's leadership directed against the centralism of Belgrade. In this sense it represented the political unity of the Croat village and city, as well as the intelligentsia's recognition of the political leadership of the former. Speaking of the Croat Bloc to his party's deputies in February 1922, Radić remarked that 'the Croat peasantry organized itself without and even against the intelligentsia on a humane and national basis, and after that it accepted the intelligentsia on its own terms ... the intelligentsia was awakened and acceded to the people.' With the creation of the Croat Bloc the HRSS was now even stronger: 'Belgrade believed that seven months of brute force [since the imposition of the Vidovdan constitution in June 1921] would be enough to liquidate the HRSS.' In fact, the HRSS had not only strengthened its own ranks, but it now headed a national movement uniting the city and the village, the intellectuals and the peasants. National unity had been achieved.[111] Indeed, the other Croat parties were forced to recognize the importance of Radić and the HRSS. 'All Croats without regard to party affiliation,' declared the main organ of the Croat Husbandmen's Party in Bosnia–Herzegovina, 'have to be at last conscious [of the fact] that Radić is today the main representative of the Croat national will, they must not see in Radić a republican or a separatist ... [rather] Radić is already today a phenomenon, that is synonymous with the very idea of Croatdom.'[112] Yet it should be stressed that the formation of the Croat Bloc evidently created apprehension in the Croat countryside. One HRSS deputy indicated that the peasants feared that the middle-class gentlemen would infiltrate the HRSS and dilute its social program. The peasants would support the Croat Bloc insofar as the bourgeois parties merely supported the HRSS's lead.[113] This was a view with which Radić and the HRSS agreed entirely. On the eve of the Croat Bloc's formation, Radić confided to his deputies that the Croat Union was not really a party but a clique of intellectuals, and that he doubted the Croat Party of Right really supported a 'peasant policy' and republicanism.[114] Be that as it may, the symbolic importance of the Croat Bloc as a united national front *vis-à-vis* Belgrade was not lost on him.

The Croat Bloc's policy amounted to a rejection of the centralist principles enshrined in the Vidovdan constitution and it maintained that an agreement with Belgrade was impossible as long as the Serbian political élite continued to view the Croats as a mere tribe of some imaginary trinomial Yugoslav nation (the opinion of the Democrats) or an object of assimilation by the dominant Serbs (a view held by many Serb Radicals). An agreement with Belgrade would be possible only after the Croatian state was recognized by Belgrade.[115] Whether Radić genuinely believed such an agreement to be possible with the likes of Pašić's NRS or the Democratic Party is difficult to ascertain, but his second round of meetings with the NRS dissident Protić in Zagreb in May 1922 confirmed his worst fears. The talks revealed no common ground on the issue of state organization. When Protić apparently suggested to Radić that he had invented the Croat people, the latter responded that the elections of November 1920 clearly demonstrated not only the existence of this people as a distinct nation, but its determination to retain its political individuality. Croat peasants had 'voted for their Croat nationality and their [republican] Croatian state.' After this meeting with Protić, Radić reiterated his view that all Serb politicians 'are largely identical, especially with regard to Croatia,' and that it would be difficult to find 'such a Serb statesman and Serb party, who will comprehend that there can be no honourable and just agreement with the Croats' until there was a recognition of Croat political rights.[116]

Radić certainly had not categorically refused any further discussions with the representatives of the Serbian parties. In the second half of 1922 he held a series of talks with the representatives of Davidović's Democratic Party (then in a government coalition with Pašić's NRS), and with Protić. These talks were initiated, as will be demonstrated, for tactical reasons on the part of both Radić and Davidović. Nevertheless, formally at least, the HRSS (and hence the Croat Bloc), refused to enter into any negotiations with the Pašić regime, a government that was not, according to the HRSS, truly representative of the Serb people.[117] In particular, Pašić and the Croatian Serb leader Pribićević, who figured prominently in Davidović's Democratic Party, were singled out as 'usurpers, parasites [*nametnici*] and tyrants. In Serbia they have no one behind them who would consider them to be *national leaders* ... [and] *outside of Serbia* everyone is against them.'[118] These remarks were buoyed by Radić's misplaced conviction throughout 1922 that new elections would bring about a radically different situation in the whole country. He predicted another over-whelming electoral victory for the HRSS in Croatia, a growing republican tide in Bosnia–Herzegovina and Dalmatia, and that the Serbian Agrarians and Republicans would make gains in Serbia of the same magnitude as the HRSS's victory in the November 1920 elections in Croatia. In Radić's opin-ion, new elections would facilitate an agreement between the Serbs and Croats, one in which the right of national self-determination for the Croats would be recognized.[119] The HRSS's continual call for new elections became part of its policy, for it believed that the corrupt and at times brutal methods of the regime and its parties would eventually translate into their electoral defeat.

Furthermore, Radić continued to believe throughout 1921–2, much as he did in 1919, that the Serbian establishment would shortly be confronted by a social revolution. He told the HRSS's deputies in December 1921 that 'the present situation among the Serbs is comparable to that of Central Europe in 1918.' Serbian policy was 'bankrupt' and would assuredly eventually end in 'catastrophe.'[120] He repeated this in late February 1922 by comparing the existing situation in Serbia to Croatia in 1918 (that is, the Green Cadre move-ment) and Russia between the two revolutions.[121] In March 1922 Radić told his deputies that 'the Serbian peasantry does not hate us, rather it sympathizes with us.' They would soon revolt against the Serbian élite: 'It seems that that which they in Belgrade want to happen to us will happen to them at the hands of the Serb people.' Croats were in a better position than the Serbs, because 'the Serb peasants have ranged against them the dynasty, the army, and the camarilla, so that the martyred peasant's and workers' question can only be solved there ... by force.' He believed that the Croats were stronger, for they had done away with 'internal injustice' by forming the supra-class Croat Bloc: 'Both the intelligentsia and workers are on the same side, with us, against the regime.'[122] Viewed in this context, the HRSS's policy of abstention became a test of endurance, for Radić certainly believed that he would outlast the major Serbian parties (NRS and Democrats), which would be either voted out of office – hence Radić's repeated calls for new elections – or ousted in a bloody confrontation by their own people. Time and European public opinion, he believed, were on his side.

Although Radić clearly expected a revolution in Serbia, he remained opposed, as he did before 1918, to the use of violence in Croatia. The HRSS leadership continued to debate the issue of tactics throughout the early 1920s. Radić was emphatic in his insistence that the HRSS confine its activism to non-violent methods and told a session of the party's deputies in late 1921 that the people should be *advised* not to respond to force with violence. The HRSS had been deluged with inquires from peasants as to what they should do with respect to paying taxes and serving in the army. One party deputy, Mato Jagatić, indicated that many men were going into the army but that most peasants were paying taxes only under duress, when gendarmes appeared to collect them. Radić did not explicitly indicate that the people should be instructed to pay taxes or to perform military service. Another prominent party figure, Djuro Basaricek, indicated that there were only two solutions to the struggle between Belgrade and the HRSS: a negotiated settlement or revolution. He was for the former but wondered aloud how the HRSS's objectives would be achieved without bloodshed. He concluded that the HRSS had to strengthen its organization and remain committed to a peaceful policy: 'Nevertheless, everything must be done to make the adversary even weaker. This is possible by refusing to pay taxes and to serve in the army ... We must be steadfast and uncompliant.' Stjepan Uroić, one of the party's more radical members and a participant in the 1920 peasant disturbances, concurred: 'As long as we go on paying taxes and serving in the army, we will continue to buttress the [Belgrade] authorities (we are paying for the gendarme's boots).'[123] The HRSS leadership thus urged non-violence, but it was certainly prepared to countenance certain forms of civil disobedience. If the reports of the regional administration and the authorities in Belgrade are any indication, then the HRSS certainly encouraged desertion. One Ministry of Internal Affairs report, basing its information on the reports of the gendarmerie in Zagreb, indicated that the HRSS's local organizations were holding dances and other social functions, especially around national holidays when soldiers were on furlough, and agitating among new recruits; the inference being that the HRSS was urging soldiers to desert.[124] Although the HRSS's goal was to reach an agreed settlement with Belgrade, it necessarily tried to weaken its adversary through all available means short of outright rebellion.

By early 1922 a negotiated settlement with Belgrade seemed impossible. Therefore, Radić once again turned his attention to European diplomacy, particularly the Genoa Conference which convened in April 1922. He clearly saw the conference as a convenient opportunity to present the Croat case, for all the major European states were in attendance, including Soviet Russia and Germany. In spite of the failure of this approach in 1919, Radić never completely abandoned his hope that the support of the European powers could be elicited. That is why Radić cautioned the Belgrade authorities that if they continued with their centralist policies and negation of the Croat people as a distinct nation, they would have to deal with 'enlightened' European public opinion.[125] In early February 1922 the Croat Bloc published a draft memorandum that it intended to send to the Genoa Conference. The memorandum essentially restated the HRSS's and Croat Bloc's earlier position: Croatia's independence was never formally ended, and as of 29 October 1918 Croatia was an independent state. Since November 1920 this state was a de facto republic that, as of June 1921, had its own constitution. The Vidovdan constitution and Belgrade's rule violated the Croats' right to self-determination and contributed to the country's political instability. The Serbian political élite was 'absorbed with the idea of a strong state ... that suffocates and demolishes completely everything around itself that is not Orthodox and Serbian,' and it had introduced 'a nation-devouring [*narodoždersku*] policy under the firm of Yugoslav *narodno jedinstvo*, a policy whose main and evident aim was entirely to destroy the Croat people.' The 'enlightened democracies' had an obligation to recognize the Croatian state within the international frontiers of the 'community' of Serbs, Croats, and Slovenes.[126]

At the end of that same month the HRSS sent a communiqué to Pašić which stated that an agreement was possible insofar as his NRS–Democratic government was willing to meet the terms enunciated in the memorandum. The HRSS also cautioned the Pašić regime that its memorandum to the Genoa Conference was only the first step in its 'foreign policy.'[127] The true purpose of this message to Pašić was to demand a Croat contingent in the Yugoslav delegation to the conference. If Pašić refused, the HRSS (and Croat Bloc) declared that it would be forced to send a memorandum to Genoa. Radić referred to the forthcoming conference as a forum where both the victors and the vanquished were meeting 'to make a lasting peace.'[128] At the March session of the Croat Bloc's meeting, one Croat prominent deputy, Matko Laginja, expressed doubts about the possibility of gaining European support: 'The regime in Serbia corresponds to the [political] situation in the rest of Europe. Everyone is looking to exploit us.' Radić agreed that Europe 'is an accessory to everything that is done in Belgrade,' but argued that it was necessary to distinguish between European governments and their peoples, for public opinion would assuredly force these governments to adopt a harsher policy *vis-à-vis* Belgrade.[129]

Pašić ignored the memorandum, however, as did the participants of the conference. Nevertheless, the entire episode prompted greater vigilance on the part of the authorities. The commander of the gendarmerie in Medjimurje reported that 'the Radićists are appealing to military deserters to gather in their native villages and to hide in their parents' homes until the weather improves, when they can hide in the forests.' The commander added that the Radićists were 'propagating among and deluding the people, that the Croat Question will be solved in Genoa.'[130] Another report concluded that 'in the last little while a marked increase in agitation on the part of the Radićists, who have despatched their agents to those villages where they have a majority, has been noticeable.' The peasant people, who were thoroughly in Radić's hands, believed that the proclamation of a republic was imminent 'and are prepared at any given moment to assist the action for a revolt and revolution [*prevrata*].'[131]

No such revolution was being planned. Apart from contributing to the anxieties of the authorities in Belgrade about a possible revolution, this episode in the HRSS's and the Croat Bloc's foreign policy was as unsuccessful as its earlier effort. Yet Radić still did not lose faith in the Western democracies, particularly Britain, especially because of the Anglo-Irish Treaty (1921) and the creation of an Irish Free State in 1922. The HRSS decided to forward another memorandum in the summer of 1922, this time to the League of Nations. Radić was evidently convinced, as he indicated in July 1922, that the European powers were becoming increasingly dissatisfied with the political situation in Yugoslavia, 'and that is why our Croat policy must be consistently *peaceful and cautious*, but also uncompromising.'[132] Just over a month later, on 13 August 1922, the HRSS formally decided to send a memorandum to the League of Nations.[133] This too proved to be an utter failure.

Defeated once again on the stage of European diplomacy, Radić had to redouble his efforts on the domestic stage. By mid-1922 he believed that an agreement resolving the country's political crisis between the HRSS and Pašić's NRS was impossible, but he had already indicated that such an agreement might be possible with Ljuba Davidović's Democrats, who were themselves at that time members of Pašić's government.[134] In actuality the chances of such an agreement were virtually non-existent, and Radić's frequent pejorative references to Pašić and Pribićević, in particular, merely reflected this. In April 1922 the Belgrade government had adopted measures to introduce a centralized system of thirty-three administrative districts and to replace the existing administrative units as prescribed by the Vidovdan constitution. Moreover, the NRS press kept dismissing Radić's 'autonomist, that is, separatist and actually regressive views regarding the organization of our new state.'[135] The 'healthy' Vidovdan constitution granted the same civil and political rights 'to all tribes and faiths.' Unfortunately, the NRS claimed, Radić was 'the representative of a confused political group,' and the leader of 'the uninformed and misled Croat masses.' His 'separatist' actions were providing the country's enemies with an opportunity to weaken it, and only 'create bad blood in the country.' The ranks of Radić's party had been joined 'by all spies and extortioners [*krvopije*].'[136] It was all too apparent, in terms of both policies and rhetoric, that there was little room for a negotiated agreement.

In spite of Radić's statements to the effect that an agreement was impossible with Pašić, in the second half of 1922 he conducted talks with representatives of Davidović's Party. The HRSS claimed that these talks were necessary to facilitate an eventual agreement to resolve the country's political crisis.[137] Radić used the talks for purely tactical reasons. He hoped that they might intensify existing divisions in the NRS–Democratic government and, ultimately, lead to new elections. Indeed, the HRSS's and Croat Bloc's options seemed limited in the second half of 1922. On the international scene the memoranda to the Genoa Conference and the League of Nations had failed to elicit any support; the HRSS thus turned to talks with the Democrats.

In early October 1922 Radić met with Pavle Andjelić, a member of Davidović's party, who tried to convince him to abandon the policy of abstention. Radić rejected such a move because his standing among the Croat peasants would be compromised thereby, for the regime was despised in the Croat countryside. A month later two other representatives of the Democratic Party, Milan Grol and Ljuba Mihailović, held talks with Radić in Zagreb, and they again urged him to end his policy of abstention, for once this happened Pašić's position would be completely undermined.[138] In mid-November Radić in turn despatched a three-man delegation of the Croat Bloc to Belgrade to continue the talks. Radić evidently hoped to undermine the position of Pribićević within the Democratic Party by arguing that the policy of centralism was subverting the possibility of a negotiated resolution to the state crisis. In late November, Radić, writing to Davidović, welcomed the latter's efforts 'to topple the present-day anti-national, reactionary and, above all, anti-Croat regime,' and to replace it with a government of 'national concentration' on the basis of 'true democracy with the objective of a sincere and lasting Croato–Serb agreement.' Radić again refused to go to Belgrade, for the regime was so detested in Croatia that Radić's appearance in Belgrade would cause 'the greatest apprehension and censure among the Croat people.' He proposed, therefore, that the current regime be brought down and a new government, excluding those elements who opposed a Croat-Serb agreement, an implicit reference to Pašić and Pribićević, be formed that would call new elections and reform the administration to ensure that those elections would be completely free.[139] Judging by Radić's second letter to Davidović, the latter had indicated his willingness to end his party's partnership with Pašić and to cooperate with the HRSS, but important differences remained over the nature of that cooperation.

Davidović clearly wanted Radić to end his policy of abstention and to form a parliamentary coalition that would undermine the NRS's position. But Radić continually refused to come to Belgrade. The state crisis, he argued, would not be resolved if the HRSS simply went to the parliament and cooperated with the Democratic Party. Although in principle committed to parliamentary action, Radić rejected parliamentary cooperation as long as the current regime was in power, and he hoped to use extra-parliamentary means to pave the way for a Croat–Serb agreement. He therefore insisted upon the concentration 'of all liberal and moral elements who have not only a progressive national, but also a progressive social, orientation,' including the Democratic Party.[140]

Both the HRSS and the Democratic Party undertook the 1922 talks for tactical reasons. For Radić, the objective was clearly to bring about new elections that might dramatically alter the situation in the parliament and ultimately pave the way for a Croat–Serb agreement. Davidović used these talks to strengthen his party's position with respect to the NRS: establishing a dialogue with Radić raised the possibility that he might be able to count on a measure of support from the HRSS. It is therefore not surprising that Davidović urged Radić to abandon his policy of abstention and promised some limited constitutional reforms in his talks with the HRSS. But the Democratic Party, which was formed on the unitarist conception of *narodno jedinstvo*, was composed of diverse elements. Pribićević's wing of the party favoured only a centralized state system, which is why he opposed an approach to Radić. The reorganization of the state along (con)federal lines would have jeopardized, in Pribićević's mind, the position of Croatia's Serbs. This explains Pribićević's willingness to cooperate with Pašić and the NRS, who wanted a centralized state order. This also explains why Davidović, while promising reform to Radić, avoided a discussion of reform within his own party or parliamentary club.[141] Open cooperation with Radić would certainly have brought about a split in the Democratic Party, which is in fact what happened in 1924.

The talks ended, therefore, without any substantive agreement. Nevertheless, in December 1922 Radić pledged to support Davidović in all his future endeavours insofar as he remained committed to reform.[142] That same month Pašić tendered his cabinet's resignation, thus ending the nearly two-year long NRS–Democratic Party partnership. On 16 December Pašić formed a NRS government, dissolved parliament, and called new elections for March 1923. This was what Radić had been waiting for throughout 1922. He now threw himself into the campaign with his usual vigour, denouncing centralism and the entire state order and its exponents, most notably Pašić and Pribićević. Radić's assessment of the HRSS's chances in the upcoming election was typically optimistic: he predicted that of the sixty-eight seats allotted to Croatia (Croatia–Slavonia), the HRSS would win at least fifty, and perhaps as many as sixty, and he announced that the HRSS was moving into new regions (Dalmatia, Bosnia–Herzegovina, Baranja, Bačka).[143]

TABLE 6.4
Election results (national, 18 March 1923), major parties, 312 seats

Party	Votes	Percentage	Seats
NRS	562,213	25.8	108
HRSS	473,333	21.8	70
Democratic Party	400,342	18.4	51
Slovenes (SLS)*	139,171	6.4	24
Bosnian Muslims	112,228	5.2	18
Džemijet	71,453	3.3	14
Serbian Agrarians**	164,602	7.6	11
Others	–	11.5	16

Sources: Gligorijević, *Parlament i političke stranke u Jugoslaviji 1919–1929*, (Belgrade, 1979), 145–149; Čulinović, *Jugoslavija izmedju dva rata* (Zagreb, 1961), 406–11.
*SLS: includes votes from Croat People's Party and Croats from Vojvodina.
**Serbian Agrarians: includes one seat and 11,023 votes from Slovene Independent Peasant Party.

TABLE 6.5
Election results in Croatia (prewar Croatia–Slavonia) and Dalmatia, 83 seats

Party	Votes	Percentage (Cr., Dalm.)	Seats
HRSS	395,534	65.9, 26.4	59
Democratic Party	97,987	15.6, 10.5	11
NRS	76,979	9.5, 22.8	11
Others	–	9.0, 40.3	2

Sources: Gligorijević, *Parlament i političke stranke u Jugoslaviji 1919–1929*, (Belgrade, 1979), 145–149; Čulinović, *Jugoslavija izmedju dva rata* (Zagreb, 1961), 406–11.

Indeed, the elections of 18 March 1923 proved to be a major victory for the HRSS; it emerged with 473,333 votes and seventy seats. Its position was tremendously strengthened for it had become the second largest party in the entire country. The HRSS was now the undisputed leader of a national mass movement: for the first time it captured a significant number of urban votes, although this had more to do with the fact that the Croat Union decided, in February 1923, not to run any candidates in the face of Radić's juggernaut. Of the HRSS's seventy seats, fifty-two came from Croatia–Slavonia. Its victory there was complete. The HRSS's remaining eighteen seats came from Bosnia–Herzegovina (9), Dalmatia (7) and Slovenia (2).[144] Of its seventy deputies,

TABLE 6.6
Election results in Bosnia–Herzegovina, 48 seats

Party	Votes	Percentage	Seats
Bosnian Muslims	112,228	29.3	18
NRS	92,623	24.4	13
HRSS	68,013	17.9	9
Serbian Agrarians	58,562	15.4	7
Serb Party	9,294	2.5	1
Others	–	10.5	0

Sources: Gligorijević, *Parlament i političke stranke u Jugoslaviji 1919–1929*, (Belgrade, 1979), 145-149; Čulinović, *Jugoslavija izmedju dva rata* (Zagreb, 1961), 406–11.

just over half – thirty-seven (52 per cent) were peasants. Intellectuals (lawyers, priests, writers, journalists, engineers, white collar officials, teachers) numbered nineteen (27 per cent). Most of the others were proprietors.[145] By 1923 Radić could legitimately refer to the HRSS not just as a party, but as a movement that had arisen above class distinctions with its main pillar in the peasantry. The HRSS had 'united the entire Croat peasantry and the majority of the working class, bourgeoisie, and intelligentsia, *therefore the entire Croat people.*'[146] The HRSS had become the agent of national integration.

The HRSS leadership viewed this electoral victory as a reconfirmation of the November 1920 vote and as a mandate for Croat self-determination.[147] On 25 March 1923 the HRSS's deputies reaffirmed the party's earlier policy and tactics. The HRSS continued to regard itself as the embodiment of and legal successor to the Croatian *Sabor* but refused to declare itself formally as such, because a declaration of this nature 'would under today's circumstances easily bring about a domestic or civil war,' something that the HRSS wished to avoid at all cost.[148] The HRSS also reaffirmed its commitment to non-violence and an 'honourable' agreement with the Serb people, but refused to recognize any of the acts of the Belgrade government as legal and binding. It concluded that if all attempts at a political agreement with the Serb parties failed, the HRSS 'will seek assistance from all European, and even other, parliaments.'[149] Within months Radić would carry out this thinly veiled threat to seek Western assistance.

The HRSS's policy in fact underwent a subtle change in the immediate aftermath of the elections. In an interview with a Belgrade paper, Radić did not categorically reject the possibility of an agreement with Pašić and the NRS. His new willingness to open a dialogue with Pašić was inspired by the election results. Pašić's NRS emerged with 108 seats, seventeen more than in the 1920 elections, whereas Davidović's Democrats, whom Radić had just recently courted, fell from ninety-two to fifty-one seats. Radić insisted that all talks were to be conducted in Zagreb, and the first step towards an agreement was for the NRS to recognize the HRSS as the only legitimate representative of the Croat people. Radić repeated his desire for a negotiated settlement with Belgrade that would guarantee the Croats' national rights. If such an agreement were impossible, 'We [HRSS] will find the path to bring about new elections,' and Radić indicated that the HRSS would 'enact an international action ... to achieve our rights.' This was yet another veiled threat to seek international support, which in a matter of months would be translated into Radić's trip abroad. In the short term Radić envisaged closer cooperation with the leaders of the Slovenes and Bosnian Muslims.[150]

To strengthen his political position, Radić joined forces with other, albeit more moderate, opposition elements, namely, Anton Korošec's Slovene People's Party (SLS, *Slovenska ljudska stranka*) and Mehmed Spaho's Yugoslav Muslim Organization (JMO, *Jugoslavenska muslimanska organizacija*), to form the Federalist Bloc.[151] Radić thus became the nexus uniting disparate political elements who for a variety of reasons were dissatisfied with the existing regime. Combined they commanded 112 of 312 seats in the Belgrade parliament, thereby potentially threatening a homogeneous NRS government (108 seats). The Pašić government was initially sufficiently alarmed at the news of this new opposition coalition, and the possibility that the HRSS would end its abstention and thus topple the NRS minority government, that it was prepared to enter into negotiations with Radić. Consequently, contacts were initiated between the HRSS and its new allies and the NRS. The negotiations culminated on 13 April 1923 with the signing of a protocol (*Markov protokol*).[152] The signatories to the protocol, the terms of which were initially kept secret, agreed to the preconditions for a national agreement between Serbs, Croats, and Slovenes. The proposed 'parcelization' of Croatia, Bosnia–Herzegovina, and Slovenia into new administrative districts, as dictated by the terms of the Vidovdan constitution, was to end, and the principles of legality, constitutionality, and just administration were to be adhered to by the NRS government. In return, the NRS was to form a homogeneous government and elect one of its deputies as the head of the parliament, unobstructed by the Federalist Bloc. Radić, anxious for a settlement, portrayed the talks as a step towards a national agreement with the Serb people, for the NRS was the largest Serb party.[153]

If Radić truly expected the NRS to hold to its agreement, and the evidence seems to suggest that he did, at least initially, he was very quickly disappointed. King Aleksandar was against the agreement and prevented Pašić from pursuing further talks.[154] In the event Pašić had little interest in either continuing the negotiations or abiding by the terms of the protocol. His immediate concern was to determine the HRSS's and the Federalist Bloc's true intent and to secure the election of a NRS deputy as head of the parliament. Once it became clear that Radić was not prepared to abandon his policy of abstention, Pašić realized that the NRS minority government was secure, at least in the short term. The protocol was therefore a dead letter. Only two days later, on 15 April, Radić, already sensing that Pašić's motives were less than sincere, and that he had been duped, delivered a vitriolic speech at a massive rally, one of the HRSS's largest in the 1920s, in Borongaj (Zagreb). Radić declared that there would never again be a royal government or administration in Zagreb and that an agreement with the NRS regime was very difficult and would not be realized in the near future. Yet he emphasized that the HRSS had an obligation to talk to the NRS as the strongest Serb party.[155] He also threatened to take his agitation to Serbia, Macedonia, and Montenegro in the next elections, to 'encircle' the NRS regime, but at that stage this was little more than an idle threat. Despite the harsh words, it appears that Radić may still have continued to believe throughout May, and perhaps even beyond, that the terms of the protocol would be implemented. Indeed, towards mid-May he despatched two HRSS representatives, Dragutin-Karla Kovačević and Juraj Krnjević, to Belgrade. After meeting with Pašić on 12 May they returned to Zagreb with the mistaken impression that he was still committed to implementing the terms of the protocol.

It was becoming increasingly evident to Radić that the NRS would not respect the terms of the protocol. His criticism of the regime sharpened, particularly after Pašić's government banned an HRSS rally in Zagreb that had been planned for 24 June. Radić interpreted this as a provocative move, and he refused to countenance any further negotiations with Pašić. On 14 July 1923, during the HRSS's Bastille Day commemorations, which in itself was a provocative act, Radić railed against the Serbian establishment in the most vituperative terms. He compared the existing state order to the Bastille and made denigrating references to the 'despotism' of the Serbian élite. For the first time he revealed the terms of the April 1923 protocol to prove that the NRS regime had no interest in genuine dialogue. But Radić was still prepared to accept a confederal arrangement.[156] He declared in conclusion that all talks with Belgrade were now off. In the absence of the real possibility of further talks with the NRS, and apparently in the fear that his personal safety was in danger,[157] Radić crossed the Drava river to Hungary on the night of 22–3 July 1923.

Radić's unexpected 'disappearance' caused a good deal of initial consternation and confusion on the part of the authorities. The head of the Fourth Gendarmerie Brigade in Čakovec reported on 2 August that Radić had left the country on 20 July.[158] Two days later, however, the head of the gendarmerie in Zagreb informed the regional administration that he was certain from all available sources 'that Stjepan Radić is hiding [in the country]. There is no proof that he would go abroad, and it is not probable.' He believed that Radić was hiding in a village, but because of 'the good organization of his party' and in light of the fact that 'individual regions are through and through in his hands, it is not difficult for him to hide before the authorities.'[159] It was only at the end of that month that the government was certain that Radić had decided to carry out his earlier threat to seek European support for his Croat republican cause.

At their session of 19 August, the HRSS's deputies formally authorized Radić's 'diplomatic action' and reaffirmed his decision of 24 June to break off talks with Belgrade. Their decision was made, they insisted, in light of the fact that not a single Serbian party had shown a genuine willingness for an agreement with the HRSS. The HRSS portrayed Radić's trip as a mission to inform European leaders about the causes of the Croat–Serb conflict and the means by which it could be resolved.[160] But evidently some elements within the HRSS opposed the trip, including Rudolf Horvat, who would distance himself from Radić with some other deputies the following year. Horvat characterized the trip as 'a cowardly move' and a 'flight.'[161] Nonetheless, Radić had closely followed European developments since the Paris Peace Conference, as demonstrated by the Croat Bloc's memoranda to the Genoa Conference and the League of Nations in 1922, and he now attempted to play the hand that he had so desperately wished for in 1919. Radić was to be seriously disappointed. He arrived in London on 17 August and immediately began a lecture tour among Labour Party politicians as well as intellectuals and societies who had an interest in Yugoslav affairs, including Noel Buxton, R.W. Seton-Watson, H. Wickham-Steed, Bertrand Russell, the Balkan Committee, and the Near East Society.

Radić kept the HRSS informed about his activities through a series of letters, over forty in total, from London, the first two of which appeared in the party newspaper *Slobodni Dom* in late August 1923. In his first letter he wrote that 'in only three days more was accomplished for our cause in London than at home in three years.' He stated in his second letter that an unnamed British diplomat told him that he had accomplished two things by coming to London: the Belgrade government would not now be able to use force against the Croats and that Croatia would achieve 'Home Rule' by the end of the year. In his thirty-first letter he finally broached the issue of abandoning the policy of abstention. The HRSS would go to Belgrade 'when we either alone or with our trustworthy allies [Slovenes and Bosnian Muslims] gain a secure majority [in the Belgrade parliament], that is, at least 160 deputies out of 313.'[162] 'My position is better every day,' Radić wrote to an associate in early November 1923, 'and the Croat Question is increasingly becoming a part of the current policy of the two Great Powers [Great Britain and France] and two other such states [probably a reference to the USSR and Italy], which can help us the most.' Radić still wanted an agreement with Belgrade, he indicated to an associate in Croatia that November, but insisted that the protocol of April 1923 first be implemented: 'I remain on the basic principle of my, that is, of our, Croat policy, that a partly limited state independence for Croatia in agreement with Serbia and without separation from her is better than unlimited Croat sovereignty, without such an agreement and in a struggle with Serbia.'[163] But all of Radić's endeavours in London were to no avail because he failed to gain any official backing for the HRSS's position, which is undoubtedly what he had wanted. In fact, Radić may well have started 'to vacillate between going and not going to the [Belgrade] parliament,' as one of his associates apparently claimed in early October 1923. It was now necessary to abstain as long as possible 'to gain as much as possible for the Croat people and to preserve their national and state individuality.'[164] Radić left London on 22 December and arrived in Vienna two days later, where he stayed until 29 May 1924.

In early 1924 Radić still maintained his willingness for a negotiated agreement. Although he remained steadfast in his views, much of the bellicose attitude of the previous summer had disappeared, undoubtedly a reflection of his failure to obtain any substantive support in London. Radić acknowledged that an agreement was possible only if the Serbs were prepared 'to recognize that we Croats were not conquered by the Serbian army and that we have a right to our national sovereignty and our territory.' This agreement would result in 'a union or confederation of states.'[165]

In January 1924 Radić elaborated a plan, supposedly the result of his consultations with political figures in London, for an agreement between Croatia and Serbia, which envisaged a common state that would be formally known as the 'Yugoslav Union,' with the Karadjordjević dynasty as its international 'symbol.' This union was to be a confederation of states providing for internal sovereignty for its constituent units. Croatia would retain its own, HRSS-sponsored constitution of 1921, a separate parliament, and become a member of the League of Nations. Defence, commerce and foreign affairs would be joint affairs. Slovenia, Bosnia-Herzegovina, Montenegro, Macedonia, and Vojvodina would also obtain autonomy.[166] Realistically, of course, Radić's plan had little chance of success, for neither the NRS nor the Democratic

Party, nor the king, would have agreed to such terms. Nevertheless, in January 1924 there was still no indication that Radić was prepared to abandon his confederalist platform. In fact, he attempted in the spring of 1924 to organize in Vienna a conference of disaffected nationalities and minority groups in the hope of drawing European attention to the stateless peoples of the continent, but was thwarted by the Austrian police.[167]

In February 1924 Radić finally decided to abandon the policy of abstention *vis-à-vis* Belgrade. This policy eventually had to give way. From the outset it was based on principle. Participating in either the Constituent Assembly or the parliament which succeeded it would have meant legitimizing the unification act of 1918. But the policy was predicated, at least in Radić's mind, on the belief that Croats would gain international backing for their cause. Such support never materialized. In London Radić was urged to abandon abstention. One British journalist wrote to Radić in March 1924 that 'if, after the next elections, you were to set up a parliament and a government at Zagreb, then the question of your recognition would arise.' He did not say that recognition would be forthcoming, only that 'the question of recognition could not arise before you have either obtained or proclaimed the autonomy of Croatia.'[168] Since Radić refused formally to proclaim the existence of a Croatian republic – he believed that such a move would likely provoke harsh reprisals from Belgrade – the question of foreign recognition remained a dead letter. Another Briton, who saw a good deal of Radić during his stay in London, concluded that the latter learned 'a good deal from his visit. He certainly realizes quite clearly now, that no one in this country will under any circumstances intervene in Jugoslavia's [*sic*] internal politics. Even those who showed the greatest sympathy with him, urged upon him most strongly the need for coming to terms with the Serbs.'[169] In this context, coming to terms with the Serbs meant, of course, going to Belgrade. Under the circumstances, the policy of abstention was fated to failure.

What is more, abstention from Belgrade was motivated by Radić's belief that the Serbian political establishment, as represented by Pašić's NRS and, to a lesser extent, Davidović's Democratic Party, would eventually be voted or ousted from office. When this was shown to be unrealistic, Radić was forced to face reality. Moreover, that reality, as contoured by the Vidovdan constitution, was in practice in no way threatened or undermined by the HRSS's passive policy of abstention. The centralist parties, especially the NRS, could implement their policies in spite of, and to a certain extent because of, the HRSS's abstention. Indeed, in mid-February 1924 the Pašić government finally did away with the Croatian regional administration in order to implement the new system of thirty-three districts. The Yugoslav authorities also formally recognized in the Italo-Yugoslav Pact of Rome (January 1924) that Rijeka (Fiume) was a part of Italy. Radić decided finally to adopt a more assertive policy; Pašić's regime had to be brought down because of its administrative parcelization of Croatia.[170] Radić was convinced the HRSS could, together with the SLS and JMO, gain two-thirds of the seats in the Belgrade parliament, and he was now prepared to send the HRSS's deputies to Belgrade to topple the minority NRS regime.[171]

Radić began holding talks in December 1923 with other political parties in order to form a new opposition front, including the SLS, JMO, and the Democratic Party. In early February he instructed the HRSS's deputies to go to Belgrade. On 8 February Maček and Krnjević submitted to parliament the HRSS's seats for verification. Abstention had come to an end, but the HRSS did not yet abandon its republican platform. In March 1924 the Opposition Bloc, composed of the Democrats, JMO, SLS, and HRSS, was formed. In late March the Opposition Bloc was weakened, however, when fifteen Democrats, led by Pribićević, seceded from the Democratic Party to constitute themselves as the Independent Democratic Party (SDS, *Samostalna demokratska stranka*). That same month the SDS joined Pašić's government, but by this stage its days were numbered. Pašić offered his cabinet's resignation on 12 April, and parliament was recessed until October 1924. Only three months later, on 24 July, did Davidović receive a mandate from the king to form a Democratic–JMO–SLS government. The HRSS pledged to support its operation but refused to participate, even though Davidović kept four ministerial portfolios vacant.

Radić's decision to send his deputies to Belgrade prompted a new wave of vigilance on the part of the authorities. They wished to determine if the nature of the HRSS's activism in the countryside had changed, and what the peasantry's disposition was to the new policy.[172] The prefect of Donja Stubica noted that there was no increased activism on the part of the HRSS in his region and that there was now little talk of a republic. Many followers still could not believe that the HRSS was going to Belgrade 'and in general there is already noticeable a certain resignation and apathy, because of the many promises that Radić has made, not a single one has of yet been realized.'[173] Another official also claimed that there was virtually no mention of a republic any longer, 'nor do the people consider it realistic.' Nonetheless, he believed that the peasantry in his region generally supported the HRSS's new policy and still expected Croatian autonomy, fewer bureaucrats, lower taxes, and other reforms.[174] The prefect of Krapina district observed that the peasants expected results from the HRSS's activism in the Belgrade parliament and still had faith in Radić, 'for of all the political parties only he is concerned about the welfare of the people, that is, the peasantry.'[175] The prefect of Sv Ivan Zelina claimed that, although the peasants were still for a republic, they supported the HRSS's new policy and expected tangible results. The prefect of Varaždin asserted that there was no talk of a republic but that the HRSS still commanded the loyalty of the region's peasants. The prefects of Samobor, Jastrebarsko, and Pregrada all reported that the HRSS's new policy had created some divisions among the HRSS's followers, who were coming to the realization that a republic would not be created, but that party discipline had prevailed.[176] What the regional administration's reports appear to indicate is that the HRSS's local activists did not make any major effort to inform the peasantry about the party's new policy, or to justify the move, that there was some opposition in the countryside to it, but that the peasantry by and large supported the decision to go to Belgrade.

Having made the decision to abandon the policy of abstention, Radić subsequently undertook another major tactical initiative by going to Soviet Russia. Because it appeared that Davidović would not yet be able to form a government at that time, Radić decided to seek support in Moscow.[177] It is unclear precisely at what point Radić was first approached by the Soviets, but he claimed that he received repeated invitations to go to the USSR from both the Presidium of the Peasant International (Krestintern), which was founded in October 1923 in Moscow, and G.V. Chicherin, the Soviet Commissar for Foreign Affairs (1918–30), in all likelihood in 1923 during his visits to London and Vienna.[178] It is important to remember that as opposed as Radić was to communism, he generally viewed events in Soviet Russia with some sympathy. He wrote in November 1922 that Bolshevik Russia had recognized the right of national self-determination to its peoples (and in theory to all peoples), which is why 'it is completely natural that we Croats respect and love this Bolshevik Russia incomparably more than the forever deceased Imperial Russia.'[179] It is also interesting to note, and almost certainly not without significance, that Radić evidently thought highly of Chicherin. Among Radić's private papers there is an article about Chicherin from a Zagreb daily, and in the margins Radić referred to Chicherin as 'a true *minister*, that is, *a servant, a worker* for his nation.'[180] It appears he may have believed that he would receive a sympathetic hearing from Chicherin.

Radić arrived in Moscow on 2 June 1924, where he was greeted – 'as a peasant leader and intrepid fighter for the liberation of the Croat peasants'[181] – by Chicherin and other Soviet officials, as well as a guard of honour. On 11 June Radić received a letter from the Polish communist Tomasz Dombal, in the name of the Krestintern's Presidium, inviting him to enrol the HRSS in that organization on his own terms. Dombal went to great lengths to allay any suspicions Radić may have had about the Krestintern and asked him to propose 'a project of our reciprocal relations and practical work.' The presidium wished to remove all obstacles 'that could in future cause undesirable disagreement between us and you.' Under these circumstances, Radić decided to join the Krestintern, which represented the culmination of his trip to Moscow. In his letter of accession of 27 June 1924 to Aleksandr Petrovich-Smirnov, the secretary of the Krestintern, Radić was careful to distance himself from any possible suggestion that the HRSS approved, tacitly or otherwise, of communist tactics or principles. Although he expressed 'complete agreement' with the Krestintern's main aims, namely, that the peasantry and workers together 'put an end to expansionist wars,' and that they 'gradually take power into their hands in all countries' to achieve social justice, Radić reiterated that the HRSS was in no way changing its program or tactics. In searching for a resolution to the Yugoslav state's internal crisis, the HRSS would employ, as was the case hitherto, 'only pacifistic means, and that only in an extreme contingency, when that pacifism is shown to be unsuccessful, will it resort to revolution.' In this context Radić indicated that his pacifism was conditional, but in reality his opposition to the use of violence as a political method remained completely intact. Furthermore, Radić reaffirmed his recognition of the Yugoslav state's international frontiers and his desire for a Croatian republic within those frontiers. Indeed, he claimed that the HRSS hoped 'to transform it [Yugoslavia] into a federal peasant republic,' that would subsequently enter into an Adriatic–Danubian federation that would stretch from Czechoslovakia to the Yugoslav federation, which was reminiscent of his musings from 1918–20. Nevertheless, he concluded by insisting that the Krestintern could not have a 'Yugoslav' representation because 'no such Yugoslavia exists.' What did exist was 'a militaristic and plundering Great Serbia under the formal name of "Kingdom of Serbs, Croats and Slovenes."'[182]

On 1 July 1924 the Presidium of the Krestintern unanimously voted to accept the HRSS as a member and embraced Radić's precondition that there could be no Yugoslav representation. It thereby endorsed fully Radić's policy of Croat national self-determination. The HRSS leadership formally approved this move on 3 August 1924, but not without some difficulty. Rudolf Horvat, Tomo Jalžabetić, and Vinko Lovreković, all of whom subsequently became dissidents, raised their opposition to this move and were mollified, albeit temporarily, only after considerable effort on the part of Radić's deputy Vladko Maček.[183]

More important than the HRSS's accession to the Krestintern was the resolution issued by the Comintern, which held its Fifth World Congress (17 June to 8 July 1924) during Radić's stay in Moscow. The Comintern's new position on the Yugoslav national question was to denounce Yugoslav unitarism and essentially to advocate the break-up of the Yugoslav state. The resolution proclaimed that the Serbs, Croats, and Slovenes were separate nations, and that 'the theory of a single trinomial nation of Serbs, Croats, and Slovenes is only a mask for Great Serbian imperialism.' Yugoslav communists were instructed to wage 'a determined struggle' against national oppression and to assist all national liberationist movements, while at the same time weaning them from the influence of the bourgeoisie. They were to adopt the slogan of national self-determination which had to be 'expressed in the form of separating Croatia, Slovenia, and Macedonia from the Yugoslav structure and in their establishment as independent republics.'[184] Hence, whereas the Yugoslav communists had in 1924 adopted federalism (though in principle recognizing the right to secession), the Comintern now was urging the destruction of Yugoslavia, a step undoubtedly initiated partly in deference to Radić.

There is no evidence to suggest that Radić attended any of the Comintern's sessions, but it seems unlikely that he was oblivious to the issues discussed at the congress or the resolution regarding the Yugoslav state. The Comintern's Yugoslav policy now overlapped to a degree with that of the HRSS, and was a victory of sorts for Radić. But it was a Pyrrhic victory with no practical benefit for the HRSS. The Comintern and KPJ were committed to overthrowing the Serbian establishment as part of their wider objective of class revolution. Because of his pacifist orientation and suspicions of the KPJ, Radić refused to countenance cooperation with the Yugoslav communists, even when it was proposed to him in late 1924. Although Radić believed that the Serbian establishment might indeed be ousted in a revolution, he evidently lost this illusion by 1924, and in the event showed no inclination personally to assist such an enterprise. What Radić wanted was not continued confrontation with Belgrade but an agreement with the Serbian establishment that would recognize Croatian state sovereignty. His trip to Moscow was designed simply as a means of attaining a measure of international legitimacy, which might in turn strengthen his bargaining position *vis-à-vis* Belgrade. Parliamentary cooperation with the KPJ was impossible, for the Yugoslav communists had no representatives in the Belgrade parliament. In mid-1924 Radić expressed interest in cooperating only with the legitimate opposition parties in Yugoslavia, above all the Democratic Party.

To justify his trip to Moscow, Radić indicated that because the process of rapprochement between the Soviets and a number of European powers, including Great Britain, had already begun, he had seen no reason why he should not go to Moscow.[185] But aside from reinforcing the Comintern's policy of the necessity of breaking up the Yugoslav state, Radić's manoeuvre had few tactical advantages. It was an act of a desperate man, and inevitably increased the suspicions of the Serbian political establishment, namely, the NRS and the king. The Kingdom of Serbs, Croats, and Slovenes maintained a hostile attitude towards the Soviets until 1941, and it had welcomed thousands of Russian émigrés after the Russian Revolution. It was this trip to Soviet Russia and the HRSS's accession to the Krestintern that ultimately provided the NRS with a suitable pretext to employ harsher measures against Radić and his republican movement.

Returning to the country on 11 August, Radić reaffirmed his support for the Davidović government, which had been formed in July. To ensure better relations between itself and Radić, in late August the Davidović government reestablished the Croatian regional administration in Zagreb. After a series of talks between the government and HRSS in early September, on 15 September 1924 the HRSS leadership formally decided to enter the government and to occupy the four vacant ministerial portfolios. The king was opposed to this move, however, and demanded a number of concessions from the HRSS, most notably that it renounce its republican platform. Davidović, eager to bring Radić into the government, sent his Minister of Internal Affairs Nastas Petrović to Zagreb to obtain concessions from Radić. During their meeting of 23 September Radić apparently indicated his willingness to recognize the state's 'integrity' and a 'monarchy of the English type,' and even expressed his desire to meet with the king.[186] Although both Davidović and Petrović were encouraged by these concessions, King Aleksandar remained suspicious of Radić's true motives and refused to allow the HRSS to join the government. On 8 October the king orchestrated the resignation of the Minister of Defence General Stevan Hadžić, who explained his resignation in terms of Radić's 'defeatist speech' on 5 October about Yugoslav policy towards Albania.[187] On 12 October Radić delivered a vitriolic speech attacking the Belgrade political establishment, for Hadžić's resignation was intended to undermine the Davidović cabinet and to prevent Radić's participation. Radić referred to Hadžić as a 'political idiot' who had been ordered to resign on the instructions of a 'criminal,' an implicit reference to Pašić. He also made implicit references to Pribićević and his followers as 'vermin,' and to the growing political influence of the court. At the same time, he urged Davidović to take a firmer stand and to resist the intrigues against his government. But in spite of his angry and bitter tone, Radić stressed that he was prepared to compromise and to recognize the Karadjordjević dynasty as the international symbol of the Yugoslav state, and emphasized his willingness to make concessions in order to reach a Croat–Serb agreement.[188]

There is a tendency in the historiography to interpret this speech as undermining the position of the Davidović government and providing the king with a pretext to move against it.[189] It has even been suggested that after this speech the king demanded Radić's arrest.[190] Even though the speech was harsh, it contained an underlying conciliatory tone and was in fact on the whole greeted favourably by Davidović's government.[191] The subsequent collapse of Davidović's government had less to do with Radić's speech than with the king's determination to prevent the HRSS from participating in that cabinet at any cost. Despite Radić's public tone, which did not portend any major change in his policy, it appears that by September–October 1924 he was prepared to abandon republicanism in favour of a parliamentary monarchy 'of the English type,' which in practice meant recognizing the Karadjordjević dynasty and the existing state system, albeit with some important alterations. He made this known to some Serbian politicians, including Petrović.[192] In the absence of foreign support, and blocked from participating in the Davidović government, Radić's options now became extremely limited.

On 15 October Davidović offered his cabinet's resignation and publicly stated that the king had asked him to do so.[193] From the day it was formed, Davidović's government had little chance of success and had no support from the king, even though it possessed a comfortable relative majority. The king confided to one politician that Davidović was naïve and that he had offered him a mandate to form a government in 1924 only 'because he wanted to demonstrate that the opposition does not have either a leader or a political man, who could bring order to the state.' The king believed that he had to work with Pašić, 'because he alone knows what he wants ... and knows what the state needs. Today he is the only man with whom one can work.'[194] With the demise of Davidović's government, Pašić again received a mandate to form a new government. The new Pašić–Pribićević minority government, formed on 6 November, was determined from the outset to break Radić's movement by using the HRSS's decision to join the Krestintern as its main weapon. With the king's assent, the parliament was recessed and new elections called for 8 February. At a cabinet session on 23 December the government decided to use the law for the protection of the state against the HRSS. The party was to be suppressed, its leadership jailed, its newspaper banned, and its archives seized – in other words, it was to be placed outside of the law. The *Obznana* (proclamation) against the HRSS, which authorized the arrest of all of its activists, was publicly announced on 1 January 1925.[195] Radić was arrested four days later, as were the most prominent leaders of the party (Vladko Maček, Josip Predavec, Juraj Krnjević, and August and Stjepan Košutić).[196] Although a Zagreb court ordered in January that they, though not Radić, be freed, they were rearrested upon their release and kept under house arrest. The Demo-

TABLE 6.7
Election results (national, 8 February 1925), major parties, 315 seats

Party	Votes	Percentage	Seats
NRS*	702,573	28.8	122
HRSS	545,466	22.3	67
Democratic Party	279,686	11.8	37
National Bloc*	210,843	9.6	33
SDS*	117,953	5.0	8
Slovenes (SLS)	105,304	4.3	20
Bosnian Muslims	132,296	5.4	15
Serbian Agrarians**	130,254	5.3	5
Others	–	7.5	8

*National Bloc (NRS–SDS joint candidates): of its 33 seats, 19 went to the NRS (giving it 141) and 14 to the SDS (Independent Democratic Party, giving it 22).
**Serbian Agrarians: includes one seat from the Slovene Independent Peasant Party.
Sources: Gligorijević, *Parlament i političke stranke u Jugoslaviji 1919–1929*, (Belgrade, 1979), 192-5; Čulinović, *Jugoslavija izmedju dva rata* (Zagreb, 1961), 454–7.

cratic Party, SLS, and JMO all condemned the *Obznana*, but this had no effect on the government's policy towards the HRSS.

The HRSS thus entered the 8 February 1925 elections with its leadership imprisoned and under tremendous political, police, and military pressure. The gendarmerie and military were activated to preserve public order, as were some Chetnik (Serb nationalist) paramilitary units. In many instances, these units prevented the HRSS and other opposition parties from organizing electoral rallies. What is more, in some parts of Croatia the government dismissed local supervisory electoral committees, dominated as they were by the HRSS, and withheld material needed to carry out the voting.[197] The Belgrade authorities also placed special emphasis on attacking the HRSS's local organizations, particularly in Dalmatia and Bosnia, where they were weakest. Over 2,000 homes were searched by the police and 2,735 HRSS local activists arrested.[198]

Despite the government's use of irregularities, the elections proved to be the greatest HRSS victory to date: 545,466 votes and sixty-seven seats. The HRSS had again penetrated a number of urban centres, particularly because many prominent members of the middle-class Croat Union, which formally adopted a republican platform in November 1924, ran on the HRSS ticket. In Croatia (Croatia–Slavonia) the HRSS won forty-five of a possible sixty-eight seats, and the remaining twenty-two seats came from Bosnia–Herzegovina (10), Dalmatia (9), and Slovenia (3). In addition to gaining over 70 per cent of

TABLE 6.8
Election results in Croatia (prewar Croatia–Slavonia) and Dalmatia, 84 seats

Party	Votes	Percentage (Cr., D.)	Seats
HRSS	442,547	60.9, 51.4	54
National Bloc*	232,811	30.7, 33.4	29
Others	71,335	8.4, 15.2	1

*National Bloc (NRS–SDS joint candidates): of its 33 seats, 19 went to the NRS (giving it 141) and 14 to the SDS (Independent Democratic Party, giving it 22).
Sources: Gligorijević, *Parlament i političke stranke u Jugoslaviji 1919–1929*, (Belgrade, 1979), 192-5; Čulinović, *Jugoslavija izmedju dva rata* (Zagreb, 1961), 454–7.

TABLE 6.9
Election results in Bosnia–Herzegovina, 48 seats

Party	Votes	Percentage	Seats
Bosnian Muslims	127,690	29.9	15
NRS*	121,291	28.2	14
HRSS	83,387	19.5	10
National Bloc*	51,759	12.2	7
Serbian Agrarians	26,326	6.2	2
Others	–	4.0	0

*National Bloc (NRS–SDS joint candidates): of its 33 seats, 19 went to the NRS (giving it 141) and 14 to the SDS (Independent Democratic Party, giving it 22).
Sources: Gligorijević, *Parlament i političke stranke u Jugoslaviji 1919–1929*, (Belgrade, 1979), 192-5; Čulinović, *Jugoslavija izmedju dva rata* (Zagreb, 1961), 454–7.

the popular vote in Zagreb and Osijek, the HRSS won over 60 per cent in the Dalmatian towns of Split and Dubrovnik.[199]

The day after the election Radić indicated to his wife that everything depended on how well Davidović's Democrats performed in the elections. He was convinced by the preliminary results that the HRSS, Slovenes (SLS), Bosnian Muslims (JMO), and Democrats would receive 172 seats, and that Pašić's NRS and Pribićević's SDS would gain only 143.[200] Radić would be greatly disappointed, however. The NRS and SDS together mustered 163 seats, obtaining a majority in the 315-seat parliament. The HRSS and its allies gained just under 140 seats. Radić was forced to deal with the NRS-led government.

The very fact that the government permitted the HRSS to run candidates in the elections demonstrates that it was not prepared to carry the *Obznana* to its logical conclusion, as had been the case with the communists in 1921. Indeed, by the second half of March, Radić began receiving emissaries of the king, like Mita Dimitrijević, Vojislav Janjić, and Toni Šlegel. At the same time, however, in mid-March the NRS-controlled verification committee of the Belgrade parliament annulled all of the HRSS's seats from the last election in order further to pressure Radić into submission. By this stage Radić was prepared to jettison his republicanism. His wife noted on 23 March that Radić was willing to recognize a British-style parliamentary monarchy, which in his mind meant, *inter alia*, local self-government, constitutional freedoms (freedom of the press and of assembly), an independent judiciary, and autonomy for the prewar Croatian Triune kingdom (Croatia–Slavonia–Dalmatia), with some minor territorial readjustments.[201] Just four days later, on 27 March, Radić's nephew Pavle Radić delivered a speech in the parliament that had been written by his uncle, in which he declared that the HRSS was abandoning its republicanism and recognizing the Karadjordjević dynasty and the Vidovdan constitution.[202] The capitulation, admittedly coerced, was now essentially complete. A month later, on 22 April, Radić told one of the king's emissaries that he renounced all autonomist schemes for Croatia.[203] Direct talks between the NRS and the HSS (*Hrvatska seljačka stranka*, Croat Peasant Party), as the party was now called, were initiated on 2 July.[204] The end result was a new NRS–HSS government, formed on 16 July and headed by Pašić. Two days later Radić was released. The idea of the Croat neutral peasant republic was finally dead.

Radić's capitulation came as a shock to many. The after-effects were to resound through the party's ranks, and indeed through political circles in the entire country. Yet the capitulation was virtually inevitable. Like Radić's policy of abstention, the demand for a republic eventually had to give way, particularly because no backing was forthcoming from abroad. In the absence of such support the republic was unrealizable, for the HRSS, in spite of its command over the Croat countryside, was too weak to achieve it unilaterally. Moreover, the Serbian political establishment demonstrated greater resilience than Radić expected. The social revolution that he anticipated in Serbia never materialized. Radić remained committed to pacifism and a negotiated settlement between Croats and Serbs, but this presupposed that the Serbian political establishment, particularly the NRS and the king, were genuinely willing to make major concessions on the issue of state organization. They were not, and Radić was consequently forced to play his only remaining card: personally to seek the assistance of 'enlightened' European opinion.

Radić believed rather naïvely that he could persuade European public and intellectual opinion to recognize the legitimacy and justness of the Croat cause, of which he was the personal embodiment, and then to assist in the realization of the republican aspirations of the Croat people. 'I am going by foot to visit the sultan, to win him over to our cause,' is how the Croat modernist critic Antun Gustav Matoš, writing before 1914, mocked Radić's belief in the power of persuasion.[205] This was no less true in 1923. When Radić's 'diplomatic mission' failed he found himself in a cul-de-sac that was to a large extent of his own making. Radić's trip to Soviet Russia completely backfired and only further stimulated the animus of the Serbian establishment. Although Radić abandoned abstention in early 1924, when the doors of government were closed to him in the autumn of that year by the court camarilla, there was little room left to manœuvre. The HRSS's new parliamentary activism was thus thwarted. The king would not countenance its participation in government as long as it remained committed to its existing platform. Radić's choices were extremely limited even before his arrest, but when that occurred in January 1925 he had to make finally a decision: capitulation, however painful, or the continuation of his republican policy, in all likelihood behind prison bars, and perhaps even the dissolution of his movement. Even though the state prosecutor concluded that the main charge against Radić, that the HRSS had become a communist organization, should be dropped for lack of sufficient evidence, he recommended prosecution on lesser counts: that Radić had incited Macedonians to revolt against the Yugoslav state, and had made slanderous remarks about the Queen in a 20 July 1923 speech.[206] Radić had been imprisoned in 1919–20 for much less than this. Capitulation seemed the only viable option.

Radić's political defeat in 1925 needs to be carefully examined. There is an exaggerated and essentially erroneous tendency in the scant Western literature to portray Radić and his policy to 1925 as erratic, obstructionist, and too inflexible, all of which contributed to his defeat and the political instability of this period.[207] His defeat of 1925 is taken by some to mean that his decision to abstain from the Constituent Assembly and parliament between 1920 and 1924 was a foolish move. But this argument misses the point. Had he gone to the Constituent Assembly the internal dynamic of the body might well have changed, but the centralist parties still would have been able, in all likelihood, to promulgate the Vidovdan constitution. And as the events of the autumn of 1924 demonstrated only too well, even when Radić evinced flexibility and agreed to participate both in parliament and government, the king would not tolerate his participation in government. Had the HRSS gone to Belgrade in 1921 and stayed there, it would have remained a perpetual outsider because of its national and republican program.

Radić's Marxist critics also assailed his policy of abstention, for by adopting this strategy he had renounced his main (and really his only) weapon against Belgrade, and was thus left defenceless against the Serbian establishment. Had he participated in the Constituent Assembly, so the argument went, he could have forced its dissolution and compelled the Serbian establishment to impose a dictatorship and put an end to the veneer of democratic parliamentarism. Radić would thereby have succeeded in revealing to the world the true nature of the Belgrade regime, and would have effectively made his case in 1920–1, instead of having to go abroad in 1923–4 to solicit Western support.[208]

This argument is not only debatable but counterfactual. Moreover, it underrates the significance of the pressures that the HRSS 'radicals' exerted on Radić. It must be stressed that Radić, despite his repeated statements about the pacifistic nature of the peasantry, was very cognizant of the existence of a radical element among the peasantry and, much more important, within the party leadership. As much as he personally sought a peaceful and negotiated settlement, he had to take into consideration those party elements who called for an uncompromising policy. A reading of the minutes of the HRSS leadership's sessions in the early 1920s reveals these internal tensions: on the one hand, talk of a negotiated settlement and non-violence, but, on the other, repeated references to the party's 'struggle' and the need to be unyielding to the end. This radical sentiment undoubtedly contributed to Radić's own intransigence. Admittedly, the policy of abstention failed to produce results. But to have gone immediately to Belgrade would have meant, certainly in Radić's mind, legitimizing the formation of a state that denied the national individuality and rights of the Croats and sanctioning a system of government for which the Croat peasantry had little sympathy, as the events of 1918 demonstrated. It would also have required a major effort on Radić's part to overcome the resistance of radical party elements. Only when Radić and the party leadership at last realized, in 1923–4, that absolutely no support could be expected from abroad, did the party finally have to acknowledge the need to abandon abstention, just as the lack of foreign support in 1919–20 forced Radić to abandon total Croat independence in favour of Yugoslav confederalism. There were no simple choices confronting Radić and the HRSS in this period.

Whatever Radić's personal or leadership shortcomings and his naïve faith in the supposed new 'moral' tenets of European diplomacy after 1919, he managed to construct a national mass movement. This was perhaps his signal accomplishment in this period, and its importance cannot be minimized. Although initially this was a rural, peasant-based movement, by 1923 the HRSS had effectively emasculated the Croat middle-class parties and thereby penetrated the Croat city, which was reconfirmed by the elections of 1925. The basis of this success was, first of all, the party's republicanism, which over-lapped with the post-war sentiments of the Croat countryside. But it was the HRSS's promotion of the concepts of 'peasant right' and 'peasant state' – embodied in the party's 1921 constitution which was disseminated throughout the countryside – that ultimately proved to be of equally decisive importance. These concepts formed the rallying call of the HRSS. Peasant hostility towards, and alienation from, the state and bureaucracy predated the world war, but after 1918 increased markedly. To rally the peasants to the national cause, Radić and the HRSS offered them a state that not only reflected their social and political interests, but safeguarded their national identity as well. As the external pressure of the new monarchical state increased – a state that denied the national individuality of the Croats – peasant social and political cohesion rose dramatically and coalesced around Radić's party. The republican peasant state could only be formed at the expense of the new, Serbian-domi-nated state. Social and national aims became intertwined and inseparable.

The HRSS also necessarily had a tremendous advantage over the Yugoslav communists. The KPJ's support of Yugoslav unitarism and its general neglect of the peasant question in the early 1920s enabled the HRSS to establish and maintain a firm hold over the Croat countryside. Radić and the HRSS viewed communist ideology and tactics as a threat to the interests of the Croat village, and even after the KPJ's adoption of federalism in 1924, Radić continued to regard the communists as a 'Serb' party who differed little from the bourgeois unitarists.[209] That is why he opposed cooperation with the KPJ, even when it was offered to him. The HRSS leadership asserted that one of its major suc-cesses in the early 1920s was in smashing the nascent 'bolshevik' organiza-tions in the countryside.[210] Thus, the two movements that, by the mid-1920s, potentially could destabilize the Yugoslav state the most, never established a common front. In the immediate post-war struggle between Wilsonian princi-ples (national self-determination) and Leninism (socialist revolution), repre-sented in the Yugoslav context by Radić and the KPJ, respectively, the HRSS won a decided victory, at least in the early 1920s.

With the creation of this mass movement the process of Croat national inte-gration was finally completed. Virtually every Croat village was penetrated by the HRSS's activists, first in Croatia proper and then eventually in Dalmatia and Bosnia–Herzegovina. It now commanded the loyalty of eight in ten Croats and was to remain, in spite of some setbacks, the only significant polit-ical force in Croatia. Compared with its status only a decade earlier, this was a revolutionary transformation. Although the dream of an independent Croat peasant republic was shattered in 1925, the peasant party's hold over the Croat countryside was not.

7

Stjepan Radić and the Croat Question, 1925–1928

The trouble with Radić is that he flutters like a butterfly from one idea or policy to another. Whenever I talk with him, I find myself almost always in agreement with the principles and views which he lays down. I even think that we have the same aims, and I certainly believe in his honesty. But he has no political ballast, and I never feel sure that he will not say something quite contradictory to the next person he meets.

R.W. Seton-Watson, 1924

I am not an evil-spirited prophet, I am, like all of us Slavs, more an optimist, but there is so much evil among us, that there will be a catastrophe one day ... Our state is not fulfilling that which was expected from it. This does not concern just the Croats, or the fact that there is no justice in this country.

Stjepan Radić, 1927

Gentlemen, this [the political situation] is wretched, this state has buried its own idea, and that broad Yugoslav idea of Strossmayer, Križanić, and others, the great Slavic idea ... is mentioned by no one, there is no trace of it. Nothing is left of the Slavic and Yugoslav idea.

Stjepan Radić, 1927

'Long live all our peasant people, long live our peasant and people's king,' were among the first words Radić uttered in July 1925 as he finally walked free from seven months of captivity.[1] Thirty-five months later Radić lay sprawled on the floor of the same Belgrade parliament that he had tried to avoid for years, the victim of an assassination attempt. If 1925 was the *année terrible* of Radić and the HSS, it was only the first of many more to come. Having abandoned republicanism and Croat self-determination, Radić appeared to have been broken politically. His volte-face caused a great deal of consternation among the HSS's deputies. Of even greater concern to Radić and the HSS was the need to assure their continued predominance over the Croat countryside. The HSS had existed for twenty years as a political outsider, untainted in peasant eyes by any association with the 'corrupt gentlemen.' And now Radić and his colleagues were entering a government with the very 'bashi-bazouks' whom they had repeatedly condemned over the last half decade. It would be no simple task to justify this latest manœuvre to his Croat peasant constituency, and no simpler, or so it seemed in 1925, to retain the HSS's status as the only significant Croat political force in the country.

Radić's defeat was a major victory for the defenders of centralism and the Vidovdan order. It was a Pyrrhic victory, however. In the event the constitutional crisis of the pre-1925 period, and with it the vexing Croat question, was set aside only temporarily. What is more, the NRS, hitherto the strongest Serbian party and the main defender of the Vidovdan order, began to implode. If there was one political actor who seemed to have emerged unscathed, indeed strengthened by the events of 1925, it was King Aleksandar. And if there is one salient attribute that characterizes Yugoslav political life after 1925, it is the growing and ever palpable influence exerted by the Yugoslav monarch over the country's political life.

In July 1925 the HSS entered government for the first time. Its influence was never altogether great, however, for the key ministerial portfolios remained in the hands of the NRS. The new government coalition, or 'R–R (Radical–Radićist) government,' as it was popularly known, was formed on 18 July 1925. The HSS received four ministerial portfolios (agrarian reform, post and telegraphs, commerce and industry, and forests and mines) and three undersecretary posts (culture, finance, social policy). This coalition was to last until late January 1927, although not without first undergoing some important changes, including Pašić's forced resignation. Radić eventually entered the government on 17 November 1925 as minister of education, raising the number of HSS portfolios to five. Between 1925 and 1927 Radić's and the HSS's public policy was one of constructive work on the basis of the constitution which they had hitherto negated. In actual fact, the NRS–HSS government had few chances for success. From the outset there was a clear-cut imbalance in the NRS's favour.

The capitulation of the HSS did not mean that it renounced the idea of constitutional reform in the longer term, particularly administrative reorganization and decentralization, although for obvious reasons the HSS did not immediately raise the issue of constitutional reform. 'National sovereignty,' Radić wrote in October 1925, 'means respect for the people's will in the whole of public life. In order for the people's will to be respected, it must be freely expressed.'[2] National sovereignty could be assured if the people organized and controlled local administration. He pledged to achieve this in cooperation with the NRS. In addition to local self-government, Radić demanded, and pledged to achieve, tax equalization and parity between Serbia and Croatia, and indeed all of the former Habsburg South Slav territories, and practical measures to improve local economic conditions. He also waged a determined campaign against government corruption, which emerged in 1926-8 as one of the most important political issues.[3] These demands invariably caused problems between the HSS and NRS and ultimately led to the demise of their coalition. None of Radić's stated aims in government were achieved. Important party differences over political principles, and the persistence of mutual suspicions, plagued the NRS–HSS regime. The NRS obstructed a number of the HSS-proposed reforms, not least because it was becoming increasingly paralyzed by internal factionalism. If Radić and his followers believed it possible to effect at least some change, and there is no reason to suspect that they did not believe change to be possible, they were soon disappointed.

Radić's immediate task was to justify to his party and following the new pact with Pašić and the NRS. The day after his release from prison Radić met with the HSS's deputies in Zagreb, where he told them that the basic character of the NRS's leaders was ethical. This was undoubtedly a startling revelation to the HSS's deputies, who had grown accustomed to hearing Radić refer to Pašić as a usurper and tyrant. Radić insisted that the NRS–HSS pact would be thoroughly enacted because it had been reached by people of an irreproachable moral and political character. The agreement was a necessity, and he cited the common social interests of the Croat and Serb peasants. The NRS was, Radić claimed, essentially a peasant party. 'An entire people,' he continued, 'cannot always be in opposition in their own state; we demand all of our rights in the state and take over all of our responsibilities.' The party had organized the Croat nation, 'and now we must work.' Although the HSS had abandoned its republicanism it retained its social and economic program.[4] This became a common theme in the HSS press, which even claimed that the NRS would gradually adopt some aspects of the HSS's program. 'It was necessary for the interests of our nation,' wrote one of the HSS's deputies, echoing Radić, 'that our party come to power once.' In government 'many of the things in our [HSS] program will be enacted.'[5] Practical work and the implementation of at least parts of its program became the stated aim of the HSS's new policy.

Radić repeatedly claimed that one of his prime reasons for coming to terms with the NRS was to avoid a conflict between Croats and Serbs. 'We wanted a republic,' he said in May 1927, but the Serbs 'did not understand us at first, and they said we were destroying the state, and there was a danger that this would come to a domestic war.' Had that occurred some followers might have incited an insurrection while others might have simply accepted defeat as a *fait accompli*.[6] Underlying these words was undoubtedly the fear that his movement faced disintegration. Radić argued that if he had not come to terms with the NRS at least one faction of his party would have. He told a session of the HSS's main committee on 21 May 1927 that the HSS deputy Nikola Nikić, one of the intermediaries between Radić and Pašić during the former's imprisonment who had, in the meantime, been ousted from the party with seven other dissidents, tried to frighten him into submission. Nikić apparently told Radić that Pašić would go to great lengths to keep him in prison if he refused an agreement with the NRS, and threatened to defect with twenty to thirty HSS dissidents and come to terms with Pašić if he did not. Radić claimed that he had to take this threat into consideration; the inference being that the party's political survival depended on an agreement with the NRS. Under the circumstances, he told his deputies, he had to do 'what my conscience, soul, intellect, experience, and far-sightedness [*sic*] prescribed.' He rejected the accusation that he had been duped and defeated by Pašić: 'I gave nothing to Pašić, [but] to the state, the king, the people, I did, and we took that which we needed the most, that is, our place as organizers of this state.' He implicitly recognized that his options in 1925 were few and that there was no other course to follow, for 'if I were continually to lead the Croat people to Calvary, this would be a crime and I would be a traitor.'[7] In spite of his comments to the effect that he had not given anything to Pašić but 'to the state,' this was clearly not the case. Pašić was as much an architect and defender of that state as any other political figure. Unsurprisingly, there was no willingness on Radić's part to acknowledge defeat or the party's or his own shortcomings or to admit that any dimension of his policy to 1924 had been questionable or contributed to the situation that led to capitulation in 1925. In actual fact, his reference to Nikić was essentially a ruse, for his capitulation came in March 1925 when his nephew Pavle Radić declared in parliament that the HSS was recognizing the existing state order, and not in July when he came to terms with the Radicals.

Radić's reasoning failed to convince all the HSS deputies. Eleven dissidents immediately broke ranks, including five former members of the Croat Union who had been elected on the HRSS ticket. They organized a conference of disaffected elements in early September 1925 and on 11 January 1926 formed the Croat Federalist Peasant Party (HFSS, *Hrvatska federalistička seljačka stranka*). The HFSS's main objectives were constitutional revision and a federal Yugoslav state in which Croatia would have its own parliament in Zagreb.

Its leaders, most notably Ante Trumbić, attacked Radić's 'levity' and argued that he was incapable of leading the Croats to the successful realization of their national aspirations. Trumbić insisted that Radić was 'demoralizing the people with his political leaps and attacks against the intelligentsia.' Reduced to its bare essence, Radić's post-1925 policy was, in the opinion of the HFSS, 'treasonable.'[8] The HFSS dissidents were only the first to depart, for another eight, led by and including Nikić, did so in July 1926. The 'old aviator,' as Radić referred to himself shortly after his release from prison, who was capable 'of making every turn-around' without crashing his plane, clearly was not able to satisfy all of his followers with his volte-face or to assuage their concerns about his leadership abilities and the Croats' predicament.[9]

The attacks against Radić's new policy came from all quarters. One dissident, who was also one of the HPSS's co-founders, claimed that Radić had become a dictator within the party who refused to consult with, let alone listen to, his deputies. Radić had premonitions about everything, but all of them ended tragically. Radić had been completely defeated for Pašić 'did not erase a comma from his Great Serbian program,' whereas Radić 'recognized everything: the dynasty, the monarchy, the centralistic Vidovdan constitution.' In twenty years of difficult struggle the party had not achieved a single success, and the only reason for this was the incompetence of its leadership, namely, Radić.[10]

Some of his more recent and militant followers, like Stjepan Uroić, came to the same conclusions about the 'charlatan' Radić.[11] What united these dissidents was their complete loss of faith in Radić's ability successfully to lead Croat policy against Belgrade.[12] One critic suggested that Radić wished to come to terms with Pašić's party in the hope of getting a few 'crumbs' for Croatia, but correctly predicted that Radić would not get a single one.[13] The general consensus among the Croat disaffected elements was that Radić had betrayed Croatdom by unconditionally recognizing the existing state order. 'The transition from monarchism across republicanism to sovietism [sic],' wrote one of Radić's bitterest critics, 'then from sovietism across republicanism to monarchism in the shortest time, demonstrates unbelievable inconsistency, it shows a political clown of a rare kind, of a peculiar and abnormal stock.'[14] This was an assessment with which virtually all of Radić's Croat critics, regardless of their political affiliation, were essentially in agreement.

The attacks from the Marxist left against Radić's new policy were equally disparaging. By 1924 the KPJ had adopted federalism and, recognizing that the national question in Yugoslavia was in many respects a peasant question, acknowledged the need to exploit the revolutionary potential of the national movements, such as Radić's HRSS. The KPJ remained committed to this line of reasoning, and in practice this meant that, even after Radić's capitulation, the Yugoslav communists were to cooperate with all nationally disaffected elements. Radić's new policy was condemned as a betrayal of the peasantry. At the KPJ's Vienna congress in June 1926, the party adopted a resolution condemning Radić and the HSS leadership. Radić's capitulation

> in the face of the Great Serbian bourgeoisie represents the most significant event in the political life of Yugoslavia from its creation ... it means the widening of the base, the strengthening of the dictatorship of the triple alliance between the monarchy, militarism, and the Great Serbian haute bourgeoisie, that in fact rule Yugoslavia. The capitulation of Radić's party means, further, the victory of the big capitalistic elements in the party, who have succeeded in placing the party in the service of their class interests. The policy of 'agreement' [between the HSS and NRS] ... was inspired mainly by the interests of the Croat haute bourgeoisie [sic], whose material and spiritual influence in Radić's party was growing on a daily basis ... [W]ith the capitulation of the HRSS the front of the oppressed nations has been broken, since its main factor, the Croat peasantry, has for the moment dropped out.[15]

That the KPJ wished to demonstrate to the Croat peasantry the perfidious nature of the Croat bourgeoisie in general and Radić in particular is understandable enough, but its explanation for Radić's capitulation was as flawed as Radić's eyesight. It failed to explain, among other things, why the former members of the Croat Union (now of the HFSS), the supposed representatives *par excellence* of the Croat bourgeoisie and erstwhile allies of Radić, joined the ranks of his most outspoken critics after 1925 and opposed the new Radić–Pašić government.

Nevertheless, the KPJ believed, much as did Radić's Croat nationalist critics, that Radić had destroyed himself politically by coming to terms with the NRS. The KPJ therefore was prepared to cooperate with the dissidents who opposed Radić's new policy, to renew 'the Croat national peasant front in the spirit of the popular slogans of the old HRSS,' but now on 'the new tactical basis of the alliance of the workers and peasants for the sake of the struggle against Serb imperialism.'[16] To that end, a number of Croat communists, particularly in Dalmatia, sought electoral alliances with dissident Radićists in what proved to be a futile policy.[17] Neither the KPJ nor his Croat opponents were able to capitalize on Radić's capitulation, or to transform his defeat into electoral gain for themselves. In spite of the KPJ's (and Comintern's) brief flirtation with Radić in 1924, after 1925 the KPJ and HSS stood, as in the immediate post-unification period, diametrically opposed to one another.

Radić and the HSS – and it should be pointed out that the overwhelming majority of the party remained loyal to him – were quick to counter-attack these accusations, whether from the Marxist left or Croat nationalist right. The HSS reminded its followers that the same Croat intellectuals who were now accusing the HSS of treason and abandoning the Croat cause had surrendered Croatia to Belgrade in 1918.[18] Radić often repeated this at his public rallies. The HSS wanted to create a sovereign Croatian republic after 1918, but this failed because 'all of the gentlemen betrayed us.' Radić added that while he was waging a struggle against Belgrade, 'these gentlemen were shooting at my back ... and now they are shooting at my chest and back. Now they say: "You wanted a republic." *Yes, we did and had we achieved a republic it would have been well.*'[19] That the HSS failed in this endeavour, its leaders argued, was really the fault of the Croat intelligentsia, because it supported unconditional unification in 1918. The HSS press once again began regularly to refer to the machinations of 'gentlemanly politics' and the 'corrupt gentlemen,' whose only goal was to exploit the peasants. Such attacks were muted between 1921 and 1925 because of the H(R)SS's cooperation with the Croat middle-class parties. Now they resurfaced with a vengeance. It was the 'corrupt' intellectuals who called on the Serbian army in 1918 'to defend the usurperous gentlemen and war plunderers from the Croat peasant people.'[20] 'Our wretched gentlemen,' Radić remarked at one of his rallies, 'fabricated the news about the supposed rebellions of the peasantry [in 1918].' At that time they invited the Serbian army 'to protect them from the Croat peasantry.' He concluded that 'our Croat gentlemen did not then need either the *Sabor* or the *ban* or democracy, because the most important thing for them was to protect themselves, with the assistance of the Serbian army ... against the social peasant wave, that is, against true [democracy].'[21] There was a good deal of truth in these accusations, which could not but have some resonance in the Croat village.

The HSS's attacks against Croatia's intellectuals were most acute in the months following the NRS–HSS agreement and on the eve of the September 1927 elections, when a number of articles appeared condemning the HFSS and the newly formed Croat Bloc (HFSS and HSP). The HSS once again returned to the 1918 unification, and reminded its followers that the 'gentlemen' handed Croatia to Belgrade in 1918, and that Radić had opposed this move. One writer argued that the HFSS 'has neither the moral nor the intellectual qualities, in spite of all of their great titles and diplomas, to participate at all in public life, let alone to be the leaders of the people.'[22] Another claimed that the only reason why the middle-class parties cooperated with the H(R)SS to 1925 was 'to get closer to the people and to displace the leadership of the

Peasant Party.' What is more, these middle-class Croat parties, it was asserted, had the support only of the banks and Jews.[23]

Radić and the HSS's position with respect to the Yugoslav communists remained unchanged after 1925. They continued to regard communism in Yugoslavia as essentially a Serbian phenomenon, a view that was shaped by the KPJ's early espousal of *narodno jedinstvo*. According to Radić, the main objective of the Yugoslav communists was still 'to supplant Croatdom and to strengthen Great Serbianism.'[24] Radić kept referring to the communists as Yugoslav unitarists, regardless of their support of federalism.[25] He also repeatedly reminded his peasant constituency that the communist ideology and program were anti-peasant, and hence dangerous. It was with such words that Radić reaffirmed his position in the countryside and reinforced the peasants' suspicions about the 'corrupt' Croat intellectuals and communists. He was for the most part successful, but as the national elections of September 1927 would show, an even greater threat than his Croat and communist opponents were peasant apathy and indifference.

The HSS went to great lengths to portray Radić's agreement with the NRS as a 'national agreement,' since it had been reached by the largest Serb and Croat parties. According to Radić there was no capitulation, for the HSS's socio-economic program had not changed.[26] In its rhetoric the HSS incredulously and unconvincingly denied that an agreement with the NRS had been reached because Radić had been imprisoned. The 'national agreement' was the result of 'general national interests.'[27] Radić stressed this point repeatedly. In the absence of an agreement 'a bloody confrontation' between Croats and Serbs would have ensued, something he wished to avoid at all cost.[28] Only in February 1928 did Radić finally concede that 'we recognized the monarchy to protect our people.'[29]

Although the HSS renounced the demand for an independent Croatian state within a Yugoslav confederation, all of its remaining program remained intact. That is hardly surprising, for the NRS demanded no more than the recognition of the Vidovdan order. Radić insisted that in government the HSS would work to implement its peasant program and preserve Croat national individuality, for 'each brother [Croat, Serb, and Slovene] must completely develop his own soul.'[30] 'We entered the government,' Radić stated a year after the formation of the NRS–HSS regime, 'as a Croat and peasant party and as a peasant and humane movement. We sought legality, equality, and humaneness for the whole state. This is being enacted.'[31] As Pavle Radić, one of the HSS's new ministers, noted: 'As far as the relations between Serbs and Croats are concerned, we stood and *stand on the viewpoint, that Serbs and Croats are – ethnically and linguistically, as in their social structure and their identical interests, the same nation.* But they had different political upbringings and organizations.' What he was saying was that Croats and Serbs were politically distinct nations and that they clearly still did not possess identical views on political matters and state organization. But if the agreement between the HSS and NRS was truly a 'national agreement,' as Radić and the HSS argued, then this begs the question of whether the Croat question had been solved. Pavle Radić indicated that it had not. But he acknowledged that 'a base can be created, so that it will never again provoke a crisis.' He added that 'our state apparatus does not function well. With the combined cooperation of the Serbs and Croats we will correct this.' When the principles of constitutional equality were finally realized, 'there will no longer be either a Croat or Serb Question.' As for the constitution, Pavle Radić stated that the question of its revision 'is not now in any way current.' There were many pressing issues, such as the consolidation of finances, agrarian reform, and building industry, that first had to be addressed.[32]

The HSS thus committed itself to practical work, implicitly envisaging eventual constitutional reform. Stjepan Radić stated in December 1926 that when three-fifths of parliament supported constitutional reform, then it would be successfully changed, but what the HSS wanted in the meantime was 'a revision of the spirit of state policy and a revision of Balkanism.'[33] Hence, the immediate task was to reform government policy, to end corruption, that is, to eliminate what Radić termed 'Balkanism,' and to create 'the foundation of a new life' in the country.[34] This new foundation was the peasant state. It is difficult to determine to what extent Radić was genuinely convinced that reform could occur, but his public statements, which are largely reinforced by his extant though hardly extensive private correspondence from this period, certainly lend the impression that he believed some reform to be possible.

In spite of the talk of 'unity' and the HSS's recognition of the Vidovdan system, after 1925 Radić remained essentially consistent with regard to his views about Croats and Serbs. As Pavle Radić's comments demonstrate, the HSS still made a distinction between Croats and Serbs in political terms, which lay at the essence of Stjepan Radić's pre-1918 espousal of *narodno jedinstvo*. Before 1918 Radić distinguished between South Slavic cultural 'oneness' and state–political dualism: from a linguistic, cultural, and sociological standpoint, Croats and Serbs were one people, but in political terms they were distinct nations that possessed two separate political traditions. Pavle Radić's comments indicate that the HSS still held to this formula, although the espousal of *narodno jedinstvo* lost its *raison d'être* with the Habsburg monarchy's demise. After 1925 – and indeed after 1918 – Radić and the HSS made virtually no references to *narodno jedinstvo*.

That is why Radić criticized elements of the Croat intelligentsia and Serbs for their interpretation of the concept of Yugoslavism. Yugoslavism could in no way be equated with the idea of nationality. 'Among the Serbs it was different. They accepted Yugoslavism as a national mark, but applied it only to us Croats ... That is why it took much time and struggle ... [to demonstrate] that Yugoslavism can be and is only a state idea [*sic*], and that the Slovenes, Croats, Serbs, and down there the Bulgars are nations. We indeed are one nation – *une nation* – but we are four nationalities. Objectively, from the standpoint of language, social composition, geography ... we are one nation for the one who views us from the outside. But we all consider ourselves to be, not only through historical development but also by our consciousness, a separate [Croat] nation unto ourselves.'[35]

Radić's volte-face in 1925 did not, therefore, represent an abandonment of Croat individuality in any way. As the Montenegrin federalist Sekula Drljević, who joined political forces with Radić in 1927, wrote in the HSS's daily in August 1927: 'Our Yugoslavism is patriotism, that is why it is tolerant. In domestic policy it means equality for all nationalities ... Their [Davidović's and Pribićević's, integral] Yugoslavism is nationalism, which can easily degenerate in domestic policy into aggressive chauvinism.' He concluded that 'our conception of our state is not a negation of the past but an organic unification of its entire diversity.'[36] The task now became to preserve that individuality as best as possible within the confines of the system established in 1921.

Of the stated objectives of the HSS after July 1925, the most important was to construct a 'peasant state' from Belgrade. Radić made repeated claims to this effect. The fundamental elements of this peasant state were supposed to be peasant participation in and control of local administration, regional self-government, the eradication of administrative arbitrariness and government corruption, the protection of peasant economic interests, and the reform of education. The peasant state, he claimed, was in the process of being formed by the HSS and NRS.[37]

This government would also work, it was claimed, gradually to reconcile Croat and Serb interests, for the basis of the NRS–HSS government were peasant right and a humane policy, as well as respect for mutual national differences.[38] Radić argued that 'the great deed of the national agreement has begun between Croatia and Serbia, between the Croat and Serb peasantry ... with the greatest sincerity, with complete mutual trust and with deep understanding of all Croat and Serb peasants.'[39] In November 1925 Radić noted that state policy had to be 'peasant based,' that is, the peasants had to control local administration, which was one of the key preconditions of general well-being.[40] The bases of the HSS–NRS agreement, according to Radić, were the principle of people's authority in local districts, the most fundamental unit of government, and the reform of finances. He insisted that all 'bashi-bazouks' had to be purged from government.[41] There was clearly a commitment on Radić's part to bring about change in the government. If Radić was initially sceptical of the possibility of reform and working with the NRS, this certainly does not emerge in any significant way, as noted earlier, through a reading of his published or unpublished correspondence. Once in government he confronted the new situation and sought to extract practical reforms. Having already committed a major volte-face, there was now, of course, a danger in once again promising too much and delivering little or nothing. But Radić's scepticism gradually became all too apparent, and he began openly to voice his dissatisfaction with the pace of reform.

Whatever Radić's initial views about the real nature of the NRS–HSS government, it seems evident that from the outset Pašić was not genuinely enthusiastic about cooperation with his new partner. In October 1925 he told a session of the NRS's parliamentary club that 'an agreement [with the HSS] was reached because the Radićists renounced all of those things that divided them from the Radicals.' The HSS abandoned its views 'about the constitution, the state, and the monarchy. We could not reject their cooperation when they presented such conditions, for they would have been justified in returning to their old program.'[42] Pašić clearly saw Radić's complete capitulation, as opposed to any concessions on his part, as the basis of the NRS–HSS government and attempted to minimize the HSS's impact on general policy. The key ministerial portfolios, especially internal and foreign affairs, remained in the NRS's hands, and with them the NRS's hegemony. In fact, Pašić claimed that he did not want an arrangement with Radić but was forced to do so under pressure from both the king and some elements within the NRS. He told one Croat politician, admittedly well after his departure from government, that he still considered Radić to be 'a destroyer of the state.' He believed it necessary 'that all means be undertaken to save the state.' Another NRS minister, Miloš Trifunović, told this same politician that Pašić frequently 'demonstrated that he is not pleased with the fact that the Radićists are members of the government.'[43] It should therefore not be surprising, and it is significant to note, that even though the criminal proceedings against Radić and the HSS leadership were dropped in July 1925, the *Obznana* of December 1924 remained in force until 4 January 1927.[44] The Pašić–Radić relationship was therefore an uneasy one between July 1925 and April 1926, when Pašić was forced out of office. By July 1926 Radić was openly declaring that one segment of the NRS was refusing all of the HSS's proposals and asserting its own influence, thus preventing any serious reform.[45]

In January 1926 Radić began voicing his demands for immediate tax parity or equalization for all parts of the country, and local self-government. Such demands only increased the suspicions of many within the NRS about Radić's true motives. It appears that one of the main reasons Radić began holding major rallies at this time, and to voice his criticism of the slow pace of reform, was to counter-act the activities of the dissidents of the recently formed HFSS. In a speech in Subotica (Bačka), Radić raised the issue of the excessive tax load of the former Habsburg areas,[46] and even called for a revision of the constitution during a speech in Dubrovnik in early February.[47]

It was during these rallies that Radić began his assault on corruption in government. It proved to be a convenient moment, for the government became embroiled in a major corruption scandal in late February 1926 involving Nikola Pašić's son Radomir (Rade), which also implicated a number of prominent NRS ministers. Radić enthusiastically joined the anti-corruption campaign. That corruption became a major political issue is hardly surprising, and that it involved the NRS is even less surprising. From an early point, the country's bureaucracy was characterized by inefficiency, nepotism, and corruption. What is more, the NRS, because of its long stint in power, had become a vehicle for upward social mobility, especially in Serbia. Though corruption was regularly debated in parliament, it was never eliminated for it was too firmly embedded.[48] The opposition began demanding a hearing into the affair in March, which prompted the government to recess parliament until early May 1926. Radić joined the opposition in its demand that the parliament be reconvened at once to investigate the corruption scandal. Under attack from a faction of his own party headed by Ljuba Jovanović, who had provoked the corruption affair by exposing it in the Belgrade press, as well as his HSS partners, Pašić offered his government's resignation on 4 April. Four days later, on 8 April, a new NRS–HSS coalition government was formed, headed by the Radical Nikola Uzunović.

Radić retained his post as minister of education in the new cabinet, but only days after Uzunović's cabinet had been formed, he again attacked corruption in government and the poor and anarchic state of government finances. The NRS minister Krsta Miletić resigned, citing Radić's comments.[49] Though he certainly contributed to the crisis, Radić was in actual fact a convenient scapegoat, for many Radicals preferred to blame him for Pašić's ouster rather than publicize even further the NRS's internal disputes, which would shortly, as will be seen, almost destroy the old NRS. Miletić's resignation prompted yet another cabinet crisis which was only resolved in late April. The HSS retained its seats in Uzunović's restructured cabinet, but Radić was replaced by another HSS deputy. Significantly, Radić demonstrated a great willingness to resolve existing differences between the NRS and HSS and insisted that the HSS had to cooperate with Uzunović to enact reform.[50] This is hardly surprising, for Pašić's forced departure finally gave Radić a much needed and seeming political victory; he could finally inform his Croat constituency that the policy of 'national agreement' was showing results. Radić publicly welcomed Pašić's departure because of the latter's unwillingness to move on HSS reform initiatives, such as local self-government and tax reform.[51]

Relations between the NRS and HSS remained understandably strained, despite Radić's affirmation of support for Uzunović. Radić certainly acknowledged the many obstacles that had to be overcome in the NRS–HSS relationship, but he believed the government coalition had to be maintained for the sake of much needed reform.[52] The chances of success were slim, however. The Uzunović government was plagued from the outset by a number of problems, above all the issue of corruption. Moreover, Uzunović, like most Radicals, clearly distrusted Radić and blamed him for Pašić's 'shameful' ouster from government. Uzunović was advised that Radić's tactics had merely changed, and that he was now trying to achieve in government what he failed to achieve in opposition: 'the destruction of every authority, even the king's.' His frequent outbursts against the gentlemen were really attacks against the administration: 'When the reputation of the state authorities is destroyed, then anything is possible ... If Radić succeeds in penetrating into Montenegro and Macedonia, then the king ... can prepare himself for a solemn escort out of the country.'[53] This opinion was essentially shared by Uzunović and most Radicals, whatever their internal party differences.

No longer a cabinet minister, Radić continued holding major rallies throughout the country, further reinforcing the NRS's suspicions. At a 24 May rally in Sombor (Bačka), Radić again addressed the need for constitutional reform. 'The Vidovdan constitution,' he said, 'has its faults, but it is the state law, and the fundamental law at that. We recognize it without secret designs and want it carried out,' but in those areas 'where it is shown not to be good, we will change it.'[54] Along with indistinct references to constitutional reform, he continued to demand an end to government corruption. In early May 1926 the HSS called for an investigation into, and supported a bill against, government corruption. The majority of Uzunović's NRS deputies voted against the bill, but a small group of NRS dissidents led by Ljuba Jovanović, who had been ousted by the Pašićists from the party, created their own parliamentary club and supported the HSS on the corruption issue. Despite the persistence of this issue, which eventually brought about the collapse of the NRS–HSS regime, the HSS remained formally committed to its working relationship with Uzunović, 'who is sincerely and consistently attempting to bring into practice the policy of national agreement.'[55]

Radić did not hide his dissatisfaction with the slow pace of change, however. In mid-July 1926 he launched one of his most acrid attacks at his NRS partner by suggesting that 'the whole state serves one part of the Radicals.' The HSS's proposals in government were not being seriously listened to, Radić explained, because of 'dark forces' within the NRS 'that determine all questions in connection to us [HSS].' Radić's diatribe was directed at the NRS's Pašićist elements, whom he identified as the main opponents of reform. Radić insisted, however, that the HSS was not attempting to create problems in the NRS–HSS relationship. What the HSS wanted was constructive work, but he added that it could not silently tolerate corruption in a government of which it was a member. It is significant that Radić now openly demanded that the *Obznana* of December 1924 against the HSS formally be annulled and correctly suggested that the NRS was keeping it active as leverage against the HSS.[56] Radić's most important concern, he asserted, was that 'legality and justice be introduced in the whole state, so that all of us will be equal.' He repeated his hope that local self-government and tax equalization would be implemented by the government.[57] These contradictory statements indicate an obvious and growing level of frustration on Radić's part. As the committee investigating the Rade Pašić affair continued dragging its feet into November 1926, Radić launched yet another attack on corruptionists in government. This prompted the resignation of Uzunović's cabinet on 6 December. Although a new NRS–HSS cabinet was worked out by late December, it would last hardly a full month.[58]

During the December cabinet crisis Radić again demonstrated a good deal of willingness to cooperate with the NRS and to pursue a conciliatory policy. It has often been asserted that throughout 1926 Radić wanted new national elections and that he was simply waiting to return to his earlier policy at an opportune moment, that is, that he was biding his time while in government until the internal contradictions of the government coalition – and the growing divisions within the NRS – brought about its demise. His frequent public rallies, reminiscent of his assemblies while still in opposition before 1925, and calls for reform in 1926 are often cited to justify this line of reasoning.[59] The facts seem to belie such an argument, however. This interpretation presupposes that Radić's political position in 1925–6 was stronger than it actually was. After the initial wave of HSS defections in the summer of 1925, the party was again confronted by internal problems in the spring and summer of 1926. The latter dissidents, unlike their earlier counterparts, did not split with Radić because of his supposed abandonment of the Croat national cause; in fact, they were prepared to cooperate with Uzunović, which lent the impression that some NRS elements were attempting to promote and exploit factionalism within the HSS. In late March 1926, before this new round of dissidence, Radić expressed some dissatisfaction, and indeed disillusionment, with certain elements within his own party. He even raised the possibility of resigning his position as president of the HSS and becoming the editor of the party's official organ *Dom*.[60] One is forced to conclude that Radić felt beleaguered and frustrated by this time.

What Radić wanted throughout 1926, and emphasized during the cabinet crisis of December 1926, and indeed all the crises of that year, was constructive parliamentary work leading to reform. Radić's conditions for a renewal of an HSS–NRS government were articulated on 23 December 1926 in a letter and accompanying memorandum to Uzunović. The HSS insisted that Uzunović's government had to complete its working program, including the implementation of local self-government and the completion of agrarian reform in Dalmatia, as well as the equalization of direct tax rates throughout the country, and was prepared to work with the NRS to achieve these ends. Radić also demanded that the *Obznana* of December 1924 be annulled (which finally occurred on 4 January 1927) and that a number of HSS activists who were tried on the basis of the *Obznana* be amnestied.[61]

Moreover, Radić openly stated that he opposed new national elections and favoured constructive parliamentary work, perhaps because he feared, at least in 1926, that his various dissidents might gain some ground at his expense. Much of the criticism that he directed at his NRS partners was assuredly done to show his Croat peasant constituency that the HSS was still working for reform. That his criticism of the government of which he was a member sharpened in late 1926 is also unsurprising, for Radić was at the time involved in a heated electoral campaign for the January 1927 district assembly elections. In mid-December 1926, at one of his electoral rallies, Radić told his audience that 'we [HSS] will not leave Belgrade to return to our old opposition.' The HSS had stayed in opposition 'for a long time, we stayed there to unite ourselves, and now that we are united, we will remain in Belgrade to organize the state.' In the same breath he added that the HSS was preparing itself for opposition 'to organize all parliamentary forces' that wanted a 'peasant state' and 'social progress.' Remaining in government would mean 'the strengthening of that spirit which we represent,' but he was under the impression that the HSS was being forced into opposition by elements within the NRS. The HSS did not have to be driven into opposition, however, because it had been 'in opposition in spirit the whole time,' which was perhaps one of Radić's most telling statements while in government.[62] Whatever his frustrations with the NRS, Radić's willingness further to cooperate with that party was undoubtedly influenced by the 10 December 1926 death of Nikola Pašić.

Radić had long viewed Pašić as an obstacle to reform, even after the latter's departure from government in April 1926. He now believed that the NRS no longer possessed an authoritative and commanding figure who could block much needed reforms.[63]

Although Radić was still prepared to cooperate with Uzunović in December 1926 and early January, the district elections of late January 1927 were accompanied by marked police brutality and electoral machinations such as arrests and the banning of rallies. Under the circumstances, and buoyed by a strong performance in these elections, on 28 January the HSS decided to end its cooperation with the NRS. The day before Radić wrote to his daughter Milica that 'we cannot and will not sanction Radical [party] electoral corruption and the reign of terror.' He observed that the NRS, unlike the HSS, had lost much ground in these elections, and foresaw another cabinet crisis within months.[64] Uzunović was now forced to form a new cabinet on 1 February with Korošec's Slovene People's Party (SLS) and the German Party. Thus ended the troubled, unworkable, and unproductive eighteen-month HSS–NRS partnership.

When that partnership was forged in 1925, Radić and the HSS appeared to have been incapacitated politically. Yet by January 1927, when Radić finally returned to the ranks of the opposition, he and the HSS seemed, despite their internal problems of the previous year, to be on more solid footing than their erstwhile, factionalized NRS ally. What is remarkable is that the HSS did as well as it did in the district elections, even though it had little to show for its stint in government other than a secondary role in Pašić's ouster and the removal of a few Croatian officials who had been appointed in the early 1920s by the despised Pribićević. It was a newly confident and invigorated Radić who met on 2 February with the HSS parliamentary club. Radić told the party's deputies that even though the HSS had broken off its cooperation with the NRS, they should not think that cooperation was impossible in the future. 'Do not say that we cannot work with the Serbs,' he said. Corruption and intrigue in government 'must not influence our relationship towards the Serb people, or Serb parties or even the Radical Party.' If circumstances forced the HSS to remain in opposition in Belgrade, 'we must further remain in power in the district parliaments, that is, we must remain at work and understand that to be in power means to be of use to the people.'[65] These words encapsulate the essence of Radić's thinking after he joined the ranks of the opposition.

After February 1927 the HSS remained active on two levels. At the national level the HSS attempted to broaden its base to other parts of the country and to forge links with those elements that were committed, at least in Radić's mind, to reform. This endeavour would mature into a proposal in the autumn of 1927 for the creation of a democratic parliamentary union. The first step in this direction was the formation on 2 February 1927 of the National Peasant Club (*Narodni seljački klub*) between the HSS and Montenegrin federalists led by Sekula Drljević.[66] At a session of the HSS's main committee in Zagreb on 21 May 1927, Radić proposed changing the party's name to the National Peasant Party (NSS, *Narodna seljačka stranka*), as it was henceforth to be known outside of Croatia and in non-Croat regions. He justified this move by claiming that the HSS was now a social and political movement that sought 'equality in the entire state and for all citizens,' which would, Radić promised, go to Montenegro, Macedonia, Serbia, and Vojvodina.[67]

At the local level, that is, in the district assemblies elected in January 1927, the HSS attempted to implement important reforms. As already noted, the HSS's performance in these elections was convincing. It received an absolute majority in the Zagreb, Osijek, Dubrovnik, and Split district assemblies, came a close second to Pribićević's Independent Democrats (SDS) in the Littoral–Krajina district, and fared respectably in the Srijem, Mostar, and Travnik districts. The HSS was once again almost exclusively a rural movement. For instance, in Zagreb district the HSS won an impressive seventy of eighty seats; the other ten, mainly urban seats went to a number of parties: the dissident HFSS, Pribićević's SDS, Ante Pavelić's Croat Party of Right, and the Yugoslav communists. The HSS's activism in these district assemblies has traditionally been neglected in the historiography.[68] This is unfortunate because these assemblies, in spite of their brief existence (1927–9), assumed a number of important functions that previously fell to the central government. One of the main aims of the HSS in these assemblies, which overlapped with its national policy, was gradually to unify the Croat districts into a single region embracing Croatia–Slavonia–Dalmatia. By employing various means the HSS was in fact able to transfer a number of economic, health, and educational functions to these assemblies.

Thus, after February 1927 the cornerstone of Radić's policy was to forge new ties and penetrate new ground and to work for reform and decentralization at the national and local levels. The HSS's new activism would occur, however, in the context of the ever-increasing political polarity between the two Serbian parties, the NRS and the Democratic Party, and the opposition, which immeasurably contributed to the country's political instability and crisis. Radić believed that the country was divided into two political camps: the NRS and the Slovene People's Party (SLS), which he identified with the status quo, and the Democratic Party and the HSS.[69] This is why he joined the parliamentary campaign, initiated by the Democrats, accusing the NRS minister of internal affairs, Boža Maksimović, of orchestrating voting irregularities

TABLE 7.1
Election results (national, 11 September 1927), 315 seats

Party	Votes	Percentage	Seats
NRS	742,111	31.9	112
Democratic Party*	381,784	16.4	59
Croat Peasant Party	367,570	15.8	61
SDS	199,040	8.6	22
Slovenes (SLS)**	139,611	6.0	21
Democratic Union*	73,703	3.2	11
Bosnian Muslims*	58,623	2.5	9
Serbian Agrarians	136,076	5.9	9
Others	–	9.7	11

Sources: Gligorijević, *Parlament i političke stranke u Jugoslaviji, 1919–1929* (Belgrade, 1979), 239-42; Čulinović, *Jugoslavija izmedju dva rata* (Zagreb, 1961), 1: 500–1.
*The Democratic Party (DS) and Bosnian Muslims (JMO) ran jointly as the 'Democratic Union.' Of its 11 seats, 9 went to the JMO (giving it 18) and 2 to the DS (giving it 61).
**Slovene People's Party (SLS): includes the votes of the clericalist Croat People's Party.

during the January elections. The campaign eventually prompted another government crisis and the break-up of the Uzunović-led coalition government. On 17 April 1927 the Radical Velimir (Velja) Vukićević, leader of a competing NRS faction, replaced Uzunović and constituted a new NRS-led government with Anton Korošec's SLS and a faction of the Democratic Party headed by Vojislav (Voja) Marinković. From the outset, the new government was weak, for neither Vukićević nor Marinković enjoyed the complete support of their respective parties. In June new elections were called for 11 September 1927.

These national elections, the last prior to the imposition of the royal dictatorship in 1929, were a turning-point of sorts for the HSS. For the first time the HSS ran candidates in Serbia, Macedonia, and Montenegro as the National Peasant Party. Radić's public and private sentiments confirm that he placed great hope in these elections. At one electoral rally he predicted that the HSS would win at least 100 seats.[70] In late June 1927 Radić wrote to his daughter Milica that 'we are much better prepared for the elections than we were in 1925.' The dissident storm had been weathered and within the leadership 'there reigns the best harmony and disposition.' Conversely, he believed that the parties of the newly formed Croat Bloc, that is, the Croat Federalist Peasant Party (HFSS) and Croat Party of Right (HSP), were in disarray and spoke with great expectation of the HSS's new activism in the non-Croat regions. He

TABLE 7.2
Election results in Croatia (prewar Croatia–Slavonia) and Dalmatia, 84 seats

Party	Votes	Percentage (Cr., Da.)	Seats
Croat Peasant Party	284,106	46.7, 37.7	53
SDS	106,933	18.1, 11.9	15
NRS	91,437	13.1, 22.2	12
Others	–	22.1, 28.2	4

Sources: Gligorijević, *Parlament i političke stranke u Jugoslaviji, 1919–1929* (Belgrade, 1979), 239-42; Čulinović, *Jugoslavija izmedju dva rata* (Zagreb, 1961), 1: 500–1.

TABLE 7.3
Election results in Bosnia–Herzegovina, 48 seats

Party	Votes	Percentage	Seats
Bosnian Muslims*	125,121	30.8	17
NRS	111,671	27.5	14
Croat Peasant Party	68,387	16.9	8
Serbian Agrarians	56,688	13.9	6
Others	–	10.9	3

Sources: Gligorijević, *Parlament i političke stranke u Jugoslaviji, 1919–1929* (Belgrade, 1979), 239-42; Čulinović, *Jugoslavija izmedju dva rata* (Zagreb, 1961), 1: 500–1.
*The Democratic Party (DS) and Bosnian Muslims (JMO) ran jointly as the 'Democratic Union.' Of its 11 seats, 9 went to the JMO (giving it 18) and 2 to the DS (giving it 61).
**Slovene People's Party (SLS): includes the votes of the clericalist Croat People's Party.

confided to his daughter that the HSS 'will certainly have ninety to one-hundred deputies, and if there is freedom [free elections], there may be significantly more.'[71] The HSS's plans in these areas proved to be an unmitigated disaster, however, partly because of the government's strong-arm tactics. In fact, Pavle Radić and other HSS activists were harassed by the police near Skopje and other areas of Macedonia, as well as in Belgrade and some parts of central Serbia.[72]

Nevertheless, the HSS still commanded a following among the overwhelming majority of Croats, although its overall vote dropped substantially. Despite Radić's typically optimistic projections, the HSS managed to gain only sixty-one seats and 367,570 votes, that is, six fewer seats and over 170,000 fewer votes than in the 1925 elections. Radić unconvincingly attributed the HSS's poorer performance to the regime's electoral machinations and to the fact many 'people were not at home, they were away at work and some emigrated to America and Australia.'[73] The HSS's urban vote, strong in 1923 and 1925, had now virtually disappeared. In Zagreb the party gained only 18 per cent of the popular vote, whereas in Osijek it polled under 11 per cent. But it still gained a respectable showing in some Dalmatian towns: Šibenik (38.2 per cent), Split (38.2 per cent), and Dubrovnik (50.4 per cent).[74] In spite of its poorer electoral performance, the HSS retained its status as the only significant political force in Croatia and, alongside the Democratic Party, the second largest party in the country. If there was any consolation in these elections, it was the fact that the Radicals too were weakened, even more so than the HSS, and that none of the HSS's dissidents managed to be re-elected. The Croat Bloc gained only two seats, both in Zagreb: Ante Trumbić of the HFSS and Ante Pavelić, the future leader of the Ustaša movement, of the HSP.

The HSS was once again primarily, if not exclusively, a rural party. This was also reflected in the occupational breakdown of the party's elected deputies in 1927: 46 per cent were peasants and approximately 39 per cent were classified as intellectuals, a term which encompassed writers, journalists, lawyers, doctors, and others who derived their livelihood from the free professions, and another 11 per cent were classified as petit bourgeois (artisans, shopkeepers).[75] The party's local leadership also retained its predominant peasant character, although admittedly the paucity of data means that a detailed study of the local leadership is difficult. That the local leadership remained committed to Radić also helps to explain why the HSS dissidents were not able to achieve any success in the 1927 elections. The importance of the local party leadership should not be exaggerated, however. In the prewar years the H(P)SS placed special emphasis on providing a voice for the local party workers through annual party assemblies, but after the war such assemblies never took place. Indeed, throughout the 1920s the party's internal machinery lost its importance. When on 21 May 1927 Radić called to session the party's Main Committee, theoretically the party's supreme body, this was its first meeting since January 1923.[76]

That the local party leadership was neglected by Radić and the central leadership was poignantly demonstrated in a May 1927 letter to Radić by Ivan Kovačević, the head of the HSS organization in Gornji Andrijevci (Slavonia). Kovačević identified himself as a party follower since 1913 who was faithfully 'executing the obligation and commands of the [central] Leadership.' 'You cannot be in every place,' he wrote to Radić, 'but the main thing is that you, the leader of the people, must know how we stand in a given region.' He suggested to Radić that the central leadership was unaware of the problems confronting the party at the local level. Kovačević bemoaned the fact that the central leadership failed to respond to his pleas to send an elected HSS deputy to rally the troops against the party dissidents. He had approached one of the HSS's most prominent deputies, Djuro Basariček, who had been in the district only twice in the past three years, but was informed that the latter had no time. The dissidents had failed, according to Kovačević, only because the local leadership responded with vigour to their challenge, for he personally had organized over thirty rallies in the district. He cautioned Radić that the HSS's reasonably solid performance in the January 1927 district elections did not mean the party could rest on its laurels; between 30 and 40 per cent of the local population had abstained from the elections. He urged Radić to send an 'agile national deputy' to the district. If the existing neglect continued, a popular conviction could soon arise that the HSS was interested in the district only for votes and was otherwise prepared to ignore the area between elections.[77] The central leadership's neglect of the local party workers was not at variance, as has already been suggested, with the populist nature of the party. The HSS's central leadership, and Radić in particular, essentially dictated policy. The local leadership was expected simply to carry out the decisions of the central leadership. Nevertheless, whatever the shortcomings of the party's organizational machinery, Radić's personal popularity was strong enough that he never lost the support of the countryside.

In the aftermath of the September 1927 elections a dramatic change occurred in the country's political alignments. The opposition parties continued to assail the new NRS-led regime of Vukićević, comprised of the SLS, JMO, and Marinković's Democratic faction. The HSS even suggested that Vukićević be hauled before the courts for violating the constitution, a reference to the government's use of the police to prevent the opposition parties from staging rallies.[78] Immediately after the elections Radić had in mind the creation of a 'Democratic–Peasant Union,' encompassing those political parties that were committed to genuine parliamentary government, the elimination of corruption, and the reform of the bureaucracy and tax system, as well as the implementation of local self-government. He was thinking primarily of a parliamentary combination between the HSS, Pribićević's SDS, Davidović's Democrats, and Jovanović's Agrarians that would be led by Davidović.[79] This effort failed but eventually led Radić to conclude a political alliance with his earlier bitter foe, Pribićević.

On 4 October 1927 Radić and Pribićević, with Sekula Drljević acting as an intermediary, met in Belgrade to discuss the political situation in the country. The meeting marked the beginning of their political cooperation. Shortly thereafter Radić claimed that the HSS had finally found 'sincere and honourable allies' in its struggle for 'justice and freedom,' allies who were brought together by the prevailing 'terror.'[80] On 22 October the HSS, SDS, and the Agrarians proposed to Davidović the creation of a coalition that would implement local self-government and tax equalization and follow through on agrarian reform. The new coalition would have enjoyed a comfortable relative majority of over 150 seats in parliament and threatened Vukićević's government.[81] The plan collapsed, however, in large part because of opposition from Marinković's faction of the Democratic Party, which was more interested in remaining in the Vukićević government for reasons of party interest.[82] On 27 October Davidović, who may well have wanted to cooperate with both the HSS and SDS, but almost certainly with the latter, rejected participation in the proposed coalition.[83]

Despite the collapse of his plans for a broader 'democratic formation,' Radić's rapprochement with Pribićević culminated on 10 November in the formation of the Peasant–Democratic Coalition (SDK, *Seljačko–demokratska koalicija*). The creation of the SDK caused a sensation. In political circles it was greeted with disbelief, for Radić and Pribićević had been implacable foes since unification, and indeed, even earlier. Their rapprochement seemed impossible from an ideological standpoint. Unsurprisingly, the formation of the SDK also caused disbelief within the HSS's ranks, for in spite of the party's recognition of the state order in 1925, Pribićević still remained the *bête noire* of the HSS. Nevertheless, the political situation in the country, that is, the hegemony of the Serbian parties and the growing realization that the political system needed immediate reform, pushed the ideological differences between the HSS and SDS to the background. Pribićević and Radić could agree that the party bureaucracy, growing corruption, and electoral machinations threatened the most basic principles of democratic and parliamentary government.[84] That is why Pribićević, who now realized that much was wrong with the very state system that he had helped to create and defend, could ask in parliament on 23 November 1927 how it was possible that Radić, who had been in government and one of the king's ministers in 1925–6, could not freely run his candidates in Macedonia in the last elections: 'Gentlemen, you have only one alternative, either to respect completely the law, the constitutional and parliamentary regime, or a dictatorship.'[85] From the outset the SDK's activism was characterized by a struggle for democratic principles, genuine parliamentarism, and equality for the country's non-Serbian regions.

In justifying this manœuvre to his followers, Radić argued that Pribićević, as the leader of Croatia's Serbs, had finally realized that Belgrade had done little for him and the non-Serbian Serbs except to exploit them. They too suffered from the centralized administrative system and unequal taxation that burdened the non-Serbian areas more excessively than it did Serbia itself. The Croats and Croatia's Serbs had to realize that the Serbian politicians 'are destroying to the foundations all sources of our well-being' in order to facilitate their transformation into 'docile political slaves.' These words suggest that Radić conceptualized the SDK as a political front that was to represent the interests of the *prečani* (formerly Habsburg) regions alone. In fact, from the beginning he made clear that the SDK 'is only the first great step towards the unification of all democracy in our state,' which demonstrates that he was still committed to a broader, country-wide alliance of all 'democratic' forces.[86]

The primary purpose of the SDK, according to Radić, was to introduce a truly democratic regime abiding by the terms of the constitution and that provided for local self-government.[87] Initially the SDK simply called for the full *implementation* of the Vidovdan constitution, although this gradually changed. Thus, Pavle Radić stated in parliament as late as 30 January 1928 that 'in the consolidation of our state it is truly about time that that which is *imperatively ordered by our Constitution* be finally legally settled, namely, that our citizens be equal, that they are placed on the same level in their rights and duties.'[88] After the cabinet crisis of February 1928, constitutional reform became one of the SDK's basic demands. The HSS and SDS agreed to act in unison in all matters. The SDK's resolution of 10 November 1927 made it known that it could participate only in such a government that would reform the existing political system in the spirit of democracy, parliamentarism, and civil equality. The SDK was, as Radić stated at its first joint session, only the first 'great step towards the unification of democratic forces in the country.' In the past two years 'and especially in the past few months, we have been in an even fiercer struggle against terror, against corruption, and against plunder. In this struggle it was clearly seen that we [HSS and SDS] have a common foundation and a common aim: the foundation is democracy, and the aim is equality.' Pribićević, seconding Radić's words, denied allegations directed from Belgrade that the SDK was a `prečani* front.' 'We do not want this,' he insisted, 'we offered the Serbians [Democrats, the opportunity] to be the central axis, to be the leadership in this concentration.' Instead of a *prečani* front, the SDK was forming a 'democratic front.' He added that circumstances had led to the creation of a de facto *prečani* front.[89] Although initially the SDK aspired to create a broad democratic bloc, such as the one proposed in October 1927, in practice it spoke for the interests of the *prečani*, particularly after February 1928 when its plans for a national democratic front collapsed.[90]

Thus, when Pribićević read on 16 December 1927 the SDK's declaration in the parliament, he called for reform and democratization in the whole country, but insisted that the non-Serbian regions had to attain equality with Serbia. The first step in this direction was to depoliticize the administration, which in practice meant eliminating the unfit and corruption-prone party bureaucracy. The SDK insisted that the existing administrative system had ruined entire regions of the country, especially Old Serbia (Kosovo) and Macedonia. It demanded a reform of the system of government in order to guarantee for the people an objective, non-party state administration for which 'the law will be the main command and that will be in harmony with the principles of human-ity and civilization, which is called for by the needs and conditions of the life of a contemporary democracy.'

The December 1927 SDK declaration also demanded 'the most complete equality of all citizens regardless of their name or region [of origin] in all areas and all manifestations of national and state life,' a reference to the dom-ination of Serbians in the state apparatus. The government had done nothing to guarantee the political and economic equality of the non-Serbian regions. The current regime was 'a hegemonistic government of one region' and did not understand the needs of the entire country. State policy had to be, not just in theory but also in practice, such that all Serbs, Croats, and Slovenes genu-inely believed that the state reflected their individual and collective interests. When they all became equal this would create 'a unity of spirit' that would in turn 'enable our state to perform its great cultural mission in Central Europe and in the European Southeast.' Pribićević concluded that the SDK would wage a determined struggle for these principles and threatened that if 'our struggle does not bring about the expected results for the people,' the SDK would 'undertake more determined and more successful means to win the vic-tory of our principles,' though what these other means were was not elabo-rated.[91] The SDK's resolutions of 21 January 1928 reaffirmed its earlier decision to act and conduct all talks with other parties in unison. It also demanded a 'government of parliamentary concentration,' that is, a govern-ment of all parties that were for immediate parliamentary work, the imple-mentation of the constitution to the letter of the law, and the respect of parliamentary principles.[92]

In line with his and the SDK's plans to unite all democratic elements, Radić did not exclude the possibility of cooperating with either of the major Serbian parties. This was a calculated tactic. Both the Democrats and Radicals were mutually and internally divided over leadership disputes and on matters of principle, the former between Davidović's 'left' and Marinković's 'right' wing, and the latter between the so-called Pašićists and Vukićević's group. Certain elements were committed to genuine parliamentary government and opposed the court's growing influence in political life, such as Davidović's faction and some Pašićists. They were repeatedly obstructed, however, by the likes of Marinković and Kosta Kumanudi of the Democrats and Vukićević, Uzunović, Boža Maksimović, and others in the NRS. Vukićević, like his predecessor Ljuba Jovanović, had once been the king's tutor; both men, and Marinković of the Democrats, had good connections to the king's inner circle. In practice they assisted the weakening of parliamentarism and strengthening of the court's influence in political life.[93] In spite of the internal fissures and mutual differences of these groups, they nevertheless generally demonstrated a large degree of uniformity with respect to what they perceived to be the state's interests. When the NRS and Democrats clashed, it was usually only for Serbian votes in parliamentary and local elections. Since most Radicals and Democrats still regarded Radić as a threat to the state's stability, cooperation with him was exceedingly difficult. The fear of some Serbian politicians of the king's growing influence in political life notwithstanding, the Serbian parties generally tended to view the king as a natural ally against Croat demands for greater autonomy.

The increasingly bitter factional struggles within the two major Serbian parties were closely tied to the king's growing political assertiveness, and this had fateful consequences for the political evolution of Yugoslavia. The king possessed an antipathy towards strong parties and political personalities. Throughout the 1920s he and his inner political circle waged a subtle campaign first to discredit and then remove all prominent political personalities, with the purpose of gradually facilitating the king's sway over the country's political life. In April 1925 King Aleksandar acknowledged that of all the political party leaders Pašić alone knew what was best for the state and thus that he had to work with him. He angrily denied, however, that he had 'fallen in love with Pašić's beard.' Aleksandar presciently observed that 'besides Pašić, there is not a single man in the Radical party who could successfully develop a political policy to the benefit of the state.' If one adds to this his conviction that the liberal Davidović was naïve and that none of the other parties had 'either a leader or a political man, who could bring order to the state,' then the king's growing concern that he personally had to exert greater influence over political life becomes comprehensible.[94] Pašić, the first victim of this campaign, was certainly cognizant of the wider political significance of the attempt to oust him from the NRS leadership. Two months before his death, he observed that his successor Uzunović was a weak authority, and that 'there is no longer a true Radical Party.' He had nothing positive to say about the current Radical leaders and was now attempting to form a new Radical 'bloc' that would complete 'the consolidation of the state.' When this bloc was formed, he promised to go to the king and 'energetically to warn him about this intolerable [political] situation, and to caution him not to toy either with the state or his position.'[95] In the event, he did see the king but died shortly thereafter, his plans to reconstruct the NRS dying with him.

It is not coincidental that the king's influence over political life became more palpable after 1925. Prior to that point Aleksandar had been committed to a working relationship with the NRS, the strongest Serbian party, because of the threat posed by Radić's republican movement. With Radić seemingly neutralized in 1925, the king moved against the NRS. Though it had its dissidents in the early 1920s (Stojan Protić, Momčilo Ivanić, Nastas Petrović), the NRS remained cohesive because of its commitment to the protection of the Vidovdan order. Now its weaknesses came to the fore. Since both the NRS and Democrats had weak party organizations, their leaders were the parties' main cohesive forces. To discredit these leaders naturally meant weakening their parties. Pašić was ousted in a carefully orchestrated campaign originating with Jovanović, a confidant of the court, who was then forced to secede from the party. By the time his faction, now headed by Vukićević, was readmitted to the NRS in February 1927, the party was factionalized beyond repair. At times the internal feuds between Vukićević and the Pašićists reached a level of recrimination resembling the earlier struggle between the NRS and the HRSS. By promoting and exploiting these differences, and thereby weakening the Serbian parties, Aleksandar emerged as the arbiter of the country's political fate. In fact, Vukićević headed his governments not because he had the backing of the majority of the NRS, but because of the king's overt support.[96]

For his part, Radić saw the factionalism as a political opportunity. Despite the occasional diatribe against the Democrats, he evidently hoped to entice Davidović into cooperation and thus to break the Serbian political front, even though such a move was strongly resisted by elements of the Democratic Party.[97] So pronounced were the internal differences between Davidović and Marinković that they brought about the resignation of the Democrats in Vukićević's government in early February 1928, forcing the Vukićević cabinet to resign. This followed on the heels of the Democratic Party's congress of 15–16 January 1928 that supported Davidović's decision to break with the NRS and to forge new ties with the opposition. At last a 'government of parliamentary concentration' of the kind that Radić and the SDK wanted seemed possible. Indeed, Radić repeatedly alluded to these mutual differences and internal party fissures, which led him to conclude in early February 1928 that the SDK was 'the key to the political situation' in the country.[98]

Although a full-blown cabinet crisis was averted until early February, both Vukićević and King Aleksandar urged Radić on 25 January to enter the government with the NRS (without the SDS), and offered the HSS three portfolios. Radić did not categorically reject cooperation with the NRS, but insisted that the SDK receive five portfolios and that its nineteen-point 'working program' be implemented. This program was an extensive list of reform projects, ranging from the reform of the tax laws and tax equality for all parts of the country, to the depoliticization of the central administration, and increased finances for district assemblies, as well as the territorial reorganization of local districts, among other things.[99] Radić refused these overtures, primarily because they were intended to split the SDK and because he hoped to come to terms with the Democrats. When Vukićević offered his cabinet's resignation in early February he again approached Radić about forming a NRS–HSS government, but was rebuffed.

When this failed King Aleksandar offered Radić a mandate on 9 February to form a coalition government. He was the first Croat to be offered this opportunity. The project failed, however, and was clearly a calculated measure on the king's part. The only way Radić could form a government was to strike a deal with Vukićević's Radicals, who demanded that he abandon his association with Pribićević's SDS. Radić refused to take such a drastic step. When he returned to meet with the king on 19 February, Radić proposed, with Pribićević's approval, the creation of a 'neutral' regime under a non-parliamentary figure, presumably a retired army officer, who would govern until the political infighting subsided and then supervise impartial elections.[100] This proved to be one of Radić's biggest political blunders, and was used by his opponents, particularly in Serbia, to question his and the SDK's commitment to parliamentarism. His suggestion also seemed to indicate that he may have viewed the king as an instrument to undermine the hegemony of the Serbian parties.

After weeks of failed negotiations, on 23 February the king offered Vukićević a mandate to form a new cabinet, which consisted of the NRS, the Democratic Party, the Slovenes (SLS), and Bosnian Muslims (JMO). By bringing the latter two parties into his cabinet, Vukićević clearly attempted to undermine the SDK's claim that it spoke for all non-Serbian lands. In spite of their participation, however, the Radicals and Democrats dominated the government. After February 1928 the political situation in the country was characterized by a growing polarization between the government parties and the SDK, which generally enjoyed the support of the Serbian Agrarians. Radić's hopes that the SDK would attract the Democrats were finally delivered a permanent blow in February 1928. The SDK interpreted this new government, with its Radical–Democratic core, as a strengthening of Serbian hegemony. Moreover, since it was a government without Croats, this in practice meant, so the SDK repeatedly argued, that it was against the Croats. Davidović in particular now became the target of numerous attacks, in large part because both

Radić and Pribićević had placed much hope in him. After February 1928 he was regularly and unjustly described as a servant of 'the worst and most inconsiderate reaction.'[101]

Although the SDK formally aspired to democratize and enact reforms in the whole country, in practice it sought to defend *prečani* interests. To this end, the SDK placed special emphasis on local activism in those *prečani* electoral districts where the NRS and Democrats had won a total of approximately fifty seats in the 1927 elections. The SDK clearly hoped to win the remaining Serb votes in the *prečani* regions away from the Serbian parties, particularly the NRS, which would invariably strengthen its future position in parliament.[102] The SDK, and the HSS in particular, believed that *prečani* interests could best be secured and defended through administrative decentralization and the implementation of local self-government. As part and parcel of this demand for local self-government among the non-Serbian areas, Radić proposed significant territorial readjustments to local administrative units. This was central to Radić's thinking, and he had raised this issue in late September 1927 when he suggested that the number of districts be reduced from thirty-three to sixteen.[103] At a rally in Dubrovnik on 27 May 1928 Radić stated that 'without wider self-government the state is going backward and not forward.' The state needed large districts: '*Croatia, Slavonia, and Dalmatia must be one district. The whole state must have four or five districts.*' The central government would retain certain political, military, as well as economic prerogatives, but otherwise all affairs would rest with the local administrative units. Moreover, the central administration had to be depoliticized. Radić repeated that what the SDK was demanding was already envisaged by the terms of the constitution, but had not been implemented.[104]

Radić developed the idea of district reorganization in more concrete terms in early June 1928 by proposing four large districts that would be based on economic, social, and geographic principles: an Adriatic–Danubian district, composed of Croatia with Dalmatia, Bosnia-Herzegovina, Montenegro, and Vojvodina; Serbia proper; southern and Old Serbia (Macedonia and Kosovo, respectively); and, finally, Slovenia. Each district would look after economic, cultural–educational, and social concerns. The legislature and executive would remain in Belgrade to look after certain matters; otherwise, the districts would take over most affairs. Radić did not elaborate in any great detail precisely what functions would be retained by Belgrade, but he emphasized that the people needed to exercise direct control over local government and insisted that 'it is necessary that we gain complete authority in our Croatian homeland.'[105] By June 1928 Radić was clearly no longer proposing merely the full implementation of the constitution, but its fundamental reform.

In its assault on Vukićević's regime, the SDK, in addition to its central demand for greater regional autonomy, directed its parliamentary activism towards three specific issues: tax equalization, condemning the police regime in the largest prison of the Belgrade city administration (the so-called Glavnjača), and, in May 1928, the Nettuno conventions.[106] Debates over these issues gradually became so bitter that parliamentary sessions often degenerated into chaos. It was during these debates that Radić and Pribićević, undeniably two of the most gifted rhetoricians on the Yugoslav political scene, excelled in exposing the inequalities of the country's political system and at the same time raising political tensions through their acerbic diatribes against the Serbian parties.

One of the most important issues that the SDK raised was the need for tax equalization. It condemned what it perceived to be the consciously exploitative economic policies of Belgrade towards the non-Serbian regions. According to the financial figures presented by the SDK for the years 1919 to 1926, the approximate tax distribution by region was as follows: Vojvodnia paid 25.75 per cent of all taxes collected, Croatia (with Dalmatia) 23.89 per cent, Serbia (with Montenegro) 22.72 per cent, Slovenia 14.08 per cent, and Bosnia–Herzegovina 13.56 per cent. The regional per capita distribution of taxes demonstrated a gross imbalance between Serbia and the non-Serbian areas: Vojvodina (1,118 dinars), Croatia (with Dalmatia) (1,051 dinars), Slovenia (1,035 dinars), Bosnia–Herzegovina (557 dinars), and Serbia–Montenegro (407 dinars).[107] The SDK also attacked Belgrade's tariff policy which severed Croatia and the former Habsburg lands from their old markets, thus producing numerous economic hardships for the inhabitants of those regions.[108] Economic exploitation had to end, the SDK argued, for whoever 'weakens and destroys, plunders, or devastates Croatia and the *prečani* areas, destroys and devastates our whole state.'[109] It was during one of the debates about economic policy, and the SDK's presentation of the incongruous tax distribution figures, that Radić launched into one of his most acrimonious attacks against the Serbian parties. 'Is this plunder or not?' Radić asked. 'No one among us will pay taxes, you'll have to send the entire army against us to collect taxes. You will see how we pay!'[110]

These remarks were made in early 1928, but when the government negotiated a new foreign loan in the spring of 1928, the SDK once again railed against Belgrade's economic policy. Radić argued that the peoples of the country would welcome such a loan only if they knew that the money would be used to assist agriculture, to build roads and railways, and to implement constructive reforms of immediate use to the peasantry. He feared, however, that most of the money would be spent on a few privileged families in Bel-

grade, particularly in light of the poor state of financial control, and on armaments. The cost of this loan would, he argued, invariably be borne by those
parts of the country that were already being economically exploited. Hence,
the SDK opposed the new loan and Radić even raised the possibility of withdrawing from parliament over this issue.[111] The SDK would return to the
question of the loan on a number of occasions. It asserted in June 1928 that the
loan was really intended to cover Serbia's prewar and wartime debts, but that
the Croats, who did not have a single individual in the government, would end
up paying for the loan in the long run.[112]

Even more important than its attacks on Belgrade's economic policies were
the SDK's assaults on the violation of individual freedoms and police brutality. In particular, the SDK launched a determined campaign against the regime
by using the Glavnjača issue (that is, the state of the prison administration in
Belgrade) to compromise the government's position among the public. The
SDK's deputies and press first raised the matter of police brutality in Belgrade's largest prison in November 1927 and kept hounding the Vukićević
government about it throughout 1928.[113] On 27 November 1927 the SDK proposed the creation of a parliamentary committee to investigate police behaviour in this particular prison.[114] On 27 February 1928 the SDK's deputies
called for a similar committee to investigate conditions in the Belgrade city
administration.[115] The government's refusal to pursue the matter led the SDK
to make continual references to the 'police regime' in Belgrade.[116] When the
SDK's deputies learned that coercive measures were regularly employed by
the police against prison inmates they again raised the issue in March 1928.[117]
The parliamentary debates over the Glavnjača issue deteriorated to such an
extent that verbal insults and threats of violence became commonplace, most
often directed from the benches of the NRS at the SDK's deputies. Once again
Radić unleashed harsh words against the regime. 'If this continues any further,' he said in relation to the violation of personal freedoms by the police,
'we will have nothing to do with you [the Serbian parties].' He added that 'we
will not allow ourselves to be trampled upon ... Keep this up, and all the people will justifiably rise up against this. I will tell you here, in the middle of the
parliament: heads will fall [glave će padati]!'[118]

In the event this remark proved to be a prescient warning. At the time, however, most observers undoubtedly dismissed it as yet more rhetorical hyper-
bole on Radić's part. There was increasingly little room for serious political
dialogue or parliamentary work. Writing in March 1928, Radić concluded that
the SDK could not find a political partner 'who could at all comprehend the
full seriousness of the [country's] internal and external situation.'[119] It was in
this context that the Vukićević government tried to ratify the Nettuno conven-

tions in the spring of 1928. Radić and the SDK believed that the conventions had no practical value for the country; in fact, they undermined its sovereignty and therefore threatened its interests. If ratified Radić believed that the conventions would facilitate Italy's economic penetration into the Balkan peninsula.[120] He pointed in particular to the clauses pertaining to the agrarian question in Dalmatia, an internal state matter, that tied this issue to the decisions of a joint Italo-Yugoslav commission. 'The peasants in Dalmatia,' Radić wrote, 'are today still serfs, it can even be said slaves, of their landlords. These landlords have for the most part opted for Italy in the firm belief that agrarian reform would not be carried out on their estates.' He could not support these conventions because the interests of the Dalmatian peasantry and the state were being undermined in favour of this former élite who controlled up to a third of the land.[121]

The SDK did not justify its opposition to the conventions on purely economic terms. It believed that the conventions secured for Italy numerous commercial privileges and would gradually lead to Italy's economic domination of the Dalmatian coast. This in turn would pave the way for Italy's future political domination of the region.[122] The SDK thus opposed the ratification and even Pribićević threatened, on 29 May 1928, that the SDK would 'use all means which stand at our disposal,' which essentially meant prolonging the ratification process through obstructionist measures in parliament, to prevent their ratification. He appealed to all of the Serbian deputies in parliament to vote against the ratification. If the conventions were ratified by a government in which there were no Croats, immeasurable harm would be done to Croat–Serb unity.[123]

The heated parliamentary debates overlapped with a wave of demonstrations against the conventions in late May in a number of urban centres, most notably in the Dalmatian towns Šibenik, Split, and Dubrovnik, as well as in Zagreb, Ljubljana, and Belgrade. On 31 May the Vukićević government called in the police to disperse the student protests in Belgrade, which invariably led to bloodshed. The SDK's deputies immediately called for the government's resignation and an investigation into its use of oppressive measures to quell the protests. On that same day and on 1 June the SDK's deputies, joined by the Serbian Agrarians, brought the parliamentary sessions to a standstill by refusing to let any of the government's deputies speak.[124] The government responded to these obstructionist tactics by excluding six SDK and two Serbian Agrarian deputies from a number of sessions of parliament; Radić had already been excluded on a number of occasions (29 February, 13 March, 4 May).[125]

Obstructionism was really the only weapon at the SDK's disposal. As an indication of the nature of the political situation, the SDK also increasingly raised the possibility of withdrawing from the parliament and Belgrade altogether if opposition to reform continued on the part of the Serbian parties. In March 1928 Radić first suggested that the SDK might withdraw from the parliament, but not Belgrade, 'because to abandon Belgrade means breaking with the court and with everyone. That is war.' That same month Pribićević too declared that the SDK was considering withdrawing from the parliament. By late May, however, as the political situation worsened, both Radić and Pribićević spoke in terms of withdrawing from Belgrade for a year or even permanently.[126] That Radić and the SDK leadership were frustrated by their inability to achieve reform is undeniable. Frustration led invariably to new invectives against the Serbian parties. 'The Radicals and Democrats are the same,' Radić declared during a parliamentary session, 'there are no real differences between them. They are purely Serbian parties, which have a Turkish ideal of the state. They want only to rule.' Rather than address the needs of and their duties to the people, they only wanted power. 'These two great parties do not have the slightest idea about what a European state is. And this is our greatest misery, this is the root of the crisis.'[127] What is more, Radić argued that failure to enact reform from above might well lead to popular discontent. He had always worked to instil in the peasants a commitment to legality and the ballot box. He regarded it his duty, however, to warn opponents of reform 'that if after all our attempts, after all our warnings there is no success, the people will not ask me, because as long as the people – who have accepted me as their practical head, their leader – ask me, all will be well, but the situation could arise in which they say: our leader is too good and we want to take action into our own hands. Gentlemen, there is already whispering about this among the people, and when the people begin to whisper something, there is no one who can stop this.'[128]

By early June parliamentary sessions had degenerated to such a level of bitter recrimination that even Radić concluded on 19 June that 'a psychological disposition for murder is being created here.'[129] That same day, twenty-four NRS and Democratic deputies presented a motion to deprive Radić of his mandate on the grounds that his behaviour was irresponsible. On the night of 19 June, Radić's Montenegrin colleague Sekula Drljević, sensing that tensions were running too high, apparently urged him not to attend any parliamentary sessions for the next few days.[130] Radić noted his concern but refused to stay away from the parliament.

The following day, on 20 June, an article written by Radić appeared in the HSS daily *Narodni val* in which he accused Vukićević of being prepared to resort to any and all means to remain in power. Rumours were rife in government circles, Radić noted, to the effect that both he and Pribićević had to be killed.[131] Radić appeared that same morning at the opening session of the parliament. One of the first speakers was the Montenegrin Serb NRS deputy Puniša Račić. Soon after he began speaking, a shouting match erupted between him and the HSS deputy Ivan Pernar. The president of the parliament, Ninko Perić, suspended the session, at which point Račić drew his pistol and began firing at the benches of the HSS. Radić was hit in the abdomen and seriously wounded. Four other HSS deputies, Djuro Basariček, Pavle Radić, Ivan Pernar, and Ivan Grandja, were shot. Pavle Radić and Basariček died instantly. Grandja and Pernar were the only ones to survive. Radić would die just over six weeks later, on 8 August.

With this crime the country's political crisis, already acute, reached a crossroads. On the day of the assassination attempt on Radić, the SDK's deputies finally carried out their threat to withdrew from Belgrade. Zagreb now formed their political centre. From this point onward the SDK demanded sweeping changes to the Vidovdan state system. According to its 21 June resolutions, the SDK refused further to participate in the Belgrade parliament, 'in which the blood of our comrades and friends, our martyrs in the struggle for equality,' had been spilled. It also refused to conduct any relations with the current government and appealed to the people to maintain order and its faith in the SDK's leadership.[132] 'We have experienced a terrible scandal,' the HSS paper *Dom* declared, 'at which distant future generations will shudder. It was precisely in this parliament that the Croats who gave this state all of their souls had to be struck down.' On 20 June the Belgrade parliament 'had ceased being a Croat parliament of equality, because the idea of brotherhood and [the Kingdom of Serbs, Croats, and Slovenes as] a Croatian state was on that day destroyed.'[133]

Pribićević was even more categorical. At the funerals of Basariček and Pavle Radić he said that the assassin's bullets were fired at 'president' Radić and the entire SDK leadership. But he observed that the bullets hit something else. 'They hit above all,' Pribićević declared, 'the present National Parliament to which, according to the decision of the SDK, we will not return. They hit, secondly, the present state order on which we worked with the best conviction, but under which we in practice experienced such inequality and subordination.' Finally, Račić's bullets 'fatally wounded the present system which always seeks its final arguments in the gun-butt and in terror, instead of searching for them in an agreement of all national forces.'[134] Not only was there no thought of returning to the Belgrade parliament, but the entire state system was called into question and its fundamental reform demanded.

Yet that same parliament kept functioning. The Vukićević government denied all suggestions of complicity in the murders and kept operating until 4 July, when Vukićević finally tendered his cabinet's resignation. On 6 July, in a symbolic though practically meaningless gesture, the king gave Radić, who seemed to be recovering from his wounds, a mandate to form a government. In line with the SDK's call for a fundamental revision of the state system, the offer was rejected. Consequently, on 27 July the Slovene leader Korošec formed a new SLS–JMO–NRS–Democrat government, really only a reconstituted version of Vukićević's cabinet, which immediately announced that parliament would reconvene on 1 August. The SDK saw this as nothing short of a provocation. According to Radić, the assassin Račić was only the executor of a plot 'conceived of and agreed to in one part of the Radical [parliamentary] club,' probably with the knowledge and approval of the president of the parliament, Nikola Perić, and Velja Vukićević.[135] Radić's position had now radicalized. According to one of his deputies, who met with Radić shortly before his death, Radić had reached the conclusion that some of the central tenets and tactics of the HSS had to be changed. Radić apparently indicated that the HSS should abandon its pacifism and 'fight with the same means as are used against us, because only then will the struggle against us be paralyzed.' Radić concluded that 'we have nothing more to look for in Belgrade.'[136] This last point should hardly be surprising, particularly in light of Radić's and Pribićević's much earlier threats to withdraw from Belgrade. Returning to Belgrade was simply not a credible alternative. Months later the HSS accused Dragomir Janković, the minister of the royal court, and Velja Vukićević of organizing the assassination.[137]

Given the SDK's perception that the assassinations were organized, it refused even to consider dialogue with the new cabinet. The Korošec regime was, according to Pribićević, 'a government of Puniša Račić, a government of the same spirit, of the same direction and policy, [as the one] which placed a revolver in the hands of Puniša Račić.'[138] It is hardly surprising, therefore, that the SDK's resolution of 1 August, which was signed by Radić as the SDK's president, concluded 'that the truncated national parliament, called to session for 1 August 1928 in Belgrade, is not authorized to reach any decisions for the whole state.' Decisions made by the Belgrade parliament were void and non-obligatory for the peoples of the non-Serbian regions. The resolution also claimed that the unification in 1918 did not mean that Croatia, the other former Habsburg lands, and Montenegro had renounced their historic state and political individualities. The diminution of these individualities was the result of Belgrade's use of both the unification act and the 1921 constitution to solidify Serbia's hegemony over the country's other regions. The resolution repeated that the bloodshed of 20 June had completely destroyed the existing state order. The SDK promised to pursue 'the most determined struggle for a new state order, which will insure full equality for all of the mentioned individualities.' The SDK also appealed to all political parties in the non-Serbian regions to join its struggle for 'a new state order,' and to the Serbian peasantry to assist in the realization of these 'great principles, which alone can save the state community.'[139] The following day the leaders of the Croat Bloc (HFSS and HSP) joined the SDK.

A full circle of sorts had now been made by the HSS. It returned to its position of the immediate post-unification period, although it did not formally demand Croat independence. But even independence was not rejected outright. Vladko Maček, Radić's successor, declared that 'we [HSS] do not want to destroy the state, we are not going outside of the state's borders, but within the borders of this state the Croat must be the only master on Croatian territory.' The Croat had to possess 'his own *Sabor*, his government, but in all other affairs, which remain common in the state, equality must be guaranteed, so that a minority cannot rule over the majority as in these last ten years.'[140] The HSS's position was strengthened by the fact that one of the key architects of that order, Pribićević, now supported its position. Although the SDK's resolution of 1 August did not explicitly call for a federal state system, undoubtedly because some elements within Pribićević's SDS opposed such a move, the HSS saw federalism as the only solution to the state crisis. Pribićević himself noted, writing from his Parisian exile in 1934, that 'these resolutions demanded a new organization of the Kingdom of Serbs, Croats, and Slovenes, in the form of federalism of the historic and national individualities in the country.' He added that perhaps the Southern Slavs 'would today be much closer to true unitarism, had they begun with a federal organization of the state that would correspond to their different historical pasts, instead of beginning with unitarism which the leading factors in Belgrade understood and realized as the hegemony of Serbia, which with the number of its citizens and its territory comprises hardly more than one fifth of the entire state.'[141] If the HSS's position had come around full circle, Pribićević had come around one hundred-eighty degrees.

After the events of 20 June there was clearly little willingness for compromise either in Belgrade or within the ranks of the HSS. There was a feeling among the HSS leaders and Croats in general that the shots fired at Radić and his colleagues were fired at the entire Croat people. This sentiment only intensified when Radić died on 8 August. His funeral on 13 August turned into a political manifestation of massive proportions, attended by about 300,000 people.[142] Even before Radić's death, and with the abstention of the SDK's deputies from Belgrade, there were renewed calls in the Belgrade press for an 'amputation.'[143] Talk of amputation was not new, for this notion had been raised at different times throughout the 1920s. Basically, amputation meant that Croatia proper, including Slovenia, but not Slavonia and Dalmatia, should be severed from the state. This would ostensibly solve the Croat question.

King Aleksander was seriously entertaining such proposals. When Pribićević had an audience with him on 9 July 1928, the king apparently raised the issue: 'You see, Mr Pribićević, you refuse to recognize that it is best to separate from the Croats. With that which will be left to us, we will at least have a firm state.' Pribićević strongly objected to such proposals, which he considered to be treasonable. When Gregor Žerjav, the leader of the Slovene section of Pribićević's Independent Democrats, had an audience with the king two days later, Aleksandar again presented the idea of separating the Serbs and Croats. The otherwise staid Žerjav replied that he saw only one solution to the current crisis, namely, the king's abdication: 'As far as I know, you are the only king in history who wants to reduce the size of his state.' At this the king, obviously offended, jumped to his feet and ordered Žerjav to leave at once.[144]

The HSS too condemned such suggestions. Maček, who upon Radić's death was almost immediately chosen to succeed him, remarked at one of his first major rallies as the HSS leader, that 'the Serbians could talk about amputation had they conquered this [land, Croatia, Slovenia, Bosnia–Herzegovina, Vojvodina], but they did not. But if they regret that we have unified – we have unfortunately regretted it – then *there can be a separation*, but there can be no amputation.' He indicated that there were only two solutions: either a 'just' agreement or separation. The various amputation schemes were interpreted as a reflection of the Serbian establishment's realization that the Croats could not be reconciled to the Vidovdan order. Belgrade had either to recognize the complete equality of the non-Serbian regions with Serbia, or agree to their separation. Upon separation, these lands would return to the status they held between 29 October and 1 December 1918, that is, as the 'State of the Slovenes, Croats, and Serbs.'[145]

It is beyond the parameters of this study to discuss in any detail the events between the summer of 1928 and the imposition of the royal dictatorship on 6 January 1929. Suffice it to say that there was no common ground between the regime parties and court in Belgrade and the SDK in Zagreb. The HSS, in a policy reminiscent of Radić's pre-1925 attempts to enlist foreign support, initiated steps to gain international support. The HSS sent its secretary Juraj Krnjević and Ivan Pernar, one of the survivors of 20 June, to the Inter-Parliamentary Union, which met in Berlin in August, and asked the union formally to condemn the events of 20 June and Belgrade policy. But the HSS mission was undertaken in its name alone, for some elements within Pribićević's SDS opposed this tactic. The HSS believed its mission was necessary because the Yugoslav delegation in Berlin no longer possessed any legitimacy. Krnjević's only success in Berlin was his meeting with the head of the German delegation.[146] The HSS subsequently sent Ante Trumbić, the former head of the Yugoslav Committee and the first foreign minister of the Yugoslav state, abroad to inform political figures about the situation in the country. Pribićević unsuccessfully attempted to win Davidović over to a common political platform with the SDK.[147] But no tangible support was forthcoming either domestically or from abroad. Throughout late 1928 the political situation deteriorated. On 1 December, the tenth anniversary of the unification, serious clashes occurred between student demonstrators and the police in Zagreb. 'The Croat Peasant Party, and with it the entire Croat people,' Maček remarked on this occasion, 'never celebrated December 1, because the entire act of December 1, 1918, was brought about without the approval of the Croat people by a numerically small intelligentsia, which was regrettably so distant from the people, that it did not bother even to consider the people's disposition.'[148] After the events of 20 June, it was naturally even less inclined to celebrate this date. On 28 December Korošec finally tendered his cabinet's resignation.

On 4 January 1929 Maček and Pribićević had separate audiences with King Aleksandar. Maček emphasized that the existing state crisis could only be resolved in accordance with the SDK's resolutions of 1 August and the state's federalization along historical–national lines. In his audience, Pribićević urged that elections be held for a new constituent assembly that would reorganize the country. On 5 January Maček again met with the king and demanded the country's federalization. He insisted that they had to return to 1918 and begin rebuilding the country from anew, 'but this time with the participation of the true representatives of the Croat people.'[149] The following day Aleksandar proclaimed the imposition of a royal dictatorship. The Vidovdan constitution was suspended and the parliament and political parties were dissolved. A new government was formed under the leadership of General Petar Živković, the commander of the Royal Guard. The Yugoslav experiment in democracy and parliamentary government had come to an end.

Radić's violent death was the turning-point in the development of the Yugoslav state. It was the end of an era. Whether or not the court was connected to this crime, King Aleksandar certainly exploited the crisis to establish the January 6 dictatorship. The Yugoslav state now lost whatever legitimacy it may have possessed among the Croats. What is more, with Radić's death Croats gained a martyr. After 20 June 1928 some of Radić's most outspoken Croat opponents, like Ante Trumbić and Ante Pavelić, quickly joined forces with the HSS, in what amounted to a demonstration of national solidarity. By all appearances, the Croat city and village stood united as never before. Moreover, Pribićević, who was as much the spokesman of Croatia's Serbs as Radić was of the Croats, now supported the HSS's call for a fundamental revision of the state order. This was the kind of unity that Radić had wanted in 1918. In death he achieved that which had eluded him in life.

Conclusion

The conflict between Serb and Croat still remains the fundamental problem, because the Jugoslav state was not in the first instance established on sound lines, and every change attempted during these eleven years has merely been a variation of the original attempt to enforce a rigid centralism, controlled by a small clique in Belgrade. The faults on both sides have been gigantic – Croat abstention in the critical years was scarcely less fatal than the tactics of Pašić and his party. But the root evil lies in the fact that Croatia (unlike Slovenia, which has gained enormously), has definitely lost much of her former position under Hungary, and has never been offered a single real concession ... It is quite true that the Croat leaders have played their cards badly and often demanded impossibilities; but the fact remains that there has never been a serious proposal from the side of Belgrade and the ruling Serbs, calculated either to flatter Croat historical sentiment or still less ensure to the Croats a due share of control over their own affairs.

R.W. Seton-Watson, 1930

With Radić's violent death in 1928 the HSS had solidified its status as the only significant political force among the Croats. By that point the HSS had penetrated virtually every village in Croatia and had taken its activism into other Croat-populated regions of the country, especially Bosnia–Herzegovina. Croat national unity had been achieved, and in August 1928 the Croat city and village stood more united than ever before. Compared with the situation just a decade earlier, this was a revolutionary transformation.

The HSS's central role in the completion of Croat national integration was based on its agrarian and national program. The party's agrarian ideology addressed the growing social, political, and economic problems of the Croat village, and its national ideology aimed to secure the political sovereignty of the Croat nation. These two components, laid out in the prewar era, were intricately interwoven. The HSS's promotion of peasant right legitimized the peasantry's right to a leading role in society and was simultaneously the economic, social, and political program of the peasant movement. It asserted the peasantry's right to greater political participation at every level of state organization, respect in society, and reform of the existing economic system. This meant providing the peasantry with more education, land, and credit, as well as cooperative action to improve its position in the marketplace. The party's ideology was both anticapitalist, in the sense that unfettered economic competition went against the notion of social justice, and antisocialist, because of the socialist–communist emphasis on collectivization, revolutionary class struggle, and the leading role of the industrial proletariat in society.

Both liberal and Marxist historians have assessed this ideological system, and all other agrarian ideologies, as quintessentially flawed and unrealizable. Moreover, agrarianism or peasantism, many have asserted, was basically an anti-modernist, and hence reactionary, ideology. In the case of the Croat peasant movement, it would be overly simplistic to conclude that it resisted the process of modernization. Like socialism and liberalism, peasantism was a response to the crisis of modernity, although not necessarily a practical or viable response. As an ideology and political movement, it attempted to chart a course to modernity for that social group which had hitherto been neglected by the political and social élites. In spite of a tendency to rail against Croatia's urban élites and industrial society, the Radićes were not luddites. As Stjepan Radić noted in 1927, the goal of the Croat peasant movement was 'to gather all of our old culture and to supplement it with new, technical progress, and to create a perfected village alongside a free normal city.'[1] To be sure, the major flaw in this ideology was the assumption that the peasant class would retain its socially dominant status indefinitely. Nevertheless, the HSS held a central role in the democratization process in Croatia by asserting the political rights of the peasant majority and facilitating the peasantry's emergence as the core of the national movement. In this respect, the peasant movement played a modernizing role in Croatian society.

The other important plank of the HSS's agrarian ideology was the peasant state. This concept was of central importance to the process of national integration, especially after Yugoslav unification in 1918. The peasantry experienced the Croatian state that began to emerge after 1868 as a new and oppressive institution. That is why it was difficult for most peasants to identify with Croatia's politically diverse intelligentsia, which the peasants increasingly associated with the city, the state, and bureaucracy. The inability of most peasants to identify with the intelligentsia, hitherto the bearer of the national idea, posed an important impediment to national integration. To mobilize peasants over to the national cause, and in order to facilitate their identification with the Croatian state, the Radićes articulated the peasant state, a state with which peasants could identify. Athough the peasant state, like peasant right, has been discussed in the historiography, the mobilizational aspect of this concept has not received sufficient attention, particularly in relation to the process of national integration. Moreover, Marxist historiography, by rejecting the peasant state as a contradiction in terms, has minimized the importance of the concept, both as the ultimate objective of the HSS and as a mobilizational instrument.

The national ideology of Stjepan Radić, and hence the national program of the peasant party, represented a synthesis of the views of Strossmayer and Starčević. Like many other Croat national ideologists, Radić acknowledged the importance of Slavic reciprocity and struck a delicate balance between Croat political rights and cultural Yugoslavism. His prewar variant of *narodno jedinstvo* was intended as a means to an end, the unification of all Croat lands within the Habsburg monarchy. Confronted by the threat of Magyar (and German) domination, he urged unity and cooperation between the Croats and Serbs. Without unity they could never hope to achieve their political rights. Unlike many other proponents of *narodno jedinstvo*, such as the prewar Nationalist Youth and some elements within the HSK, as well as the post-war Democrats, Radić's variant never carried with it unitarist implications. He always remained within the political framework of Croatia. That is why his jettisoning of *narodno jedinstvo* was relatively painless after 1918.

Radić was certainly a Croat nationalist, but his deeply rooted commitment to Christian ethics and democratic principles meant that Radić's nationalism never degenerated into chauvinism. Even after 1918 he remained committed to his Slavophile ideas and recognized that Croats and Serbs, in linguistic and even cultural terms, formed part of a larger Slavic family. During the height of the struggle against Belgrade for a Croatian republic in the early 1920s, when Radić often resorted to bitter invective against Belgrade, he always distinguished between the Serbs as a people (the peasantry) and the Serbian establishment, which he viewed as being thoroughly corrupt. His Slavophile sentiments notwithstanding, Radić never believed that the South Slavs' political individualities and historical identities should be sacrificed – as indeed they could not – for the sake of, or subsumed within, this greater (South) Slavic community. The nationalist antagonism between Croats and Serbs over the issue of state organization, which was at the core of the national question in Yugoslavia, could only be resolved, at least in Radić's mind, if each national group respected the political individuality and rights of the others.

The Yugoslav state would not be able to secure political stability and legitimacy, and to evolve along democratic lines, as long as the rights of any of its constituent peoples went unrecognized. This was the underlying theme in Radić's policies in the 1920s.

The Yugoslav integralist intelligentsia, on the other hand, which was certainly not renowned for its tolerance or commitment to democratic principles, wanted those very individualities and identities to be erased for the purposes of the greater, Yugoslav good. Yugoslavia's intellectuals were 'intolerant, often irascible, largely ignorant of history, narrowly rationalistic, and unduly impressed with the superiority of Western Europe.' Moreover, they saw themselves 'as engineers who would pull a passive backward country into modernity, if need be by force.'[2] The peasants, on the other hand, who comprised the vast majority of the population, had only a vague, if any, comprehension of the Yugoslav idea – and it should be stressed that Yugoslavism remained a phenomenon of the intelligentsia – and were being asked to sacrifice their own, recently acquired national identity for the sake of a concept which they did not truly fathom. When that concept descended from the nebulous realm of ideas to the hard ground of reality in 1918, Croat peasants experienced the Yugoslav state as a new affliction, even more burdensome than the defunct Habsburg monarchy. Moreover, the Yugoslav state quickly came to be dominated by Great Serbian elements, namely, the NRS, which sought a highly centralized state in order to preserve Serbia's pre-eminent role and to safeguard Serb unification which had been achieved in 1918.

Radić's historic significance emerges in this context. In 1918 the revolt of the Croat peasants demonstrated the existence of a wide chasm between the Croat city and village. Possessing a republican platform and the concepts of peasant right and peasant state, Radić offered the peasants a program which affirmed not only their social, political, and economic rights, but their national identity as well. As Maček correctly noted in 1928, Radić 'was the only member of the Croat intelligentsia who in 1918 raised high the flag of Croat freedom, whereas the others went mad for the nebulous Yugoslavism.'[3] Burdened throughout the 1920s by pressures from the new monarchical Yugoslav state, the Croat peasantry's social and political cohesion increased tremendously and coalesced around 'the party of Radić.' In spite of the ongoing process of economic differentiation in the countryside after 1918, the peasants demonstrated the strength of traditional rural ties and acted in unison under Radić's leadership. By 1920, and even more so by 1925, Radić's juggernaut had emasculated the other Croat parties, who were grudgingly forced to recognize his leadership. This was based on their realization that Radić's party was the only political force of significance in Croatia, as well as their own disenchantment with

Yugoslav unitarism. Even his Croat critics recognized that Radić had come to represent the Croat nation's resistance to Belgrade's state centralism.[4] By the early 1920s Radić's name had become synonymous with Croatdom and the preservation of Croat national individuality, and thereafter the HSS would remain the only significant political party in Croatia, at least until the Second World War. By the mid-1920s Croat national integration had been completed under the aegis of the HSS. Indeed, in early 1925 the HSS (at that time, still the HRSS) central leadership could claim that 'the Croat Republican Peasant Party has become the Croat people.'[5] This claim was essentially correct.

Despite its firm hold over the Croatian countryside, Radić's party was never able to enact its program. Although the peasant movement undermined the legitimacy of the Yugoslav state before 1925, in reality it never posed as serious a danger as the authorities believed. Committed to a pacifist platform, Radić never earnestly countenanced the use of violence. He was a committed parliamentarian and evinced a great deal of tactical flexibility, certainly more than is normally recognized in the historiography. Radić always spoke of 'just' and 'honourable' agreements, of compromise solutions. Yet his parliamentary activism, which only truly began in the second half of 1925, was thwarted by the same forces that had brought him to heel in the first place. The NRS–HSS government, in spite of Radić's comments to the contrary, was an unworkable association from its inception. That little was accomplished during the HSS's only stint in government is hardly surprising, because for the most part Pašić, who did not want Radić in government in the first place, was not prepared to move on any major reforms, and the NRS became increasingly immobilized because of internal problems.

Radić's experience between 1925 and 1928 is instructive. The consistent criticism directed at Radić and his movement by contemporaries – whether Yugoslav or Western – and historians alike is that he committed an egregious error by abstaining from Belgrade in the first years of the new state. Had he gone to Belgrade, Seton-Watson and many others have argued, the political system would not have had such a pronounced Serbian bent. This argument is not only counterfactual, but underrates the significance of the pressures exerted on Radić by the more radical HSS elements, and overrates the commitment to state reform among the two major Serbian parties. This argument also fails to take into account the structural flaws of the Yugoslav parliamentary system and the powerful role of King Aleksandar. In the event, after Radić went to Belgrade in 1925 and worked for reform, whether within government or in opposition together with his new Croatian Serb ally Pribićević, reform proved to be no simple matter. Some elements within the NRS, like Stojan Protić, realized in the early 1920s that strict centralism was unworkable and threatened the constitutional liberties of all the country's citizens, including the Serbs. But he was unable to find sufficient support for constitutional reform within the NRS, and eventually was forced to recognize the Vidovdan system.[6] Among the Democrats, on the other hand, Ljuba Davidović was amenable to limited reform, but was thwarted first by Pribićević's faction (1919-24) and then by Marinković's (1926-8). Under the circumstances, the determined assault that Radić and Pribićević launched to enact constitutional reform was bound to fail horribly. Radić the parliamentarian was foiled again, this time by the growing influence of the court and its factions within the NRS and Democratic Party. The king's role was paramount and ultimately jeopardized parliamentarism. His decision in 1924 to oust Davidović's government was not unconstitutional, but it certainly demonstrated that he was prepared and more than willing to topple a government with a comfortable relative majority if only because he disagreed with its policies. Aleksandar's actions in 1924 set an ominous precedent for the future. Even the arch-centralist Nikola Pašić was forced by 1926 to fight a desperate and ultimately futile rearguard action againt Aleksandar's anti-NRS intrigues. As for Radić, by 1928 he appeared, as he had before 1925, to be enough of a threat to the Serbian establishment that his liquidation became only a question of time. Rumours were rife in the spring of 1928 of possible assassination attempts against both Radić and Pribićević. The bullets that were fired at Radić on 20 June only confirmed the truth of those rumours.

The Serbian Agrarian leader Dragoljub Jovanović observed that the month of June was fatal for peasant leaders.[7] Like the Bulgarian peasantist Alexander Stamboliski, who was killed in June 1923, Radić would succumb to the forces of reaction in the month of June. Jovanović might also have added that the month of June was fatal for the first Yugoslav state. The Vidovdan constitution (June 1921) had a deleterious impact on the evolution of the Yugoslav state in the 1920s. The shots fired in the parliament in June 1928 eventually killed not only Radić, but the democratic experience in the Kingdom of Serbs, Croats, and Slovenes, for the two were intimately tied, although Radić died five months before the latter. With Radić's violent death the Yugoslav state stood at the crossroads, a fact that was not lost on contemporaries. The existing political system had broken down completely. In 1928 Yugoslavia's first and only ostensibly democratic decade ended in political failure, and Croat–Serb relations now reached their nadir.

Jovanović astutely pointed out that Radić's greatest success was in drawing the village away from communism, clericalism, and the extremist Croat nationalists. If there was one leader among the Croats who was for a sincere agreement with the Serbs, it was Radić. Jovanović was correct, and this undoubtedly explains why the Croat nationalist right, which was a *quantité négligeable* in the 1920s, remained very critical of Radić and believed he was incapable of achieving Croatian statehood. Jovanović now wondered, and he was certainly not alone, who could take up the task of channelling and normalizing the Croat peasant movement, and he feared that Croat peasants would gradually be won over by extremists of the left and right. The murder of Radić would undermine Croat–Serb relations and haunt the Great Serbian establishment. His sentiments were echoed by Miroslav Krleža, otherwise one of Radić's most prominent and prescient critics. Krleža suggested that Radić was perhaps the only political figure in the country who could, with his naïve romanticism and Slavophile views, still bridge the gap that divided Zagreb and Belgrade. He saw no other political figure on the landscape who could possibly fill that role. In spite of his dislike for Radić and his ideology, even Krleža had to admit after Radić's death that 'the people returned his sincere love with love.' His fellow writer August Cesarec wrote of the 'tragic death of the uncrowned king of Croatia' who had died in the struggle 'for humanity and the equality of all citizens.'[8] In death Radić's stature grew tremendously.

   Radić martyrization meant that his name would continue to command enormous political capital. But what was and is Radić's legacy? His party certainly played the central role in Croat national integration and mobilization, but beyond that, discussing his legacy is problematical. Even his followers drew rather different conclusions after his death as to the course that he himself would have followed. This assuredly stems primarily from Radić's numerous seemingly contradictory statements. One could easily skim his published works and speeches and extract remarks to support one of any number of positions. Radić frequently denounced 'Balkanism' and yet at times, often in the same breath, called for unification with the Bulgars. He travelled to the Soviet Union, but repeatedly denounced communism as a purely negative social movement. He was always a practising Christian, but consistently denounced the clergy, be it Catholic or Orthodox. He was a committed pacifist, and yet his rhetoric was often inflammatory. In late 1927 he said in the Belgrade parliament that the Yugoslav idea was already dead, but in February 1928 he told two Americans, Charles A. Beard and George Radin, that 'the unity of the Yugoslavs is permanently established.'[9] It was often difficult to distinguish between rhetoric and conviction. One should therefore not be surprised that during the Second World War, both the Croat wing of the Partisan resistance movement and the radical-right Ustaše used his name in an attempt to win the hearts and minds of Croat peasants, while at the same time subverting the ideals for which he stood.[10] As a result, Radić's legacy has been very much politicized, not least by post–Second World War scholars in the former

Yugoslavia. Indeed, even in the Croatia of the 1990s a number of political parties of quite different and seemingly opposing perspectives have laid claim to Radić's legacy.[11]

Radić's most important ideals were always a Croatian peasant state and the implementation of peasant right within that state. The underlying objective of these ideals was to provide the Croat peasants with a greater role in politics and society, and to affirm their national identity and sovereignty. The HSS acted as a vehicle through which the peasants could attempt to achieve these objectives. But if the HSS claimed to assert the rights of peasants in society, it was only natural that it provide peasants with a leading role within the party. This it did only to a limited extent. Peasants constituted a majority of the party's central leadership and elected deputies; the internal make-up of the party reflected the existing social composition of Croatian society.

There was an unseemlier side. Even though the peasant movement asserted the rights of the peasantry, and thus provided a powerfully democratic and progressive impetus to Croatian political life, the HSS never developed an internal democratic machinery. Although this was certainly not the original intention of Radić, by the late 1920s the party had become, in effect, an unofficial autocracy. The local peasant leadership was slighted and lost much of its earlier significance. Sessions of the main assemblies and main committees, frequent before 1914, ceased almost completely after 1918. This stemmed, in part, from the general political circumstances of the early 1920s. It was never remedied in Radić's lifetime, however, nor were any major initiatives undertaken to reverse this trend. In fact, the process only intensified under Maček's leadership between 1928 and 1941, although this undemocratic tendency also reflected the period. Radić often confronted the party with *faits accompli*: in 1923 when he left for London, in 1924 when he went to Soviet Russia, in 1925 when he came to terms with Pašić's party, and again in 1927 when he came to terms with Pribićević. Moreover, towards the end of his life a virtual cult of personality had developed around Radić. On the occasion of his fifty-seventh birthday, just days before the assassination attempt, the HSS's main organ ran poems and odes to 'the Leader' Radić. This was a testament to Radić's towering presence within the party–movement. Indeed, in many ways he was the party. But it also testifies to the fact that the party had become internally undemocratic. To a certain extent this was a reflection of Radić's character. Radić remained very much the idealist and never managed to leave the village either emotionally or intellectually. That is why it has often been asserted, and not without some truth, that Radić was able to divine and to articulate intuitively the inarticulate desires of the Croat village. He saw himself as an interpreter of the people's will. But having divined and articulated, Radić now commanded. Or to cite one of his oldest associates, Radić had become a virtual dictator within the party.[12]

Despite this undemocratic trend within 'the party of Radić,' it carried out a veritable national revolution among Croats, and in this respect it played a decisively progressive historical role, acknowledged even by its Marxist critics.[13] It achieved complete mastery over the Croat national movement, and in fact became synonymous with that movement, at least until 1941. Given his stature as the leader of the first Croat national mass movement, Radić is regarded in Croatia today as an important progenitor of Croatia's more recent drive for independence in the 1990s. The reality is that by bringing together for the first time peasants and intellectuals into one mass movement that aspired towards Croat independence, Radić and the party facilitated the completion of Croat national integration.

Radić, who was always the driving spirit within the party, remains something of an enigma. That he possessed a powerful will and exerted a tremendous moral authority over his followers is obvious enough. Where and how did he acquire these attributes? The Croat writer Ljubo Weisner pondered these questions. 'What is it that drives the half-blind Stjepan Radić forward ... from one suffering to the next, from one persecution to another, through insane asylums, police prisons, jails, in never-ending danger of some ambush or open attack on the part of some poor devil, who does not understand him, because he is a talent isolated in a mass? ... Why does this man, who does not even see the masses who come to listen to him at his rallies, but hears them like the roar of an ocean, always rush forward with his ideals, in the danger that he'll parish, so long as his ideals will be realized?'[14] Weisner did not offer any answers, for Radić seemed to him to be a mystery. In fact, there really was no mystery, and there was always an internal logic to Radić's actions. At an early age Radić acquired a passionate and sincere devotion to his constituency. He wished to achieve peasant affirmation in a society that had a highly disparaging view of peasants.

It was his devotion to the people that separated Radić from most of the Croat intelligentsia. In late 1895, as Radić and his associates sat in prison, Živan Bertić remarked to Radić that 'our old men say that we were [and are] a nation, whereas we young men believe that we will become a nation.' A new national intelligentsia 'is being born from among our generation, which will win the bureaucrats over to the people and raise the people to the level of the gentlemen.'[15] Unlike the older generation of the intelligentsia, Radić and the *mladi* believed that the essence of political activism consisted of practical work among the people. Yet by the 1920s Bertić was referring to his old friend Radić as a demagogue.[16] That was because Radić went one step further than his colleagues: he asserted that the intelligentsia had to go to the people and learn from the people, that it had to follow the pulse of the people.

Radić never lost his faith in the peasantry, either in its supposedly superior moral virtues or in its potential political power, that is, if only it could be mobilized. In this respect Radić remained naïvely idealistic; this stemmed from his romantic view of the peasantry and his Christian beliefs. The experiences of the 1920s disproved the accuracy of his earlier assertions. In that decade the Croat peasantry was finally organized and became a political force, but this did not translate into a real share of political power or the realization of the party's socio-economic program. Radić always seemed to believe that the Croat peasant movement that he led would prevail, if for no other reason than because its 'mission,' to use his words, was 'just' and 'honourable.' Profoundly convinced of the justness of his Croat national and peasant cause – this was the internal logic propelling Radić from his earliest days – he always moved forward in the belief that victory was not far off. In the end, however, Radić the idealist and romantic was delivered a fatal blow. Radić's fate had ominous implications for Croatia and Yugoslavia. History would regrettably show that, in an age dominated by ideological extremes, those forces in Yugoslavia committed to violent change would dominate the political stage. In this respect, Radić's violent demise presaged by just over a decade an equally violent end for the movement that he had founded.

Notes

1 Introduction and Historical Background

1 The literature on modern nations and nationalism is immense, and only some of the most recent and major works can be cited here. See Peter Alter, *Nationalism* 2d ed. (London, 1994); Ernest Gellner, *Nations and Nationalism* (Oxford, 1983); Eric J. Hobsbawm, *Nations and Nationalism since 1780* (Cambridge, 1990); C.A. Kupchan (ed.), *Nationalism and Nationalities in the New Europe* (Ithaca and London, 1995); the works of Anthony D. Smith: *Nationalism in the Twentieth Century* (Oxford, 1979); *Theories of Nationalism*, 2nd ed. (London, 1983), *The Ethnic Origins of Nations* (Oxford, 1986), and *National Identity* (London, 1991); and P.F. Sugar and I.J. Lederer, *Nationalism in Eastern Europe* (Seattle, 1969). For the emergence of national ideologies in Croatia and the other South Slav lands, see the excellent study by Ivo Banac, *The National Question in Yugoslavia: Origins, History, Politics*, 2nd ed. (Ithaca and London, 1988); and the very important studies by Mirjana Gross, 'Croatian National-Integrational Ideologies from the End of Illyrism to the Creation of Yugoslavia,' *Austrian History Yearbook* 15–16 (1979–80): 3–33, and Charles Jelavich, *South Slav Nationalisms: Textbooks and Yugoslav Union before 1914* (Columbus, Ohio, 1990).
2 On the advice of Professor Paul R. Magocsi, I have adopted the terminology employed in his study, *The Shaping of a National Identity: Subcarpathian Rus', 1848–1948* (Cambridge and London, 1978).
3 Smith, *National Identity*, 72.
4 Miroslav Hroch, *Social Preconditions of National Revival in Europe: A Comparative Analysis of the Social Composition of Patriotic Groups among the Smaller European Nations* (Cambridge, 1985), 22–4.
5 Miroslav Hroch, 'National Self-Determination from a Historical Perspective,' *Canadian Slavonic Papers* 37, nos. 3–4 (1995): 293.

6 Mirjana Gross, 'O integraciji hrvatske nacije,' in *Društveni razvoj u Hrvatskoj (od 16 stoljeća do početka 20 stoljeća)*, ed. M. Gross (Zagreb, 1981), 183. See also her article, 'The Integration of the Croatian Nation,' *East European Quarterly* 15, no. 2 (1981): 209–225.

7 Banac, *The National Question in Yugoslavia*, 73.

8 Gross, 'O integraciji hrvatske nacije,' 183–4.

9 For studies of Gaj and the Illyrianist movement, see Josip Horvat, *Ljudevit Gaj: Njegov život, njegovo doba* (Zagreb, 1975); Elinor M. Despalatović, *Ljudevit Gaj and the Illyrian Movement* (New York, 1975); and the works of Jaroslav Šidak, 'Ilirski pokret,' in *Društveni razvoj u Hrvatskoj*, 191–230; *Studije iz hrvatske povijesti XIX stoljeća* (Zagreb, 1973), 95–124, 195–220; and, *Hrvatski narodni preporod: Ilirski pokret* (Zagreb, 1988).

10 Mirjana Gross, 'O društvenim procesima u sjevernoj Hrvatskoj u drugoj polovici 19 stoljeća,' in *Društveni razvoj u Hrvatskoj*, 353–4. According to Gross, up to the 1860s the bureaucrats and clergy were the most important groups within the intelligentsia. With the secularization of education and the creation of the University of Zagreb in the 1870s, teachers and lawyers became more prominent.

11 Gross, 'O integraciji hrvatske nacije,' 185.

12 For works on Strossmayer, Rački, and their 'Yugoslavism' (*jugoslovjenstvo*), see J.J. Strossmayer and Franjo Rački, *Politički spisi*, compiled by Vladimir Košćak (Zagreb, 1971); Jaroslav Šidak, *Studije iz hrvatske povijesti XIX stoljeća* (Zagreb, 1973), 45–84; and Petar Korunić, *Jugoslavizam i federalizam u hrvatskom nacionalnom preporodu, 1835–1875* (Zagreb, 1989).

13 Banac, *The National Question in Yugoslavia*, 89–91. As Šidak notes, the contemporary emphasis on state right and so-called historic nations, especially in Magyar and German circles, meant that Strossmayer and Rački had to avail themselves of the principle of state right, for it was a powerful legitimizing factor in the national cause. Šidak, *Studije iz hrvatske povijesti XIX stoljeća*, 55.

14 For studies of Starčević and his movement, see Mirjana Gross, *Povijest pravaške ideologije* (Zagreb, 1973); M. Gross, 'O nacionalnoj ideologiji A. Starčevića i E. Kvaternika,' *Časopis za suvremenu povijest* 4, no. 1 (1972): 25–46; Ante Starčević, *Politički spisi*, comp. Tomislav Ladan (Zagreb, 1971); and Josip Horvat, *Ante Starčević: Kulturno-povjesna slika* (Zagreb, 1940). A brief clarification of the term state right, as opposed to states' rights or state rights, is in order. The term should not be employed in the plural, simply because a state can have only one state right. See Ivo Banac, 'Nationalism in Southeastern Europe,' in *Nationalism and Nationalities in the New Europe*, 112.

15 For the terms of the *Nagodba* and the implications this agreement had on Croatia, see Josip Šarinić, *Nagodbena Hrvatska: Postanak i osnove ustavne organizacije* (Zagreb, 1972).

16 Šarinić, *Nagodbena Hrvatska*, 294–300; J. Šidak, M. Gross, I. Karaman, and D. Šepić, *Povijest hrvatskog naroda g. 1860–1914* (Zagreb, 1968), 38–43.

17 M. Gross and A. Szabo, *Prema hrvatskome gradjanskom društvu: Društveni razvoj u civilnoj Hrvatskoj i Slavoniji šezdeseti i sedamdeseti godina 19 stoljeća* (Zagreb, 1992), 232–3.

18 Šidak et al., *Povijest hrvatskog naroda*, 125; Šarinić, *Nagodbena Hrvatska*, 265–6; Igor Karaman, 'Problemi ekonomskog razvitka hrvatskih zemalja u doba oblikovanja gradjansko-kapitalističkog društva do prvog svjetskog rata' (hereafter, 'Problemi'), in *Društveni razvoj u Hrvatskoj*, 321–5.

19 For a brief political profile of Mažuranić, see Šidak, *Studije iz hrvatske povijesti XIX stoljeća*, 279–308. For an excellent discussion of these reforms, see Gross and Szabo, *Prema hrvatskome gradjanskom društvu*, 369–423.

20 Šarinić, *Nagodbena Hrvatska*, 260.

21 Gross and Szabo, *Prema hrvatskome gradjanskom društvu*, 419.

22 Ibid., 401–2.

23 Ibid., 404.

24 Šidak et al., *Povijest hrvatskog naroda*, 87.

25 Gross and Szabo, *Prema hrvatskome gradjanskom društvu*, 415–18, 422.

26 Gross, 'O društvenim procesima u sjevernoj Hrvatskoj u drugoj polovici 19 stoljeća,' 361.

27 Gross and Szabo, *Prema hrvatskome gradjanskom društvu*, 465–71.

28 Šidak et al., *Povijest hrvatskog naroda*, 99.

29 Ibid., 104–5.

30 Ibid., 123–4. For details relating to the electoral system, see Janko Ibler, *Hrvatska politika, 1903–1906* (Zagreb, 1914), vol. 1, 522.

31 Šidak et al., *Povijest hrvatskog naroda*, 131.

32 Gross and Szabo, *Prema hrvatskome gradjanskom društvu*, 151. For studies of Croatia's Serbs, see Drago Roksandić, *Srbi u Hrvatskoj: Od 15. stoljeća do naših dana* (Zagreb, 1991); Mato Artuković, *Ideologija srpsko-hrvatskih sporova: Srbobran, 1884–1902* (Zagreb, 1991); Tomislav Markus, 'Mihailo Polit-Desančić i srpski nacionalizam 1861 godine,' *Časopis za suvremenu povijest* 26, no. 3 (1994): 487–500; and the two studies by Nicholas Miller, 'Two strategies in Serbian politics in Croatia and Hungary before the First World War,' *Nationalities Papers* 23, no. 2 (1995): 327–51; *Between Nation and State: Serbian Politics in Croatia before the First World War* (Pittsburgh, 1997).

33 Gross and Szabo, *Prema hrvatskome gradjanskom društvu*, 270–1.

34 Ibid., 276, 497; Artuković, *Ideologija srpsko-hrvatskih sporova*, 23.

35 Artuković, *Ideologija srpsko-hrvatskih sporova*, 14–15, 50–5.

36 Ibid., 142–3, 152–4.

37 Ibid., 168–93, 208.

38 Ibid., 214–17.

39 Šidak et al., *Povijest hrvatskog naroda*, 133.

40 Ibid., 145.

41 Ibid., 147–8, 157–8.

42 For works relating to Croatian Social Democracy, see the two articles by Mirjana Gross, 'Neke karakteristike socijalne demokracije u Hrvatskoj i Slavoniji,' *Historijski zbornik* 5, nos. 3–4 (1952): 311–23; and, 'Socijalna demokracija prema nacionalnom pitanju u Hrvatskoj 1890–1902,' *Historijski zbornik* 9 (1956): 1–29; and, Vitomir Korać, *Povjest radničkog pokreta u Hrvatskoj i Slavoniji od prvih početaka do ukidanja ovih pokrajina 1922 godine*, 3 vols. (Zagreb, 1929–33).

43 Šidak et al., *Povijest hrvatskog naroda*, 201.

44 Korać, *Povjest radničkog pokreta u Hrvatskoj i Slavoniji*, vol. 3, 270.

45 Šidak et al., *Povijest hrvatskog naroda*, 204.

46 Ibid., 311.

47 Artuković, *Ideologija srpsko-hrvatskih sporova*, 241–5.

48 For a discussion of the Serb Independents' activism in 1903–5, see Gordana Krivokapić, 'Skupštinski pokret i politička aktivnost Srpske samostalne stranke u Kraljevini Hrvatskoj i Slavoniji 1903–1905 godine,' *Radovi Zavoda za hrvatsku povijest* 22 (1989): 95–111.

49 Hroch, *Social Preconditions of National Revival in Europe*, 180.

50 For a discussion of the peasantry and the agrarian economy in this period, see Manuela Dobos, 'The Nagodba and the Peasantry in Croatia-Slavonia,' in *The Peasantry of Eastern Europe*, vol. 1, *Roots of Rural Transformation*, ed. Ivan Volgyes (New York, 1979), 79–107; the relevant sections of the excellent study by Jozo Tomasevich, *Peasants, Politics and Economic Change in Yugoslavia* (Stanford, 1955); and V.I. Freidzon, 'Razvitie kapitalizma v horvatskoi derevne i polozhenie krestian v Horvatii v konce XIX – nachale XX veka,' *Uchenye zapiski Instituta slavianovedeniia* 10 (1954): 72–137. For a very useful study of the development of the agrarian economy in Slavonia, see Igor Karaman, 'Privredni položaj Slavonije u Habsburškoj monarhiji pod nagodbenim sistemom (1868–1918)' (hereafter, 'Privredni položaj'), *Zbornik Historijskog instituta Slavonije* 4 (1966): 283–374.

51 Šidak et al., *Povijest hrvatskog naroda*, 128. Up to 1892 the Austro-Hungarian currency was the gulden (Hung., forint), but in that year the Dual Monarchy adopted the gold standard and the gulden was replaced by the krone (Hung., korona).

52 David F. Good, *The Economic Rise of the Habsburg Empire, 1750–1914* (Berkeley and Los Angeles, 1984), 170–1.

53 Dobos, 'The Nagodba and the Peasantry in Croatia-Slavonia,' 88–9. The land tax was by far the largest direct tax, whereas indirect taxes were levied on a variety of goods and services: salt, tobacco, liquor distillation, charges for bureaucratic services, and others.

54 Tomasevich, *Peasants, Politics and Economic Change in Yugoslavia*, 182.
55 Ibid., 184–9.
56 One yoke (*jutro*) is about 0.58 hectares. Ibid., 205, Table 5.
57 Gross and Szabo, *Prema hrvatskome gradjanskom društvu*, 387–97.
58 Šidak et al., *Povijest hrvatskog naroda*, 129. See also Karaman, 'Problemi,' 311–14.
59 Karaman, 'Privredni položaj,' 366–7.
60 Tomasevich, *Peasants, Politics and Economic Change in Yugoslavia*, 204–5.
61 Ibid., 166–7.
62 Dobos, 'The Nagodba and the Peasantry in Croatia-Slavonia,' 90–1. In the first post-*Nagodba* decade alone, tax arrears grew by 130 per cent.
63 Ivan Kovačević, *Ekonomski položaj radničke klase u Hrvatskoj i Slavoniji 1867–1914* (Belgrade, 1972), 31.
64 Šidak et al., *Povijest hrvatskog naroda*, 325. See also Karaman, 'Problemi,' 326–8. A number of Czech banks, particularly the Prague-based Živnostěnská banka pro Čechy a Moravu and the Ústřední banka českych spořitelen, invested large amounts of money in Croatia in the decade before 1914 and played an important role in the development of Croatian banking (ibid., 328).
65 Šidak et al., *Povijest hrvatskog naroda*, 141, 319.
66 Tomasevich, *Peasants, Politics and Economic Change in Yugoslavia*, 157. Karaman provides a figure of 41.4 per cent population increase between 1869 and 1910. Karaman, 'Privredni položaj,' 288.
67 For the urbanization process and the changes in the structure of Croatia's towns in this period, see Božena Vranješ-Šoljan, *Stanovništvo gradova banske Hrvatske na prijelazu stoljeća: Socijalno-ekonomski sastav i vodeći slojevi, 1890–1914* (Zagreb, 1991).
68 Šidak et al., *Povijest hrvatskog naroda*, 75, 139–41.
69 Dragutin Pavličević, 'Gospodarske prilike Civilne Hrvatske (1860–1873) s posebnim osvrtom na agrarnu proizvodnju,' *Radovi Zavoda za hrvatsku povijest* 22 (1989): 135–6.
70 For the process of industrialization in this period, see Igor Karaman, *Industrijalizacija gradjanske Hrvatske (1800–1941)* (Zagreb, 1991), 46ff.; also of importance is his earlier study *Privreda i društvo Hrvatske u 19 stoljeću* (Zagreb, 1972).
71 Kovačević, *Ekonomski položaj radničke klase u Hrvatskoj i Slavoniji*, 39–41; Karaman, 'Privredni položaj,' 322–3.
72 Good, *The Economic Rise of the Habsburg Empire*, 146.
73 Vladimir Žerjavić, 'Kretanje stanovništva i demografski gubici Republike Hrvatske u razdoblju 1900–1991 godine,' *Časopis za suvremenu povijest* 25, nos. 2–3 (1993): 77. For an analysis of emigration trends, see Ivan Čizmić, 'O iseljavanju iz Hrvatske u razdoblju 1880–1914,' *Historijski zbornik* 27–8 (1974–5): 27–47.

Čizmić estimates that in the period between 1880 and 1910, 211,796 people emigrated from Croatia-Slavonia. If one includes data from the other Croat lands (Dalmatia, Istria) for the same period, the total exceeds 300,000 (ibid., 31).

74 Tomasevich, *Peasants, Politics and Economic Change in Yugoslavia*, 250.

75 Dragutin Pavličević, *Narodni pokret 1883 u Hrvatskoj* (Zagreb, 1980), 290–2, 352–3.

76 Cited in Dobos, 'The Nagodba and the Peasantry in Croatia-Slavonia,' 95. Mirjana Gross sums up the peasant's predicament as follows: 'For their catastrophic situation the peasants no longer blamed the feudal lords alone. They gained the experience that the administrative organs, in which the urban intelligentsia was growing in number, did not help them at all and that their usurers were tied to the city by different means ... that is how the typical hatred of the small peasant towards all social classes in the city originated.' Gross, 'O društvenim procesima u sjevernoj Hrvatskoj u drugoj polovici 19 stoljeća,' 357.

77 Pavličević, *Narodni pokret 1883 u Hrvatskoj*, 357.

2 Stepjan Radić: The Formative Years

1 For works relating to Radić's youth, see the relevant sections of his autobiography in Stjepan Radić, *Politički spisi*, compiled by Zvonimir Kulundžić (Zagreb, 1971), 51–99; the excellent article by Vladimir Košćak, 'Mladost Stjepana Radića,' *Hrvatski znanstveni zbornik* 1, no. 2 (1971): 123–64; the brief biography by Bogdan Krizman in Stjepan Radić, *Korespondencija Stjepana Radića 1885–1928* (hereafter *Korespondencija*), 2 vols., compiled by Bogdan Krizman (Zagreb, 1972–3), vol. 1, 25–38; and, Dragan Bublić, *Ogled o životu i smrti Stjepana Radića* (Zagreb, 1943). The most recent and best account of the various influences that shaped Radić's views is Branka Boban, 'Stjepan Radić: Opus, utjecaji i dodiri,' *Radovi Zavoda za hrvatsku povijest* 22 (1989): 147–210.

2 Stjepan Radić, *Uzničke uspomene*, 3rd ed. (Zagreb, 1971), 205, 259.

3 Stjepan Radić, 'Moji susreti s našim biskupom,' *Novi Vienac* 1, no. 8 (1905): 124.

4 Radić, *Korespondencija*, 74–5.

5 Radić, *Politički spisi*, 53–4.

6 Ibid., 56; Radić, 'Moji susreti s našim biskupom,' 127.

7 Radić, *Korespondencija*, 328. This was a reference to the Czech historian and politician František Palacký. He became prominent during the revolutions of 1848–9 and is perhaps best known for articulating his 'Austro-Slav' political program.

8 There has been some debate regarding the date of Radić's first trip to Russia, some placing it in 1888 and others in 1889. But based on Radić's published correspondence, one is compelled to agree with Bogdan Krizman that this occurred in the summer of 1889. See Radić, *Korespondencija*, 26, 77–8. Yet Radić places the date

in 1888. See Radić, *Politički spisi*, 55–6; 'Moji susreti s našim biskupom,' *Novi Vienac* 1, no. 9 (1905): 135; and, Ivan Očak, 'Stjepan Radić i Rusija,' *Radovi Zavoda za hrvatsku povijest* 25 (1992): 103–22.

9 'The Russians are not the most cultured,' Antun wrote to Stjepan in Nov. 1894, 'perhaps you mean some other culture – Slavic ... The Africans have land, perhaps even more than the Russians. The question is, in whose hands is this land and what is done with it ..., [and] where did you learn that there is no chasm between the intelligentsia and the people among the Russians? What is intelligent [in Russia] – is the same as in Western Europe.' Although himself 'fond' of the Russians, he believed that Stjepan's conceptions about Russia were ill-informed and naïve. Radić, *Korespondencija*, 125.

10 Radić, *Uzničke uspomene*, 187.

11 Radić, *Politički spisi*, 58.

12 Arhiv Hrvatske (hereafter, AH), Rukopisna Ostavština Antuna, Pavla i Stjepana Radića, Box 9: no. 6, Rukopisi dvaju članaka Stjepana Radića o Vlasima, 1892.

13 Stjepan Radić, *Najjača stranka u Hrvatskoj* (Rijeka, 1902), 29.

14 Radić, *Korespondencija*, 85.

15 Ibid., 87–8.

16 On the margins of an Aug. 1888 letter that Stjepan received from his brother, he wrote, 'Yes, my Antun, my Mentor. Thank you, brother.' Ibid., 75.

17 Radić, *Politički spisi*, 59–60.

18 Radić, *Korespondencija*, 92. As in 1888, Strossmayer again provided Radić with some money to cover the cost of his trip to Prague. Radić, 'Moji susreti s našim biskupom,' 138.

19 Radić, *Korespondencija*, 94.

20 Ibid., 93. Supilo wrote, 'I regret to inform you that from among our students [in Dubrovnik], not a single one plans to go to Prague.' He concluded his letter as follows, 'Please accept a Croat greeting from your devoted F. Supilo, who knows that you suffer because of traitors' (ibid., 94).

21 See, e.g., the letter that Radić received from his colleague Kaurić on 5 Jan. 1894. Kaurić goes to great lengths to apologize for not visiting or writing to Radić: 'Knowing your resoluteness – I am convinced that, because of my silence, you have placed me in that category of people, whom you branded as submissive and selfish, because they are afraid to visit you in prison.' Ibid., 110.

22 Ibid., 102, 109.

23 Ibid., 121.

24 Radić, *Uzničke uspomene*, 269–70.

25 Povijesni Arhiv, Zagreb, Fond Stjepana Radića i HSS (hereafter, PA-Z, HSS), Box 1: no. 50, Antun Radić to Stjepan Radić, 26 Nov. 1894. Throughout this study, emphasis is always in the original unless otherwise noted.

26 Radić, *Korespondencija*, 153.

27 Ibid., 146, 151.

28 Radić, *Korespondencija*, 155. For a discussion of the demonstration, see Ljerka Racko, 'Spaljivanje madjarske zastave 1895 godine u Zagrebu,' *Radovi Zavoda za hrvatsku povijest* 23 (1990): 233–45.

29 The term is taken from István Deák, *The Lawful Revolution: Louis Kossuth and the Hungarians, 1848–1849* (New York, 1979).

30 Radić, *Korespondencija*, 156, 173.

31 Stjepan Radić, 'O modernoj naobrazbi kod nas Hrvata,' *Hrvatska misao* 4, no. 7 (1905): 293–4.

32 Cited in Jaroslav Šidak, 'Idejno sazrijevanje Stjepana Radića,' in his *Studije iz hrvatske povijesti XIX stoljeća* (Zagreb, 1973), 385 n29. For works relating to Masaryk, see Marie Neudorfl, *Masaryk's Understanding of Democracy Before 1914* (Pittsburgh, 1989); the essays in *T.G. Masaryk (1850–1937)*, vol. 1, *Thinker and Politician*, ed. S.B. Winters (London, 1990), and vol. 2, *Thinker and Critic*, ed. R.B. Pynsent (London, 1989); and H. Gordon Skilling, *T.G. Masaryk: Against the Current, 1882–1914* (University Park, Pa., 1994).

33 Radić, *Korespondencija*, 158, 160–1.

34 By April 1896 there were already about twenty Croat students at Prague University, among whom Živan Bertić, Milan Heimrl, Svetimir Korporić, and Milan Krištof – all Radić's former cellmates – were the most prominent. 'Your wish has therefore come true,' Krištof wrote to Radić, 'that as many of us as possible come here and that a Croat colony be created here forever.' Prague had an immediate impact on them; they were impressed 'by the city itself, the industrially and intellectually more progressive life, and along with all of this the great hospitality and simplicity of Czech men and women, [Czech] national pride and the Czech spirit.' Ibid., 185.

35 But not before visiting Strossmayer, who was evidently pleased by the flag-burning of Oct.; he told Radić that he and his colleagues had 'removed the stone from the grave in which our cowardly intelligentsia had been buried alive.' With Strossmayer's blessing, Radić set out for Russia. Radić, 'Moji susreti s našim biskupom,' 139.

36 Radić, *Korespondencija*, 191, 208.

37 Ibid., 208–9.

38 Antun Radić, 'Studij slavenskih naroda' (1900), in his *Sabrana djela*, vol. 17, *O ruskoj književnosti* (Zagreb, 1937), vi–vii.

39 Radić, 'O modernoj naobrazbi kod nas Hrvata,' 294–5.

40 Radić, *Korespondencija*, 209.

41 Radić, *Politički spisi*, 65.

42 Radić, *Korespondencija*, 230.

43 Bogdan Krizman, 'Stjepan Radić na Pariškoj političkoj školi,' *Naše teme* 15, no. 6 (1971): 1075 n7. In mid-Sept. 1896 Radić indicated that he might again try to enrol at Prague University, but judging by Antun's letter to Stjepan of 14 Nov., Stjepan was already thinking of going to Paris. Antun advised him not to go to Paris but to appeal to the University of Zagreb to readmit him as a regular student. Radić, *Korespondencija*, 220, 226.

44 Radić, 'O modernoj naobrazbi kod nas Hrvata,' 295; Radić, *Korespondencija*, 237. Born in France, Pinkas was a Young Czech deputy and chairman of the Alliance française in Prague and the most noted Czech francophile. See B.M. Garver, *The Young Czech Party, 1874–1901, and the Emergence of a Multi-Party System* (New Haven and London, 1978), 138.

45 Stjepan Radić, 'Tko je mene školovao,' *Hrvatska misao*, 4, no. 6 (1905): 287–8.

46 Founded in 1871, the Sciences Po recruited its professors from the Faculty of Law, Collège de France, government ministries, the diplomatic corps, and the captains of French banking and industry. It was a necessary stepping stone to the best jobs in the French civil service. Since it was a private institution, recruitment was for the most part limited to the upper-middle-class élite. See Terry Nichols Clark, *Prophets and Patrons: The French University and the Emergence of the Social Sciences* (Cambridge, Mass., 1973) 112–13; R.D. Anderson, *France, 1870–1914: Politics and Society* (London, 1977), 81.

47 Radić, *Politički spisi*, 65.

48 He subsequently published a version of the thesis as 'Južni Slaveni, njihovo narodno jedinstvo i njihova snaga,' *Hrvatska misao*, 4, nos. 2–4 (1904–5): 49–66, 97–112, 145–63, which will be discussed later in this chapter and in Chapter 4.

49 For a discussion of French influences on Radić, see Boban, 'Stjepan Radić,' 188–200.

50 Krizman, 'Stjepan Radić na Pariškoj političkoj školi,' 1090.

51 See the letter from Svetimir Korporić to Radić (22 June 1896) and the latter's letter to Marija Dvořák (2 Sept. 1896) in Radić, *Korespondencija*, 199, 217.

52 See, e.g., the letter from Franjo Poljak to Stjepan Radić (11 July 1899), in which he refers to Radić as 'the leader.' Antun Radić was less than pleased by his brother's planned participation with *Hrvatska misao* and told him in Oct. 1896 that no one would take it seriously. Ibid., 225, 343.

53 Milan Marjanović, *Stjepan Radić* (Belgrade, 1937), 44.

54 PA-Z, HSS, Box 14: no. 53.5, 'Bilješke razne, 16 June [1896].'

55 Živan Bertić, *Hrvatska politika* (Zagreb, 1927), 10, 12–13.

56 'Što hoćemo?' *Hrvatska misao*, 1, no. 1 (1897): 1.

57 Radić, *Korespondencija*, 264, 273, 313.

58 Many of the *mladi*, like Ivan Lorković, did not expect anything positive from the intelligentsia. He told Radić that he hated the intelligentsia because he loved the

people. Even Radić, though he wanted a rapprochement with the older intelligentsia, believed that foreign cultural influences were so strong among the intelligentsia, and the old bureaucratic and noble traditions so firmly rooted, that most intellectuals refused to see the peasant as anything other than a born thief and a common criminal. Radić, *Korespondencija*, 296–7, 327.

59 'Što hoćemo,' 2–4.
60 Bertić, *Hrvatska politika*, 13–14.
61 Ibid., 17–18.
62 'Novo Doba,' *Novo Doba* 1, no. 1 (1898): 1–4.
63 Ivan Lorković, the leader of the Zagreb wing of the *mladi*, wrote to Radić in June 1897 of the 'third period of our [national] awakening,' which had commenced in 1895 and was led by the *mladi*. Radić, *Korespondencija*, 275.
64 'Novo doba,' 4–5.
65 On 5 Jan. 1897 Radić and a number of his colleagues met with Masaryk, evidently to discuss their new journal *Hrvatska misao*. Moreover, it is almost certainly not a coincidence that *Novo doba* had the name it did, for it was probably modelled on the Czech periodical *Naše doba* (Our era), co-founded by Masaryk in the early 1890s. Radić, *Korespondencija*, 238.
66 Ibid., 155. For studies of the *Moderna* and the *mladi* in general, see Milan Marjanović, *Hrvatska moderna*, 2 vols. (Zagreb, 1951); Stanislav Marijanović, *Fin de siècle hrvatske moderne: Generacije 'mladih' i časopis 'Mladost'* (Osijek, 1990); Ivo Frangeš, *Povijest hrvatske književnosti* (Zagreb-Ljubljana, 1987), 227–83; and Branka Pribić, 'Idejna strujanja u hrvatskoj kulturi od 1895 do 1903,' *Časopis za suvremenu povijest* 4, no. 1 (1972): 87–129.
67 Šidak, 'Idejno sazrijevanje Stjepana Radića,' 381.
68 Stjepan Radić, 'Hrvatski ideali,' *Hrvatska misao* 1, no. 1 (1897): 5–6.
69 Ibid., 8–9.
70 Cited in Šidak, 'Idejno sazrijevanje Stjepana Radića,' 385.
71 Stjepan Radić, 'O pripravi za rad u narodnoj politici,' *Novo doba* 1, nos. 8–10 (1898): 321–2.
72 Radić, *Korespondencija*, 209.
73 Cited in Šidak, 'Idejno sazrijevanje Stjepana Radića,' 384.
74 Radić, *Korespondencija*, 363.
75 Stjepan Radić, 'Hrvatski ideali,' *Novo doba* 1, no. 1 (1898): 6–8.
76 Ibid., 8–9.
77 Stjepan Radić, 'O pripravi za rad u narodnoj politici,' *Novo doba* 1, nos. 8–10 (1898): 322.
78 Radić, 'Hrvatski ideali,' *Novo doba* 1, no. 2 (1898): 55–6.
79 Radić, 'O pripravi za rad u narodnoj politici,' *Novo doba* 1, nos. 3–4 (1898): 126–7.

80 Radić, 'O pripravi za rad u narodnoj politici,' *Novo doba* 1, nos. 6–7 (1898): 274–5.

81 Cited in Šidak, 'Idejno sazrijevanje Stjepana Radića,' 384.

82 Ibid., 385 n29.

83 Writing about the potential consequences of the Russo-Japanese war and the revolutionary events in Russia, an anonymous writer (probably Radić) asserted in the peasant party-affiliated press that Russia's enemies wanted her to be weakened: 'This unconcealed happiness of our national enemies tells us of a danger which threatens all Slavs, if Russia were not to remain what she is [a great power].' The type of government in Russia mattered less than a Russian victory over Japan, for a Russian defeat would invariably weaken all the Slavs. 'Rusija i Slaveni,' *Hrvatske novine*, 18 Feb. 1905, 1.

84 Stjepan Radić, 'Kako sam postao svoj gospodar,' *Božićnica za 1922 g.* (Zagreb, 1921), 59–60.

85 The only serious investigation of Radić's anti-Semitism is provided by Ivo Goldstein, 'Stjepan Radić i Židovi,' *Radovi Zavoda za hrvatsku povijest* 29 (1996): 208–16. Goldstein correctly notes that Radić's anti-Semitism waned over the years, especially after 1918, although he avoids a discussion of the delicate issue of Jewish assimilation in Croatia and Radić's views on this matter. Harriet Pass Freidenreich observes, much like Goldstein, that although Radić 'occasionally resorted to anti-Semitic demagoguery ... he should not be considered in the same class as other blatantly anti-Semitic politicians elsewhere in Eastern Europe at the time.' See H.P. Freidenreich, *The Jews of Yugoslavia: A Quest for Community* (Philadelphia, 1979), 172. The literature on anti-Semitism in Croatia is not extensive. The most recent and useful work is the collection of essays in *Antisemitizam, Holokaust, Antifašizam*, ed. Ognjen Kraus (Zagreb, 1996), particularly the essays by Ivo Goldstein, 'Antisemitizam u Hrvatskoj' (12–52), and Luka Vincetić, 'Antisemitizam u hrvatskoj katoličkoj štampi do Drugoga svjetskog rata' (54–63).

86 In 1906 Radić reviewed, translated, and published a chapter from Otto Weininger's anti-Semitic book *Geschlecht und Charakter*, 6th ed. (Berlin, 1905) in a Croatian journal. Radić's article was posthumously published as a brochure in 1937. Weininger's book had, by Radić's own admission, a 'powerful impression' on him, and he uncritically adopted most of Weininger's views as legitimate. Stjepan Radić, 'Židovstvo kao negativni elemenat kulture,' *Hrvatsko kolo* 2 (1906): 454–63; and *Židovstvo kao negativni elemenat kulture* (Zagreb, 1937).

87 Radić, *Židovstvo kao negativni elemenat kulture*, 8–10, 13–15.

88 Ibid., 6.

89 'Novi Starčevićev program,' *Dom*, 17 Mar. 1909, 1–2.

90 Antun Radić, 'Dom i rod,' *Dom*, 4 Apr. 1901, cited in Antun Radić, *Sabrana djela*, vol. 3, *Dom 1901* (Zagreb, 1936), 120–1.

91 Radić, *Židovstvo kao negativni elemenat kulture*, 16.

92 For works relating to Antun Radić, see Antun Barac, *Dr Antun Radić u hrvatskoj književnosti* (Zagreb, 1937); the two works by N. Matanić, *Dr Antun Radić: Njegove misli i njegovo značenje* (Zagreb, 1940) and *Dr. Antun Radić kao pisac i mislilac* (Zagreb, 1940); Stjepan Kranjčević, 'Dr Ante Radić,' *Književnik* 9, no. 2 (1936): 49–64; Ljubica Vuković-Todorović, *Hrvatski seljački pokret braće Radića: Antun Radić* (Belgrade, 1940), 51 ff.; and Elinor M. Despalatovic, 'The Peasant Nationalism of Ante Radić,' *Canadian Review of Studies in Nationalism* 5 (1979): 86–98.

93 Antun Radić, 'Kako čovjek postaje čovjek. Pogled na razvoj kulture i civilizacije,' *Božićnica za 1910 g.* (Zagreb, 1909), 63.

94 Ibid., 63–5, 69.

95 Antun Radić, 'Osnutak i značenje hrvatsko-slavonskoga gospodarskoga društva,' in *Sabrana djela*, vol. 18, *Dodatak* (Zagreb, 1939), 403.

96 Antun Radić, '*Život' t.j. Smrt hrvatskoga preporoda?* (Zagreb, 1899). *Život* (Life) was the main organ of the *Moderna*.

97 Ibid., 9–12.

98 Stjepan Radić, 'Zadaća "Novoga Vienca,"' *Novi Vienac* 1, no. 12 (1905): 191–2.

99 Radić, *Korespondencija*, 354.

100 PA-Z, HSS, Box 1: no. 54, Antun Radić to Stjepan Radić, 3 Sept. 1901. Junije Palmotić (1607–57), Ivan Gundulić (1589–1638), and Andrija Kačić Miošić (1704–60) were all prominent Dalmatian Croat writers.

101 See, e.g., the undated letter that he received from his associates Nikola Fugger and Živan Bertić, which reveals important differences between Radić and the *mladi*. Radić, *Korespondencija*, 352–3.

102 PA-Z, HSS, Box 1: no. 106, Živan Bertić to Stjepan Radić, 26 Mar. 1898. Bertić was referring to a draft of Radić's article, 'O pripravi za rad u narodnoj politici,' which appeared in numbers 3–4, 6–7, and 8–10 of *Novo doba* (1898).

103 Živan Bertić, 'Dom,' *Hrvatska misao* 1, no. 4 (1902): 124–5.

104 'Predsjednik seljačke stranke kao književnik i kao knjižar,' *Božićnica za 1914 g.* (Zagreb, 1913), 39–40.

105 Cited in Josip Horvat, *Supilo: Život jednoga hrvatskog političara* (Zagreb, 1938), 68.

106 Radić, 'Kako sam postao svoj gospodar,' 58–61.

107 Radić, *Korespondencija*, 303, 136.

108 'Predsjednik seljačke stranke kao književnik i knjižar,' 40.

109 PA-Z, HSS, Box 1: no. 54, Antun Radić to Stjepan Radić, 3 Sept. 1901.

110 Radić, *Korespondencija*, 364.

111 'Glavno obilježje i osnovni nacrt našega rada,' in ibid., 375–6.

112 Stjepan Radić, *Za jedinstvo Hrvatske opozicije na narodnjačkom (demokratskom) i slavenskom osnovu* (Zagreb, 1903), 20.

113 AH, Rukopisna Ostavština Antuna, Pavla i Stjepana Radića, Box 9: no. 94, 'Rukopis Stj. Radića: Osnova za gospodarsku, narodnu i političku obranu proti madjarskoj političkoj sili,' no date.

114 Cited in Šidak, 'Idejno sazrijevanje Stjepana Radića,' 386.

115 Stjepan Radić, *Hrvatski pokret godine 1903: Politička razprava* (Allegheny, Pa., n.d.), 54–5. For a brief discussion of Radić's activities during the national movement of 1903, see Vaso Bogdanov, *Hrvatski narodni pokret 1903–4* (Zagreb, 1961), 238–43.

116 Stjepan Radić, 'Hrvatski narod i njegovo vodstvo,' *Hrvatska misao* 3, no. 4 (1904): 200–10. In this article, published in January 1904, Radić reiterated his belief that foreign influences were so deeply rooted among the (older) intelligentsia, that it refused even to consider the sentiments of the peasants, whom it still regarded as vulgar and stupid. But the events of 1903 would give rise to a new, people's intelligentsia and political leadership (ibid., 204, 206–9).

117 Radić, *Politički spisi*, 71–2; Radić, *Korespondencija*, 33.

118 Radić, *Korespondencija*, 393–5. This was the central argument in his pamphlet *Najjača stranka u Hrvatskoj* (Zagreb, 1902).

119 See, e.g., the letters from Šandor Bresztynszky, the head of the united opposition (1902–3), to Radić of 28 Mar. and 4 June 1902, in ibid., 382–3, 386.

120 Ibid., 340–1.

121 Ibid., 389.

3 Agrarianism and National Integration

1 For studies of agrarian movements in East Central Europe, see Ghita Ionescu, 'Eastern Europe,' in *Populism: Its Meaning and National Characteristics*, ed. Ernest Gellner and Ghita Ionescu (New York, 1969), 97–121; the collection of essays in *The Peasantry of Eastern Europe*, vol. 1, *Roots of Rural Transformation*, ed. Ivan Volgyes (New York, 1979); G.M. Dimitrov, 'Agrarianism,' in *European Ideologies*, ed. Felix Gross (New York, 1948), 391–452; David Mitrany, *Marx against the Peasant* (New York, 1961); John D. Bell, *Peasants in Power: Alexander Stamboliski and the Bulgarian Agrarian National Union, 1899–1923* (Princeton, NJ, 1977); G.D. Jackson, Jr., *Comintern and Peasant in East Europe, 1919–1930* (New York, 1966), and his 'Peasant Political Movements in Eastern Europe,' in *Rural Protest: Peasant Movements and Social Change*, ed. H.A. Landsberger (London, 1974), 259–315.

2 On the establishment of the HPSS, see Bogdan Krizman, 'Osnivanje Hrvatske pučke seljačke stranke (1904–1905),' *Radovi Instituta za hrvatsku povijest* 2 (1972): 105–79; V.I. Freidzon, 'Sotsial'no-politicheskie vzgliady Antuna i Stepana Radichei v 1900-kh godakh i vozniknovenie khorvatskoi krest'ianskoi partii

(1904–1905),' *Uchenye zapiski Instituta slavianovedeniia* 20 (1960): 275–305; and Stjepan Gaži, 'Beginning of the Croatian Peasant Party: A Historico-Political Study,' *Journal of Croatian Studies* 3–4 (1962–3): 19–32. The literature about the HPSS and the Radićes, particularly from the interwar era, is abundant, although much of it is either panegyrical or disparaging. In the former category, see the two works by Rudolf Herceg, *Seljački pokret u Hrvatskoj* (Zagreb, 1923), and *Nemojmo zaboraviti: Hrvatska politika mora biti seljačka* (Zagreb, 1928); Ante Hikec, *Radić: portrait historijske ličnosti* (Zagreb, 1926); Ivo Šarinić, *Ideologija hrvatskog seljačkog pokreta* (Zagreb, 1935); and Imbro Štivić, *Život i djelo braće Radića* (Zagreb, 1940). In the latter category, see August Cesarec, *Stjepan Radić i Republika* (Zagreb, 1925). Also worthy of mention are Milan Marjanović, *Stjepan Radić* (Belgrade, 1937); and Ljubica Vuković-Todorović, *Hrvatski seljački pokret braće Radića* (Belgrade, 1940). For more recent studies, see the essays in Franjo Gaži and Stjepan Radić (eds.), *Stjepan Radić* (Zagreb, 1990), although many of the articles in this work are reprinted from the interwar era; the introductory essay by Bogdan Krizman in Radić, *Korespondencija*, vol. 1, 25–70; the two articles by Branka Boban, 'Stjepan Radić – opus, utjecaji i dodiri,' *Radovi Zavoda za hrvatsku povijest* 22 (1989): 147–210, and 'Shvaćanja Antuna i Stjepana Radića o mjestu i ulozi seljaštva u gospodarskom, društvenom i političkom životu,' *Radovi Instituta za hrvatsku povijest* 12 (1979): 265–304; Stjepan Gaži, 'Stjepan Radić: His Life and Political Activities (1871–1928),' *Journal of Croatian Studies* 14–15 (1973–4): 13–73; and Robert G. Livingston, 'Stjepan Radić and the Croatian Peasant Party, 1904–1929' (doctoral dissertation, Harvard University, 1959).

3 'Hrvatska Pučka Seljačka Stranka,' *Hrvatska misao* 4, no. 4 (1905): 173.
4 Antun Radić, 'Pučka politika,' *Hrvatska misao* 4, no. 6 (1905): 259–65.
5 Antun Radić, *Sabrana djela*, vol. 7, *Seljački nauk* (Zagreb, 1936), 77; Stjepan Radić, 'Strašan poraz gospodske politike,' *Dom*, 22 May 1907, 1.
6 Antun Radić, *Sabrana djela*, vol. 7, 158; Antun Radić, 'Pučka politika,' *Hrvatski narod*, 12 Jan. 1905, 1.
7 'Hrvatska Pučka Seljačka Stranka,' *Hrvatski Narod*, 23 Feb. 1905, 1.
8 Stjepan Radić, 'Kako se danas brani domovina,' *Hrvatska misao* 3, no. 11 (1904): 644–5.
9 Stjepan Radić, 'K osnivanju hrvatske seljačke stranke,' *Hrvatska misao* 3, no. 10 (1904): 580–1; see also, 'Neoborivi temelji velikomu djelu,' *Hrvatska misao* 4, no. 7 (1905): 321.
10 Radić, 'K osnivanju hrvatske seljačke stranke,' 583; Stjepan Radić, 'Izlaz iz današnjega meteža,' *Hrvatska misao* 3, no. 8 (1904): 456–7.
11 Antun Radić, 'Što ćemo prije?' *Dom*, 23 Dec. 1908, 2.
12 Radić, 'K osnivanju hrvatske seljačke stranke,' 584.
13 Stjepan Radić, 'Živi narod,' *Dom*, 8 Sept. 1909, 1–2.

14 Antun Radić, 'Na trećoj glavnoj skupštini Hrvatske pučke seljačke stranke,' *Dom*, 24 Aug. 1907, 1.

15 Antun Radić, 'Pučka politika,' *Hrvatski Narod*, 12 Jan. 1905, 1.

16 Radić, *Sabrana djela*, vol. 7, 35.

17 Radić, 'Izlaz iz današnjega meteža,' 462.

18 Radić, 'K osnivanju hrvatske seljačke stranke,' 586. See also, Stjepan Radić, 'Živjela seljačka Hrvatska,' *Dom*, 25 Aug. 1909, 1–2.

19 Radić, 'Izlaz iz današnjega meteža,' 470.

20 For the Radićes' views pertaining to the working class, see Branka Boban, 'Shvaćanja Antuna i Stjepana Radića o mjestu i ulozi radničke klase u društvu (do 1918 god.),' *Radovi Instituta za hrvatsku povijest* 15 (1982): 131–62.

21 See, e.g., August Cesarec, 'Ideologija HRSS ili put u – Bačvu,' in *Djela Augusta Cesarca*, vol. 4, *Rasprave, Članci, Polemike. Nacionalni, socijalni i kulturni problemi Jugoslavije*, ed. Vice Zaninović (Zagreb, 1971), 223–8; and Vaso Bogdanov, *Historija političkih stranaka u Hrvatskoj od prvih stranačkih grupiranja do 1918* (Zagreb, 1958), 782–9. For a comparative Marxist account of the region's peasantist ('bourgeois agrarian') movements, see M.M. Goranovich, *Krakh zelenogo internatsionala, 1921–1938* (Moscow, 1967).

22 Radić, *Sabrana djela*, vol. 7, 90.

23 Fran Škrinjar, 'Skupština u Sv. Ivanu Žabnu,' *Dom*, 3 July 1907, 3.

24 Fran Škrinjar, 'Prigovori proti seljačkoj stranci,' *Dom*, 11 Sept. 1907, 2; see also, Adam Neferanović, 'Jesmo li staležka stranka,' *Dom*, 29 May 1907, 3.

25 Radić, *Sabrana djela*, vol. 9, *Za seljačku politiku* (Zagreb, 1938), 203, 211.

26 Josip Predavec, *Agrarizam kao svjetski pokret i glavne seljačke gospodarske potrebe u Hrvatskoj* (Zagreb, 1911), vi.

27 Stjepan Radić, 'Kako je bilo na trećoj glavnoj skupštini HPSS,' 4 Sept. 1907, 1.

28 Djuro Basariček, 'Treba li staležka organizacija?' *Dom*, 9 Oct. 1907, 2.

29 Stjepan Radić, 'Kako je bilo na glavnoj skupštini,' *Dom*, 1 Sept. 1909, 2.

30 Antun Radić, 'Praváši proti seljačkoj banki,' *Dom*, 18 Oct. 1911, 1. Antun Radić denied that the HPSS was attempting to widen the chasm between the intelligentsia and peasantry: 'Borba za "korito,"' *Dom*, 12 Jan. 1910, 1.

31 Radić, *Sabrana djela*, vol. 7, 15, 36–7, 40–1, 97–101; Stjepan Radić, 'O seljačkom pravu na zemlju, na vladu i na poštovanje u družtvu,' *Dom*, 18 Sept. 1907, 1–2; Stjepan Radić, 'Za seljačko pravo,' *Dom*, 9 Nov. 1910, 1.

32 Tomasevich, *Peasants, Politics, and Economic Change in Yugoslavia*, 204.

33 Radić, *Sabrana djela*, vol. 7, 45, 121; Stjepan Radić, *Seljačko pravo u sto pitanja i sto odgovora* (Zagreb, 1913), 8–10; Predavec, *Agrarizam kao svjetski pokret*, 7–20.

34 Radić, *Sabrana djela*, vol. 4: *Dom 1902* (Zagreb, 1937), 274.

35 Radić, *Seljačko pravo*, 10–11.

36 Stjepan Radić, 'Zašto kod nas u Hrvatskoj ima toliko gulionica?' *Dom*, 27 Sept. 1911, 1.

37 Radić, *Seljačko pravo*, 11–16; Predavec, *Agrarizam kao svjetski pokret*, 30–44; Stjepan Radić, 'Za seljačko pravo,' *Dom*, 9 Nov. 1910, 1.

38 Stjepan Radić, 'Prva narodna potreba i četiri glavne seljačke potrebe,' *Dom*, 20 Sept. 1911, 1; Antun Radić, 'Pravaši proti seljačkoj banki,' *Dom*, 18 Oct. 1911, 1–2.

39 Radić, 'Kako se danas brani domovina,' 654; Stjepan Radić, 'O seljačkom pravu na zemlju, na vladu i na poštovanje u družtvu,' *Dom*, 11 Sept. 1907, 1.

40 The Croat Peasant Union was to provide inexpensive credit, as well as homestead and livestock insurance, to the peasantry, sell peasant goods at local markets, and fund peasant economic schools and courses. To raise capital the HPSS planned to sell 2,000 shares at 100 Austro-Hungarian crowns each, but the project was abandoned. Only in 1935, with the creation of 'Economic Concord' (*Gospodarska Sloga*), were the party's long-standing plans for an economic organization realized. See Antun Radić, 'Na trećoj glavnoj skupštini' and 'Hrvatski Seljački Savez,' *Dom*, 24 Aug. 1907, 1; 'Kako je bilo na trećoj glavnoj skupštini HPSS,' *Dom*, 4 Sept. 1907, 1–3.

41 Antun Radić, 'U kojem se smjeru imadu preurediti naše obćine?' *Dom*, 14 Dec. 1910, 1.

42 Radić, *Sabrana djela*, vol. 7, 44–8.

43 Radić, 'K osnivanju hrvatske seljačke stranke,' 588–9.

44 Antun Radić, 'Narod i vlada,' *Božićnica za 1910 g.* (Zagreb, 1909), 82; and Radić, *Sabrana djela*, vol. 7, 48–50.

45 Stjepan Radić, 'Hrvatski milijuni,' *Božićnica za 1910 g.* (Zagreb, 1909), 21–5. Stjepan Radić devoted much attention to the issue of finance, particularly the economic and financial relationship between Croatia and Hungary, and authored a major monographic study entitled *Današnja financijalna znanost* (Zagreb, 1908), for which he was awarded the Count Janko Drašković literary prize by Matica Hrvatska (Croat Literary–Cultural Foundation).

46 Stjepan Radić, 'O seljačkom pravu na zemlju, na vladu i na poštovanje u družtvu,' *Dom*, 18 Sept. 1907, 1–2.

47 Stjepan Radić, 'Naše obćine,' *Dom*, 20 July 1910, 1.

47 Radić, *Sabrana djela*, vol. 7, 50.

49 Antun Radić, 'Preuredjenje županijskih skupština,' *Dom*, 20 Mar. 1907, 1–2.

50 Radić, *Sabrana djela*, vol. 7, 118–19; Antun Radić, 'U kojem se smjeru imadu preurediti naše obćine,' *Dom*, 14 Dec. 1910, 1; Radić, *Seljačko pravo*, 26–9.

51 Radić, *Sabrana djela*, vol. 7, 58, 118.

52 Vladko Maček, *Memoari*, ed. Boris Urbić (Zagreb, 1992), 23.

53 Stjepan Radić, 'Korjen našemu narodnome zlu,' *Dom*, 4 Apr. 1913, 1.

54 Radić, *Sabrana djela*, vol. 7, 92.

55 Stjepan Radić, 'Zar čemo natrag u tminu?' *Dom*, 16 April 1913, 1.

56 Radić, *Sabrana djela*, vol. 7, 52–5, 119. See also, Stjepan Radić, 'Govor narod-noga zastupnika Stjepana Radića, izrečen u hrvatskom državnom saboru dne 12 svibnja 1910,' *Božićnica za 1911 g.* (Zagreb, 1910), 6–9.

57 Radić, *Seljačko pravo*, 29–32.

58 Radić, 'Govor narodnoga zastupnika Stjepana Radića,' 19.

59 For a discussion of the `peasant state,' see Branka Boban, 'O osnovnim obilježjima 'seljačke države' u ideologiji Antuna i Stjepana Radića,' *Radovi Instituta za hrvatsku povijest* 13 (1980): 51–88.

60 Stjepan Radić, 'Državna i narodnostna ideja s gledišta socijalne znanosti,' *Mjesečnik pravničkog družtva* 35, no. 6 (1909): 556–9.

61 Boban, 'O osnovnim obilježjima "seljačke države" u ideologiji Antuna i Stjepana Radića,' 68.

62 For the party's constitution, see 'Temeljni nauk ili program Hrvatske republikanske seljačke stranke (HRSS),' *Božićnica za 1923 g.* (Zagreb, 1922), 49–63. It is repro-duced in Ivan Mužić, *Stjepan Radić u Kraljevini Srba, Hrvata i Slovenaca*, 4th ed. (Zagreb, 1990), 303–25.

63 I.F. Lupis, 'Natrag k polju. Slom industrijalizma,' *Dom*, 23 Aug. 1911, 1; '"Budalaština!,"' *Dom*, 20 Sept. 1911, 1; and, 'Poljodjelstvo i fabrike,' *Dom*, 25 Oct. 1911, 1.

64 Radić, 'Govor narodnoga zastupnika Stjepana Radića,' 16, 27.

65 Antun Radić, 'Gospodarstvo, trgovina i novčarstvo,' and 'Radničko "pitanje,"' *Sabrana djela*, vol. 3, *Dom 1901* (Zagreb, 1936), 89, 263–4; 'Hrvatska industrija,' *Hrvatski narod*, 30 Mar. 1905, 1.

66 Radić, *Sabrana djela*, vol. 7, 83.

67 Ibid., vol. 4, 359–60; vol. 2, 340.

68 Stjepan Radić, 'Što je to gospodska politika,' *Dom*, 29 Jan. 1908, 2. For the HPSS's exploration of the relationship between Jewry and liberalism (esp. the lib-eral Viennese press), see 'Židovska politika,' *Dom*, 20 Nov. 1907, 1; Antun Radić, 'Židovska preuzetnost u Hrvatskoj,' *Dom*, 15 July 1908, 1; and Radić, *Sabrana djela*, vol. 3, 325.

69 PA-Z, HSS, Box 1: no. 54, letter from Antun to Stjepan Radić, 3 Sept. 1901, Zagreb.

70 Radić, *Sabrana djela*, vol. 6, 314; vol. 2, 340.

71 Ibid., vol. 2, 222.

72 Ibid., vol. 5, 206.

73 Stjepan Radić, 'Rauch, Frank i Supilo,' *Dom*, 24 June 1908, 1.

74 'Židovi u Hrvatskoj,' *Dom*, 6 Mar. 1907, 2.

75 Antun Radić admitted in 1903 that until very recently he had had no idea what

socialism truly represented, and although he read a good deal on the subject to remedy his ignorance, his knowledge of the subject apparently remained rather limited. See Radić, *Sabrana djela*, vol. 5, 50.

76 Zorica Stipetić, *Komunistički pokret i inteligencija: Istraživanja ideološkog i političkog djelovanja inteligencije u Hrvatskoj, 1918–1945* (Zagreb, 1980), 82.

77 Baćuška, 'Hrvatska pučka seljačka stranka,' *Hrvatska misao* 4, no. 4 (1905): 174. See also Radić, *Sabrana djela*, vol. 3, 263; and, Stjepan Radić, 'Gradjanska, radnička i seljačka pučka politika,' *Hrvatske novine*, 8 Mar. 1906, 1.

78 Radić, *Sabrana djela*, vol. 2, 50–1.

79 Stjepan Radić, 'Zašto seljački stalež mora biti glavni temelj hrvatskoj narodnoj politici,' *Dom*, 19 June 1907, 2–3; 'Hrvatska pučka seljačka stranka,' *Dom*, 18 Mar. 1908, 3.

80 Radić, *Sabrana djela*, vol. 7, 17, 37.

81 Stjepan Radić, 'Za napredak bez revolucije proti aristokratizmu,' *Hrvatska misao* 4, no. 1 (1904): 7.

82 Ibid., 9. See also, Stjepan Radić, 'Proti tiraniji i proti revoluciji,' *Hrvatska misao* 4, no. 6 (1905): 242–5, and Stjepan Radić, *Hrvatski politički katekizam* (1913; reprint, Opatija, 1995), 212–19.

83 Radić, *Sabrana djela*, vol. 7, 126. See also, Stjepan Radić, 'Plemićki ponos i seljačka sviest,' *Hrvatski narod*, 19 Jan. 1905, 1.

84 Radić, *Sabrana djela*, vol. 7, 177.

85 Stjepan Radić, 'Dajte seljaku zemlje,' *Dom*, 3 Apr. 1907, 1.

86 'Zašto u cieloj našoj carevini manjina gazi većinu,' *Dom*, 23 Sept. 1908, 1–2. See also, Radić, *Sabrana djela*, vol. 7, 94–101.

87 Radić, *Sabrana djela*, vol. 7, 93. Although the Radićes' anticlericalism has been addressed in the historiography, the importance of Christian morality on their political activism has not received the same attention. For their anticlericalism, see Zvonimir Kulundžić, *Ante Radić i klerikalci* (Zagreb, 1951); and, Viktor Novak, *Magnum Crimen: Pola vijeka klerikalizma u Hrvatskoj* (Zagreb, 1948), 205–52. For a more detailed analysis of Stjepan Radić's religious convictions and his views pertaining to Catholicism, see Jure Krišto, 'Hrvatsko katoličanstvo i ideološko formiranje Stjepana Radića (1893–1914),' *Časopis za suvremenu povijest* 23, no. 2–3 (1991): 129–65.

88 'Katolik sa strane' [Anonymous], 'Jaki preokret u mišljenju talijanskih katolika,' *Hrvatska misao* 4, no. 6 (1905): 285–6.

89 Stjepan Radić, 'Pripravljamo se za mir i slobodu,' *Dom*, 2 Oct. 1918, 1.

90 'Što mora znati o HPSS svaki njezin pristaša,' *Hrvatski narod*, 9 Feb. 1905, 2.

91 Stjepan Radić, 'Najbolje mjerilo za hrvatske političke stranke,' *Dom*, 13 Jan. 1909, 1–2; Fran Škrinjar, 'Hrvatska pučka seljačka stranka i svećenstvo,' *Dom*, 30 Jan.

1907, 2; Josip Brnardić, 'Gospodska politika, svećenstvo i hrvatska pučka seljačka stranka,' *Dom*, 3 Apr. 1907, 1–2.

92 'Prva naša briga,' *Hrvatski narod*, 22 Mar. 1905, 1.

93 'Katolik sa strane,' '"Konfesijonalna i narodna," "katolička i politička" stranka – nesmisao i nemogućnost!' *Hrvatska misao* 4, no. 7 (1905): 300–1.

94 Stjepan Radić, 'Seljačka stranka i Srbi,' *Dom*, 6 Nov. 1907, 1–2.

95 'Hrvatstvo,' *Hrvatstvo*, 2 Jan. 1905, 1.

96 J. Šafran, 'Za katoličku organizaciju,' *Hrvatstvo*, 18 July 1905, 1–2.

97 'Politika i modernizam,' *Hrvatstvo*, 15 July 1905, 1. See also, J. Šafar, 'Još o katoličkoj organizaciji,' *Hrvatstvo*, 29 July 1905, 1.

98 'Hrvatska katolička stranka?' *Hrvatstvo*, 26 Apr. 1905, 1.

99 From the Latin *furtim*, meaning an act done secretly (by trickery) or by theft. The nickname was derived from the fact that the clericalists tried to elicit the blessing of Bishop Josip Juraj Strossmayer for their political organization and claimed that he had signed on to the party. Strossmayer denied this, however, and claimed that they had obtained his signature by *furtim*, that is, by trickery.

100 'Hrvatska pučka seljačka stranka,' *Hrvatstvo*, 5 Apr. 1905, 2.

101 'Domaće vijesti,' *Hrvatstvo*, 26 Apr. 1905, 4.

102 Josip Posilović, 'Naši dopisi,' *Hrvatstvo*, 17 May 1905, 3.

103 Radić, *Sabrana djela*, vol. 7, 61–3, 112–17.

104 In 1905 the HPSS had three affiliated papers: *Hrvatski narod*, which had merged in Dec. 1904 with Antun Radić's *Dom* (1899–1904) to become the official party organ, *Hrvatske novine*, and the journal *Hrvatska misao*. In early Dec. 1905 *Hrvatski narod* ceased being the party's official organ because of a split in the HPSS's central leadership. From that point until late 1906 *Hrvatske novine* acted as the main party organ, which was subsequently superseded in that function by the resurrected *Dom*. *Hrvatska misao*, which was aimed at Croatia's intelligentsia, ceased publication in 1906 because of its sharply declining readership.

105 Radić, *Sabrana djela*, vol. 7, 65–8.

106 'Hrvatska pučka seljačka stranka, *Hrvatski narod*, 23 Feb. and 27 Apr. 1905, 1; 'Naš program pred sudom,' *Hrvatski narod*, 29 June 1905, 1.

107 'Hrvatska Pučka Seljačka Stranka,' *Hrvatske novine*, 19 Aug. 1905, 1.

108 'Vijesti iz domovine i iz drugih slavenskih krajeva,' *Hrvatske novine*, 19 Aug. 1905, 3.

109 'Hrvatska Pučka Seljačka Stranka,' *Hrvatski narod*, 24 Aug. 1905, 1. See also, 'Progoni hrvatske pučke seljačke stranke,' *Hrvatska misao* 4, no. 12 (1905): 572.

110 'Domaći viestnik,' *Hrvatske novine*, 3 May 1906, 3.

111 AH, Rukopisna Ostavština Antuna, Pavla i Stjepana Radića, Box 1: nos. 149 and 152, letters from Stjepan Hrastovec and Lovro Kranjec to Stjepan Radić, [22 Dec.?] 1911 and 28 Dec. 1911, Dubrava.

112 Ibid., Box 2: no. 123, 'Čija je dužnost braniti prava kraljevine Hrvatske?', no date, but before 1914, Zagreb.

113 Rudolf Herceg, *Seljački pokret u Hrvatskoj* (Zagreb, 1923), 25.

114 AH, Rukopisna Ostavština Antuna, Pavla i Stjepana Radića, Box 2: nos. 27–45, Autobiografija Stjepana Radića pisana 1924 g.

115 'Prva glavna skupština hrvatske pučke seljačke stranke,' *Hrvatski narod*, 21 Sept. 1905, 1.

116 'Glavna skupština hrvatske pučke seljačke stranke,' *Hrvatske novine*, 9 Sept. 1905, 1.

117 Stjepan Radić, 'Prva godišnjica hrvatske pučke seljačke stranke,' *Hrvatske novine*, 14 Dec. 1905, 1.

118 'Druga glavna skupština hrvatske pučke seljačke stranke,' *Dom*, 15 Sept. 1906, 1.

119 'Prva glavna skupština hrvatske pučke seljačke stranke,' *Hrvatske novine*, 23 Sept. 1905, 1; 'Prva glavna skupština hrvatske pučke seljačke stranke,' *Hrvatski narod*, 21 Sept. 1905, 1.

120 'Druga glavna skupština hrvatske pučke seljačke stranke,' *Dom*, 15 Sept. 1906, 1; see also, Antun and Stjepan Radić, *Što je i što hoće Hrvatska pučka seljačka stranka* (Zagreb, 1908), 142.

121 'Prva glavna skupština hrvatske pučke seljačke stranke,' *Hrvatski narod*, 21 Sept. 1905, 1.

122 Stjepan Radić, 'Prva godišnjica hrvatske pučke seljačke stranke,' *Hrvatske novine*, 14 Dec. 1905, 1.

123 Antun and Stjepan Radić, *Što je i što hoće*, 144; 'Druga glavna skupština hrvatske pučke seljačke stranke,' *Dom*, 15 Sept. 1906, 1; 'Kako je bilo na trećoj glavnoj skupštini HPSS,' *Dom*, 4 Sept. 1907, 1–3.

124 Antun and Stjepan Radić, *Što je i što hoće*, 141.

125 Antun Radić, 'Šesta glavna skupština HPSS,' *Dom*, 8 Feb. 1912, 1–2. On the commissariat, which will be discussed in the next chapter, see Šidak et al., *Povijest hrvatskog naroda*, 276–9, 284–92.

126 'Neoborivi temelji velikomu djelu,' 325.

127 'Prva glavna skupština hrvatske pučke seljačke stranke,' *Hrvatski narod*, 21 Sept. 1905, 2.

128 'Hrvatska pučka seljačka stranka,' *Dom*, 11 and 18 Sept. 1907, 2, 3.

129 Livingston, 'Stjepan Radić and the Croatian Peasant Party 1904–1929,' 663.

130 Stjepan Radić, 'Nećemo i ne možemo propasti,' *Dom*, 9 Nov. 1911, 1.

131 Antun Radić, 'Za moć seljačtva,' *Dom*, 5 July 1911, 1.

132 For an excellent analysis of the Green Cadre movement, see Ivo Banac, '"Emperor Karl Has Become a Comitadji": The Croatian Disturbances of Autumn 1918,' *Slavonic and East European Review*, 70, no. 2 (1992): 284–305.

133 'Hrvatsko seljačtvo organizirano za borbu i prosviećeno za sporazum,' *Slobodni Dom*, 17 Dec. 1922, 1–2.
134 August Cesarec, *Stjepan Radić i Republika* (Zagreb, 1925), in *Djela Augusta Cesarca*, 340–1.

4 Stepjan Radić, Croatianism, Yugoslavism, and the Habsburg Monarchy

1 Scotus Viator (pseud. of R.W. Seton-Watson), *Racial Problems in Hungary* (London, 1908), 418.
2 From the introduction to the German edition of his book *The Southern Slav Question* (1913), cited in R.W. Seton-Watson, *German, Slav, and Magyar: A Study in the Origins of the Great War* (London, 1915), 120.
3 For Radić's national ideology, see Ivo Banac, *The National Question in Yugoslavia: Origins, History, Politics* (Ithaca, 1988), 104–5, 231–4; Radić, *Korespondencija*, vol. 1, 25–70; Ljubica Vuković-Todorović, *Sveslovenstvo Stjepana Radića* (Belgrade, 1940); and, Boban, 'Stjepan Radić,' 147–210.
4 For the new course, see Rene Lovrenčić, *Geneza politike 'Novog kursa'* (Zagreb, 1972); and, Šidak et al., *Povijest hrvatskog naroda*, 152–5, 211–13.
5 For studies relating to these two individuals, see Ante Smith Pavelić, *Dr Ante Trumbić. Problemi hrvatsko-srpskih odnosa* (Munich, 1959); Frano Supilo, *Politički spisi*, compiled by Dragovan Šepić (Zagreb, 1970), 7–95.
6 Mirjana Gross, *Vladavina Hrvatsko-srpske koalicije, 1906–1907* (Belgrade, 1960), 5–6.
7 Pavelić, *Dr Ante Trumbić*, 15.
8 Gross, *Vladavina Hrvatsko-srpske koalicije*, 11–12, 14, 19–20. On 14 Nov. 1905 representatives of both the Croat and Serb parties met in Zadar (Dalmatia), where they concluded that Croats and Serbs were one people and should cooperate to bring about Dalmatia's unification with Croatia. The official language of united Croatia would be 'Croatian or Serbian' and both the Latin and Cyrillic scripts would be taught in schools (ibid., 19–20).
9 Ibid., 21–2. The new course was welcomed by the Magyar opposition. Trumbić and Supilo hoped to come to a formal agreement with the Magyars and even met with their more prominent leaders, like Ferenc Kossuth, Albert Apponyi, and others. The proposed joint conference and formal agreement between the Magyar opposition and the HSK never materialized, however (ibid., 54–5).
10 Živan Bertić, *Hrvatska politika* (Zagreb, 1927), 19.
11 Gross, *Vladavina Hrvatsko-srpske koalicije*, 70, 81.
12 Banac, *The National Question in Yugoslavia*, 98–99.
13 Gross, *Vladavina Hrvatsko-srpske koalicije*, 226. Tripartite rule, as understood in Croatia, meant the creation of a Greater Croatia, encompassing Croatia-Slavonia,

Dalmatia, Istria, the Slovene lands and Bosnia-Herzegovina, and its constitutional elevation to a status equal to that of 'Austria' and Hungary.

14 Šidak et al., *Povijest hrvatskog naroda*, 238–9.

15 Ibid., 248.

16 Gross, *Povijest pravaške ideologije*, 338–9, 350–1.

17 Ibid., 362. Like the Frankists, the Croat clericalists' goal was a Greater Croatia within a reorganized Habsburg monarchy. With the party merger of 1910, Aleksandar Horvat and Vladimir Prebeg replaced the ailing Frank as party leader, although the Christian Social Party of Right's followers were still popularly known as Frankists. On the clericalists and their merger with the Frankists, see Gross, *Povijest pravaške ideologije*, 331f.

18 Ibid., 354, 360.

19 Ibid., 369, 370–2.

20 Ibid., 404–5.

21 Acting on instructions from the Hungarian government, Cuvaj proclaimed the commissariat on 3 Apr. 1912. Cuvaj introduced press censorship and banned all public rallies, thus effectively establishing an absolutist regime in Croatia-Slavonia. With the appointment of Skerlecz to the position of commissar (later *ban*) in the summer of 1913, political freedoms were gradually reintroduced. For a discussion of these events, see Šidak et al., *Povijest hrvatskog naroda*, 276–9, 284–92.

22 For detailed studies of the revolutionary youth and their ideological development, see the excellent article by Mirjana Gross, 'Nacionalne ideje studentske omladine u Hrvatskoj uoči I. svjetskog rata,' *Historijski zbornik* 21–2 (1968–9): 75–144; and, Vice Zaninović, 'Mlada Hrvatska uoči I. svjetskog rata,' *Historijski zbornik* 11–12 (1958–9): 65–104.

23 Gross, 'Nacionalne ideje,' 112–24, 127–34. It should be noted that after the second Balkan war many Young Croats returned to the Starčevićist fold, their brief flirtation with Yugoslavism being punctured by the Serbo-Bulgarian conflict. Others did not abandon Yugoslavism outright, although they now advocated a different form. No longer advocates of the 'hybridization' of the South Slavs, they still believed that Croat individuality could be preserved under the rubric of Yugoslavism.

24 Stjepan Radić, 'Južni Slaveni, njihovo narodno jedinstvo i njihova snaga,' *Hrvatska misao* 4, no. 2 (1904): 55.

25 Stjepan Radić, 'O pripravi za rad u narodnoj politici,' *Novo doba* 1, nos. 8–10 (1898): 323.

26 Radić, 'Južni Slaveni, njihovo narodno jedinstvo i njihova snaga,' 63. See also, Stjepan Radić, *Savremena Evropa ili Karakteristika evropskih država i naroda* (Zagreb, 1905), 246.

27 Radić, *Politički spisi*, 264.

28 Ibid., 145–6.
29 Ibid., 148.
30 Ibid., 270–2.
31 Ibid., 272.
32 Radić, 'Uzroci hrvatsko-srbskomu sporu i njegovo rješenje ili Hrvatsko državno pravo i srbska iredenta,' *Hrvatska misao* 5, no. 3 (1905): 158–60.
33 Radić, *Uzničke uspomene*, 91.
34 Radić, 'Što vi zapravo mislite o srbskom pitanju?' *Hrvatska misao* 4, no. 4 (1905): 183–5.
35 Stjepan Radić, 'Govor narodnoga zastupnika Stjepana Radića, izrečen u hrvatskom saboru dne 12 svibnja 1910,' *Božićnica za 1911 g.* (Zagreb, 1910), 66–9.
36 Radić, 'Uzroci hrvatsko-srbskomu sporu,' 161.
37 'Hrvati, Slaveni i Austrija,' *Dom*, 18 Nov. 1908, 1.
38 Radić, 'Što vi zapravo mislite o srbskom pitanju?,' 180–1.
39 Ibid., 177, 179.
40 Radić, *Uzničke uspomene*, 92.
41 'Hrvatska pučka seljačka stranka: Tri osobito uspjela sastanka u Peterancu, u Drnju i Novomgradu podravskom,' *Hrvatske novine*, 2 Sept. 1905, 1.
42 Antun Radić, 'Poslie skupštine,' *Hrvatski narod*, 5 Oct. 1905, 2.
43 Stjepan Radić, '"HPSS podkapa temelje srbskom opstanku,"' *Hrvatske novine*, 3 May 1906, 1; Stjepan Radić, 'Seljačka stranka i Srbi,' *Dom*, 6 Nov. 1907, 1–2.
44 Antun Radić, 'Poslie skupštine,' *Hrvatski narod*, 5 Oct. 1905, 2.
45 'Hrvatska pučka seljačka stranka,' *Hrvatski narod*, 16 Mar. 1905, 2. See also, 'Hrvatska pučka seljačka stranka,' *Hrvatski narod*, 23 Feb. 1905, 2; 'Hrvatska pučka seljačka stranka,' *Hrvatski narod*, 30 Mar. 1905, 1–3.
46 'Vijesti iz domovine i iz drugih slavenskih krajeva,' *Hrvatske novine*, 22 Apr. 1905, 3; 'Hrvatska pučka seljačka stranka: Četiri pouzdana sastanaka u našem kraju,' *Hrvatske novine*, 26 Aug. 1905, 1–2. Mile Srdić, another HPSS Serb sympathizer, helped to organize meetings in villages around the town of Bjelovar, and some Serbs were elected as party confidants. Peroslav Ljubić, 'Hrvatska pučka seljačka stranka,' *Hrvatske novine*, 1 Apr. 1905, 1; 'Pouzdani sastanak u Kapeli,' *Hrvatske novine*, 9 Sept. 1905, 1.
47 'Hrvatska pučka seljačka stranka,' *Hrvatski narod*, 3 Jan. 1905, 1.
48 For interpretations about Radić's plans for the monarchy's reorganization, see Stjepan Matković, 'Vidjenje Stjepana Radića o preobražaju Habsburške monarhije 1905–1906,' *Časopis za suvremenu povijest* 25, no. 1 (1993): 125–39; and, Bogdan Krizman, 'Plan Stjepana Radića o preuredjenju Habsburške monarhije,' *Istorija XX veka: zbornik radova* 12 (1972): 31–84.
49 Stjepan Radić, 'Hrvatsko pitanje s evropskoga slavenskoga gledišta,' *Hrvatska misao* 4, no. 11 (1905): 481–91.

50 Radić, *Uzničke uspomene*, 80. For Radić Austria was 'a mere geographic appellation,' the main merit of which was that it possessed a Slavic majority (ibid., 88–9).

51 Radić argued that the Slavs were 'numerically, by our [geographic] position, our education, property, and reputable work so strong that the Magyars together with the Germans would not be able to commit any violence or injustice against us, if only we all worked together in Vienna and Pest on the basis of a populist Slavic policy.' The Germans and Magyars had prevailed over the Slavs because 'we [Slavs] have hitherto always divided ourselves into two, three [camps], and some supported the Germans and others the Magyars.' What was needed, he believed, was Slavic unity. 'Kad u našoj carevini ne će imati vlasti samo Magjari i Niemci?' *Hrvatske novine*, 12 Apr. 1906, 1.

52 Stjepan Radić, *Slavenska politika u Habsburžkoj monarkiji* (Zagreb, 1906), 13.

53 Ibid., 15. For more on Radić's views of Slavic reciprocity and the need for political cooperation among the monarchy's Slavs, see his *Moderna kolonizacija i Slaveni* (Zagreb, 1904), 232–40, 250–2.

54 Radić, *Slavenska politika u Habsburžkoj monarkiji*, 40. Common 'civil' matters included uniform legislation pertaining to freedom of the press and association as well as a single Imperial electoral law. Language, peasant, and worker rights, and bureaucratic responsibility would all fall under Imperial jurisdiction. Trade and finance were to be common affairs.

55 Ibid., 48, 52–3.

56 Ibid., 37–8.

57 Ibid., 39.

58 Ibid., 43, 46–7.

59 Ibid., 68–9.

60 Ibid., 69. Slavdom was a means by which each Slav nation could strengthen itself, yet remain true to its unique national attributes. No Slav nation should sacrifice its name or history to Slavdom. 'No one enters a society to be weaker,' Radić wrote, 'people gather so as to be stronger by association, and so the Croats are moving towards the great Slavic family, so that in this great Slavic family they may be Croats, and Croats to the end.' Stjepan Radić, *Mir, pravica i sloboda* (Zagreb, 1917), 38–9.

61 Radić, 'Naša carevina kao federalistička ili savezna država,' *Božićnica za 1910 g.* (Zagreb, 1909), 9.

62 Radić, 'Treće pismo iz Zlatnoga Praga,' *Dom*, 23 Oct. 1910, 2.

63 Radić, 'Naša carevina kao federalistička ili savezna država,' 9.

64 One of the most prominent reform proposals to emerge at this time was associated with the Romanian intellectual A. Popovici. In his *Die Vereinigten Staaten von Gross-Österreich* (1906), Popovici proposed a common Austrian state with a strong central government, a single parliament elected on the basis of universal

manhood suffrage, and with German as the official language. He also proposed the creation of sixteen provinces to replace the existing units; he did away with historic borders and the principle of state right. For a discussion of the reform proposals, see Matković, 'Stjepan Radić o preobražaju Habsburške monarhije,' 130–2; and, Oscar Jászi, *The Dissolution of the Habsburg Monarchy* (Chicago, 1929), 245, 399.

65 'Hrvatska pučka seljačka stranka spram drugih stranaka,' *Hrvatske novine*, 25 Mar. 1905, 1.

66 Antun Radić, 'Magjaronstvo,' *Hrvatski narod*, 13 July 1905, 1.

67 For the Radićes' and HPSS's assessment of the Rijeka Resolution and the new course, see Radić, 'Uzroci hrvatsko-srbskomu sporu,' 152–4; Stjepan and Antun Radić, *Hrvati i Magjari ili Hrvatska politika i "Riečka rezolucija"* (Zagreb, 1905); 'Hrvatska opet na razkršću,' *Hrvatska misao* 4, no. 5 (1905): 216–20; 'Riečka rezolucija s gledišta realne politike evropske, slavenske i hrvatske,' *Hrvatska misao* 5, no. 2 (1905): 88–108; Stjepan Radić, 'Tri slavenska bedema proti pangermanizmu,' *Hrvatska misao* 5: nos. 8–10 (1906): 449–58; and, Stjepan Radić, 'Hrvatska prema Ugarskoj i prema ostaloj monarkiji,' *Hrvatska misao* 5, no. 6 (1906): 346–55. For an analysis of their opposition to the new course, see Stjepan Matković, 'Odnos braće Radić prema politici "novoga kursa" na primjenu Riječke i Zadarske rezolucije,' *Časopis za suvremenu povijest* 26, no. 3 (1994): 475–85.

68 Stjepan Radić, *Savremena ustavnost. Temelji, načela, jamstvo, obilježje* (Zagreb, 1910), 128.

69 'Politička nevjera,' *Hrvatske novine*, 14 Oct. 1905, 1. Even after the utter collapse of the new course in 1907, Radić continued to hound the HSK's politicians for not condemning the Magyar oligarchy's treatment of the non-Magyars. When Father Andrej Hlinka of the Slovak People's Party was imprisoned in Hungary in late 1907, Radić delivered one of his customary philippics against the HSK and the Magyar élite. Stjepan Radić, 'Bez duše i bez pameti,' *Dom*, 4 Dec. 1907, 1.

70 See, e.g., Robert S. Wistrich, 'The Jews and Nationality Conflicts in the Habsburg Lands,' *Nationalities Papers* 22, no. 1 (1994): 119–39.

71 Stjepan Radić, 'Tko u istinu vlada našom carevinom?' *Dom*, 10 June 1908, 1; and, 'Izbori u Ugarskoj,' *Dom*, 8 June 1910, 1.

72 'Pod bečkim cesarom,' *Dom*, 3 Dec. 1903, cited in Antun Radić, *Sabrana djela*, vol. 5, 351.

73 'Hrvatska carevinska politika,' *Dom*, 28 Feb. 1912, 2.

74 Stjepan Radić, 'Proglas saborske većine na narod,' *Dom*, 25 Mar. 1908, 1.

75 Stjepan Radić, 'Svezani branitelji Hrvatske,' *Dom*, 21 Oct. 1908, 1–2.

76 Antun Radić, 'Pogibeljna politička spekulacija,' *Dom*, 11 Nov. 1908, 1.

77 Stjepan Radić, 'Sramotna trgovina s narodom,' *Dom*, 25 Nov. 1908, 1. See also, Radić's *Živo hrvatsko pravo na Bosnu i Hercegovinu* (Zagreb, 1908), written shortly after the monarchy's annexation of Bosnia-Herzegovina.

78 Antun Radić, 'Pogibeljna politička spekulacija,' *Dom*, 11 Nov. 1908, 1. For Radić's views about Frank, see Radić, *Frankova politička smrt* (Zagreb, 1908).

79 Antun Radić, 'Srbi – gospodari u Hrvatskoj,' *Dom*, 10 Feb. 1909, 2.

80 Stjepan Radić, 'Divljačtvo naših "frankovaca,"' *Hrvatske novine*, 8 July 1905, 1.

81 'Hrvatska pučka seljačka stranka,' *Dom*, 9 Dec. 1908, 1.

82 'Parnica proti obtuženim Srbima,' *Dom*, 22 Apr. 1909, 1.

83 Stjepan Radić, 'Jedan narod ali dvije politike,' *Dom*, 22 Sept. 1909, 1.

84 Ibid., 1–2; Stjepan Radić, 'Naputak za saborske izbore,' *Dom*, 19 Oct. 1910, 2.

85 Antun Radić, 'Ban Tomašić odlazi,' *Dom*, 20 July 1910, 1.

86 Stjepan Radić, 'Ban Tomašić, hrvatsko-srbska koalicija i seljačka stranka,' *Dom*, 31 Aug. 1910, 1.

87 Stjepan Radić, 'Naputak za saborske izbore,' *Dom*, 19 Oct. 1910, 2.

88 Antun Radić, 'Ban Tomašić i koalicija,' *Dom*, 9 Nov. 1910, 2.

89 Cited in Bogdan Krizman, 'Pogovor: Skica za biografiju Svetozara Pribićevića, 1875–1936,' in Svetozar Pribićević, *Diktatura kralja Aleksandra* (Zagreb, 1990), 278.

90 Banac, *The National Question in Yugoslavia*, 171.

91 Krizman, 'Pogovor,' 282.

92 Živan Bertić, *Hrvatska politika* (Zagreb, 1927), 26–8, 31.

93 Stjepan Radić, 'Za politiku bana Jelačića,' *Dom*, 10 Feb. 1909, 1.

94 Stjepan Radić claimed that the HPSS adopted 'the strong consciousness about the Croat state from the former Party of [Croat State] Right, and a sincere feeling of Slavic reciprocity from the former Independent National Party.' 'Hrvatska pučka seljačka stranka,' *Hrvatski narod*, 16 Feb. 1905, 1; 'Izborni sastanak u Sunji,' *Hrvatske novine*, 27 May 1905, 2.

95 Stjepan Radić, 'Velika izborna skupština u Bjelovaru,' *Hrvatske novine*, 28 June 1906, 1.

96 Stjepan Radić, 'Kako je bilo na glavnoj skupštini,' *Dom*, 1 Sept. 1909, 1–2.

97 Vladimir Košćak writes, e.g., that in the period before 1918 Radić went through two stages of political development: 'He started ... as a follower of Strossmayer and Rački, animated by Slavdom, but after 1904 when he founded the peasant party, he moved closer to the *pravaši*, fighting against the Croato-Serb Coalition and its Yugoslav unitarist platform.' Jere Jareb claims that the HPSS was, with its Habsburg loyalism and commitment to Austrian federalism, closest to the Frankists in the 1904–18 era. Robert Livingston argues that the Bosnian annexation crisis and Zagreb treason trial 'transformed the HPSS attitude toward the Serbs, and turned it away from the Yugoslav view expressed in the 1905 [party] program toward an attitude akin to that of the Frankists.' In fact, although the HPSS's opposition to the HSK's policies in practice gradually compelled it to greater cooperation with the state right parties, *ideologically* it remained closer to Strossmayer-

Rački than to Starčević and the *pravaši*. V. Košćak, 'Formiranje hrvatske nacije i slavenska ideja,' in Strossmayer and Rački, *Politički spisi*, 41–2; J. Jareb, *Pola stoljeća hrvatske politike 1895–1945: Povodom Mačekove autobiografije* (1960, reprint; Zagreb, 1995), 19; and Livingston, 'Stjepan Radić and the Croatian Peasant Party,' 159, 200.

98 Antun Radić, 'Obračunajmo,' *Dom*, 10 Nov. 1909, 1–2.

99 Stjepan Radić, 'Stranka bez blagoslova,' *Dom*, 17 Nov. 1909, 1–2; Stjepan Radić, 'Što su nama Hrvatima Starčevići,' *Božićnica za 1910 g.* (Zagreb, 1909), 54–6. In his obituary of Strossmayer, Stjepan Radić called him a great patriot and cultural worker whose political thought was based on Croat state right (political Croatism), the unity and cooperation of the South Slavs, and the brotherhood of all Slavs, ideas which the HPSS was propagating among the peasants. Stjepan Radić, 'Josip Juraj Štrosmajer,' *Hrvatski narod*, 13 Apr. 1905, 1.

100 'Političke viesti,' *Dom*, 11 Oct. 1911, 3.

101 Antun Radić, 'Pravaši i seljačtvo,' *Dom*, 8 June 1910, 1–2.

102 Stjepan Radić, 'Politička znanost, odvažnost i razboritost,' *Dom*, 1 Mar. 1911, 1.

103 Stjepan Radić, 'Bit će dobro jer dobro radimo,' *Dom*, 7 Feb. 1913, 1. Radić greeted the Bulgarian advance on Adrianople as a great victory for 'the whole of Slavdom.' *Dom*, 31 Mar. 1913, 2.

104 Stjepan Radić, 'Braća i nebraća,' *Dom*, 9 July 1913, 1.

105 Stjepan Radić, 'Spremaju se velike stvari, svi Hrvati za Hrvatsku,' *Dom*, 17 June 1914, 1.

106 Stjepan Radić, 'Najveća i najpogibeljnija politička zabluda,' *Dom*, 15 Apr. 1914, 2.

107 Ibid.

108 Mirko Najderfer, 'Narodno jedinstvo i koalicija,' *Dom*, 22 Apr. 1914, 2.

109 Stjepan Radić, 'Pravaška i seljačka stranka,' *Dom*, 6 May 1914, 2.

110 Stjepan Radić, 'Za ujedinjenje hrvatske domovine i za oslobodjenje seljačkog naroda,' *Dom*, 13 May 1914, 1.

111 Antun Radić, 'Najveće uzdanice Hrvatske i ciele carevine – nema više!' *Dom*, 1 July 1914, 1. Stjepan Radić's comments are taken from an untitled article-obituary from the front page of the same issue. According to Vladko Maček, Radić's close collaborator and eventual successor, at the outset of the Great War Radić told him that he hoped the monarchy would be thoroughly defeated but remain intact. Such a defeat would, he believed, force the dynasty to reorganize the monarchy internally. A complete victory by Imperial Germany and the monarchy would be a 'catastrophe' for all of the nations of the monarchy, except for the Germans and Magyars. The collapse of the monarchy, on the other hand, would be a catastrophe for all of its peoples, including the Germans and Magyars. Vladko Maček, *Memoari*, ed. Boris Urbić (Zagreb, 1992), 38.

112 Antun Radić, 'Poslie skupštine,' *Hrvatski narod*, 5 Oct. 1905, 2.

5 The Revolt of the Masses

1 José Ortega y Gasset, *Revolt of the Masses* (New York, 1932), 18.

2 The figure (estimate) for military losses is taken from Žerjavić, 'Kretanje stanovništva i demografski gubici Republike Hrvatske u razdoblju 1900–1991,' 78–9. According to Jozo Tomasevich, the figure for military casualties for all of the monarchy's South Slavs is circa 150,000. See Tomasevich, *Peasants, Politics, and Economic Change in Yugoslavia*, 223–5. For a discussion of the economic exactions and effects of the war on the peasantry, see the relevant sections of Tomasevich's study (pp. 217–32).

3 Victor-L. Tapié, *The Rise and Fall of the Habsburg Monarchy* (New York, 1971), 375.

4 For an assessment of the programs and wartime policies of the different parties in Croatia, see the two articles by Bogdan Krizman, 'Stranke u Hrvatskom saboru za vrijeme I svjetskog rata,' *Zgodovinski časopis* 19–20 (1965–6): 375–90; 'Hrvatske stranke prema ujedinjenju i stvaranju jugoslavenske države,' in *Politički život Jugoslavije*, 93–128; and, his much more extensive monographic study, *Hrvatska u prvom svjetskom ratu: Hrvatsko-srpski politički odnosi* (Zagreb, 1989). See also, Dragovan Šepić, 'Hrvatska politika i pitanje jugoslavenskog ujedinjenja 1914–1918,' 389–94, 400–5; and, Josip Horvat, *Politička povijest Hrvatske* (1936; reprint; Zagreb, 1989), 332–83.

5 Bertić, *Hrvatska politika*, 37.

6 For an account of Radić's wartime policy, see the two articles by Bogdan Krizman, 'Stjepan Radić i Hrvatska pučka seljačka stranka u prvom svjetskom ratu,' *Časopis za suvremenu povijest* 2, no. 2 (1970): 99–166; 'Stjepan Radić 1918 godine,' *Historijski pregled* 5, no. 3 (1959): 266–95; and, Branka Boban, 'Stjepan Radić u Saboru Kraljevine Hrvatske, Slavonije i Dalmacije,' *Radovi Zavoda za hrvatsku povijest* 29 (1996): 186–207.

7 Stjepan Radić, *Mir, pravica i sloboda* (Zagreb, 1917), 73.

8 Radić's remarks of 16 and 17 June 1915 in the *Sabor*, cited in Krizman, *Hrvatska u prvom svjetskom ratu*, 91, 95–6.

9 Stjepan Radić, 'Hrvatski sabor za hrvatsko jedinstvo i za hrvatsku samostalnost u monarkiji,' *Dom*, 16 June 1915, 1.

10 *Dom*, 27 Aug. 1914, 1. Just weeks earlier Radić again claimed that Franz Ferdinand had intended to reorganize the monarchy and unify the Croat lands in the autumn of 1914. Stjepan Radić, 'Sad se sve zna,' *Dom*, 8 July 1914, 1.

11 Krizman, 'Stjepan Radić i Hrvatska pučka seljačka stranka u prvom svjetskom ratu,' 122.

12 This was a recurring theme in the HPSS press. See, e.g., Stjepan Radić, 'Ruska zemlja, rusko seljačtvo i dvie ruske revolucije,' *Dom*, 4 Apr. 1917, 1; 'Za što je

uspjela ruska revolucija,' *Dom*, 2 May 1917, 1–3; and, Stjepan Radić, 'Ruska revolucija – škola za sve narode,' *Dom*, 31 May 1917, 1.

13 Cited in Krizman, *Hrvatska u prvom svjetskom ratu*, 128.

14 Radić, *Mir, pravica i sloboda*, 19, 21–3.

15 Stjepan Radić, 'Ruska revolucija na svom vrhuncu,' *Dom*, 30 Jan. 1918, 1.

16 'Svjetska politika u svjetskom ratu,' *Dom*, 1 June 1918, 1.

17 Stjepan Radić, 'Ruska revolucija i novo medjunarodno pravo,' *Dom*, 28 Feb. 1918, 1.

18 'Ruska revolucija i Hrvatska seljačka stranka,' *Dom*, 6 Feb. 1918, 1.

19 'Likvidacija (obračun) svjetskog rata, hrvatski narodni i državni tip (uzor) i slavenska koncentracija,' *Dom*, 12 July 1918, 1.

20 The May Declaration is reproduced in Ferdo Šišić, *Dokumenti o postanku kraljevine Srba, Hrvata i Slovenaca, 1914–1919* (Zagreb, 1920), 94.

21 Gross, *Povijest pravaške ideologije*, 414–15; Krizman, 'Hrvatske stranke prema ujedinjenju i stvaranju jugoslavenske države,' 113–15; and, Šepić, *Italija, saveznici i jugoslavensko pitanje*, 189–238.

22 Cited in Krizman, *Hrvatska u prvom svjetskom ratu*, 116.

23 Stjepan Radić, *Temelji za budućnost Hrvatske, Habsburžke monarkije i ciele Evrope* (Zagreb, 1917), 41, 95.

24 Cited in Krizman, *Hrvatska u prvom svjetskom ratu*, 128.

25 Radić, *Mir, pravica i sloboda*, 72.

26 Maček, *Memoari*, 43–4.

27 For the J.O., see Vaso Bogdanov, Ferdo Čulinović and Marko Kostrenčić (eds.), *Jugoslavenski odbor u Londonu* (Zagreb, 1966); Milada Paulová, *Jugoslavenski odbor* (Zagreb, 1925); and, Ljubo Leontić, *O Jugoslavenskom odboru u Londonu* (Zagreb, 1961).

28 On the role of these British intellectuals, see Hugh Seton-Watson and Christopher Seton-Watson, *The Making of a New Europe: R.W. Seton-Watson and the Last Years of Austria-Hungary* (London, 1981); and Henry Wickham Steed, *Through Thirty Years, 1892–1922: A Personal Narrative*, vol. 2 (London, 1924). Their main organ, the journal entitled *The New Europe*, called for the destruction of the Habsburg monarchy well before this became a war aim of the Entente. See, 'The reorganization of Europe,' *The New Europe*, 1, no. 4 (9 Nov. 1916): 97–104; and, 'The Fate of Austria,' *The New Europe*, 2, no. 21 (8 Mar. 1917): 232–3. For British policy and the monarchy, see Harry Hanak, *Great Britain and Austria-Hungary during the First World War: A Study in the Formation of Public Opinion* (London, 1962).

29 For the Niš Declaration, see Dragoslav Janković, 'Niška deklaracija (Nastajanje programa jugoslovenskog ujedinjenja u Srbiji 1914 godine),' *Istorija XX veka: zbornik radova* 10 (1969): 7–111. For a more detailed discussion of Serbia's war aims, see Milorad Ekmečić, *Ratni ciljevi Srbije 1914* (Belgrade, 1973); Dragoslav

Janković, *Srbija i jugoslovensko pitanje 1914–1915 godine* (Belgrade, 1973); and, Dragoljub Živojinović, 'Ratni ciljevi Srbije i Italija (1917),' *Istorija XX veka* 1, no. 1 (1983): 9–23.

30 Janković, 'Niška deklaracija,' 106–7.

31 Ibid., 83.

32 Dragovan Šepić, 'Hrvatska politika i pitanje jugoslavenskog ujedinjenja 1914–1918,' in *Društveni razvoj u Hrvatskoj*, 380.

33 For the complications arising from Italian participation in the war, see Dragovan Šepić, *Italija, saveznici i stvaranje jugoslavenske države 1914–1918* (Zagreb, 1970); and, his 'Jugoslavensko pitanje u politici Saveznika 1914–1918,' in *Politički život Jugoslavije*, 179–99.

34 Banac, *The National Question in Yugoslavia*, 120–1.

35 For the issue of South Slav POWs in Russia, see Ivo Banac, 'South Slav Prisoners of War in Revolutionary Russia,' in *Essays on World War I: Origins and Prisoners of War*, ed. S.R. Williamson, Jr., and Peter Pastor (New York, 1983), 119–48. As Professor Banac observes, 'Only a narrow layer of intelligentsia among these men [South Slav POWs] supported the ideal of South Slav unification. The Croat and Slovene rank and file remained skeptical. Partly for this reason only some 85 Croat and Slovene soldiers had joined a total of 5,365 volunteers by mid-Mar. 1916 ... This imbalance was less pronounced by the end of the war, but the Serbs continued greatly to outnumber the other South Slavs in the volunteer corps, which totaled some 42,000 men at its peak in early 1917' (ibid., 125).

36 The best study of the Corfu Declaration is Dragoslav Janković's *Jugoslovensko pitanje i krfska deklaracija 1917 godine* (Belgrade, 1967).

37 H. Wickham Steed, *Through Thirty Years, 1892–1922: A Personal Narrative*, vol. 1 (New York, 1925), 235. This was the last meeting between the two men and sheds important light on Pašić's thoughts about Yugoslav unification. When Steed urged Pašić to grant official recognition to the J.O. as the representative of the Habsburg monarchy's South Slavs, the latter responded that 'the Serbian Government could not regard the Austro-Hungarian Yugoslavs as requiring any such special recognition. It had always been the idea of Serbia to liberate them from the Hapsburg yoke and Serbia alone was qualified to do so.' Steed also pointed out that the historic individualities of the Habsburg South Slavs, such as the Croatian Triune kingdom, should be respected in the future Yugoslav state, but this upset Pašić, who rejected the idea completely. The meeting ended on bitter terms, and Steed wrote that 'I never saw, or wished to see, M. Pashitch [*sic*] again' (ibid., 235–239).

38 Stjepan Radić, 'Hrvatsko državno pravo kao cimer protuslavenskoj srpskoj politici,' *Dom*, 12 Sept. 1917, 1–2.

39 Krizman, 'Stjepan Radić i Hrvatska pučka seljačka stranka u prvom svjetskom ratu,' 144.

40 Stjepan Radić, 'Najzreliji narod slavenski,' *Dom*, 3 Apr. 1918, 1.

41 Ibid.

42 Krizman, 'Stjepan Radić 1918 godine,' 272–3.

43 Krizman, 'Stjepan Radić i Hrvatska pučka seljačka stranka u prvom svjetskom ratu,' 148–9.

44 Stjepan Radić, 'Jedinstvena politika Čeha i Hrvata,' *Dom*, 24 Apr. 1918, 1.

45 Stjepan Radić, 'Trostruka prisega i političke stranke u banskoj Hrvatskoj,' *Dom*, 24 Apr. 1918, 3.

46 Krizman, 'Stjepan Radić i Hrvatska pučka seljačka stranka u prvom svjetskom ratu,' 150.

47 Stjepan Radić, 'Pogled po širokom svietu i narodna politika hrvatska,' *Dom*, 17 May 1918, 1.

48 Stjepan Radić, 'Svjetska politika u svjetskom ratu,' *Dom*, 1 June 1918, 2.

49 Stjepan Radić, 'Pogled po širokom svietu i narodna politika hrvatska,' *Dom*, 17 May 1918, 1.

50 Stjepan Radić, 'Svjetska politika u svjetskom ratu,' *Dom*, 1 June 1918, 1–2.

51 Stjepan Radić, 'Likvidacija (obračun) svjetskog rata, hrvatski narodni i državni tip (uzor) i slavenska koncentracija,' *Dom*, 12 July 1918, 1–2.

52 Krizman, 'Stjepan Radić i Hrvatska pučka seljačka stranka u prvom svjetskom ratu,' 153.

53 Stjepan Radić, 'Za veliku slavensku narodnu slogu ili za trojni savez češko-poljsko-jugoslavenski,' *Dom*, 22 Aug. 1918, 1–2.

54 'Hrvatska pučka seljačka stranka u petoj ratnoj godini,' *Dom*, 29 Aug. 1918, 1.

55 'Važan politički razgovor urednika najvećih bečkih novina s predsjednikom seljačke stranke,' *Dom*, 29 Aug. 1918, 4. Radić repeated that the Croats, Serbs, Slovenes, and Bulgars were, from a linguistic and sociological standpoint, one nation, that is, their 'national-cultural' interests were the same, but that this did not mean that their political traditions and individualities should be obliterated or subsumed within the Yugoslav framework.

56 Banac, *The National Question in Yugoslavia*, 127.

57 He had no relation whatsoever to the infamous leader of the Ustaša movement.

58 'Poruka seljačkomu narodu o Narodnom Vieću i o narodnom oslobodjenju, o zajednici s Česima i Poljacima, o skorom miru i o seljačkom pravu,' *Dom*, 9 Oct. 1918, 1.

59 Krizman, 'Stjepan Radić i Hrvatska pučka seljačka stranka u prvom svjetskom ratu,' 156.

60 For recent studies of this 'interim' state and the events between 19 Oct. and 1 Dec. 1918, see Ljubo Boban, 'Kada je i kako nastala Država Slovenaca, Hrvata i Srba,' and Hodimir Sirotković, 'O nastanku, organizaciji, državnopravnim pitanjima i sukcesiji Države SHS nastale u jesen 1918,' *Časopis za suvremenu povijest* 24, no.

3 (1992): 45–60, 61–74; and Stanislava Koprivica-Oštrić, 'Konstituiranje Države Slovenaca, Hrvata i Srba 29 listopada 1918 godine,' *Časopis za suvremenu povijest* 25, no. 1 (1993): 45–72. For older works, see Bogdan Krizman, '"Prevrat" u Zagrebu i stvaranje Države Slovenaca, Hrvata i Srba u listopadu 1918 godine,' *Zbornik Historijskog instituta Slavonije* 6 (1968): 173–243; and the relevant sections of his *Raspad Austro-Ugarske i stvaranje jugoslavenske države* (Zagreb, 1977).

61   For the Geneva Conference, see Dragoslav Janković, 'Ženevska konferencija o stvaranju jugoslovenske zajednice 1918 godine,' *Istorija XX veka: zbornik radova* 5 (1963): 225–60.

62   Dragoslav Janković and Bogdan Krizman (eds.), *Gradja o stvaranju jugoslovenske države (1 I.–20 XII. 1918)* (hereafter *Gradja*), vol. 2 (Belgrade, 1964), 576.

63   Stjepan Radić, *Seljačka sviest i narodna volja: Put k seljačkoj republici* (Zagreb, 1923), 28–31, 36.

64   Stjepan Radić, 'Čiji smo sada?' *Dom*, 4 Nov. 1918, 1.

65   'Hrvatski seljaci – američki republikanci,' *Dom*, 4 Nov. 1918, 1. 'We want American democracy,' Radić said, 'we want, seek, and demand republican freedom' (ibid.). When he heard of the proclamation of the Czechoslovak republic, Radić welcomed the news and added 'that we Croats, and let us hope all Yugoslavs, will follow this example.' Stjepan Radić, 'Živjela češko-slovačka republika!' *Dom*, 9 Nov. 1918, 1.

66   Krizman, 'Stjepan Radić i Hrvatska pučka seljačka stranka u prvom svjetskom ratu,' 158.

67   Ibid., 158 n 265. Krizman claims that this was related to him by his father, Hinko Krizman, and Srdjan Budisavljević, both of whom were members of the National Council's Central Committee.

68   Stjepan Radić, 'Hoćemo u jugoslavenskom jedinstvu svoju hrvatsku državu,' *Dom*, 21 Nov. 1918, 2–3.

69   Radić, *Seljačka sviest i narodna volja*, 10. Radić incorrectly asserted here that the HPSS formally adopted a republican platform at this session of its Main Assembly. This actually occurred in Dec. 1920.

70   'Glavna skupština seljačke stranke,' *Dom*, 28 Nov. 1918, 2–3.

71   Ibid., 4.

72   Stjepan Radić, 'Poziv na osnutak dnevnih seljačkih novina pod imenom "Republika,"' *Dom*, 28 Nov. 1918, 1.

73   Jareb, *Pola stoljeća hrvatske politike*, 20.

74   Ivo Banac, '"Emperor Karl has become a Comitadji": The Croatian Disturbances in the Autumn of 1918,' *Slavonic and East European Review* 70, no. 2 (1992): 285, 286 n4.

75   Cited in ibid., 289.

76 Banac, *The National Question in Yugoslavia*, 130.
77 Janković and Krizman, *Gradja*, 666.
78 Banac, *The National Question in Yugoslavia*, 129–30.
79 Janković and Krizman, *Gradja*, 547–8.
80 Banac, 'Emperor Karl has become a Comitadji,' 297–8.
81 Janković and Krizman, *Gradja*, 665–6.
82 Ibid., 548–9, 628.
83 Ibid., 629.
84 Ibid., 707.
85 Cited in Banac, 'Emperor Karl has become a Comitadji,' 300.
86 Janković and Krizman, *Gradja*, 708.
87 Ibid., 550.
88 Stjepan Radić, 'Ne zakapajmo svoje mlade slobode!' *Dom*, 9 Nov. 1918, 1.
89 'Glavna skupština seljačke stranke,' *Dom*, 28 Nov. 1918, 2–3.
90 Janković and Krizman, *Gradja*, 397, 556.
91 Stjepan Radić, 'O političkom vodstvu u seljačkoj demokraciji,' *Dom*, 24 Dec. 1918, 1.
92 'Republika ili slobodna narodna država i konštituanta ili narodni revolucionarni sabor!' *Dom*, 31 Dec. 1918, Appendix.
93 Rudolf Horvat, 'Savezna republikanska Jugoslavija,' *Dom*, 31 Dec. 1918, 2.
94 For the events of 5 Dec., see Krizman, *Hrvatska u prvom svjetskom ratu*, 361–80.

6 The Neutral Croat Peasant Republic and the Politics of Mobilization

1 For studies of the early years of the new state and all of its major political groups, see the excellent work by Banac, *The National Question in Yugoslavia*, 141ff.; Ferdo Čulinović, *Jugoslavija izmedju dva rata*, vol. 1 (Zagreb, 1961), which surveys political developments in the 1920s; Branislav Gligorijević, 'Parlamentarni sistem u Kraljevini SHS (1919–1929),' in *Politički život Jugoslavije*, 365–88; and his *Parlament i političke stranke u Jugoslaviji 1919–1929* (Belgrade, 1979); the relevant sections of Branko Petranović, *Istorija Jugoslavije 1918–1978* (Belgrade, 1978); Josip Horvat, *Politička povijest Hrvatske 1918–1929* (1938, reprint; Zagreb, 1989); Rudolf Horvat, *Hrvatska na mučilištu* (1942, reprint; Zagreb, 1992); and Wayne S. Vucinich, 'Interwar Yugoslavia,' in *Contemporary Yugoslavia: Twenty Years of Socialist Experiment*, ed. W. S. Vucinich (Berkeley, 1969).

2 Banac, *The National Question in Yugoslavia*, 153. For a discussion of the policy of centralization in Croatia, see Bosiljka Janjatović, 'Karadjordjevićevska centralizacija i položaj Hrvatske u Kraljevstvu (Kraljevini) SHS,' *Časopis za suvremenu povijest* 27, no. 1 (1995): 55–76. The HPSS quickly denounced the often brutal behaviour of Serbian troops and the beatings inflicted on Croat peasants. See,

'Zar turska strahovlada umjesto evropske slobode?' *Dom*, 16 Jan. 1919, 1–2.

3 Bogumil Hrabak, 'Zapisnici sednica Davidovićeve dve vlade od avgusta 1919 do februara 1920,' *Arhivski vjesnik* 13 (1970): 49.

4 'Elaborat francuske vojnoobaveštajne službe od 5. avgusta 1919. godine o srpsko-hrvatskim odnosima,' cited in Djordje Stanković, *Nikola Pašić i Hrvati, 1918–1923* (Belgrade, 1995), 368–9.

5 Steed, *Through Thirty Years*, 238.

6 'Ustavno pitanje i zagrebački kongres,' *Zastava*, 22 Sept. 1922, 1, cited in Stanković, *Nikola Pašić i Hrvati*, 452.

7 'Novi blok,' *Samouprava*, 1 Apr. 1923, 1, cited in ibid., 463, 465.

8 'Srpski "imperijalizam" i srpski "balkanizam,"' *Samouprava*, 13 June 1923, 1, cited in ibid., 476, 478.

9 'Da se zna,' *Samouprava*, 27 June 1923, 1, cited in ibid., pp. 479–80.

10 'Izdajica,' *Riječ Srba-Hrvata-Slovenaca*, 22 Mar. 1919, 1.

11 'Iškariot,' *Novosti*, 1 Apr. 1919, 1.

12 B. K., 'Hipnotizer hrvatskih masa,' *Novi list* (Belgrade), 1 Apr. 1923, 1.

13 For the Democrats, see Branislav Gligorijević, *Demokratska stranka i politički odnosi u Kraljevini Srba, Hrvata i Slovenaca* (Belgrade, 1970); Hrvoje Matković, *Svetozar Pribićević i Samostalna demokratska stranka do šestojanuarske diktature* (Zagreb, 1972); and Ljubo Boban, *Svetozar Pribićević u opoziciji, 1928–1936* (Zagreb, 1973), 1–13. For a comparison of the views of the NRS and DS on the national question, see Branislav Gligorijević, 'Razlike i dodirne tačke u gledištu na nacionalno pitanje izmedju Radikalne i Demokratske stranke 1919–1929,' *Jugoslovenski istorijski časopis*, no. 4 (1969): 153–158. For the journal *Nova Evropa*, see Ivo Ćurčin, 'The Yugoslav *Nova Evropa* and its British Model: a Case of Cross-Cultural Influence,' *Slavonic and East European Review* 68, no. 3 (1990): 461–75. For *Nova Evropa*'s views with respect to Radić, see Branka Boban, '"Nova Evropa" o Stjepanu Radiću: Časopis "Nova Evropa" (1920–1928) o Stjepanu Radiću,' *Radovi Zavoda za hrvatsku povijest* 24 (1991): 119–48.

14 For studies of the early communist movement, see Ivo Banac, 'The Communist Party of Yugoslavia during the period of legality (1919–1921),' in *The Effects of World War I: The Class War after the Great War; The Rise of Communist Parties in East Central Europe, 1919–1921*, ed. Ivo Banac (Brooklyn, 1983), 188–230. For studies of the KPJ in the interwar era, see Ivo Banac, *With Stalin Against Tito: Cominformist Splits in Yugoslav Communism* (Ithaca and London, 1988), 45–116; Rodoljub Čolaković, Dragoslav Janković, and Pero Morača (eds.), *Pregled istorije Saveza komunista Jugoslavije* (Belgrade, 1963); Stanislav Stojanović (ed.), *Istorija Saveza komunista Jugoslavije: Kratak pregled* (Belgrade, 1976); Ivan Avakumović, *History of the Communist Party of Yugoslavia*, vol. 1 (Aberdeen, 1964); and Aleksa Djilas, *The Contested Country: Yugoslav Unity and Communist*

Revolution, 1919–1953 (Cambridge, Mass., and London, 1991), 49–102. For studies of the KPJ's attitude towards the national question, see Banac, *The National Question in Yugoslavia*, 328–39; Dušan Lukač, *Radnički pokret u Jugoslaviji i nacionalno pitanje 1918–1941* (Belgrade, 1972); Gordana Vlajičić, *KPJ i nacionalno pitanje u Jugoslaviji* (Zagreb, 1974); Janko Pleterski, *Komunistička partija Jugoslavije i nacionalno pitanje 1919–1941* (Belgrade, 1971); and Paul Shoup, *Communism and the Yugoslav National Question* (New York, 1968).

15 For specific works relating to the relationship between the KPJ and Radić, see Slavoljub Cvetković, 'Stjepan Radić i komunistički pokret, 1923–1925,' *Istorija XX veka: zbornik radova* 12 (1972): 375–402; Nada Sokolić-Jaman, 'Komunistička štampa u Hrvatskoj o djelatnosti Stjepana Radića, 1918–1925,' *Radovi Instituta za hrvatsku povijest* 6 (1974): 273–313; and, Mužić, *Stjepan Radić u Kraljevini Srba, Hrvata i Slovenaca*, 341–51.

16 In Jan. 1923 the communists formed a legal party, the Independent Workers' Party of Yugoslavia (NRPJ, *Nezavisna radnička partija Jugoslavije*). For the sake of simplicity, KPJ will be used throughout to refer to the Yugoslav communists.

17 'Na rad u mase!' and 'Radićeva "pobeda" u Hrvatskoj,' *Borba*, 24 Mar. 1923, 1, cited in Cvetković, 'Stjepan Radić i komunistički pokret,' 384–5 n31.

18 Kosta Novaković, 'Nacionalno pitanje u Jugoslaviji: Autonomija ili federacija,' *Radnik-Delavec*, 28 Oct. 1923, cited in Banac, *With Stalin against Tito*, 56.

19 'Rezolucija o Nacionalnom pitanju,' in *Istorijski arhiv*, 68, 70–1.

20 'Rezolucija o Agrarnom pitanju u Jugoslaviji i o radu na selu,' in *Istorijski arhiv*, 78–80.

21 August Cesarec, *Stjepan Radić i Republika* (Zagreb, 1925) in *Djela Augusta Cesarca*, vol. 4, *Rasprave, članci, polemike. Nacionalni, socijalni i kulturni problemi Jugoslavije*, ed. Vice Zaninović (Zagreb, 1971), 404.

22 Cesarec, 'Ideologija HRSS ili put u – Bačvu,' in ibid., 232.

23 Cesarec, *Stjepan Radić i Republika*, 374.

24 For an excellent study of the HZ, see Hrvoje Matković, 'Hrvatska zajednica: prilog proučavanju političkih stranaka u staroj Jugoslaviji,' *Istorija XX veka: zbornik radova* 5 (1963): 5–136.

25 AH, Rukopisna Ostavština Djure Šurmina, Box 3: Opći spisi, 1919–20: Nacrt programa Hrvatske zajednice, June 1919.

26 'Seljačka stranka pred zagrebačkim gradjanstvom i radničtvom,' *Slobodni Dom*, 1 Dec. 1920, 4.

27 AH, Rukopisna Ostavština Djure Šurmina, Box 4: nos. 110 and 121, Dr Damjan Sokol and Stjepan Sanić to Djuro Šurmin, 1 and 6 Jan. 1923, respectively.

28 Stjepan Sarkotić, *Radićevo izdajstvo* (Vienna, 1925), 27, 9.

29 PA-Z, HSS, Box 2: no. 933/3, 'Prava revolucija seljačkog naroda u Hrvatskoj,' 21 Mar. 1920, Zagreb.

30 Ibid.

31 'Drugi predsjednikov pohod u Srijem,' *Dom*, 7 July 1927, 4.

32 Ibid.

33 Stjepan Radić, *Seljačka sviest i narodna volja. Put k seljačkoj republici* (Zagreb, 1923), 54.

34 'Hrvatsko seljačtvo organizirano za borbu i prosviečeno za sporazum,' *Slobodni Dom*, 17 Dec. 1922, 1–2.

35 AH, Rukopisna Ostavština Antuna, Pavla i Stjepana Radića, Box 2: no. 177, 'Uputa organizacijama Hrvatske republikanske seljačke stranke,' 25. XII. 1922.

36 Radić, *Korespondencija*, vol. 2, 151.

37 Ibid., 166.

38 *Nauk i program Hrvatske Pučke Seljačke Stranke* (Zagreb, 1919), cited in Radić, *Sabrana djela*, vol. 7, 169–70.

39 'Poruka zastupničke republikanske većine banske Hrvatske regentu Aleksandru,' cited in Ivan Mužić, *Stjepan Radić u Kraljevini Srba, Hrvata i Slovenaca*, 4th ed. (Zagreb, 1990), 300.

40 Radić, *Korespondencija*, 271.

41 PA-Z, HSS, Box 2: no. 904/46, Zapisnik XXI sjednice zastupničke većine banske Hrvatske, 25 Nov. 1922, pp. 2–3.

42 Radić, *Korespondencija*, 104–5.

43 Ibid., 509.

44 Ibid., 141. 'My soul aches,' he wrote to his wife only three days later, 'when I see that these bashi-bazouks are doing to us *to a hair the same thing* that the Magyars were doing to the Slovaks; except that our misfortune lies in the fact that we are "brothers," we are "one," so that one cannot criticize this' (ibid., 144).

45 Horvat, *Hrvatska na mučilištu*, 64–6.

46 Radić, *Korespondencija*, 151.

47 Horvat, *Hrvatska na mučilištu*, 86.

48 Rudolf Herceg, *Seljački pokret u Hrvatskoj* (Zagreb, 1923), 32.

49 For a study of the PNP, see Neda Engelsfeld, *Prvi parlament Kraljevstva Srba, Hrvata i Slovenaca. Privremeno Narodno Predstavništvo* (Zagreb, 1989). The regional distribution of seats in the PNP was as follows: Serbia (with Macedonia), 108; Croatia (with Medjimurje, Rijeka and Istria), 66; Bosnia-Herzegovina, 42; Slovenia, 32; Vojvodina, 24; Dalmatia and Montenegro, 12 each. Its deputies were representatives of the prewar regional parliaments. The PNP, which began its deliberations on 1 Mar. 1919 and was dissolved on 28 Nov. 1920, had the task of preparing the groundwork for the Constituent Assembly and drafting an electoral law.

50 Horvat, *Hrvatska na mučilištu*, 83–4.

51 Radić believed he was arrested because of his party's decision to collect signatures in support of Croat independence. His associate Rudolf Horvat says that Radić

translated the 8 Mar. resolution into French and passed it on to the French mission in Zagreb, which prompted the authorities to detain him. See Radić, *Politički spisi*, 92; and, Horvat, *Hrvatska na mučilištu*, 84. Horvat's claim is supported by Čedomil Mitrinović, *Životni krugovi hrvatstva* (Belgrade, 1938), 338.

52 Radić, *Korespondencija*, 123.

53 Ibid., 127–9, 257.

54 Ibid., 137, 142, 149, 165.

55 Ibid., 181–2. Moreover, he believed that the Paris peacemakers would insist on the demilitarization of the former Habsburg territories, which 'must also embrace Yugoslavia, that is, the territory of the Slovenes, Croats, and Serbs of the former monarchy ... The demilitarization of this Yugoslavia = the departure of Serbian detachments from Croatia' (ibid., 148).

56 Ibid., 227, 324, 469. This plebiscite would determine two things: first, whether the people wanted a republic – and he was certain that they did; and, second, if they were for or against union with Serbia (ibid., 248–50, 489–90).

57 Ibid., 224.

58 Mužić, *Stjepan Radić u Kraljevini Srba, Hrvata i Slovenaca*, 46–7.

59 Radić, *Korespondencija*, 157.

60 Ibid., 146, 272.

61 Ibid., 515.

62 For a discussion of this rebellion and its significance, see Banac, *The National Question in Yugoslavia*, 248–60. For an additional, though much briefer, treatment of this revolt, as well as the various oppressive measures adopted in the countryside in the immediate post-unification period, see Bosiljka Janjatović, 'Represija spram hrvatskih seljaka 1918–1921,' *Časopis za suvremenu povijest* 25, no. 1 (1993): 25–43.

63 Stjepan Buć, 'Najveći talijanski list o hrvatskom pitanju,' *Slobodni Dom*, 16 Jan. 1924, 2–3.

64 'Drugi predsjednikov pohod u Srijem,' *Dom*, 7 July 1927, 4.

65 Radić, *Korespondencija*, 152, 159, 280–3, 431.

66 This was demonstrated by his letter of 3 Jan. 1920, in which he wrote of the need for an economic union between Austria and a neutral peasant republic of Croatia, as well as plebiscites in the South Slavic areas of the former Habsburg monarchy that might lead to the formation of 'a federal peasant republic of Yugoslavia = Croatia-Slovenia-Bosnia.' On 14 Jan. 1920, he wrote: 'The more I think about our political position, the clearer I see that the Entente cannot *now* solve our Croat question *by itself*, but only in connection with the whole Yugoslav question of the former monarchy. If these Yugoslavs *gather around Croatia* ... they will neither want nor be able to bother us, so that a Croat spirit will prevail in this Yugoslavia' (ibid., 455, 473). Radić first raised the issue of such a 'Danu-

bian federation' – an 'economic' and 'financial' union – in a letter of 22 May 1919 (ibid., 152).

67 Ibid., 196, 202, 231, 240.

68 Ibid., 148. In Jan. 1920 Radić again expressed the belief that a revolution would occur and compared conditions in Serbia to those in Russia between the Feb. and Oct. 1917 revolutions (ibid., 475).

69 Ibid., 184–5, 220–1, 237. In two other letters Radić added that revolution was imminent in Serbia and that he believed the Hungarian communists to be in contact with, and perhaps even financing, the Yugoslav communists (ibid., 252, 254).

70 Ibid., 140. Nonetheless, during the 1920s Radić seemed to believe that the Russian peasants were gradually achieving their rights in Soviet Russia, a view that may not have been entirely unwarranted to the outside observer during the period of the New Economic Policy (NEP). As late as Dec. 1927 Radić expressed the view that Soviet Russia was becoming a 'peasant democracy.' Radić, 'Sovjetska Rusija za podpunu seljačku demokraciju,' *Dom*, 14 Dec. 1927, 2.

71 'Mi i komunisti,' *Slobodni Dom*, 21 Apr. 1920, 2.

72 Martin Crnčić, 'Nešto o komunizmu i o rušenju kapitalizma,' *Slobodni Dom*, 26 May 1920, 1.

73 Stjepan Uroić, 'Gospodsko i radničko viećanje o suzbijanju skupoće,' *Slobodni Dom*, 12 May 1920, 2–3.

74 Uroić, 'Gospodska politika, sama laž i prevara,' *Slobodni Dom*, 26 May 1920, 1.

75 'Iz HPSS (kratke viesti),' *Dom*, 19 Mar. 1920, 4.

76 Radić, *Korespondencija*, 254. This view was shaped by the close cooperation in 1919 of Korać's socialists and the Democrats in the PNP. For his part, Korać dismissed as 'nebulous' Radić's notion of a 'peasant state order,' and erroneously interpreted his opposition to the state as hatred of Serbs. Vitomir Korać, 'Slom radićevštine,' *Socijalistički kalendar za 1927* (Belgrade, 1926), 25–6.

77 Radić, *Korespondencija*, 252.

78 'Predsjednik Hrvatske seljačke stranke pred sudom,' *Slobodni Dom*, 21 July 1920, 7.

79 'Osamsatni govor obtuženog narod. zast. Stjepana Radića pred zagrebačkim sudben. stolom dne. 9 srpnja 1920,' *Slobodni Dom*, 4 Aug. 1920, 2.

80 'Osamsatni govor obtuženoga narod. zastup. Stjepana Radića pred zagrebačkim sudben. stolom dne. 9 srpnja 1920,' *Slobodni Dom*, 11 Aug. 1920, 2.

81 'Osamsatni govor obtuženog nar. zast. Stj. Radića ...,' *Slobodni Dom*, 17 Nov. 1920, 3.

82 'Četiri pitanja i četiri odgovora,' *Slobodni Dom*, 30 July 1922, 2–3. For the issue of confederalism versus federalism, see also Stjepan Buć, 'U formi možda i federacija, ali u stvari konfederacija,' *Slobodni Dom*, 12 Nov. 1922, 1–2. For a discussion of Radić's confederalist proposal of 1922, see Jere Jareb, 'Stjepan Radić predlaže konfederaciju 1922,' *Hrvatska revija* 18, no. 4 (1968): 518–24.

83 Radić, *Korespondencija*, 38. For an assessment of Radić's activism leading up to the 1920 elections, see Hrvoje Matković, 'Stjepan Radić u izbornoj 1920 godini,' *Časopis za suvremenu povijest*, 24, no. 3 (1992): 75–86.

84 See Ferdo Čulinović, *Jugoslavija izmedju dva rata*, vol. 1 (Zagreb, 1961), 308–13.

85 'Seljačka stranka prema konstituanti,' *Jutarnji List*, 1 Dec. 1920, 3.

86 PA-Z, HSS, Box 2: no. 904/38, 'Zaključci HRSS na izvanrednoj glavnoj skupštini 8. XII. 1920.'

87 Ibid.

88 'Poruka zastupničke republikanske većine ...,' cited in Mužić, *Stjepan Radić u Kraljevini Srba, Hrvata i Slovenaca*, 294.

89 Ibid., 299–300.

90 Ibid., 301–302.

91 Ibid., 73. Radić dismissed the approaches of both the Republicans and Agrarians because he regarded them as supporters of state centralism. He referred to the Janus nature of the Republicans; when their leaders were in Zagreb, they spoke of a united Serb-Croat republican front, but when they returned to Belgrade they acted like Great Serbs. The Agrarians, he noted, were no better, and pointed to their support for 'Pašić's constitution.' PA-Z, HSS, Box 14: Zapisnik šeste sjednice republikanske većine banske Hrvatske, 14–15 May 1921.

92 Radić, *Politički spisi*, 362.

93 Mužić, *Stjepan Radić u Kraljevini Srba, Hrvata i Slovenaca*, 304. The HRSS's constitution has been reprinted in full in Mužić's book, and all citations here (n94 and n95) are taken from his study. For the original version, see 'Temeljni nauk ili program Hrvatske republikanske seljačke stranke (HRSS),' *Božićnica za 1923 g.* (Zagreb, 1922), 49–63.

94 Cited in ibid., 305.

95 Ibid., 306–7.

96 Arhiv Instituta za suvremenu povijest (hereafter, AISP), Zbirka gradjanskih stranaka, VI-C, Box 1: Okružnica Predsjedništva kr. hrv.-slav. zemaljske vlade svim velikim županima (osim bjelovarskog) i povjereniku za Medjimurje (Broj 3319 Pr 1921), 4 Mar. 1921, Zagreb.

97 AISP, VI-C, Box 1: Okružnica Predsjedništva kr. hrv.-slav. zemaljske vlade o zabrani skupštine Radićeve stranke (Broj 813 Res 1921), 31 May 1921, Zagreb.

98 AISP, VI-C, Box 1: Okružnica Predsjedništva kr. hrv.-slav. zemaljske vlade u kojoj se upozorava na rad poslanika Radićeve stranke i mjere koje treba poduzeti (Broj 9603 Pr. 1921), 23 June 1921, Zagreb.

99 PA-Z, HSS, Box 17: Kr. državno nadodvjetništvo: Sudbena istraga proti Milanu Galoviću i drugih (Broj 24 Prs.-1921), p. 7.

100 AISP, VI-C, Box 1: Pokrajinska uprava za Hrvatsku i Slavoniju izvještava o tajnim sastancima seljačke stranke bez dozvole vlade i o mjerama vlade (Broj 8414 Pr. 1923), 9 Sept. 1923, Zagreb.

101 Ibid. Čimić was not the only one to argue that Radić's popularity was linked to the poor state of the administration. The Yugoslav integralist intelligentsia stressed the same point: when the administration was depoliticized and force eliminated, Radić's support would wane. See, e.g., Ć.[určin], 'Lutanje g. Radića,' *Nova Evropa* 10, no. 5 (11 Aug. 1924): 131–4.

102 AISP, VI-C, Box 1: Ministarstvo unutrašnjih dela Pokrajinskoj upravi u Zagrebu (Broj 16060/8414 Pr.), 19 Sept. 1923, Belgrade.

103 AISP, VI-C, Box 1: Sreski poglavar u Novom Marofu gosp. dru. E. Čimiću (Broj 120 Prs. 1924), 21 Mar. 1924, Novi Marof.

104 AISP, VI-C, Box 1: Sreski poglavar sreza Varaždina gosp. dru. E. Čimiću (Broj 129 Pr., 1924), 22 Mar. 1924, Varaždin.

105 Banac, *The National Question in Yugoslavia*, 403–4.

106 PA-Z, HSS, Box 14: no. 54, Zapisnik šeste sjednice republikanske većine banske Hrvatske, 14–15 May 1921, pp. 4–5.

107 Petranović, *Istorija Jugoslavije*, 54, 76; Gligorijević, *Parlament i političke stranke u Jugoslaviji*, 278–279; and, Gligorijević, 'Parlamentarni sistem u Kraljevini SHS,' 373–82.

108 'Najglavnije stvari, koje sam kazao g. Protiću,' *Slobodni Dom*, 5 Sept. 1921, 1. Protić and Radić met three times that summer (28 July, 14 and 17 Aug.). For a discussion of Protić's motives and the talks, see Djordje Stanković, 'Neuspeh Stojana Protića u okupljanju političkih snaga radi rešavanja hrvatskog pitanja 1921,' *Istorijski glasnik* 24 (1971), no. 1: 7–34. For Protić's views, see Banac, *The National Question in Yugoslavia*, 167–9.

109 On the formation of the Croat Bloc, see Radić, *Korespondencija*, 75–6. The Croat Husbandmen's Party (HTS) also joined the bloc. It was close to the HZ and sought to organize Bosnia-Herzegovina's Croats. The HRS joined the bloc in early 1922. For a detailed study of the HRS, see Bosiljka Janjatović, *Politika HSS prema radničkoj klasi* (Zagreb, 1983).

110 'Što je hrvatski blok?' *Slobodni Dom*, 6 Feb. 1922, 2.

111 PA-Z, HSS, Box 2: no. 904/44, Zapisnik XV sjednice zastupničke većine banske Hrvatske, 25 Feb. 1922, p. 7.

112 'Radić i Hrvatstvo,' *Hrvatska Sloga*, 26 Mar. 1921, 1.

113 PA-Z, HSS, Box 2: no. 904/43, Zapisnik XI sjednice zastupničke većine banske Hrvatske, 17 Dec. 1921, p. 8.

114 Ibid., Box 14: no. 54, Zapisnik šeste sjednice republikanske većine banske Hrvatske, 14–15 May 1921.

115 'Šestnaesta sjednica hrvatske republikanske zastupničke većine (Šesta skupna sjednica Hrvatskog bloka),' *Slobodni Dom*, 2 Apr. 1922, 4.

116 'U čem je Protić sličan Pribićeviću,' *Slobodni Dom*, 4 June 1922, 2.

117 'Četiri zaključka 17. sjednice Hrvatske republikanske većine (7 sjednica Hrvatskog bloka),' *Slobodni Dom*, 21 May 1922, 2.

118 'Pašić i Pribićević, Protić i Davidović,' *Slobodni Dom*, 29 October 1922, 4.

119 See, e.g., 'Trostruka osuda beogradskih vlastodržaca,' *Slobodni Dom*, 23 April 1922, 1–2.

120 PA-Z, HSS, Box 2: no. 904/43, Zapisnik XI sjednice zastupničke većine banske Hrvatske, 17 Dec. 1921, p. 2.

121 Ibid., no. 904/44, Zapisnik XV sjednice zastupničke većine banske Hrvatske, 25 Feb. 1922, p. 8.

122 Ibid., no. 904/45, Zapisnik XVI sjednice zastupničke većine banske Hrvatske, 25 Mar. 1922, pp. 2–3.

123 Ibid., no. 904/43, Zapisnik XI sjednice zastupničke većine banske Hrvatske, 17 Dec. 1921, pp. 1–2, 5–8.

124 AISP, VI-C, Box 1: Ministarstvo unutrašnjih dela Kr. SHS javlja Pokrajinskoj upravi o velikoj podršci koju Radić ima u inteligenciji (Broj 14462), 23 Aug. 1923, Belgrade.

125 'Još jedna opomena beogradskim vlastodržcima,' *Slobodni Dom*, 23 Jan. 1922, 2–3.

126 'Nacrt spomenice hrvatskoga bloka,' *Slobodni Dom*, 20 Feb. 1922, 2–3.

127 'Poruka beogradskim vlastodržcima i poslanica američkim Hrvatima,' *Slobodni Dom*, 6 Mar. 1922, 1–2.

128 PA-Z, HSS, Box 2: no. 904/44, Zapisnik XV sjednice zastupničke većine banske Hrvatske, 25 Feb. 1922, pp. 2–3.

129 Ibid., no. 904/45, Zapisnik XVI sjednice zastupničke većine banske Hrvatske, 25 Mar. 1922, pp. 7–8.

130 AISP, VI-C, Box 1: Komanda murske posade šalje povjereniku za Medjimurje izvještaj o radu Radićevih agenata na odcjepljenju Hrvatske (Broj 733/168 Prs.), 7 April 1922, Varaždin.

131 AISP, VI-C, Box 1: Komanda medjimurskog odsjeka dostavlja povjereniku za Medjimurje izvještaj štaba murske posade o agitaciji i antidržavnom radu Radićevih agenata (Broj 1870/286 Prs.), 24 June 1922, Varaždin.

132 'Osamnaesta sjednica hrvatskog narodnoga zastupstva,' *Slobodni Dom*, 9 July 1922, 4.

133 'Hrvatsko narodno zastupstvo za pravo samoodredjenja naroda hrvatskoga,' *Slobodni Dom*, 3 Sept. 1922, 1–2.

134 'Osamnaesta sjednica hrvatskog narodnoga zastupstva,' *Slobodni Dom*, 9 July 1922, 3–4.

135 'Srpski "imperijalizam" i srpski "balkanizam,"' *Samouprava*, 13 June 1923, 1, cited in Stanković, *Nikola Pašić i Hrvati*, 476.

136 'Na prekretnici,' *Samouprava*, 13 Sept. 1923, 1, and 'Radić i lojalnost,' *Straža*, 2 Nov. 1921, 1, cited in ibid., 488–9, 425–6.

137 'Treći seljački republikanski Božić,' *Slobodni Dom*, 24 Dec. 1922, 2. For an analysis of these talks and Davidović's motives, see Branislav Gligorijević, 'Politička previranja u Demokratskoj stranci na pitanju taktike prema Hrvatskom bloku u drugoj polovini 1922,' *Istorija XX veka: zbornik radova* 8 (1966): 165–269. For an analysis of the evolving relationship between the Democrats and the HRSS in this period, see B. Gligorijević, 'Neki aspekti na odnose izmedju Demokratske stranke i Hrvatske republikanske seljačke stranke (1919–1925),' *Istorija XX veka: zbornik radova* 12 (1972): 355–72.

138 Gligorijević, 'Politička previranja u Demokratskoj stranci,' 210, 225.

139 Radić, *Korespondencija*, 565–6.

140 Ibid., 567–8.

141 Gligorijević, 'Politička previranja u Demokratskoj stranci,' 266.

142 Radić, *Korespondencija*, 569.

143 'Narode Hrvatski!' *Slobodni Dom*, 11 Feb. 1923, 1. For an analysis of the HRSS's activism in Bosnia-Herzegovina, see Tomislav Išek, *Djelatnost Hrvatske seljačke stranke u Bosni i Hercegovini do zavodjenja diktature* (Sarajevo, 1981).

144 See Livingston, 'Stjepan Radić and the Croatian Peasant Party, 1904–1929,' 414; Čulinović, *Jugoslavija izmedju dva rata*, 405–12.

145 These figures are based on the social breakdown provided by Rudolf Herceg, 'HRSS na izborima dne 18 ožujka 1923,' *Božićnica za 1924 g.* (Zagreb, 1923), 84–92.

146 PA-Z, HSS, Box 14: no. 47, Preko pola milijuna naroda na velikim skupštinama HRSS (no date, but likely 1923, on the eve of the elections).

147 'Proglas HRSS poslije izbora,' *Slobodni Dom*, 30 Mar. 1923, 1–2.

148 Radić, *Politički spisi*, 394–8.

149 'Zaključci hrv. narodn. zast. izabranog dne. 18. ožujka 1923,' *Slobodni Dom*, 20 Mar. 1922, 1.

150 *Novosti*, 24 Mar. 1923, 1.

151 For the SLS and JMO, see Banac, *The National Question in Yugoslavia*, 340–51, 359–77; Atif Purivatra, *Jugoslavenska muslimanska organizacija u političkom životu Srba, Hrvata i Slovenaca* (Sarajevo, 1974).

152 For a discussion of these negotiations, see Mužić, *Stjepan Radić u Kraljevini Srba, Hrvata i Slovenaca*, 116–20; Radić, *Korespondencija*, 84–5; and, Lazar Marković, *Jugoslovenska država i hrvatsko pitanje, 1914–1929* (Belgrade, 1935), 235–9.

153 'Na putu k hrvatsko-srbskomu sporazumu,' *Slobodni Dom*, 16 May 1923, 2.

154 Mužić, *Stjepan Radić u Kraljevini Srba, Hrvata i Slovenaca*, 120.

155 Radić, *Politički spisi*, 419–22. For a discussion of the significance and impact of this speech, see Bosiljka Janjatović, 'Stjepan Radić i kraljevski panduri: odjeci Borongajske skupštine 1923,' *Časopis za suvremenu povijest* 26, no. 2 (1994): 277–97.

156 'Sloboda i narodna prava,' *Jutarnji list*, 15 July 1923, 4–6.
157 'Gdje je predsjednik HRSS Stj. Radić,' *Slobodni Dom*, 15 Aug. 1923, 6–7. When asked by the head of the Zagreb police about Radić's trip, the HRSS deputy (and Radić's son-in-law) August Košutić told him that Radić left the country with a British passport, although he did not know where it had been obtained, because the HRSS's Main Committee was convinced that Radić would shortly be arrested and sent to Belgrade, where he would in all likelihood be killed. According to Robert Livingston, Maček told him that Radić had obtained a false passport in the name of Stjepan Fleissig from the Hungarian authorities. AISP, VI-C, Box 1: Predsjednički ured kr. redarstvenog ravnateljstva u Zagrebu gosp. dru. E. Čimiću (Broj 10362 Prs. 1923), 28 Aug. 1923, Zagreb; and, Livingston, 'Stjepan Radić and the Croatian Peasant Party, 1904–1929,' 443.
158 AISP, VI-C, Box 1: IV. žandarmerijska brigada dostavlja Predsjedništvu Pokrajinske uprave za Hrvatsku i Slavoniju o prelasku Stjepana Radića u Madjarsku ilegalno (Broj 948 Pr. 1923), 2 Aug. 1923, Čakovec.
159 AISP, VI-C, Box 1: Predsjednički ured kr. redarstvenog ravnateljstva u Zagrebu gosp. dru. E. Čimiću (Broj 9686 Pr. 1923), 4 Aug. 1923, Zagreb.
160 'Četvrta sjednica hrvatskoga narodnoga zastupstva,' and Rudolf Herceg, 'Razvoj novije hrvatske politike i Radićev sadašnji posao,' *Slobodni Dom*, 22 Aug. 1923, 1–2.
161 AISP, VI-C, Box 1: Predsjednički ured kr. redarstvenog ravnateljstva u Zagrebu gosp. dru. E. Čimiću (Broj 9818 Prs. 1923), 9 Aug. 1923, Zagreb.
162 'Pisma iz Londona,' *Slobodni Dom*, 29 Aug. and 21 Nov. 1923, 2–4, 2.
163 Radić, *Korespondencija*, 579.
164 AISP, VI-C, Box 1: Predsjednički ured kr. redarstvenog ravnateljstva u Zagrebu Predsjedništvu Pokrajinske uprave za Hrvatsku i Slavoniju u Zagrebu (Broj 11733 Prs. 1923), 11 Oct. 1923, Zagreb. These comments were related on 6 Oct. to a police informant by an unnamed associate of Radić.
165 Stjepan Buć, 'Najveći talijanski list o hrvatskom pitanju,' *Slobodni Dom*, 16 Jan. 1924, 2–3.
166 'Temelji za sporazum izmedju Hrvatske i Srbije za konsolidaciju Jugoslavije, zadovoljstvom svih njezinih naroda,' cited in Radić, *Korespondencija*, 90–1.
167 Mužić, *Stjepan Radić u Kraljevini Srba, Hrvata i Slovenaca*, 336.
168 AH, Rukopisna Ostavština Antuna, Pavla i Stjepana Radića, Box 9: no. 180, David Mitrany to Stjepan Radić, 7 Mar. 1924. According to Radić's son Vladimir, Radić was urged in London to pursue a parliamentary path and abandon the policy of abstention. Ibid., Box 2: nos. 420–3, Vladimir Radić, 'Stjepan Radić u Moskvi 1924 g.,' no date.
169 *R. W. Seton-Watson i Jugoslaveni: Korespondencija, 1906–1941* (Zagreb, 1976), 115.

170 'Pašićevu parcelatorsku vladu treba srušiti,' *Slobodni Dom*, 23 Jan. 1924, 1.

171 Radić, *Korespondencija*, 90.

172 AISP, VI-C, Box 2: Okružnica velikog župana zagrebačke oblasti o potrebi kontrole rada i agitaciji članova HRSS (Broj 102 Pr. ovž. 1924), 18 Mar. 1924, Zagreb.

173 AISP, VI-C, Box 2: Sreski poglavar u Donjoj Stubici gosp. dru. E. Čimiću (Broj 108 Prs 1924), 22 Mar. 1924, Donja Stubica.

174 AISP, VI-C, Box 2: Sreski poglavar u Novom Marofu gosp. dru. E. Čimiću (Broj 120 Prs 1924), 21 Mar. 1924, Novi Marof.

175 AISP, VI-C, Box 2: Sreski poglavar u Krapini (Broj 96 Prs 1924), 1 Apr. 1924, Krapina.

176 AISP, VI-C, Box 2: Predstojništvo kr. kotarske oblasti u Sv. Ivanu Zelini (Broj 126 Prs. 1924), 21 Mar. 1924, Sv. Ivan Zelina; Sreski poglavar sreza Varaždina (Broj 129 Prs. 1924), 22 Mar. 1924, Varaždin; Kr. kotarski oblast u Samoboru (Broj 116 Prs. 1924), 28 Mar. 1924, Samobor; Sreski poglavar u Jastrebarskom (Broj 59 Prs. 1924), 29 Mar. 1924, Jastrebarsko; Sreski poglavar Pregrade (Broj 118 Prs. 1924), 29 Mar. 1924, Pregrada.

177 For Radić's trip to Soviet Russia, see Mužić, *Stjepan Radić u Kraljevini Srba, Hrvata i Slovenaca*, 152–65; Mira Dimitrijević-Kolar, 'Put Stjepana Radića u Moskvu i pristup Hrvatske republikanske seljačke stranke u Seljačku internacionalu,' *Časopis za suvremenu povijest* 4 (1972), no. 3: 7–29; Mira Dimitrijević-Kolar, 'Prepiska izmedju Stjepana Radića i Seljačke internacionale u Moskvi 1924. godine,' *Časopis za suvremenu povijest* 4 (1972), no. 1: 148–65.

178 AH, Rukopisna Ostavština Antuna, Pavla i Stjepana Radića, Box 2: nos. 27–45, Autobiografija Stjepana Radića pisana 1924 g., ispravljena njegovom rukom u zatvoru 1925 godine.

179 'Boljševička (Lenjinova) Rusija i nacionalistička (Kemalova) Turska,' *Slobodni Dom*, 26 Nov. 1922, 4.

180 PA-Z, HSS, Box 14: no. 57 ('Čičerin,' *Jutarnji list*, 3 June 1920, reprinted from the French paper *Excelsior*, with Radić's notes in the margins).

181 Ibid., Box 17: Kr. Državno nadodvjetništvo u Zagrebu, Kazneni predmet proti Stjepanu Radiću (Broj I. 46-1925/R47-1924), Tomasz Dombal to Stjepan Radić, 7 June 1924. This and other letters cited here are not in the original, but are taken from copies reproduced in the state prosecutor's ninety-six page report about Radić's anti-state activities.

182 Ibid., pp. 5–6. Dombal to Radić, 11 June 1924; Radić to Aleksandr Petrovich-Smirnov, 27 June 1924.

183 AISP, VI-C, Box 2: Predsjednički ured kr. redarstvenog ravnateljstva velikom županu zagrebačke oblasti (Broj 5664 Prs. 1924), 6 Aug. 1924. For Maček's account of the 3 Aug. meeting, see Vladko Maček, 'Sedam izgubljenika – sedam gladnih godina,' *Slobodni Dom*, 1 Jan. 1925, 6–7.

184 'Rezolucija V. kongresa Kominterne o Nacionalnom pitanju u Jugoslaviji,' in *Istorijski arhiv Komunističke partije Jugoslavije*. Vol. 2: *Kongresi i zemaljske konferencije KPJ, 1919–1937*, ed. Moša Pijade (Belgrade, 1950), 420–421.

185 PA-Z, HSS, Box 17: 'Kr. Državno Nadodvjetništvo u Zagrebu,' pp. 15–16.

186 Radić, *Korespondencija*, 42.

187 Branislav Gligorijević, 'O pitanju ulaska predstavnika HRSS u Davidovićevu vladu 1924 i o krizi i padu te vlade,' *Istorija XX veka: zbornik radova* 7 (1965): 376–377; Gligorijević, *Demokratska stranka*, 419–20.

188 AISP, VI-C, Box 2: Govor predsjednika HRSS g. Stjepana Radića na javnoj skupštini u Vrpolju dne 12 listopada 1924 (Broj 4893 Prs), pp. 3–5, 8–10, 12–15, 19, 25.

189 See, e.g., Čulinović, *Jugoslavija izmedju dva rata*, 433; Matković, 'Hrvatska zajednica,' 121; and, Marjanović, *Stjepan Radić*, 155.

190 Mužić, *Stjepan Radić u Kraljevini Srba, Hrvata i Slovenaca*, 182.

191 Gligorijević, *Demokratska stranka*, 421.

192 See Gligorijević, 'O pitanju ulaska,' 375. For an account of the Radić-Petrović talks, see 'Nastas Petrović i predsjednik HRSS,' *Slobodni Dom*, 22 Apr. 1925, 3–4; and, 'Život i rad predsjednika prije 15 godina,' *Dom*, 22 June 1927, 10.

193 Gligorijević, 'O pitanju ulaska,' 379. On the role of the leadership of the Yugoslav military in undermining Davidović's government, see Branislav Gligorijević, 'Uloga vojnih krugova u "rešavanju" političke krize 1924 godine,' *Vojnoistorijski glasnik* 23, no. 1 (1972): 161–86.

194 AH, Rukopisna Ostavština Djure Šurmina, Box 5: no. 12, 'Političke bilješke 1906–1936,' 25 Apr. 1925.

195 AISP, VI-C, Box 3: Okružnica velikog župana zagrebačke oblasti kojom se odredjuje rasturanje HRSS radi članstva u komunističkoj internacionali (Broj 3 Pr. v.ž. 1925), 2 Jan. 1925.

196 Radić, *Korespondencija*, 98–9.

197 On the regime's strong-arm tactics and the role of paramilitary units, see Nadežda Jovanović, *Politički sukobi u Jugoslaviji, 1925–1928* (Belgrade, 1974), 47–53. Jovanović incorrectly claims, based on the reports of Croatia's district officials, that the HRSS formed secret armed resistance units, and cites some instances of Croat peasant resistance in 1925. Although there were undeniably local acts of resistance on the part of Croat peasants, the local administration tended grossly to exaggerate the threat of rebellion posed by the HRSS throughout the early 1920s.

198 Mita Dimitrijević, *Mi i Hrvati: Hrvatsko pitanje (1914–1939). Sporazum sa Hrvatima* (Belgrade, 1939), 151–5. On the *Obznana*'s impact on the HRSS in Bosnia-Herzegovina, see Tomislav Išek, 'Primjena Obznane na HRSS i posledice za njene pristaše u Bosni i Hercegovini,' *Časopis za suvremenu povijest* 3, no. 1 (1971): 27–57.

199 Čulinović, *Jugoslavija izmedju dva rata*, 453–7.

200 Radić, *Korespondencija*, 600.

201 Ibid., 604.

202 Mužić, *Stjepan Radić u Kraljevini Srba, Hrvata i Slovenaca*, 199.

203 Gligorijević, *Demokratska stranka*, 458.

204 For a discussion of the various manœuvres between the regime and Radić during the latter's stint in prison, see Dimitrijević, *Mi i Hrvati*, 162–86; Bogdan Krizman, 'Izaslanik kralja Aleksandra kod Stjepana Radića u zatvoru 1925 godine,' *Mogućnosti* 18 (1971), no. 9: 1087–1109; Bogdan Krizman, 'Dva pisma Toni Šlegela o razgovorima sa Stjepanom Radićem u zatvoru 1925,' *Časopis za suvremenu povijest* 2 (1974), no. 2: 125–38; and, Hrvoje Matković, 'Stjepan Radić pod Obznanom 1925. godine,' *Mogućnosti* 18, nos. 7–9 (1971): 844–913, 987–1052, 1109–1146.

205 Cited in Banac, *The National Question in Yugoslavia*, 96.

206 The state prosecutor urged dropping the charge that the HRSS had established combat groups through its local organizations. Similarly, although there was evidence that Radić met in 1923–4 with agents of the Hungarian government, he concluded that there was no proof of an agreement between Budapest and the HRSS directed against Belgrade. PA-Z, HSS, Box 17: 'Kr. Državno Nadodvjetništvo u Zagrebu,' pp. 20, 36–8, 67–92. On the state prosecutor's report, see Bernard Stulli, 'Izvještaj državnog nadodvjetnika u Zagrebu od 27. VI. 1925 o stanju istrage protiv Stjepana Radića,' *Arhivski vjesnik* 14, no. 14 (1971): 135–200.

207 See, e.g., Joseph Rothschild, *East Central Europe between the Two World Wars* (Seattle and London, 1974), 226; Alex N. Dragnich, *Serbs and Croats: The Struggle in Yugoslavia* (New York, 1992), 40–4, 49–52; and Djilas, *The Contested Country*, 79.

208 Cesarec, *Stjepan Radić i Republika* in *Djela Augusta Cesarca*, 369–71.

209 In 1924 Radić kept referring to the Yugoslav communists 'as defenders of the contrived official trinomial nation,' and as 'centralists' who are 'defenders of the violently imposed state unity.' He was incorrect, of course, but this line of thinking continued to shape his attitude towards the KPJ. As late as 1927 he was still referring to the Yugoslav communists as centralists. See 'Seljačka internacionala i Komunistička internacionala,' *Slobodni Dom*, 25 June 1924, 1–2; 'Naše radništvo i naš seljački pokret,' *Narodni val*, 21 July 1927, 1–3.

210 Stjepan Uroić, 'Vlastodržci i boljševizam,' *Slobodni Dom*, 28 Jan. 1925, 5.

7 Stepjan Radić and the Croat Question

1 'Hrvatsko-srbski sporazum i nova vlada,' *Dom*, 22 July 1925, 1.

2 'Narodni suverenitet, narodni vladar i narodni sporazum,' *Dom*, 7 Oct. 1925, 1.
3 'Seljačka i hrvatska čovječanska politika u narodnom sporazumu,' *Dom*, 2 Dec. 1925, 4.
4 Radić, *Korespondencija*, 105.
5 Martin Crnčić, 'Uspjeh seljačke politike je osiguran,' *Dom*, 20 Jan. 1926, 4.
6 'Dvije veličanstvene skupštine HSS u Donjoj Podravini,' *Dom*, 18 May 1927, 2.
7 'Sjednica glavnoga odbora HSS,' *Dom*, 22 May 1927, 2–3.
8 AISP,VI-C, Box 3: Sreski poglavar sreza Veliko-goričkog Predsjedničkom uredu Velikog župana zagrebačke oblasti (Broj 8052/6468 Pr.), 25 Aug. 1927; Sresko poglavarstvo u Velikoj Gorici Predsjedničkom uredu gospodina Vel. župana zagrebačke oblasti (Broj 5446/4479 Pov.), 15 June 1927. For a discussion of the HFSS, see Ljubomir Antić, 'Hrvatska federalistička seljačka stranka,' *Radovi Instituta za hrvatsku povijest* 15 (1982): 163–222.
9 Radić, *Korespondencija*, 106–7.
10 Fran Škrinjar, *Zašto sam ostavio Radića* (Zagreb, 1927), 6–7, 21.
11 Stjepan Uroić and Ivan Peršić, *Stjepan Radić proti Zagrebu* (Zagreb, 1927), 7–8.
12 Ivan Lončarević, 'Zašto smo ostavili g. Stjepana Radića?' *Novosti*, 3 Sept. 1926, 2.
13 J. Prodanović, 'Snaga bez očiju: Politika Stjepana Radića i njegove družine,' *Nova Evropa* 11 (21 April 1925), no. 12: 383.
14 Stjepan Sarkotić, *Radićevo izdajstvo* (Vienna, 1925), 6.
15 'Rezolucija o političkoj situaciji i zadacima partije,' in *Istorijski arhiv*, 106–7.
16 Ibid., 109.
17 Banac, *With Stalin against Tito*, 59.
18 M. Crnčić, 'Uspjeh seljačke politike je osiguran,' *Dom*, 20 Jan. 1926, 3; and, K. Brkljačić, 'Nova osnova za prevaru seljaka,' *Dom*, 24 Feb. 1926, 3–4.
19 'Hrvatsko Zagorje za seljačku monarhiju, za iskreni i pošteni sporazum,' *Dom*, 1 Sept. 1926.
20 Mijo Pavlek, 'Starinska gospodska navala i moderna seljačka odbrana,' *Dom*, 11 May 1927, 1. One of the most frequent contributors of the articles in this vein was Ivo Šarinić, who subsequently authored two monographic studies about the HSS's ideology, *Ideologija hrvatskog seljačkog pokreta* (Zagreb, 1935); and *Hrvatska seljačka demokracija* (Zagreb, no date).
21 'Temelji naše unutrašnje i vanjske državne politike,' *Dom*, 9 July 1927, 2. Nothing was supposed about the 1918 peasant disturbances. In spite of his cited remarks, Radić was clearly aware of this fact. He remarked in another speech that wherever the HSS was organized, 'nothing happened in the autumn of 1918 either to the most odious Jews or bureaucrats.' 'Drugi predsjednikov pohod u Srijem,' *Dom*, 7 July 1927, 4.
22 See J. Krnjević, 'Cvijet hrvatske inteligencije,' *Narodni val*, 21 July 1927, 2; and,

Vladko Radić, 'Što vrijede i kakva su to ferijalsko-blokaška gospoda,' *Narodni val*, 28 July 1927, 2.

23 'I službene brojke dokazuju,' *Narodni val*, 15 Sept. 1927, 1.

24 Stjepan Radić, 'Radnički i seljački pokret u stranom svijetu i kod nas,' *Božićnica za 1927 g.* (Zagreb, 1926), 60–1.

25 See, e.g., Stjepan Radić, 'Naše radništvo i naš seljački pokret,' *Narodni val*, 21 July 1927, 1–3.

26 Miško Račan, 'Likvidacija i kapitulacija,' *Dom*, 7 Oct. 1925, 2.

27 Miško Račan, 'Sporazum Hrvatske i Srbije ne potječe iz sile nego iz obće narodnih interesa,' *Dom*, 28 Oct. 1925, 1–2.

28 'Mi smo sporazum htjeli,' *Dom*, 5 Aug. 1925, 3.

29 *Stenografske beleške Narodne skupštine Kraljevine Srba, Hrvata i Slovenaca* (hereafter, *Stenografske beleške*), Redovni saziv za 1927/8, vol. 3 (Belgrade, 1928), 201.

30 'Slovenija, seljačka politika i narodni sporazum,' *Dom*, 25 Nov. 1925, 1.

31 'Tri najvažnija govora predsjednika HSS u najgornjem Hrvatskom Primorju,' *Dom*, 28 July 1926, 2.

32 'Naš seljački ministar o narodnom sporazumu pred vanjskim svietom,' *Dom*, 5 Aug. 1925, 1.

33 'Tri skupštine HSS u Zagrebu,' *Dom*, 22 Dec. 1926, 6.

34 'Predsjednik HSS o najvažnijim narodnim potrebama,' *Dom*, 21 July 1926, 1.

35 'Sjednica glavnoga odbora HSS,' *Dom*, 22 May 1927, 2.

36 Sekula Drljević, 'Zašto seljački pokret pobjedjuje,' *Narodni val*, 7 Aug. 1927, 2.

37 'Stvaranje seljačke države,' *Dom*, 12 Aug. 1925, 1–2.

38 'Seljačtvo kao organizator i kontrola svoje države,' *Dom*, 16 June 1926, 1–2.

39 'Hrvatska seljačka fronta narodnog sporazuma,' *Dom*, 9 Sept. 1925, 1.

40 'U seljačkoj državi – jedino seljačka politika,' *Dom*, 18 Nov. 1925, 3.

41 'Narod pozdravlja Radića kao predstavnika hrvatstva, čovječnosti i seljačke politike,' *Dom*, 10 Feb. 1926, 1–2.

42 Cited in Čulinović, *Jugoslavija izmedju dva rata*, vol. 1, 482.

43 AH, Rukopisna Ostavština Djure Šurmina, Box 5: no. 12, Političke bilješke 1906–36, 12 Sept. and 18 Oct. 1926. Pašić hesitated until late June 1925 before deciding to come to terms with the HSS. It appears he would have preferred maintaining his ties with Pribićević's SDS. See Gligorijević, *Parlament i političke stranke u Jugoslaviji*, 203.

44 Radić, *Korespondencija*, 634.

45 'Veliki politički govor predsjednika HSS,' *Dom*, 14 July 1926, 2.

46 'Srijem, Banat i Bačka – tri srdca seljačka,' *Dom*, 20 Jan. 1926, 1–3.

47 Although urging a faster pace of reform, in a speech in Sarajevo on 31 Jan. 1926 Radić still referred to the NRS as the HSS's 'natural ally.' *Dom*, 3 Feb. 1926, 4–5.

48 On corruption in general and the NRS, see Petranović, *Istorija Jugoslavije*, 79–82.

49 'Govor predsjednika HSS u Pakracu,' *Dom*, 14 April 1926, 1–2; and, 'Korupciju treba satrti i izkorijeniti,' *Dom*, 19 Apr. 1926, 1–2.

50 'Odgovor na nekoja važna politička pitanja,' *Dom*, 5 May 1926, 3–4. After this cabinet crisis was resolved, and in spite of any differences, Radić claimed that he agreed in everything with Uzunović. 'Predsjednik HSS o najvažnijim narodnim potrebama,' *Dom*, 21 July 1926, 2.

51 'Radna vlada narodnoga sporazuma,' *Dom*, 7 April 1926, 2. Though welcoming Pašić's departure from office, Radić was willing to cooperate with that part of the NRS that was against corruption and for reform. Ivo Šarinić, 'Uzkrsni pohod HSS u Hrvatsko Primorje,' *Dom*, 7 Apr. 1926, 4.

52 'Za iskreni sporazum, za poštenu borbu proti korupciji te za brz i plodonosan rad u parlamentu,' *Dom*, 28 Apr. 1926, 2–4.

53 AH, Rukopisna Ostavština Djure Šurmina, Box 5: Politički spisi, 17 Sept. 1926, Šurmin's comments to Uzunović.

54 'Nije velik narod u slavi nego u kulturi,' *Dom*, 9 June 1926, 1–2.

55 'Zaključci Hrvatskog seljačkog kluba,' *Dom*, 14 July 1926, 1.

56 'Veliki politički govor predsjednika HSS,' *Dom*, 14 July 1926, 2–3.

57 'Tri najvažnija govora predsjednika HSS u najgornjem Hrvatskom Primorju,' *Dom*, 28 July 1926, 2.

58 Čulinović, *Jugoslavija izmedju dva rata*, 486–7.

59 See, e.g., Mužić, *Stjepan Radić u Kraljevini Srba, Hrvata i Slovenaca*, 209–20; and, Stjepan Gazi, 'Stjepan Radić and the Croatian Question. A Study in Political Biography,' (doctoral dissertation, Georgetown University, 1962), 291. Radić's wife, writing shortly after his death, referred to the Pašić-Radić pact of 1925 as an 'unfortunate Byzantine "agreement,"' which undoubtedly contributed to the above interpretation. Marija Radićeva, 'Iz mojih uspomena,' *Dom*, 26 Sept. 1928, 2.

60 Radić, *Korespondencija*, 610.

61 Pavle Radić and Dragutin Kovačević, 'Memorandum Hrvatskoga seljačkoga kluba,' *Dom*, 22 Dec. 1926, 1–2; Radić, *Korespondencija*, 629–34.

62 'Tri skupštine HSS u Zagrebu,' *Dom*, 22 Dec. 1926, 6.

63 Radić, *Korespondencija*, 109.

64 AH, Rukopisna Ostavština Antuna, Pavla i Stjepana Radića, Box 1: no. 116, Stjepan Radić to Milica Radić-Vandekar, 27 Jan. 1927.

65 Radić, *Korespondencija*, 110.

66 Radić had indicated during the Dec. 1926 cabinet crisis that he was forming a National Peasant Club with Drljević and Jovanović, the leader of the Serbian Agrarians, but it did not materialize at that time because the HSS renewed its cooperation with the NRS. 'Tri skupštine HSS u Zagrebu,' *Dom*, 22 Dec. 1926, 4; Sekula Drljević, 'Zašto seljački pokret pobjedjuje,' *Narodni val*, 7 Aug. 1927, 2.

67 'Sjednica glavnoga odbora HSS,' *Dom*, 22 May 1927, 3, 6.
68 There have been some recent useful works in this area, however. See Mira Kolar-
   Dimitrijević (ed.), *Radićev Sabor, 1927–1928: Zapisnici Oblasne skupštine zagrebačke oblasti* (Zagreb, 1993); and, Franko Mirošević, 'Politički program skupštine
   dubrovačke oblasti 1927–1928,' *Časopis za suvremenu povijest* 24, no. 3 (1992):
   117–27.
69 Radić, *Korespondencija*, 110. Although he did not say so explicitly at the time,
   Radić certainly included the Serbian Agrarians and, more importantly, Pribićević's
   SDS within the 'democratic camp.' In spite of Pribićević's past record, Radić noted
   that he was now fighting government corruption and demanding administrative
   reform (ibid., 110–11). In 1927, at a conference in Bled (Slovenia), the SLS had
   renounced much of its earlier autonomist platform, which is why Radić now associated that party with the status quo.
70 At a mid-Aug. rally Radić predicted that the Serbian Agrarians would win 30 to 40
   seats and the Democrats close to 100, and that after the elections the HSS would
   seek out 'the most similar' allies (Democrats, Agrarians) and form a government
   'of work, justice, and freedom' that would implement local self-government and
   tax equality for all parts of the country. 'Sav narod jednodušan proti Vukićevićevoj
   igri sa ustavom,' *Narodni val*, 19 Aug. 1927, 1, 3.
71 AH, Rukopisna Ostavština Antuna, Pavla i Stjepana Radića, Box 1: nos. 114–115,
   Stjepan Radić to Milica Radić-Vandekar, 25 June 1927.
72 Čulinović, *Jugoslavija izmedju dva rata*, 498; Gligorijević, *Parlament i političke
   stranke u Jugoslaviji*, 238.
73 'Prva sjednica hrvatskih seljačkih zastupnika,' *Dom*, 28 Sept. 1927, 1.
74 On the election results, see Čulinović, *Jugoslavija izmedju dva rata*, 497–503.
75 Livingston, 'Stjepan Radić and the Croatian Peasant Party,' 663.
76 Radić, *Korespondencija*, 111.
77 Ibid., 643–5.
78 'S Vukićevićem pod Optužbu mjesto u suradnji s njim,' *Narodni val*, 17 Sept.
   1927, 2.
79 'Prva sjednica hrvatskih seljačkih zastupnika,' *Dom*, 28 Sept. 1927, 1–2.
80 'Što će to sad biti u Beogradu?' *Dom*, 19 Oct. 1927, 1.
81 'Parlamentarni rad i nastup stotine seljačkih zastupnika,' *Dom*, 3 Nov. 1927, 2.
82 Gligorijević, *Parlament i političke stranke u Jugoslaviji*, 245. For a more detailed
   discussion of the differences within the Democratic Party over the issue of cooperation with the HSS, SDS and the Agrarians, see Gligorijević, *Demokratska stranka
   i politički odnosi u Kraljevini Srba, Hrvata i Slovenaca*, 487–95.
83 Radić, *Korespondencija*, 113.
84 For an analysis of Pribićević's thinking at this time and his rapprochement with
   Radić, see the two works by Hrvoje Matković, *Svetozar Pribićević i Samostalna*

demokratska stranka do šestojanuarske diktature, 204–13; and, 'Stjepan Radić i Svetozar Pribićević u jugoslavenskoj politici od ujedinjenja do šestojanuarske diktature,' *Jugoslovenski istorijski časopis* 7, no. 4 (1969): 148–53.

85 *Stenografske beleške*, 1927/1928, vol. 1, 300.

86 'Seljačko-demokratska koalicija,' *Dom*, 16 Nov. 1927, 1–2.

87 'Hrvati i Srbi u Vojvodini,' *Dom*, 2 May 1928, 3. See also, Svetozar Pribićević, *Diktatura kralja Aleksandra* (Zagreb, 1990), 48–52.

88 *Stenografske beleške*, 1927/1928, vol. 2, 310.

89 'Duh i značenje Seljačko-demokratske koalicije,' *Narodni val*, 13 Nov. 1927, 1–2.

90 M. Bartulica, 'Prečanska Jugoslavija,' *Narodni val*, 24 Feb. 1928, 1–2.

91 *Stenografske beleške*, 1927/1928, vol. 2, 154–5.

92 'Prva sjednica u glavnom gradu Hrvatske,' *Narodni val*, 22 Jan. 1928, 1, 8; and, 'Velike linije seljačke demokratske politike,' *Dom*, 25 Jan. 1928, 4.

93 For a discussion of the factionalism within the NRS and Democratic Party and the king's role, see Gligorijević, *Parlament i političke stranke u Jugoslaviji*, 204–10, 245–7; Petranović, *Istorija Jugoslavije*, 76–8; and, Jovanović, *Politički sukobi u Jugoslaviji*, 121–31, 142–55, 171–80.

94 AH, Rukopisna Ostavština Djure Šurmina, Box 5: Političke bilješke, 25 Apr. 1925, King Aleksandar's comments to Šurmin.

95 Ibid., Box 5: Političke bilješke, 18 Oct. 1926, Pašić's comments to Šurmin. After being forced from office in Apr. 1926, Pašić managed in turn to force Jovanović and his followers out of the NRS. According to Branislav Gligorijević, by ousting Jovanović, Pašić believed he was counteracting the king's growing influence within the NRS. Gligorijević, *Parlament i političke stranke*, 207–8.

96 Jovanović, *Politički sukobi u Jugoslaviji*, 206. The Vukićević-Pašićist feud within the NRS was so volatile that, according to Jovanović, during the 1927 national elections Vukićević employed the police and electoral irregularities to prevent some Pašićists from holding rallies and running against his own candidates.

97 Stjepan Radić, 'Hrvatska seljačka stranka i ujedinjena demokracija,' *Božićnica za 1928 g.* (Zagreb, 1927), 128.

98 'Ne u parlamentu nego u kutu,' *Narodni val*, 5 Jan. 1928, 2; and, 'Seljačko-demokratska koalicija glavni faktor u svem političkom životu,' *Dom*, 1 Feb. 1928, 2.

99 'Osnov na kojem se je imao postići sporazum za koncentraciju u sadanjoj vladi,' *Narodni val*, 28 Jan. 1928, 2.

100 Jovanović, *Politički sukobi u Jugoslaviji*, 260–1.

101 'Privremena radna vlada – stalnog nerada, bezzakonja i nasilja,' and 'Komedija je odigrana,' *Narodni val*, 24 Feb. 1926, 1–2. For Davidović, see M. Bartulica, 'Korošec i Davidović,' *Narodni val*, 9 Mar. 1928, 2.

102 M. Bartulica, 'Kako da se oslobodimo srbijanske hegemonije?' *Dom*, 21 Mar. 1928, 2.

103 'Prva sjednica hrvatskih seljačkih zastupnika,' *Dom*, 28 Sept. 1927, 2.

104 'Manifestacije hrvatske seljačke misli u Dubrovnika,' *Dom*, 30 May 1928, 3.

105 'Predsjednikov 57. rodjendan,' *Dom*, 13 June 1928, 2.

106 The Nettuno Conventions refer to the thirty-two conventions, signed in July 1925 in Nettuno (Italy) between the Yugoslav and Italian states, that were designed to regulate issues of mutual concern not addressed in the Rome and Belgrade conventions of 1924. The task of ratifying the conventions fell to Vukićević's government. In most Croat circles the conventions were interpreted as being detrimental to Croat interests.

107 The cited figures were presented by the SDK deputies Ivan Krajač and Svetislav Popović on 4 Nov. 1927 and 26 Jan. 1928, respectively. It should be noted, however, that there were some differences between Krajač's and Popović's figures; whereas the average national tax rate was given as 468 dinars by Krajač, Popović cited the figure of 645.56 dinars. See *Stenografske beleške*, 1927/8, vol. 1, 113, and vol. 2, 285–6. The SDK argued that had Croatia-Slavonia contributed the same proportion of taxes as Serbia in the 1919–26 period, it would have paid approximately 686 million dinars less than it actually did. Krajač cited Article 116 of the constitution which stated that the tax obligation was to be equally distributed throughout the country. If the government accepted the need for tax equalization, he argued, it would not be making concessions to anyone. Rather, it would simply be adhering to the terms of the Vidovdan constitution. In line with the SDK's policy at the time, Krajač insisted that the Vidovdan constitution be treated as 'the holiest law.' See *Stenografske beleške*, 1927/8, vol. 1, 112. For a discussion of the financial and economic inequalities between Serbia and the non-Serbian regions, see Rudolf Bićanić, *Ekonomska podloga hrvatskog pitanja* (Zagreb, 1938).

108 'Pod balkanskim režimom,' *Narodni val*, 21 Apr. 1928, 1.

109 'Stočetrdeset zastupnika u obrani od cincarske pljačke,' *Dom*, 14 Dec. 1927, 1.

110 *Stenografske beleške*, 1927/8, vol. 3, 177.

110 'Rotšildov zajam,' *Narodni val*, 29 Apr. 1928, 1.

112 Ivo Šarinić, 'Ovako se ne može ni ne smije,' *Narodni val*, 20 June 1928, 2.

113 See, e.g., 'Grozote beogradske Bastille,' *Narodni val*, 7 Feb. 1928, 1; and, 'Glad i Glavnjača,' *Narodni val*, 2 Mar. 1928, 1–3.

114 *Stenografske beleške*, 1927/1928, vol. 2, 28.

115 Ibid., 1927/8, vol. 4, 12–13.

116 Ibid., 21–2.

117 Ibid., 1927/8, vol. 5, 8.

118 Ibid., 1927/8, vol. 3, 201.

119 'Situacija je sve oštrija i sve teža,' *Narodni val*, 14 Mar. 1928, 1.

120 'Političke i kulturne vijesti,' *Dom*, 28 Mar. 1928, 10.

121 'Rotšildov zajam,' *Narodni val*, 29 Apr. 1928, 2.

122 'Političke i kulturne vijesti,' *Dom*, 30 May 1928, 6.

123 *Stenografske beleške*, 1927/1928, vol. 8, 191–2.

124 Ibid., 237. See also 'Političke i kulturne vijesti,' *Dom*, 6 June 1928, 6.

125 'Političke i kulturne vijesti,' *Dom*, 13 June 1928, 6.

126 'Situacija je sve oštrija i sve teža,' *Narodni val*, 14 Mar. 1928, 1; *Stenografske beleške*, 1927/8, vol. 4, 158–9; and, 'Manifestacije hrvatske seljačke misli u Dubrovniku,' *Dom*, 30 May 1928, 3.

127 *Stenografske beleške*, 1927/8, vol. 1, 78.

128 Ibid., vol. 3, 229.

129 Ibid., vol. 8, 525.

130 Sekula Drljević, '20. lipanj godine 1928.,' *Božićnica za 1929* (Zagreb, 1928), 95.

131 'Paklenski plan Velje Vukićevića,' *Narodni val*, 20 June 1928, 1. Rumours about assassination plots against Radić and Pribićević began circulating months earlier. 'Političke i kulturne vijesti,' *Dom*, 21 Mar. 1928, 13.

132 Radić, *Korespondencija*, 116–17.

133 M. Bartulica, 'Veličanstveno hrvatsko jedinstvo,' *Dom*, 11 July 1928, 3. The day after the murders an article appeared in the NRS organ *Jedinstvo* that described Radić's characterization of Serbia as insulting towards all Serbs. 'Must even this be tolerated,' the author asked, 'so that a national deputy and former minister, the leader of a party, the leader of the Croat people, can shamefully and obscenely defame the ideal and heroic history of Serbia, *undoubtedly one of the most majestic tales of all times and all peoples.*' Vladimir Ristović, 'Stjepan Radić, agent provokator,' *Jedinstvo*, 21 June 1928, 1. Emphasis in the original. Although not explicitly condoning Račić's actions, *Jedinstvo* argued that Radić had provoked the whole affair. The author of this article, Ristović, who was also the paper's editor, was murdered on 5 Aug. by Josip Sunić, an HSS follower, while on a visit to Zagreb. For a discussion of political reactions in Yugoslavia to the assassination attempt on Radić, see Nadežda Jovanović, 'Prilog proučavanju odjeka atentata u Narodnoj skupštini 20. juna 1928.,' *Časopis za suvremenu povijest* 2, no. 1 (1970): 61–75.

134 'Veličanstveni sprovod hrvatskih mučenika,' *Narodni val*, 24 June 1928, 3.

135 AH, Rukopisna Ostavština Antuna, Pavla i Stjepana Radića, Box 1: nos. 133–8, Zapisnik od 24. VII. 1928. o saslušanju Stjepana Radića kao svjedoka. For a discussion of Radić's account of the assassination attempt, see Josipa Paver, 'Još jedna verzija zapisnika saslušanja Stjepana Radića o atentatu u Narodnoj skupštini u Beogradu 20 lipnja 1928,' *Časopis za suvremenu povijest* 4, no. 1 (1972): 165–77.

136 Ivan Krajač, 'Dvije političke sinteze,' *Hrvatska revija* 11, no. 11 (1938): 566.
137 'Političke i kulturne vijesti,' *Dom*, 26 Sept. 1928, 5.
138 'Slavlje hrvatske kulture i seljačke svijesti,' *Dom*, 24 Oct. 1928, 3.
139 Radić, *Korespondencija*, 118–19. The resolution is reprinted in Maček, *Memoari*, 79; and, Pribićević, *Diktatura kralja Aleksandra*, 78–9. In mid-Aug. Korošec's government ratified the Nettuno Conventions in the truncated parliament, which was greeted by the SDK as a provocation.
140 'Pravac hrvatske politike,' *Dom*, 12 Sept. 1928, 2.
141 Pribićević, *Diktatura kralja Aleksandra*, 80.
142 Maček, *Memoari*, 81.
143 Čulinović, *Jugoslavija izmedju dva rata*, 544–7.
144 Pribićević, *Diktatura kralja Aleksandra*, 71–4.
145 'Pravac hrvatske politike,' and 'Političke i kulturne vijesti,' *Dom*, 12 Sept. 1928, 2, 5.
146 Maček, *Memoari*, 83; and, Juraj Krnjević, 'Beogradski zločin oštro osudjen na sastanku 37. parlamenata iz svih dijelova svijeta,' *Dom*, 5 Sept. 1928, 2–3.
147 Krizman, 'Pogovor,' in Pribićević, *Diktatura kralja Aleksandra*, 295–6. For Trumbić's mission, see B. Krizman, 'Trumbićeva misija u inozemstvu uoči proglašenja šestojanuarske diktature,' *Historijski pregled* 3 (1962): 176–202; and, Todor Stojkov, 'O spoljnopolitičkoj aktivnosti vodjstva seljačko-demokratske koalicije uoči šestojanuarske diktature,' *Istorija XX veka: zbornik radova* 9 (1968): 293–336.
148 'Političke i kulturne vijesti,' *Dom*, 28 Nov. 1928, 9.
149 Maček, *Memoari*, 84–5; and, Pribićević, *Diktatura kralja Aleksandra*, 84–6.

8 Conclusion

1 'Drugi predsjednikov pohod u Srijem,' *Dom*, 7 July 1927, 4.
2 Banac, *The National Question in Yugoslavia*, 225.
3 AISP, VI-C, Box 4: Sreski poglavar u Zagrebu Velikom županu zagrebačke oblasti (Broj 249 Pres. 928/5667 Pov.), 9 Sept. 1928. Maček's comments are taken from his speech of 8 Sept. 1928 in Zagreb.
4 Mate Drinković, *Hrvatska i državna politika* (Zagreb, 1928), 72.
5 Rudolf Herceg and Stjepan Buć, 'Hrvatski narod pod "Obznanom,"' *Slobodni Dom*, 28 Jan. 1925, 2.
6 Stanković, 'Neuspeh Stojana Protića,' 31–2.
7 Dragoljub Jovanović, 'Stjepan Radić,' *Rad*, 1 July 1928, 1–2, cited in his *Sloboda od straha: Izabrane političke rasprave*, compiled by N. Jovanović and B. Jakšić (Belgrade, 1991), 197–205. All of Jovanović's cited comments in this chapter are taken from this article.

8 Miroslav Krleža, 'Stjepan Radić na odru 8 VIII 1928,' in his *Deset krvavih godina i drugi političkih eseji*, vols. 14–15 of *Sabrana djela Miroslava Krleže* (Zagreb, 1971), 263, 280–2; and August Cesarec, 'Nad grobom sudbonosne žrtve,' in *Stjepan Radić*, ed. Franjo Gaži and Stjepan Radić (Zagreb, 1990), 157–8.

9 Cited in 'Autobiography of Stephen Raditch: With an Introduction by Charles A. Beard,' *Current History* 29 (Oct. 1928): 83.

10 A number of HSS local party activists, like Filip Lakuš, joined the Croat Partisans during the Second World War. He argued that if Radić were alive, he too would support the kind of revolution launched by the communists. At the same time, Ante Pavelić, the leader of the Ustaše, insisted that the Ustaša movement was committed to implementing the social program of Stjepan Radić. When the Ustaša-sponsored Croatian *Sabor* was convened in Feb. 1942, a number of former Radićists, like Rudolf Horvat, Miško Račan, Stjepan Uroić, and Mato Jagatić, occupied front-benches. See Jill Irvine, *The Croat Question: Partisan Politics in the Formation of the Yugoslav Socialist State* (Boulder, Colorado, 1993), 149; Ante Pavelić, *Ustaška misao: Poglavnikovi govori od 12. X. 1941. do 12. IV. 1942.* (Zagreb, 1942), 19; and *Brzopisni zapisnici prvog zasjedanja Hrvatskog sabora u Nezavisnoj Državi Hrvatskoj godine 1942* (Zagreb, 1942), 10–11.

11 Zoran Batušić, 'Stjepan Radić: Čovjek za sva vremena,' *Danas*, no. 486 (11 June 1991), 63–5.

12 Škrinjar, *Zašto sam ostavio Radića*, 6–7.

13 Cesarec, *Stjepan Radić i Republika* in *Djela Augusta Cesarca*, 340–1, 346.

14 Ljubo Weisner, 'Radić: portrait historijske ličnosti,' *Novosti*, 12 Jan. 1926, 3.

15 Stjepan Radić, *Praški zapisi* (Zagreb, 1985), 161.

16 Živan Bertić, *Hrvatska politika* (Zagreb, 1927), 12. The Yugoslav integralist intelligentsia also argued that Radić's success was to be found in his demagogic appeals to the people, as well as his supposed exploitation of the peasantry's traditional animosity towards the educated élite. Radić was 'only an organizer of the negative and tribal tendencies' of the Croat peasants. See M.[ilan] Ć.[určin], 'Smrt Ivana Lorkovića: Tragedija hrvatske inteligencije,' *Nova Evropa* 12, no. 5 (11 Mar. 1926): 133; and Ć.[určin], 'Lutanje g. Radića,' *Nova Evropa* 10, no. 5 (11 Aug. 1924): 131.

Bibliography

The research for this study was undertaken at the Archive of Croatia and the Historical Archive of Zagreb, which house the Private Papers of Antun, Pavle, and Stjepan Radić, and the Stjepan Radić and Croat Peasant Party Collection, respectively. These collections contain Stjepan Radić's letters, diary, prison notes, correspondence, and miscellaneous party material. Use has also been made of the Archive of the Institute of Contemporary History, in particular the Bourgeois Parties Collection (Group VI-C). This collection, which has now been moved to the Archive of Croatia, contains reports from, and communications between the Croatian district officials, gendarmerie, the head of the Croatian regional administration, as well as the Ministry of Internal Affairs in Belgrade. It is of great relevance for an analysis of how the Yugoslav authorities perceived the organizational structure and activism of the HSS. Finally, the Private Papers of Djuro Šurmin, housed in the Archive of Croatia, have also been examined. Šurmin was one of the Croato-Serb Coalition's most influential politicians, and after the war a member of the Croat Union. In 1924 he left that party to join the Pašić-Pribićević government which imprisoned Radić. Use has been made of his political notes from the 1920s, particularly since Šurmin interacted closely with King Aleksandar, Nikola Pašić, and many Serb Radicals, like Nikola Uzunović.

A thorough reading of the HSS's press has also been undertaken. In the first two years of its existence, the party had two papers and one journal: *Hrvatski narod* (1904–5); *Hrvatske novine* (1904–6); and, *Hrvatska misao* (established in 1902, but a party organ only from 1904 to 1906). In 1906 the weekly newspaper *Dom* became the party's official organ. It has been examined for the years 1906–28. There are important gaps, however. The University of Zagreb's newspaper repository does not contain complete holdings for 1915–16 and 1924. Because *Dom* was temporarily banned in 1919 by the Yugoslav authorities, there is no complete holding for that year. Some extant issues from those years can be found, however, in the above-mentioned archival collections. In 1927 the HSS launched its daily newspaper *Narodni val*, which has been examined for the period 1927–8. The party almanac *Božičnica* has also been examined for the years 1910–29. Finally, it must be emphasized that the Radićes, and particularly Stjepan, were prolific writers. I have attempted to incorporate as many of their works as was feasible.˘

Of the published sources, by far the most useful is Stjepan Radić's two-volume correspondence for the years 1885–1928, which was meticulously compiled by the late Bogdan Krizman. The stenographic records of the Belgrade parliament have also been examined, but only for 1927–8, the period of Radić's second opposition. The collection of documents compiled by Bogdan Krizman and Dragoslav Janković relating to the creation of the Yugoslav state in 1918 is also helpful, particularly the reports of Croatia's district officials about the peasant disturbances of 1918. As to the secondary sources, I have listed all the works which are of importance for the study of Stjepan Radić and HSS in the period from 1904 to 1928.

Archival Sources

Arhiv Hrvatske (AH, Archive of Croatia), Zagreb

Rukopisna Ostavština Antuna, Pavla i Stjepana Radića (Private Papers of Antun, Pavle, and Stjepan Radić)
Rukopisna Ostavština Dr Djure Šurmina (Private Papers of Dr Djuro Šurmin)

Povijesni Arhiv-Zagreb (PA-Z, Historical Archive of Zagreb), Zagreb

Fond Stjepana Radića i HSS (Stjepan Radić and HSS Collection)

Arhiv Instituta za Suvremenu Povijest (AISP, Archive of the Institute of Contemporary History), Zagreb

Zbirka Gradjanskih Stranaka, Grupa VI-C, Hrvatska Seljačka Stranka (Bourgeois Parties Collection, Group VI-C, Croat Peasant Party)

Works by Antun and Stjepan Radić

Radić, Antun. *Sabrana Djela*, 19 vols. Zagreb, 1936–9.
– *'Život' t.j. Smrt hrvatskoga preporoda?* Zagreb, 1899.

– *Matica Hrvatska*. Zagreb, 1906.
– *Osnova za sabiranje i proučavanje gradje o narodnom životu*. Zagreb, 1929.
Radić, Stjepan. *Devet seljačkih zastupnika izabranih prvi put po proširenom izbornom pravu u Banskoj Hrvatskoj: Pogled na politički njihov rad*. Zagreb, 1912.
– *Jakost i temelj Hrvatske*. Zagreb, 1907.
– *Što je i što hoće HPSS*. Zagreb, 1908.
– *Kako ćemo iz našeg zla u dobro*. Sisak, 1902.
– *Moderna kolonizacija i Slaveni*. Zagreb, 1904.
– *Najjača stranka u Hrvatskoj*. Rijeka, 1902.
– *Hrvati i Srbi*. Zagreb, 1902.
– *Za jedinstvo hrvatske opozicije na narodnjačkom (demokratskom) i slavenskom osnovu*. Zagreb, 1903.
– *Hrvatski pokret godine 1903. Politička razprava*. Zagreb, 1904.
– *Kako se danas brani domovina*. Zagreb, 1904.
– *Židovstvo kao negativni elemenat kulture*. Zagreb, 1937.
– *Politički spisi*. Compiled by Zvonimir Kulundžić, Zagreb, 1971.
– *Savremena Evropa ili karakteristika evropskih država i naroda*. Zagreb, 1905.
– *Frankova politička smrt*. Zagreb, 1908.
– *Današnja financijalna znanost*. Zagreb, 1908.
– *Češki narod na početku XX stoljeća*. Zagreb, 1910.
– 'Državna i narodnostna ideja s gledišta socijalne znanosti.' *Mjesečnik pravničkog društva* 35, nos. 4–10 (1909): 378–85, 445–62, 551–67, 657–64, 774–99, 947–62, 1040–54.
– 'O svjetskoj radničkoj i seljačkoj revoluciji,' and 'Radnička i seljačka revolucija poslie svjetskog rata,' in C. Seignobos and A. Métin, *Najnovija svjetska poviest od 1815 do 1900*, trans. from the French by S. Radić. Zagreb, 1921, introduction and 589–93.
– *Javna politička poruka probudjenoj seljačkoj braći naročito u Americi i po ostaloj tudjini*. Zagreb, 1913.
– *Za lakši i bolji seljački život ili najpotrebnija uputa o seljačkoj prosvjeti i seljačkom osiguranju*. Zagreb, 1913.
– *Temelji za budućnost Hrvatske, Habsburške monarkije i ciele Evrope*. Zagreb, 1917.
– *Seljačka svijest i narodna volja. Put k seljačkoj republici*. Zagreb, 1923.
– *Slavenska politika u Habsburžkoj monarkiji*. Zagreb, 1906.
– *Mir, Pravica i Sloboda*. Zagreb, 1917.
– *Gospodska politika bez naroda i proti narodu*. Zagreb, 1920.
– *Sovjetska Rusija i seljačko pravo*. Zagreb, 1944.
– *Uzničke uspomene*. 3rd ed. Zagreb, 1971.
– *Živo hrvatsko pravo na Bosnu i Hercegovinu*. Zagreb, 1908.

– 'Autobiography of Stephen Raditch: With an Introduction by Charles A. Beard.'
  Current History 29, no. 1 (1928–9): 82–106.
– *Praški zapisi: autobiografska proza*. Zagreb, 1985.
Radić, Stjepan et al., *Federalizam naše carevine i narodno oslobodjenje*. Zagreb, 1910.

Published Primary Sources

*Brzopisni zapisnici prvog zasjedanja Hrvatskog državnog sabora u Nezavisnoj Državi
  Hrvatskoj godine 1942*. Zagreb, 1942.
Dimitrijević-Kolar, Mira (ed.). *Radićev Sabor 1927–1928*. Zagreb, 1993.
Janković, D., and B. Krizman, (eds.). *Gradja o stvaranju jugoslovenske države (1. I. –
  20. XII. 1918)*, 2 vols. Belgrade, 1964.
Pijade, Moša (ed.). *Istorijski arhiv Komunističke partije Jugoslavije*. Vol. 2: *Kongresi i
  zemaljske konferencije KPJ 1919–1937*. Belgrade, 1950.
Radić, Stjepan. *Korespondencija Stjepana Radića 1885–1928*, comp. Bogdan Kriz-
  man, 2 vols. Zagreb, 1972–3.
R.W. Seton-Watson and the Yugoslavs: Correspondence. 2 vols. London, 1976.
Seton-Watson, Hugh, and Christopher Seton-Watson (eds).
Stenografske beleške Narodne skupštine Kraljevine Srba, Hrvata i Slovenaca, Redovni
  saziv. Belgrade, 1926–8.

Secondary Sources

Memoirs

Jovanović, Dragoljub. *Sloboda od straha: Izabrane političke rasprave*, comp. N.
  Jovanović and B. Jakšić. Belgrade, 1991.
Maček, Vladko. *Memoari*, ed. Boris Urbić. Zagreb, 1992.
– *In the Struggle for Freedom*. New York, 1957.
Meštrović, Ivan. *Uspomene na političke ljude i dogadjaje*. 2nd ed. Zagreb, 1992.
Pribićević, Svetozar. *Diktatura kralja Aleksandra*. Zagreb, 1990.

Books

Aleksić, Dušan. *Stjepan Radić*. Belgrade, 1928.
Alter, Peter. *Nationalism*. 2nd ed. London, 1994.
Artuković, Mato. *Ideologija srpsko-hrvatskih sporova: Srbobran, 1884–1902*. Zagreb,
  1991.
Avakumović, Ivan. *History of the Communist Party of Yugoslavia*. Aberdeen, Scotland,
  1964.

Badalić, J. *Hrvatska svjedočanstva o Rusiji*. Zagreb, 1945.

Banac, Ivo. *The National Question in Yugoslavia: Origins, History, Politics*. 2nd ed. Ithaca and London, 1988.

– *With Tito against Stalin: Cominformist Splits in Yugoslav Communism*. Ithaca and London, 1988.

Barac, Antun. *Dr Ante Radić u hrvatskoj književnosti*. Zagreb, 1937.

Bell, John D. *Peasants in Power: Alexander Stamboliski and the Bulgarian Agrarian National Union, 1899–1923*. Princeton, NJ, 1977.

Bertić, Živan. *Hrvatska politika*. Zagreb, 1927.

Bićanić, Rudolf. *Ekonomska podloga hrvatskog pitanja*. 2nd ed. Zagreb, 1938.

– *Agrarna kriza u Hrvatskoj, 1873–1895*. Zagreb, 1937.

– *Kako živi narod. Život u pasevnim krajevima*. Vol. 1. Zagreb, 1936.

– *How the People Live: Life in the Passive Regions*, ed. by J.M. Halpern and E.M. Despalatović. Amherst, Mass., 1981.

Boban, Ljubo, *Maček i Politika HSS, 1928–1941*. 2 vols. Zagreb, 1974.

– *Svetozar Pribićević u opoziciji, 1928–1936*. Zagreb, 1973.

Bogdanov, Vaso. *Likovi i pokreti*. Zagreb, 1957.

– *Historija političkih stranaka u Hrvatskoj od prvih stranačkih grupiranja do 1918*. Zagreb, 1958.

– *Hrvatski narodni pokret, 1903–4*. Zagreb, 1961.

Bublić, Dragan. *Tamnice Stjepana Radića*. Zagreb, 1929.

– *Ogled o životu i smrti Stjepana Radića*. Zagreb, 1943.

Cesarec, August. *Stjepan Radić i republika*. Zagreb, 1925.

– *Djela Augusta Cesarca*. vol. 4: *Rasprave, članci, polemike. Nacionalni, socijalni i kulturni problemi Jugoslavije*. Zagreb, 1971.

Čolaković, R., D. Janković, and P. Morača (eds.). *Pregled istorije Saveza komunista Jugoslavije*. Belgrade, 1963.

Čubrilović, Vaso. *Politička prošlost Hrvata*. Belgrade, 1939.

Čulinović, Ferdo. *Jugoslavija izmedju dva rata*. 2 vols. Zagreb, 1961.

Despalatović, Elinor M. *Ljudevit Gaj and the Illyrian Movement*. New York, 1975.

Dežman, M., and R. Maixner (eds.). *Obzor. Spomen-knjiga, 1860–1935*. Zagreb, 1936.

Dimitrijević, Mita. *Mi i Hrvati: Hrvatsko pitanje, 1914–1939. Sporazum sa Hrvatima*. Belgrade, 1939.

Djilas, Aleksa. *The Contested Country: Yugoslav Unity and Communist Revolution, 1919–1953*. Cambridge, Mass., and London, 1991.

Djordjević, D. (ed.). *The Creation of Yugoslavia, 1914–1918*. Santa Barbara, 1980.

Dražić, Ambroz. *Tko je Stjepan Radić?* Dubrovnik, 1925.

Dragnich, Alex N. *The First Yugoslavia: Search for a Viable Political System*. Stanford, 1983.

– *Serbia, Nikola Pašić, and Yugoslavia*. New Brunswick, NJ, 1974.

Drinković, Mate, *Hrvatska i državna politika*. Zagreb, 1928.

Drljević, Sekula. *Balkanski sukobi 1905–1941*. 1944; reprint Zagreb, 1991.

Ekmečić, Milorad. *Ratni ciljevi Srbije, 1914*. Belgrade, 1973.

– *Stvaranje Jugoslavije, 1790–1918*. Belgrade, 1989.

Engelsfeld, Neda. *Prvi parlament Kraljevstva Srba, Hrvata i Slovenaca: Privremeno narodno predstavništvo*. Zagreb, 1989.

Fiegenwald, Vladimir. *Položaj seljaštva u staroj Jugoslaviji*. Zagreb, 1952.

Frangeš, Ivo. *Povijest hrvatske književnosti*. Zagreb-Ljubljana, 1987.

Gaži, Franjo, and Stjepan Radić (eds.). *Stjepan Radić*. Zagreb, 1990.

Gellner, E., and Ghita Ionescu (eds.). *Populism: Its Meaning and National Characteristics*. London, 1970.

Gligorijević, Branislav. *Parlament i političke stranke u Jugoslaviji, 1919–1929*. Belgrade, 1979.

– *Demokratska stranka i politički odnosi u Kraljevini Srba, Hrvata i Slovenaca*. Belgrade, 1970.

– *Kominterna, jugoslovensko i srpsko pitanje*. Belgrade, 1992.

Goranovich, Maksim M. *Krakh zelenogo internatsionala, 1921–1938*. Moscow, 1967.

Gross, Mirjana. *Povijest pravaške ideologije*. Zagreb, 1973.

– *Vladavina Hrvatsko-srpske koalicije, 1906–1907*. Belgrade, 1960.

– (ed.) *Društveni razvoj u Hrvatskoj (od 16 stoljeća do početka 20 stoljeća)*, Zagreb, 1981.

Gross, M., and A. Szabo. *Prema Hrvatskome gradjanskom društvu: Društveni razvoj u civilnoj Hrvatskoj i Slavoniji šezdeseti i sedamdeseti godina 19 stoljeća*. Zagreb, 1992.

Herceg, Rudolf. *Svjetski rat i problem nove države*. Zagreb, 1919.

– *Nemojmo zaboraviti: Hrvatska politika mora biti seljačka*. Zagreb, 1921.

– *Seljački pokret u Hrvatskoj*. Zagreb, 1923.

Hikec, Ante. *Radić: Portrait historijske ličnosti*. Zagreb, 1926.

Hlača, Dragutin. *Stjepan Radić i njegov politički rad*. Zagreb, 1923.

Hobsbawm, E.J. *Nations and Nationalism since 1780: Programme, Myth, Reality*. Cambridge, 1990.

Horvat, Josip. *Politička povijest Hrvatske*. 2 vols. 1936–8; reprint Zagreb, 1989.

– *Stranke kod Hrvata i njihova ideologija*. Belgrade, 1939.

– *Ante Starčević: Kulturno-povjesna slika*. Zagreb, 1940.

– *Ljudevit Gaj: Njegov život, njegovo doba*. Zagreb, 1975.

– *Hrvatski panoptikum*. Zagreb, 1965.

– *Živjeti u Hrvatskoj: Zapisi iz zavičaja, 1900–1941*. Zagreb, 1981.

Horvat, Rudolf. *Hrvatsko pitanje*. Zagreb, 1923.

– *Hrvatska na mučilištu*. 1942; reprint Zagreb, 1992.

Hroch, Miroslav. *Social Preconditions of National Revival in Europe: A Comparative*

Analysis of the Social Composition of Patriotic Groups among the Smaller European Nations. Cambridge, 1985.

Ibler, Janko. *Hrvatska politika, 1903–1906.* Zagreb, 1914.

Irvine, Jill. *The Croat Question: Partisan Politics in the Formation of the Yugoslav Socialist State.* Boulder, Col., 1993.

Išek, Tomislav. *Djelatnost HSS u Bosni i Hercegovini do zavodjenja diktature.* Sarajevo, 1981.

Iveković, Mladen. *Hrvatska lijeva inteligencija 1918–1945.* 2 vols. Zagreb, 1970.

Ivšić, Milan. *Diljem sela.* Zagreb, 1935.

– *Seljačka politika: Gospodarski život na selu.* Zagreb, 1938.

– *Seljačka politika: Društveni život na selu.* 2 vols. Zagreb, 1937.

Jackson, George D. *Comintern and Peasants in Eastern Europe, 1919–1930.* New York, 1966.

Janjatović, Bosiljka. *Politika HSS prema radničkoj klasi.* Zagreb, 1983.

Janković, Dragoslav. *Srbija i jugoslovensko pitanje, 1914–1915 godine.* Belgrade, 1973.

Jareb, Jere. *Pola stoljeća hrvatske politike, 1895–1945: Povodom Mačekove autobiografije.* 1960; reprint Zagreb, 1995.

Jászi, Oszkar. *The Dissolution of the Habsburg Monarchy.* Chicago and London, 1929.

Jelavich, Charles. *South Slav Nationalisms: Textbooks and Yugoslav Union before 1914.* Columbus, Ohio, 1990.

Johnson, Chalmers. *Peasant Nationalism and Communist Power.* Stanford, 1962.

Jovanović, Nadežda. *Politički sukobi u Jugoslaviji, 1925–1928.* Belgrade, 1974.

Jukić, Ilija. *Pogledi na prošlost, sadašnjost i budućnost hrvatskog naroda.* London, 1965.

Karaman, Igor. *Industrijalizacija gradjanske Hrvatske, 1800–1941.* Zagreb, 1991.

Keršovani, Otokar. *Povijest Hrvata.* Rijeka, 1971.

Konjhodžić, Mahmud. *Seljački pokret u Hrvatskoj.* Zagreb, 1940.

Korać, Vitomir. *Povjest radničkog pokreta u Hrvatskoj i Slavoniji od prvih početaka do ukidanja ovih pokrajina 1922 godine.* 3 vols. Zagreb, 1929–33.

Korunić, Petar. *Jugoslavizam i federalizam u hrvatskom nacionalnom preporodu 1835–1875.* Zagreb, 1989.

Kovačević, Ivan. *Ekonomski položaj radničke klase u Hrvatskoj i Slavoniji, 1867–1914.* Belgrade, 1972.

Kovačić, Matija. *Od Radića do Pavelića.* Munich, 1970.

Kranjčević, Stjepan. *Hrvatski seljački pokret.* Zagreb, 1937.

Krestić, Vasilije. *Ugarsko-hrvatska nagodba 1868 godine.* Belgrade, 1969.

Krišto, Jure. *Prešućena povijest: Katolička crkva u hrvatskoj politici, 1850–1918.* Zagreb, 1994.

Krizman, Bogdan. *Raspad Austro-ugarske i stvaranje jugoslavenske države*. Zagreb, 1977.
– *Hrvatska u prvom svjetskom ratu: Hrvatsko-srpski politički odnosi*. Zagreb, 1989.
Krleža, Miroslav. *Sabrana djela*. Vols. 1–50. Zagreb, 1975–87.
Kujundzić, Nedjeljko. *Pedagogija braće Radić*. Zagreb, 1990.
Kulundžić, Zvonimir. *Ante Radić i klerikalci*. Zagreb, 1951.
– *Atentat na Stjepana Radića i njegova prava pozadina*. Zagreb, 1967.
– *Politika i korupcija u kraljevskoj Jugoslaviji*. Zagreb, 1968.
– *Živi Radić: Uoči stote obljetnice rodjenja hrvatskog velikana*. 2nd ed. Zagreb, 1971.
– *Radić i njegov republikanski ustav*. Zagreb, 1991.
Leontić, Ljubo. *O Jugoslavenskom odboru u Londonu*. Zagreb, 1961.
Lovrenčić, Rene. *Geneza politike novog kursa*. Zagreb, 1972.
Lukač, Dušan. *Radnički pokret u Jugoslaviji i nacionalno pitanje, 1918–1941*. Belgrade, 1972.
Magocsi, Paul R. *The Shaping of a National Identity: Subcarpathian Rus', 1848–1948*. Cambridge, Mass., and London, 1978.
Marijanović, S. *Fin de siècle hrvatske moderne: Generacije mladih i časopis 'Mladost.'* Zagreb, 1990.
Marinčić, Ivan. *Gdje su i u čemu su uspjesi vodstva HSS od 1907 do 1927*. Zagreb, 1927.
Marjanović, Milan. *Hrvatski pokret*. Dubrovnik, 1904.
– *Savremena Hrvatska*. Belgrade, 1913.
– *Stjepan Radić*. Belgrade, 1937.
– *Hrvatska moderna*. 2 vols. Zagreb, 1951.
Marković, Lazar. *Jugoslavenska država i hrvatsko pitanje, 1914–1929*. Zagreb, 1935.
Maštrović, Ljubomir. *Socijalno i političko učenje Stjepana Radića u izvornoj reči*. Belgrade, 1940.
Matanić, Nikola. *Dr Antun Radić o narodnoj i seljačkoj kulturi*. Zagreb, 1940.
– *Dr Antun Radić o socijalnom pitanju*. Zagreb, 1940.
– *Antun Radić: Njegove misli i njegovo značenje*. Zagreb, 1940.
– *Dr Antun Radić o rodoljublju*. Zagreb, 1940.
Miller, Nicholos J. *Between Nation and State: Serbian Politics in Croatia before the First World War*. Pittsburgh, 1997.
Mirković, M. *Ekonomska historija Jugoslavije*. Zagreb, 1958.
Mitrany, David. *Marx against the Peasant: A Study in Social Dogmatism*. New York, 1961.
Mitrinović, Čedomil. *Životni krugovi hrvatstva*. Belgrade, 1938.
Murgić, Božidar. *Život, rad i misli Dr. Ante Radića*. Zagreb, 1937.
Mužić, Ivan. *Hrvatska politika i jugoslavenska ideja*. Split, 1969.
– *Stjepan Radić u kraljevini Srba, Hrvata i Slovenaca*. 4th ed. Zagreb, 1990.

Nehajev, Milutin. *Političke silhuete.* Zagreb, 1945.

Neudorfl, Marie. *Masaryk's Understanding of Democracy before 1914.* Pittsburgh, 1989.

Novak, Viktor. *Magnum crimen: Pola vijeka klerikalizma u Hrvatskoj.* Zagreb, 1948.

Ostovic, Pavle. *The Truth About Yugoslavia.* New York, 1952.

Paulova, Milada. *Jugoslavenski odbor.* Zagreb, 1925.

Pavelić, Ante. *Putem hrvatskog državnog prava: Članci, govori, izjave, 1918–1929.* Madrid, 1977.

– *Ustaška misao: Poglavnikovi govori od 12. X. 1941 do 12. IV. 1942.* Zagreb, 1942.

Pavelić, Ante Smith. *Dr Ante Trumbić: Problemi hrvatsko-srpski odnosa.* Munich, 1959.

Pavličević, Dragutin. *Narodni pokret 1883 u Hrvatskoj.* Zagreb, 1980.

Pavlowitch, Stevan K. *Yugoslavia.* London, 1971.

Petranović, Branko. *Istorija Jugoslavije, 1918–1978.* Belgrade, 1980.

Pleterski, Janko. *Komunistička partija Jugoslavije i nacionalno pitanje, 1919–1941.* Belgrade, 1971.

Predavec, Josip. *Agrarizam kao svjetski pokret i glavne seljačke potrebe u Hrvatskoj.* Zagreb, 1911.

– *Selo i seljaci.* Zagreb, 1934.

Preradović, Petar. *Hrvatski seljački pokret gledan sa strane.* Zagreb, 1939.

Pynsent, R.B. (ed.). *T.G. Masaryk (1850–1937).* Vol. 2. *Thinker and Critic.* London, 1989.

Radićeva Politička Baština i budućnost Hrvatske: Simpozij Hrvatske seljačke stranke povodom 60-e obljetnice Radićeve smrti. Brussels, 1988.

Radošević, Miško. *Republika svemu svijetu dika i HRSS i Treća Internacionala.* Zagreb, 1924.

– *Osnovi savremene Jugoslavije: Političke ideje, stranke i ljudi u XIX i XX veku.* Zagreb, 1935.

Raos, Predrag. *Hrvatskim mučenicima: Spomenpis na tragične dogadjaje u lipnju i kolovozu 1928.* Zagreb, 1991.

Roksandić, Drago. *Srbi u Hrvatskoj: Od 15. stoljeća do naših dana.* Zagreb, 1991.

Rothschild, Joseph. *East Central Europe between the Two World Wars.* Seattle, 1974.

Sarkotić, Stjepan. *Radićevo izdajstvo.* Vienna, 1925.

Seton-Watson, R.W. *Racial Problems in Hungary.* London, 1908.

– *Corruption and Reform in Hungary.* London, 1911.

– *The South Slav Question and the Habsburg Monarchy.* London, 1911.

– *Absolutism in Croatia.* London, 1912.

– *German, Slav and Magyar: A Study in the Origins of the Great War.* London, 1915.

Shoup, Paul. *Communism and the Yugoslav National Question.* New York, 1968.

Sisarić, Ivan. *Hrvatski mit XX stoljeća: Ideologija hrvatskog seljačkog pokreta. Apologij hrvatskog nacionalizma.* Zagreb, 1938.

Skilling, G.H. *T.G. Masaryk: Against the Current, 1882–1914*. University Park, Pa., 1994.

Smith, Anthony D. *Nationalism in the Twentieth Century*. Oxford, 1979.

– *Theories of Nationalism*. 2nd. ed. London, 1983.

– *The Ethnic Origins of Nations*. Oxford, 1986.

– *National Identity*. London, 1991.

Smodlka, Josip. *Izabrani spisi*. comp. I. Perić and H. Sirotković. Split, 1989.

Stanić, Eugen. *Stjepan Radić o sovjetskoj Rusiji*. Zagreb, 1945.

Stipetić, Zorica. *Komunistički pokret i inteligencija*. Zagreb, 1980.

Stojanović, S. (ed.). *Istorija Saveza komunista Jugoslavije: Kratak pregled*. Belgrade, 1976.

Stojsavljević, Bogdan. *Seljaštvo Jugoslavije, 1918–1941*. Zagreb, 1952.

– *Prodiranje kapitalizma u selo, 1919–1929*. Zagreb, 1965.

Strižić, Živko. *Tako je Radić počeo ...* Zagreb, 1992.

Supilo, Frano. *Politika u Hrvatskoj*. Zagreb, 1953.

– *Politički spisi. Članci, govori, pisma, memorandumi*. comp. Dragovan Šepić. Zagreb, 1970.

Szporluk, Roman. *The Political Thought of Thomas G. Masaryk*. New York, 1987.

Šarinić, Ivo. *Ideologija hrvatskog seljačkog pokreta*. Zagreb, 1935.

– *Hrvatska seljačka demokracija*. Zagreb, n.d.

Šarinić, Josip. *Nagodbena Hrvatska: Postanak i osnove ustavne organizacije*. Zagreb, 1972.

Šidak, Jaroslav, Mirjana Gross, Igor Karaman and Dragovan Šepić. *Povijest hrvatskog naroda, 1860–1914*. Zagreb, 1968.

Šidak, J. *Studije iz Hrvatske povijesti XIX stoljeća*. Zagreb, 1973.

– *Hrvatski narodni preporod: Ilirski pokret*. Zagreb, 1988.

Škrinjar, Fran. *Zašto sam ostavio Radića*. Koprivnica, 1927.

Štivić, Imbro. *Život i djelo braće Radića*. Zagreb, 1940.

Taletov, P.S. *Savremeni političari Stjepan Radić, Ljuba Davidović, Nastas Petrović*. Belgrade, 1928.

Tasić, F. *Socijalna ideologija i nacionalizam Antuna Radića*. Belgrade, 1940.

Tomasevich, Jozo. *Peasants, Politics and Economic Change in Yugoslavia*. Stanford, 1955.

Uroić, Stjepan, and Ivan Peršić. *Stjepan Radić proti Zagrebu*. Zagreb, 1927.

Vlajičić, Gordana. *KPJ i problemi revolucije: Rasprave o idejnom i organizacijskom razvitku KPJ izmedju dva svjetska rata*. Zagreb, 1979.

– *KPJ i nacionalno pitanje u Jugoslaviji*. Zagreb, 1974.

Volgyes, Ivan (ed.). *The Peasantry of Eastern Europe*. Vol. 1: *Roots of Rural Transformation*. Vol. 2: *Twentieth-Century Developments*. New York, 1979.

Vranješ-Šoljan, Božena. *Stanovništvo gradova banske Hrvatske na prijelazu stoljeća: Socijalno-ekonomski sastav i vodeći slojevi, 1890–1914.* Zagreb, 1991.

Vuković-Todorović, Ljubica. *Hrvatski seljački pokret braće Radića: Antun Radić.* Belgrade, 1940.

– *Sveslovenstvo Stjepana Radića.* Belgrade, 1940.

Wandruszka, Adam, and Peter Urbanitsch (eds.). *Die Habsburgermonarchie, 1848–1918.* Vol. 3. *Die Völker des Reiches.* pt. 1. Vienna, 1980.

Winters, S.B. (ed.). *T.G. Masaryk.* Vol. 1. *Thinker and Politician.* London, 1990.

Articles

Antić, Ljubomir. 'Hrvatska federalistička seljačka stranka.' *Radovi Instituta za hrvatsku povijest* 15 (1982): 163–222.

Banac, Ivo. '"Emperor Karl Has Become a Comitadji": The Croatian Disturbances of Autumn 1918.' *Slavonic and East European Review* 70, no. 2 (1992): 284–305.

– 'The Communist Party of Yugoslavia during the Period of Legality (1919–1921).' In *The Effects of World War I: The Class War after the Great War. The Rise of Communist Parties in East Central Europe, 1918–1921.* ed. Ivo Banac, 188–230. Brooklyn, NY, 1983.

– 'South Slav Prisoners of War in Revolutionary Russia.' In *Essays on World War I: Origins and Prisoners of War.* ed. S.R. Williamson, Jr., and Peter Pastor, 119–48. New York, 1983.

– 'Nationalism in Southeastern Europe.' In *Nationalism and Nationalities in the New Europe.* ed. Charles A. Kupchan, 107–21. Ithaca and London, 1995.

Boban, Branka. 'Shvaćanje Antuna i Stjepana Radića o mjestu i ulozi seljaštva u gospodarskom, društvenom i političkom životu.' *Radovi Instituta za hrvatsku povijest* 12 (1979): 265–304.

– 'O osnovnim obilježjima "seljačke države" u ideologiji Antuna i Stjepana Radića.' *Radovi Instituta za hrvatsku povijest* 13 (1980): 51–88.

– 'Shvaćanje Antuna i Stjepana Radića o mjestu i ulozi radničke klase u društvu (do 1918 god.).' *Radovi Instituta za hrvatsku povijest* 15 (1982): 131–62.

– 'Stjepan Radić – opus, utjecaji i dodiri.' *Radovi Zavoda za hrvatsku povijest* 22 (1989): 147–210.

– '*Nova Evropa* o Stjepanu Radiću.' *Radovi Zavoda za hrvatsku povijest* 24 (1991): 119–48.

Boban, Ljubo. 'Kada je i kako nastala Država Slovenaca, Hrvata i Srba.' *Časopis za suvremenu povijest* 24, no. 3 (1992): 45–60.

[Bonifačić, Ante]. 'Les idées du mouvement paysan croate: Antoine et Étienne Radić.' *Le monde slave* 15, no. 1 (1938): 342–69.

Cesarec, August. 'Stjepan Radić u Austriji.' *Književna Republika* 1, book 1, no. 1 (1923): 20–8.

– 'Stjepan Radić u Jugoslaviji.' *Književna Republika* 1, book 1, no. 2–3 (1923): 77–91.

– 'Stjepan Radić u Hrvatskoj (kritika republikanca o republikancu).' *Književna Republika* 2, book 1, no. 3 (1924): 85–100.

– 'Stjepan Radić (njegovo historijsko mjesto i značenje).' *Književna Republika* 2, book 1, no. 7 (1924): 258–71.

– 'Stjepan Radić ili likvidator Stjepana Radića.' *Književna Republika* 2, book 2, no. 7 (1925): 296–305.

Cvetković, Slavoljub. 'Stjepan Radić i komunistički pokret 1923–1925.' *Istorija XX veka: zbornik radova* 12 (1972): 375–402.

Čizmić, Ivan. 'O iseljavanju iz Hrvatske u razdoblju 1880–1914.' *Historijski zbornik* 27–8 (1974–5): 27–47.

Ćurčin, Ivo. 'The Yugoslav *Nova Evropa* and Its British Model: A Case of Cross-Cultural Influence.' *Slavonic and East European Review* 68, no. 3 (1990): 461–75.

Despalatovic, Elinor M. 'The Peasant Nationalism of Ante Radić.' *Canadian Review of Studies in Nationalism.* 5 (1979): 86–98.

Dobos, Manuela. 'The Nagodba and the Peasantry in Croatia-Slavonia.' In *The Peasantry of Eastern Europe.* Vol. 1. *Roots of Rural Transformation.* ed. Ivan Volgyes, 79–107. New York, 1979.

Engelsfeld, Neda. 'Rad kluba komunističkih poslanika u plenumu Ustavotvorne skupštine (u prosincu 1920 i u siječnju 1921).' *Radovi Instituta za hrvatsku povijest* 2 (1972): 181–262.

Freidzon, V.I. 'Sotsial'no-politicheskie vzgliady Antuna i Stepana Radichei v 1900-kh godakh i vozniknovenie khorvatskoi krest'ianskoi partii (1904–1905).' *Uchenye zapiski Instituta slavianovedeniia* 20 (1960): 275–305.

– 'Razvitie kapitalizma v horvatskoi derevne i polozhenie krestian v Horvatii v konce XIX – nachale XX veka.' *Uchenye zapiski Instituta slavianovedeniia* 10 (1954): 72–137.

Gabelica, Ivan. 'Politička misao Stjepana Radića.' *Marulić*, no. 1 (1989): 7–31.

Gaži, Stjepan. 'Beginning of the Croatian Peasant Party: A Historico-Political Study.' *Journal of Croatian Studies* 3–4 (1962–3): 19–33.

– 'Stjepan Radic: His Life and Political Activities (1871–1928).' *Journal of Croatian Studies* 14–15 (1973–4): 13–73.

Gligorijević, Branislav. 'O pitanju ulaska predstavnika HRSS u Davidovićevu vladu 1924 i o krizi i padu te vlade.' *Istorija XX veka: zbornik radova* 7 (1965): 345–406.

– 'Politička previranja u Demokratskoj stranci na pitanju taktike prema Hrvatskom bloku u drugoj polovini 1922.' *Istorija XX veka: zbornik radova* 8 (1966): 165–269.

– 'Razlike i dodirne tačke u gledištu na nacionalno pitanje izmedju Radikalne i

Demokratske stranke, 1919–1929.' *Jugoslovenski istorijski časopis* 1969, no. 4: 153–158.

- 'Neki aspekti na odnose izmedju Demokratske stranke i Hrvatske republikanske seljačke stranke (1919–1925).' *Istorija XX veka: zbornik radova* 12 (1972): 355–74.
- 'Uloga vojnih krugova u "rešavanju" političke krize 1924 godine.' *Vojnoistorijski glasnik* 23, no. 1 (1972): 161–86.
- 'Parlamentarni sistem u Kraljevini SHS (1919–1929).' In *Politički život Jugoslavije 1914–1945*. ed. Aleksandar Acković, 365–88. Belgrade, 1973.
Gross, Mirjana. 'Nacionalne ideje studentske omladine u Hrvatskoj uoči I svjetskog rata.' *Historijski zbornik* 21–2 (1968–9): 75–144.
- 'Neke karakteristike socijalne demokracije u Hrvatskoj i Slavoniji.' *Historijski zbornik* 5, nos. 3–4 (1952): 311–23.
- 'Socijalna demokracija prema nacionalnom pitanju u Hrvatskoj 1890–1902.' *Historijski zbornik* 9 (1956): 1–29.
- 'Hrvatska uoči aneksije Bosne i Hercegovine.' *Istorija XX veka: zbornik radova* 3 (1962): 153–274.
- 'Hrvatska politika velikoaustrijskog kruga oko prijestolonasljednika Franje Ferdinanda.' *Časopis za suvremenu povijest* 2, no. 1 (1970): 9–74.
- 'Social Structure and National Movements among the Yugoslav Peoples on the Eve of the First World War.' *Slavic Review* 36, no. 4 (1977): 628–43.
- 'Croatian National-Integrational Ideologies from the End of Illyrism to the Creation of Yugoslavia.' *Austrian History Yearbook* 15–16 (1979–80): 3–33.
- 'On the integration of the Croatian Nation: A Case Study in Nation Building.' *East European Quarterly* 15, no. 2 (1981): 209–25.
- 'O integraciji hrvatske nacije.' In *Društveni razvoj u Hrvatskoj (od 16 stoljeća do 20 stoljeća)*. ed. M. Gross, 175–90. Zagreb, 1981.
- 'The Union of Dalmatia with Northern Croatia: A Crucial Question of the Croatian National Integration in the Nineteenth Century.' In *The National Question in Europe in Historical Context*. ed. Mikuláš Teich and Roy Porter, 270–92. Cambridge, 1993.
Hrabak, Bogumil. 'Zapisnici sednica Davidovićeve dve vlade od avgusta 1919 do februara 1920.' *Arhivski vjesnik* 13, no. 13 (1970): 7–92.
Hroch, Miroslav. 'National Self-Determination from a Historical Perspective.' *Canadian Slavonic Papers* 37, nos. 3–4 (1995): 283–99.
Išek, Tomislav. 'Stjepan Radić kao politički mislilac.' *Časopis za suvremenu povijest* 4, no. 1 (1972): 187–199.
- 'Primjena Obznane na HRSS i posljedice za njene pristaše u Bosni i Hercegovini.' *Časopis za suvremenu povijest* 3, no. 1 (1971): 27–57.
Ivanić, Momčilo. 'Stjepan Radić.' *Srpski književni glasnik* 25, no. 6 (1928): 442–9.
Ivančević, Dušan. 'Stjepan Radić i njegova "mirotvorna republika",' *Srpski književni glasnik* 10, nos. 7–8 (1923): 525–34, 603–8.

Ivić, Stjepan. 'Stjepan Radić – borac za demokratske interese hrvatskog naroda.' *Naše teme* 15, no. 6 (1971): 971–84.

Janjatović, Bosiljka. 'Karadjordjevićevska centalizacija i položaj Hrvatske u Kraljevstvu (Kraljevini) SHS.' *Časopis za suvremenu povijest* 27, no. 1 (1995): 55–76.

– 'Stjepan Radić i kraljevski panduri: odjeci Borongajske skupštine 1923.' *Časopis za suvremenu povijest* 26, no. 2 (1994): 277–97.

– 'Represija spram hrvatskih seljaka 1918–1921.' *Časopis za suvremenu povijest* 25, no. 1 (1993): 25–43.

– 'Radnička politika HSS 1921–1941.' *Časopis za suvremenu povijest* 5, no. 1 (1973): 65–83.

Janković, Dragoslav. 'Društveni i politički odnosi u Kraljevstvu Srba, Hrvata i Slovenaca uoči stvaranja Socijalističke partije Jugoslavije (komunista).' *Istorija XX veka: zbornik radova* 1 (1959): 7–147.

– 'Ženevska konferencija o stvaranju jugoslovenske zajednice 1918 godine.' *Istorija XX veka: zbornik radova* 5 (1963): 225–60.

– 'Niška deklaracija (nastajanje programa jugoslovenskog ujedinjenja u Srbiji 1914 godine).' *Istorija XX veka: zbornik radova* 10 (1969): 7–111.

– 'Srbija i stvaranje Jugoslavije.' In *Politički život Jugoslavije 1914–1945*. ed. A. Acković, 49–74. Belgrade, 1973.

Jareb, Jere. 'Stjepan Radić predlaže konfederaciju 1922.' *Hrvatska revija* 18, no. 4 (1968): 518–24.

– 'Tri dokumenta o dodirima Stjepana Radića s Talijanima, 1923–1924.' *Hrvatska Revija* 18, no. 4 (1968): 524–33.

Jelavich, Charles. 'The Croatian Problem in the Habsburg Empire in the Nineteenth Century.' *Austrian History Yearbook* 3 (1967): 82–115.

Jovanović, Nadežda. 'Prilog proučavanju odjeka atentata u Narodnoj skupštini 20. juna 1928.' *Časopis za suvremenu povijest* 2, no. 1 (1970): 61–75.

Karaman, Igor. 'Privredni položaj Slavonije u Habsburškoj monarhiji pod nagodbenim sistemom, 1868–1918.' *Zbornik Historijskog Instituta Slavonije* 4 (1966): 283–374.

Kolar-Dimitrijević, Mira. 'Prepiska izmedju Stjepana Radića i Seljačke internacionale u Moskvi 1924 godine.' *Časopis za suvremenu povijest* 4, no. 1 (1972): 148–65.

– 'Put Stjepana Radića u Moskvu i pristup Hrvatske republikanske seljačke stranke u Seljačku internacionalu.' *Časopis za suvremenu povijest* 4, no. 3 (1972): 7–29.

Koprivica-Oštrić, Stanislava. 'Konstituiranje Države Slovenaca, Hrvata i Srba 29 listopada 1918 godine,' *Časopis za suvremenu povijest* 25, no. 1 (1993): 45–71.

Korać, Vitomir. 'Slom radićevštine.' In *Socijalistički radnički kalendar za godinu 1927*, 25–7. Belgrade, 1926.

Kosor, Josip. 'Stjepan Radić.' *Hrvatska revija* 1, nos. 1–2 (1928): 117–73.

Košćak, Vladimir. 'Mladost Stjepan Radića.' *Hrvatski znanstveni zbornik* 1, no. 2 (1971): 123–64.

Krajač, Ivan. 'Dvije političke sinteze: I. Tomo Masaryk II. Stjepan Radić.' *Hrvatska revija* 11, no. 11 (1938): 561–7.

Kranjčević, Stjepan. 'Dr Ante Radić.' *Književnik* 9, no. 2 (1936): 49–64.

Krišto, Jure. 'Hrvatsko katoličanstvo i ideološko formiranje Stjepana Radića (1893–1914).' *Časopis za suvremenu povijest* 23, nos. 1–3 (1991): 129–65.

Krivokapić, Gordana. 'Skupštinski pokret i politička aktivnost Srpske samostalne stranke u Kraljevini Hrvatskoj i Slavoniji 1903–1905 godine.' *Radovi Zavoda za hrvatsku povijest* 22 (1989): 95–111.

Krizman, Bogdan. 'The Croatians in the Habsburg Monarchy in the Nineteenth Century.' *Austrian History Yearbook* 3 (1967): 116–59.

– 'Izaslanik kralja Aleksandra kod Stjepana Radića u zatvoru 1925.' *Mogućnosti* 28, no. 9 (1971): 1087–1109.

– 'Osnivanje Hrvatske pučke seljačke stranke, 1904–1905.' *Radovi instituta za hrvatsku povijest* 2 (1972): 105–79.

– 'Osnivanje Narodnog Vijeća Slovenaca, Hrvata i Srba u Zagrebu 1918.' *Historijski zbornik* 7 (1954): 23–32.

– 'Plan Stjepana Radića o preuredjenju habsburške monarhije.' *Istorija XX veka: zbornik radova* 12 (1972): 31–84.

– 'Početak rada Narodnog Vijeća SHS u Zagrebu 1918 godine.' *Historijski pregled* 1, no. 2 (1954): 39–47.

– 'Politička misao Stjepana Radića.' *Naše teme* 15, no. 3 (1971): 502–14.

– 'Stjepan Radić i Hrvatska pučka seljačka stranka u prvom svjetskom ratu.' *Časopis za suvremenu povijest* 2, no. 2 (1970): 99–166.

– 'Stjepan Radić 1918 godine,' *Historijski pregled*. 5, no. 3 (1959): 266–96.

– 'Stjepan Radić na Pariškoj političkoj školi, 1897–1899.' *Naše teme*. 15, no. 6 (1971): 1072–1090.

– 'Stranke u Hrvatskom saboru za vrijeme I svjetskog rata.' *Zgodovinski časopis*. 19–20 (1965–6): 375–90.

– 'Dva pisma Toni Schlegela o razgovorima sa Stjepanom Radićem u zatvoru 1925.' *Časopis za suvremenu povijest* 2, no. 2 (1974): 125–38.

Krleža, Miroslav. 'O Stjepanu Radiću (Asocijacije povodom Hikčeve knjige).' *Književna republika* 3, no. 1 (1926): 22–47.

– 'Stjepan Radić na odru.' *Književnik* 1, no. 6 (1928): 193–203.

Krnjević, Juraj. 'Deset godina hrvatske politike.' *Hrvatska revija* 2, no. 1 (1929): 1–5.

Kulundžić, Zvonimir. 'O vezama frankovaca i radikala od god. 1918 do 1941.' *Historijski zbornik* 17 (1964): 311–17.

Laxa, Eugen. 'Stjepan Radić i preporod hrvatskog seljaštva. O 100-godišnjici njegova rodjenja.' *Hrvatska revija* 20, no. 4 (1970): 609–27.

Markus, Tomislav. 'Mihailo Polit-Desančić i srpski nacionalizam 1861 godine.' *Časopis za suvremenu povijest* 26, no. 3 (1994): 487–500.

Matijević, Zlatko. 'Nastanak dviju političkih stranaka bosansko-hercegovački Hrvata (1919–1920).' *Časopis za suvremenu povijest* 24, no. 3 (1992): 87–97.

Matković, Hrvoje. 'Stjepan Radić i Svetozar Pribićević u jugoslavenskoj politici od ujedinjenja do šestojanuarske diktature.' *Jugoslovenski istorijski časopis* 7, no. 4 (1969): 148–153.

– 'Hrvatska Zajednica: Prilog proučavanju političkih stranaka u staroj Jugoslaviji.' *Istorija XX veka: zbornik radova* 5 (1963): 5–136.

– 'Veze izmedju frankovaca i radikala od 1922–1925.' *Historijski zbornik* 15 (1962): 41–59.

– 'Stjepan Radić u izbornoj 1920. godini.' *Časopis za suvremenu povijest* 24, no. 3 (1992): 75–86.

Matković, Stjepan. 'Odnos braće Radić prema politici "novoga kursa" na primjenu Riječke i Zadarske rezolucije.' *Časopis za suvremenu povijest* 26, no. 3 (1994): 475–85.

– 'Vidjenje Stjepana Radića o preobražaju Habsburške monarhije, 1905–1906.' *Časopis za suvremenu povijest* 25, no. 1 (1993): 125–39.

Meštrović, Matthew M. 'The Elections of 1923 in the Kingdom of the Serbs, Croats and Slovenes.' *Journal of Croatian Studies* 1 (1960): 44–52.

Miller, Nicholas. 'Two Strategies in Serbian Politics in Croatia and Hungary before the First World War,' *Nationalities Papers* 23, no. 2 (1995): 327–51.

Mirošević, Franko. 'Borba za općinsku samoupravu u južnoj Dalmaciji od 1919 do 1929,' *Radovi Zavoda za hrvatsku povijest* 23 (1990): 149–61.

– 'Politički program skupštine dubrovačke oblasti 1927–1928.' *Časopis za suvremenu povijest* 24, no. 3 (1992): 117–27.

Morović, Hrvoje. 'Stjepan Radić pod Obznanom 1925 godine: Iskazi Stjepana Radića pred sudom za zaštitu države o boravku u Moskvi 1924.' *Mogućnosti* 18, no. 7 (1971): 844–913.

– 'Stjepan Radić pod Obznanom 1925 godine: II. Iskazi Stjepana Radića o njegovom boravku u Londonu 1923 godine.' *Mogućnosti* 18, no. 8 (1971): 987–1052.

– 'Stjepan Radić pod Obznanom: III. Prilozi.' *Mogućnosti* 18, no. 9 (1971): 1109–1146.

Mužić, Ivan. 'Katolicizam Stjepana Radića.' *Tavelić* 16, no. 4 (1976): 100–2.

– 'Državno uredjenje ili ustav Neutralne Seljačke Republikanske Hrvatske.' *Mogućnosti* 18, no. 9 (1971): 1147–66.

Nehajev, Milutin. 'Stjepan Radić.' *Hrvatsko Kolo* 3 (1928): 5–24.

Nikolić, Vinko. 'Pola stoljeća hrvatske politike: Razgovor s drom. Stjepanom Bućem.' *Hrvatska revija* 18, no. 1 (1968): 47–68.

Očak, Ivan. 'Stjepan Radić i Rusija.' *Radovi Zavoda za hrvatsku povijest* 25 (1992): 103–22.

Paver, Josipa. 'Još jedna verzija zapisnika saslušanja Stjepana Radića o atentatu u Narodnoj skupštini u Beogradu 20. lipnja 1928.' *Časopis za Suvremenu Povijest* 4, no. 1 (1972): 165–79.

Pavličević, Dragutin. 'Gospodarske prilike Civilne Hrvatske (1860–1873) s posebnim osvrtom na agrarnu proizvodnju.' *Radovi Zavoda za hrvatsku povijest* 22 (1989): 133–46.

Racko, Ljerka. 'Spaljivanje madjarske zastave 1895 godine u Zagrebu.' *Radovi Zavoda za hrvatsku povijest* 23 (1990): 233–45.

Radica, Bogdan. 'Dvije hrvatske politike prema fašističkoj Italiji: Stjepan Radić odbija suradnju s Mussolinijem.' *Hrvatska revija* 19, no. 3 (1979): 424–27.

Seton-Watson, Robert W. 'Jugoslavia and the Croat Problem.' *Slavonic Review* 16, no. 2 (1937): 102–12.

Sirotković, Hodimir. 'O nastanku, organizaciji, državopravnim pitajima i sukcesiji Države SHS nastale u jesen 1918.' *Časopis za suvremenu povijest* 24, no. 3 (1992): 61–74.

Smodlaka, Josip. 'Značaj Radićeve pobjede u Dalmaciji.' *Srpski književni glasnik* 9, no. 5 (1923): 371–8.

Sokolić-Jaman, Nada. 'Komunistička štampa u Hrvatskoj o djelatnosti Stjepana Radića (1918–1925).' *Radovi Instituta za hrvatsku povijest* 6 (1974): 273–313.

Stanković, Djordje D. 'Kriza radikalsko-demokratske koalicije 1921 i hrvatsko pitanje.' *Jugoslovenski istorijski časopis*, no. 1–2 (1972): 79–91.

– 'Neuspeh Stojana Protića u okupljanju političkih snaga radi rešavanja hrvatskog pitanja 1921 godine.' *Istorijski glasnik*, no. 1 (1971): 7–34.

Stipetić, Zorica, and M. Maticka. 'Odnos selo-grad u interpretaciji intelektualaca Hrvatske u medjuratnom razdoblju.' *Časopis za suvremenu povijest* 1, no. 1 (1974): 7–25.

Stulli, Bernard. 'Izvještaj državnog nadodvjetnika u Zagrebu od 27. VI. 1925. o stanju istrage protiv Stjepana Radića.' *Arhivski vjesnik* 14 (1971): 135–200.

Šepić, Dragovan. 'Jugoslavenski pokret i Milan Marjanović 1901–1919.' *Zbornik Historijskog instituta jugoslavenske akademije* 3 (1960): 531–61.

– 'The Question of Yugoslav Union in 1918.' *Journal of Contemporary History* 3, no. 4 (1968): 29–43.

– 'Hrvatska politika i pitanje jugoslavenskog ujedinjenja 1914–1918.' In *Društveni razvoj u Hrvatskoj (od 16 stoljeća do 20 stoljeća).* ed. M. Gross, 373–416. Zagreb, 1981.

Šimončić-Bobetko, Zdenka. 'Motrišta političkih stranaka u Hrvatskoj o agrarnom pitanju (1918–1931).' *Časopis za suvremenu povijest* 24, no. 3 (1992): 129–47.

Tudjman, Franjo. 'Stjepan Radić i hrvatska državnost. O stotoj obljetnici rodjenja Stjepana Radića.' *Kritika* 4, no. 18 (1971): 386–401.

Vucinich, W.S. 'Interwar Yugoslavia.' In *Contemporary Yugoslavia: Twenty Years of Socialist Experiment.* ed. W.S. Vucinich, 59–118. Berkeley, 1969.

Wiesner, Ljubo. 'Stjepan Radić i A. G. Matoš' *Savremenik* 21, nos. 8–9 (1928): 387–90.

Zaninović, Vice. 'Mlada Hrvatska uoči I svjetskog rata.' *Historijski zbornik* 11–12 (1958–9): 65–104.

Žerjavić, Vladimir. 'Kretanje stanovništva i demografski gubici Republike Hrvatske u razdoblju 1900–1991 godine.' *Časopis za suvremenu povijest* 23, nos. 2–3 (1993): 65–85.

Newspapers/Periodicals

Božićnica (Zagreb, 1910–28)
Dom/Slobodni Dom (Zagreb, 1906–28)
Hrvatska misao (Prague, 1897)
Hrvatska misao (Zagreb, 1902–6)
Hrvatski narod (Zagreb, 1904–5)
Hrvatske novine (Virje, 1904–6)
Hrvatstvo (Zagreb, 1904–5)
Narodni val (Zagreb, 1927–8)
Nova Evropa (Zagreb, 1921–8)
Novi vienac (Zagreb, 1905)
Novo doba (Prague, 1898)

Unpublished Doctoral Dissertations

Gazi, Stjepan. 'Stjepan Radić and the Croatian Question: A Study in Political Biography.' PhD diss., Georgetown University, 1962.

Livingston, Robert G. 'Stjepan Radić and the Croatian Peasant Party, 1904–1929.' PhD diss., Harvard University, 1959.

Lukac, Iva. 'Stjepan Radić and the Croatian Peasant Party, 1914–1928.' PhD diss., University of Cincinatti, 1989.

Schmidt, Katherine A. 'Croatian Peasant Party in Yugoslav Politics.' PhD diss., Kent State University, 1984.

Index